T0301254

SOLIDARITY STORIES

SOLIDARITY

STORIES

AN ORAL HISTORY OF THE ILWU

HARVEY SCHWARTZ

UNIVERSITY OF WASHINGTON PRESS   *Seattle & London*

© 2009 by the University of Washington Press
Printed in the United States of America by Consolidated Printers, Inc., Berkeley, California
Design by Thomas Eykemans
12 11 10 09   5 4 3 2 1

University of Washington Press
P.O. Box 50096, Seattle, WA 98145 U.S.A.
www.washington.edu/uwpress

LIBRARY OF CONGRESS CATALOGING-IN-PUBLICATION DATA

Schwartz, Harvey.
Solidarity stories : an oral history of the ILWU / Harvey Schwartz.
    p. cm.
Includes bibliographical references and index.
ISBN 978-0-295-98883-2 (hbk. : alk. paper)
ISBN 978-0-295-98884-9 (pbk. : alk. paper)
    1. International Longshoremen's and Warehousemen's Union—History.   2. Labor
unions—United States—History.   3 Labor movement—United States—History.   I. Title.
HD6515.L821577   2009
331.88'113871640973—dc22   2008054050

The paper used in this publication is acid-free and 90 percent recycled from at least 50
percent post-consumer waste. It meets the minimum requirements of American National
Standard for Information Sciences—Permanence of Paper for Printed Library Materials,
ANSI Z39.48–1984.

To ILWU people everywhere
on the seventy-fifth anniversary
of the 1934 strike

CONTENTS

ABBREVIATIONS

AALA   African American Longshoremen's Association
AALPS   Afro-American Labor Protective Society
AFL   American Federation of Labor
AFL-CIO   American Federation of Labor–Congress of Industrial Organizations (the two groups merged in 1955)
ANG   American Newspaper Guild
AP   Associated Press
AYC   American Youth Congress
BALHW   Bay Area Labor History Workshop
BN   Burlington Northern Railroad
CAWIU   Cannery and Agricultural Workers Industrial Union
CCLLA   Copra Crane Labor Landmark Association
CDC   California Democratic Council
CIO   Committee for Industrial Organization (1935–38, thereafter Congress of Industrial Organizations)
CLRC   Coast Labor Relations Committee
CLS   California Labor School
CP   Communist Party
DOL   U.S. Department of Labor
ERA   Equal Rights Amendment
FEPC   Fair Employment Practices Committee
FLSA   Fair Labor Standards Act
FTA   Food, Tobacco, Agricultural and Allied Workers
HUAC   House Un-American Activities Committee
IBEW   International Brotherhood of Electrical Workers

IBL	International Brotherhood of Longshoremen
IBU	Inlandboatmen's Union
ILA	International Longshoremen's Association
ILGWU	International Ladies Garment Workers Union
ILWU	International Longshoremen's and Warehousemen's Union (1937–97, thereafter International Longshore and Warehouse Union)
ISO	International Safety Organization
IUMMSW	International Union of Mine, Mill and Smelter Workers
IWA	International Woodworkers of America
IWW	Industrial Workers of the World
JLSAC	Joint Longshore Strike Assistance Committee
JMSC	Joint Marine Strike Committee
KKK	Ku Klux Klan
LRC	Labor Relations Committee
M & M	Mechanization and Modernization Agreement
MCS	Marine Cooks and Stewards Association of the Pacific Coast, CIO (1937–45, thereafter National Union of Marine Cooks and Stewards)
MEBA	Marine Engineers' Beneficial Association
MFOW	Marine Firemen, Oilers, Watertenders and Wipers Association
MFP	Maritime Federation of the Pacific
MMP	Masters, Mates and Pilots
MWIU	Marine Workers Industrial Union
NAACP	National Association for the Advancement of Colored People
NCDC	Northern California District Council
NIRA	National Industrial Recovery Act, 1933
NLRA	National Labor Relations Act, or Wagner Act, 1935 (compromised by Taft-Hartley Act, 1947)
NLRB	National Labor Relations Board
NRA	National Recovery Administration
OSHA	Occupational Safety and Health Administration
PCLB	Pacific Coast Labor Bureau
PGP	Pay Guarantee Plan
PMA	Pacific Maritime Association
PW	*People's World* newspaper
SIU-AG	Seafarers International Union–Atlantic and Gulf District
SSA	Stevedoring Services of America
SUP	Sailors Union of the Pacific
SWLSA	Southwest Labor Studies Association
TOOR	Tenants and Owners in Opposition to Redevelopment
UCAPAWA	United Cannery, Agricultural, Packing and Allied Workers of America
UE	United Electrical, Radio and Machine Workers of America

UFCW	United Food and Commercial Workers
UFW	United Farm Workers
UPW	United Public Workers
WLB	War Labor Board
WMC	War Manpower Commission
WPA	Works Progress Administration
YCL	Young Communist League

Seattle ILWU Local 19 workers and supporters marching against the Iraq war, May Day, 2008. Photo by Grant Haller. *Seattle Post-Intelligencer.*

SOLIDARITY STORIES

1948 maritime strike, Portland, Oregon. *Left to right*: Don Wollan, John Fougerouse, Marion Lee Howton, Kenny Ford, Kneeland Stranahan, George Morgan, Tommy George, Olaf Rasmussen, and James Fantz. ILWU Library, San Francisco.

INTRODUCTION

THE MYSTIQUE OF THE INTERNATIONAL LONGSHORE AND WAREHOUSE UNION (ILWU) has stirred the passions of its defenders and enemies alike for decades. Harry Renton Bridges, the longtime ILWU leader, felt that much of the militant left-wing union's unique strength and ability to command a following came from its tradition of membership participation. "It was about democracy," he suggested in 1984, looking back at the union's origins in the 1930s. "We said that the rank and file had the right to decide, and if you gave them the facts, they'd make the right decision."

One decision the rank and file made was to support the union's left-wing leaders and their politics. ILWU members were fiercely loyal, even when they disagreed with Bridges or other leaders on specific policies. When forces outside the union charged that Bridges was a Communist, the membership defended him vigorously. As they said on the waterfront, "He may be a bastard, but he's our bastard."

Perhaps union democracy had much to do with this loyalty. It's easier to buy into something when you have a say, when your voice matters, and when you have some sense of control over your destiny. This oral history of the ILWU largely represents the voices of all those rank-and-file members who have supported the union with vigor, pride, and passion for the past seventy-five years. Important pioneer leaders are certainly heard from in these pages too, but the chorus is one of worker pride in belonging to and participating in the ILWU.

Leadership, of course, still merits attention. When Bridges led thousands of waterfront workers to victory in the great West Coast maritime strike of 1934, he became a national figure, a labor celebrity, and something of a folk hero. The Australian-born seaman turned San Francisco longshore worker and leader was only thirty-three at the time. In 1973 he was seventy-two and had been president of the International Longshoremen's and Warehousemen's Union (as the organization was called then) for thirty-six years. The survivor of four Pacific Coast longshore strikes and twenty years of proto-McCarthyite witch hunts that had targeted him for deportation until 1955, he remained a living symbol of militant unionism.

So on May 3, 1973, when Bridges addressed the ILWU International convention in San Francisco, he spoke with authority to the union's highest policy-making body. Drawn from the ILWU's West Coast, Alaskan, Hawaiian, and Canadian components, or locals, elected delegates had convened to work on committees that would generate resolutions and then cast votes determining the direction of the union for the immediate future. Commenting on his union's legacy on that occasion, Bridges credited the rank and file with the ILWU's long record of success. "I know who wrote the history of this union," he said. "It was the people down there facing the guns and doing a few other things." A moment later, to make sure everyone got the point, he added, "There's all kinds of people that have done as much as me to build this union."

This book is filled with the recollections of the kinds of men and women Bridges had in mind. As befits his historic role, Bridges gets the first and last words. But in between, dozens of other ILWU officers, organizers, activists, and rank and filers tell their stories about life at work, on the picket line, and in the union. What emerges is a broad picture of what the ILWU has meant to generations of workers. In comparison, the narrow Cold War–era question of whether Bridges ever belonged to the American Communist Party, which long preoccupied government agents, media people, and many scholars, seems unimportant.

Taken together, these reminiscences depict the idealism and heritage of an organization that has long stood not only for union democracy but also for dignity on the job, racial equality, freedom from corruption, and international solidarity. The union vigorously condemned fascism in the 1930s. Between 1936 and 1939, it raised funds toward the Spanish Republic's defense against the fascist rebellion of General Francisco Franco. Like the Old Left, the ILWU initially supported neutrality in World War II, but it enthusiastically backed the Allied cause when the United States entered the fray in 1941.

Since the Second World War, the union has consistently campaigned for the peaceful resolution of U.S. overseas conflicts from Vietnam to Iraq. For thirty years, the ILWU has criticized and sometimes boycotted military dictatorships in places like Chile and El Salvador and actively supported beleaguered unionists, from the dockers of Liverpool, England, to members of the Maritime Union of Australia. Recently the union has condemned the abuses of human and labor rights inherent in the international corporate push toward globalization, free trade agreements, and privatization.

The ILWU also officially opposed racial and other kinds of discrimination from 1934 onward. It tried to organize black and white workers in the South nearly a decade before the Congress of Industrial Organizations (CIO) launched the better-known Operation Dixie in 1946–47, which failed in part because its top leadership avoided organizing blacks and whites together, as historian Michael K. Honey and others have shown. The ILWU actively supported the civil rights movement of the 1960s, and in the 1980s it opposed apartheid in South Africa by boycotting ships from that country. During 2000–2001, it worked diligently in defense of members of the predominantly black International Longshoremen's Association (ILA) local in Charleston, South Carolina.

In many ways, the ILWU is unique among American labor organizations. Historically more left of center, it has also demonstrated an uncommon ability to overcome adversity. In 1949–50, five years before the American Federation of Labor (AFL) and the CIO merged, the CIO purged eleven of its member unions for alleged Communist influences. Those eleven were then raided by both the AFL and the CIO. The United Electrical, Radio, and Machine Workers of America (UE) and the ILWU were the only ones to survive. The UE lost much of its membership, power, and influence. Only the ILWU remained almost entirely intact.

Thus the institutional record of the ILWU is unusual within the American labor movement. Still, in the broadest sense, but especially on the level of the individual rank and filer's work experience, the testimonies in this book re-create the world of the millions of American union members who were witnesses, activists, or leaders during organized labor's mid-twentieth-century heyday.

All but one of the oral history profiles in this book first appeared in somewhat different form as articles in the ILWU International newspaper, *The Dis-*

patcher, between 1994 and 2007. That series of articles had its origins in a major oral history project the union undertook in partnership with the University of California, Berkeley, between 1981 and 1986. A discussion of the methodology used in that project, in the preparation of the *Dispatcher* articles, and in this text is located in "A Note on Sources" near the back of this book. Since interviewees sometimes use specialized terms or slang, there is also a glossary toward the back of the book, which readers can consult for explanations of perplexing references.

The oral histories presented here cover most of the union's industrial jurisdiction and geography in generally chronological order. The ILWU's long-held policy of welcoming diversity is much in evidence, too, for there are testimonies here from workers with African, Chinese, European, Filipino, Hispanic, Japanese, and Native Hawaiian backgrounds. These testimonies describe the workers' experiences in their own words with an immediacy rarely found in secondary histories. Eugene D. Vrana, a former longshore worker and the ILWU's director of educational services, librarian, and archivist, called them "the real history of the union," despite the existence of a large and well-regarded body of academic literature on the organization.

Throughout the book I have tried to highlight paramount themes in ILWU history, including the origins of the union, organizing, strikes, radicalism, race, ethnicity, gender issues, and perseverance in the face of adversities like the 1950s red scare. The ILWU's concern with discrimination is worth considering. At times, the International union's strict antidiscrimination policy met local resistance, so this book includes considerable testimony about the ways in which unionists experienced and dealt with this tension.

In the great majority of instances, the union has, in the parlance of the waterfront, managed to "do the right thing." But it goes further than that. As a colleague once remarked to me, "The ILWU is a symbolic union; it always stood for something." What she meant was that the union has historically had a social vision and has campaigned for universal social justice. In traditional labor jargon, the ILWU was always far more than a conservative business union, although it was usually good at shop-floor representation and collective bargaining, too.

Bridges summarized much of this vision himself while addressing the ILWU International Convention in 1957. "We stand," he said, "as we always stood, with the working people of our own country and the working people of the world. We intend to go forward, and we can always be sure of one thing: There will be a place for us somewhere, somehow, as long as we recognize and see to it that the working people must always struggle on, fight for everything they have, and everything they hope to get, for dignity, equality, democracy, to oppose war and to bring to the whole world a better life."

These sentiments are implied in the union's official slogan, borrowed from the pre–World War I radical Industrial Workers of the World (IWW), the famous Wobblies: "An injury to one is an injury to all."[1] The vision is clear in the oral history testimonies in this volume. It is a vision that the U.S. labor movement has long had to offer, notwithstanding its own shortcomings and the distortions of its corporate detractors. Nelson Lichtenstein, the biographer of United Auto Workers leader Walter Reuther, recently characterized this wide-ranging social vision as "the old dream of an industrial democracy, animated by a mass of alert citizen-workers." Lichtenstein describes this vision in his masterly 2002 analysis of organized labor's rise and decline, *State of the Union: A Century of American Labor.* "By the early 1950s," he writes, collective bargaining, a business or "firm-centered set of bargaining arrangements 'free' of overt politicization, was all that remained of the old idea of an industrial democracy."[2] This is emphatically not the case for the ILWU, which was never typical of the majority of American unions.

In *State of the Union*, Lichtenstein also contends that the rights-consciousness movements of recent decades—that is, social justice movements for particular groups defined by race, ethnicity, gender, and so on—while presenting legitimate demands, have sometimes taken the attention of workers and their supporters away from labor's traditional goal of solidarity. If this is true, perhaps the ILWU's history, as reflected in these pages, will remind readers of the tradition of solidarity and provide a model of what a labor union should be.

That rights consciousness and rights rhetoric can and should be adopted by labor is another point Lichtenstein makes in *State of the Union*. In its effort to embrace rights consciousness, along with its historic sponsorship of diversity, civil rights, and nondiscrimination, the ILWU has already tried to do this. For example, in 1997 the union changed its famous name, becoming the International Longshore and Warehouse Union, to reflect its search for gender equality. Here again, the ILWU can serve as a model to others.

Lichtenstein emphasizes further that an insistence on internal union democracy is central to the process of rebuilding America's unions. This, he writes, "is vital to restoring the social mission of labor and returning unions to their social-movement heritage."[3] Other prominent labor observers such as Kim Moody agree that union democracy is key to union vigor. In this area, too, the ILWU provides a model for emulation, for it has practiced union democracy throughout its history.

Recent academic evidence supports this claim. In February 2006, at a Seattle conference, Margaret Levi, David J. Olson, and a team of their University of Washington students showcased the results of their Union Democracy Reexamined Project (UDRP), a major, multiyear study of the ILWU. Their examination of ILWU convention proceedings since 1938 and other sources indicated that in consistently conducting open debates, respecting minority opinions, and holding clean elections, the ILWU has done much to safeguard its democratic tradition.

The oral history of the ILWU, I believe, can play a role in the revitalization of today's union movement.[4] My hope is that this book and the vision it reflects will prove informative, useful, and even inspiring to unionized and non-unionized workers alike, to labor activists, teachers, students, and researchers, and to all those other interested good people outside the labor and academic communities.

1

LONGSHORE

THE SAN FRANCISCO BAY AREA

THE ORGANIZING MOVEMENT THAT LED TO THE FORMATION OF THE ILWU started in San Francisco. Here Harry Bridges rose to prominence, and here the 1934 West Coast maritime strike led to one of the few major citywide general strikes in U.S. history. It was here also, under Bridges's leadership, that the union's policy of opposition to discrimination originated. So our story begins in San Francisco, with three sections featuring Bridges's recollections of his early days on the waterfront, the unionization drive he led, and the 1934 strike.

When Bridges started longshoring in the 1920s, San Francisco was the leading port on the West Coast. The container revolution that made Oakland the bigger Bay Area port was forty years in the future. Most shipborne cargo was stowed or unpacked manually. In the great majority of situations, workers used handheld longshore hooks to maneuver heavy goods. Loads of cargo typically were put into slings and moved to and from ships' holds by steam-driven winches. Working this break bulk cargo, as it was called, required strength and skill.[1]

HARRY BRIDGES: THE BEGINNING OF THE UNION, 1924–1933

Bridges recalls the hard life of longshore workers when there was no employee-controlled union. He describes how a disreputable, ostensibly autonomous but actually company-dominated union known as the Blue Book exploited water-

Longshore workers handling a sling load of eight 160–pound coffee sacks, 1937. Photo by Otto Hagel. Copyright 1998 Center for Creative Photography, University of Arizona Foundation.

front workers in San Francisco between 1919 and 1934.[2] The background for this recollection is a longshore industry that was notorious for its corrupt hiring practices, brutally long shifts with no overtime pay, speed-ups, or dangerously fast-paced work sessions, and callous shipowner disregard for job safety.

The ILWU leader also reviews the 1933 revival of the nearly defunct Pacific Coast District of the International Longshoremen's Association (ILA), which would represent California, Oregon, and Washington waterfront workers in 1934. This organization became the ILWU in 1937 when it left the ILA, an AFL affiliate, and switched to the new and more progressive Committee for Industrial Organization.

Bridges was a twenty-one-year-old, Australian-born ex-sailor when he started longshoring on the San Francisco waterfront in 1922. He had rejected his father's Melbourne real estate business, gone to sea at seventeen, and joined the Australian seamen's union.[3] Bridges had participated in the 1921 U.S. sailors' strike while

*in New Orleans and briefly enrolled in the IWW. We pick up his narrative in
1924, as he recalls an effort to organize a dock workers' union in the Bay City.*

Harry Bridges

We set up for the ILA union in 1924, prior to Labor Day, because we did march
in the Labor Day parade. We had a membership of about four hundred. No
contracts, 'cause we had a company union. It was set up after the 1919 longshore
strike that was lost. You had to be a member of the company union to get work.
It was a closed shop. We used to dodge paying as much as we could.

So we joined the Labor Day parade from the Ferry Building up Market
Street to city hall. The company and union officers stood on the sidelines and
marked down all the names they could. I don't know how they got mine; I
wasn't anything special.

I was blacklisted, but I had enough to get by on, what with the Japanese
lines, an occasional unscheduled tramp ship that was gonna go to, say, Japan
or Australia, the Alaska Packer Line, and some luck in the card games. Various
shipping groups, like the Japanese lines, did not have to go along with the
company union.

We'd load their drums of lubricating oil, mostly from Richmond. We'd load
cans of gasoline and kerosene in woodwork cases with two five-gallon cans in
each case. Goddamn right they were heavy!

The ship'd be up there in Richmond a week, usually, loading top to bottom.
See, if you caught one of them, that would be good for a pretty good payday.
You make fifty or sixty bucks on a ship like that alone.

It was awfully hard with the goddamn company union officials, but they
were so busy watching card games and catching the chicks and making dough
that they couldn't take care of these other things, like the tramp ships. They
had a good enough thing without that.

Later on I was in the company union, and I was no longer blacklisted. I
used to work on the San Francisco waterfront then for California Stevedore
and Ballast—that was the biggest stevedore company. I used to work the steel
ships, the Argonaut Line, and a whole slew of things.

On paper, some of the company union conditions were very good. It was
like some of the labor laws of Mexico; they were wonderful laws, but they
weren't enforced.

"Belly packing" cargo on the waterfront, 1930s. Photo by Otto Hagel. Courtesy Labor Archives and Research Center, San Francisco State University. Copyright 1998 Center for Creative Photography, University of Arizona Foundation.

The company union officials would come down to knock you off the job for not paying dues. When they caught up with you, you had to pay a year's dues, see—nine bucks. And that's all you got out of that; you didn't get nothing out of the union. The ones that were in the know went along with it and did get some service from the business agents. But if you had a beef against the company, everybody knew in advance that if you went to the company union and made a beef, you lost your job.

I broke my foot in '29 working in the hold. I was standing there on a pile, and we let a load go out, and my foot got jammed between two cases that came together. I worked for a couple days with it—couldn't afford to lay off, you see? But it swelled up so high that I couldn't work down there, so the boss put me on the deck. I couldn't even stand that.

At that time you were so afraid of reporting an injury that you stayed away. This is also part of the company union thing. You cost the company money by claims for injury, and the company's insurance rates went up. So the word was around that you didn't go and make a claim for injury. That's the reason I waited for two or three days, but the foot got swollen so badly I couldn't limp around anymore.

When I did go on disability, I was getting twenty-five bucks a week under worker's compensation. Finally the doctor ordered me back to work. I didn't want to go. Twenty-five dollars for doing nothing was more than I would make on the waterfront the way it was, see?

When the 1929 crash came, and the Depression set in, what we were doing on the waterfront was struggling to make a buck, just trying to get a day's work. I was married to Agnes then, and we were losing our house. Couldn't afford to keep it anymore. After that we moved down to a little flat on Harrison Street, and when that got too expensive—twenty-five bucks a month—we moved next door for fifteen.

In '32 there was a program put together for city relief where you could go to work on certain projects for one week and you got three weeks of groceries. I entered the program and went to work at the foot of Seventh Street tearing down some old stables. The foreman saw I was pretty handy as a rigger. He said he needed me, so I actually stayed on and worked about a month, which set me up for three months of supplies at a bag of groceries every week.

The shape-up for longshore hiring back then was right there at the Ferry Building, on the block between Market and Mission Streets. On the other side of Market there was another part of the shape-up. Certain longshore gangs— that's what the work groups were called—used to shape-up there.[4]

After seven thirty in the morning, when there was no more picking up, then you'd go around and stand in front of the docks—you'd know, where the ships were—in the hope that they'd need a few extra men. There was a smaller shape-up in front of the docks, see?

In the big shape-up, you just stood there and waited for the gang boss. If you were in a gang, when you knocked off the day before, the order from the gang boss was, "Ferry Building in the morning." And that meant you'd be right across the street from the Ferry Building at six thirty, seven o'clock, to get your order to get on at work, or the boss would come around and say, "Such and such a dock, eight o'clock." Or twelve o'clock, or whatever it was.

Otherwise, they'd say, "Okay, go home. Nothing today." Then, if your boss said that, you might go around seeing if some other boss needed some extras, see? After that was done, you'd hang around in the shape-up and see if you could go to work somewhere else. And if you couldn't, then you'd go down beside the docks where there were ships, and there was a possibility of a few extra men needed.

In those tough times, once you got a job in a gang, you stayed there, because they were valuable jobs. There's about sixteen men in a gang. I was working in a steady gang for American-Hawaiian Steamship Company just before the 1934 strike. We was the star gang—the top-producing gang—at Pier 26. We worked number two hatch. There were steady gangs and what we called "fou fous," or casuals. Every company had a nucleus of steady gangs that worked all the time.

Along the waterfront near the shape-up, there were bootleg joints, book-making joints, and poolrooms. These were places we hung out at. We'd hang out at Paddy Hurley's bootleg joint, just drink there, and chew the rag. [This was during Prohibition, 1919–33, when liquor was illegal.] At one period, I kept on going to Paddy's about once every week, borrowing money from him. He'd scream like hell. I was into him for about sixty or seventy dollars. I'd get ten bucks a week, and that was what we lived on. That was the same period I lost the house.

We used to cash payroll brass checks at Paddy Hurley's. Hurley did business with the company union, cashing brass checks. When you got a job, and you went to work, the boss had a bunch of brass checks. He'd give you a brass check and he'd put his name on it. That was to show it was a payroll check. It was a brass check with a number on it, you see? It had a hole in the top so you could put it on a key chain or something. You could take it down to the boot-legger and cash it in.[5]

The bootleg joint didn't take nothing out of your check before drinks. But you had to spend at least fifty cents. When you spent fifty cents, you got two shots of bootleg at twenty-five cents each and then one on the house. Then the bootlegger used the company union agent to go down and collect his money from the stevedoring company. There was other guys that used to cash in brass checks down there, too, and take a 20 percent payment.

In the latter part of '32, at the time of Franklin D. Roosevelt being elected president, all over the country there was the beginning of talk about labor unions, the right of workers to organize, and all that jazz. On the waterfront there was a lot of talk on the job. The Marine Workers Industrial Union [MWIU] was talked about. That was a national Communist Party [CP] union.[6] It had been organizing and was doing a pretty good job.

At the end of '32, early '33, we started to meet down at the Albion Hall. It was just a rank-and-file group. Later we called ourselves the Committee of 500. [The committee actually had only about fifty members.] It was more or less under the direction of the MWIU and more or less indirectly under Party leadership. But that did not mean that all members of the group were members of the Party.

We were just a bunch of rank and filers with what experience we had. There were not many around who'd been involved in strikes. We used to have all kinds of people at the meetings. Everybody was welcome. Of course, later on, the charge was that it was a Party group, but it was really a fraction that included non-Party members.

In '33 we took over the MWIU paper, *The Waterfront Worker*. The MWIU was putting out *The Waterfront Worker* for the longshoremen. We used to read it, too. But it was mostly concerned with seamen and international affairs, like revolutions overseas. So it did not fit the situation. The decision was made to concentrate on the longshoremen.

When we started to print *The Waterfront Worker*, it was a tremendous success. Everybody who worked on or near the waterfront read it.

We'd grind *The Waterfront Worker* out. All of us worked on it—John Schomaker, Schomaker's wife, who was a typist and a stenographer, Henry Schmidt and I, and others. B. B. Jones, too. Some of the guys could type—including me, with one finger. We made a stencil each time and hand-cranked the paper out from a mimeograph machine.

All we said on the top of the paper was "Put out by a group of rank-and-file longshoremen." It was anonymous—we were afraid of being attacked and of being blacklisted again—but most everybody was getting an inkling of who was running the goddamn thing. We did name the bosses, the finks, and so forth and report their speed-ups, chiseling, forcing payoffs, and things like that.

We had young guys from Skid Row that would come down and sell the paper. At first it was a penny—then the price was raised 100 percent to two cents. The guys'd get about fifty cents for the job. They'd sell the paper during the shape-up and then around the docks.

The Waterfront Worker was clumsy and amateurish, but it had an important role in organizing the waterfront. And it played a tremendous role in getting the workers organized coastwise, or across the entire West Coast industry.

The guys in the other ports that were in cahoots with us would watch for the papers. They would distribute them in the so-called fink halls, which were waterfront employer hiring halls that existed in all the other ports. That made it easy to distribute, because that was the central place where all the longshoremen gathered, like the shape-up here.

See, *The Waterfront Worker* was loaded aboard vessels. You'd put bundles aboard the ships. We'd just leave them in the hull. There'd be a bundle for the guys in the other ports to pick up and read. There was a handful of guys in all the ports that knew the score. They would go aboard the ships and look for the papers. Then they would distribute them.

The first issue that came up was to urge the guys to join the ILA. Now this created a collision with the MWIU. We said, the MWIU is one union of seamen, longshoremen, everything. That's not good, it won't work. We should forget the idea of the MWIU and having the longshoremen and seamen in one union. Instead, we should go along and build the union of longshore on an industry-wide basis like the pattern of the East Coast ILA.

I used my experience as a former Wobbly and member of the seamen's union, a veteran of the '21 sailors' strike, and being an Australian, to get one union of longshoremen only. Being Australian helped because, especially on the waterfront here, Australia was well known as a union country. The one group of seamen and longshoremen that supported the 1919 San Francisco longshore strike, which was lost, was the Australian unionists.

Our difficulty was urging guys to join the ILA even though we took nothing back attacking it. It was a lousy, rotten, racketeering organization. We said, "We don't deny that, but let's join it. Just get in there and change it. Let's go in and take it over." The guys thought I was crazy, but we did. We took it over on the West Coast.[7]

The ILA Pacific Coast District had autonomy. There'd been a battle back around 1908 when the whole ILA was organized on the West Coast, and the West Coast got autonomy within the ILA International structure. Technically speaking, we were in full command. We eventually prevailed.

So in '33, we're out to sea. We had a meeting at the Labor Temple in San Francisco, and we were sworn into the union with the oath of obligation. We were in the ILA, District 38, San Francisco Local 79 [ILA 38–79]. The initiation fee to join the union, I think, was fifty cents. Dues were a dollar a month. And as long as you signed up, you could delay paying the dues, see?

I recall a meeting that must have been later on in '33 with a report from Henry Melnikow, a Pacific Coast Labor Bureau [PCLB] economist who represented us. It was about these National Recovery Administration [NRA] code hearings in Washington, D.C.[8] This was settling the thing by government decree. We, down below, said that's another lot of bullshit. The only thing that'll do the goddamn trick is to get organized, see, and negotiate—and strike if need be.

HARRY BRIDGES: THE COMING OF THE BIG STRIKE, 1933–1934

In this section, Bridges traces the union's progress from 1933 through the first five weeks of the 1934 strike, when twelve thousand longshoremen, joined by thousands of seafaring unionists, tied up shipping along the entire West Coast. Among other revelations, he explains why he pushed hard for the concept of a coastwise longshore contract, which has provided the foundation for the ILWU's waterfront power ever since.

Harry Bridges

In 1933 there was a hearing before a NRA board to listen to charges against the company union of the Port of San Francisco. This challenge was organized by our first local ILA officials. The ILA argument was that the company union was illegitimate. The board found in favor of the company union, saying it was a legitimate union and its contract with the shipowners was good.

Our Committee of 500 group was saying—and especially me, with my Wobbly background—that we should put all our reliance on the solidarity of the rank and file and strike clout, and that all those hearings were a lot of shit. The guys who were our early ILA officials had faith in the new NRA code. They thought, "All you had to do was take a vote, and when they took the vote, the shipowners had to deal with you."

We took a position, "To hell with that." This is what we adopted. On a certain day we'd go down to the docks—the guys used to gather at the docks in a shape-up—and we'd say, "All right. All those guys that are members of the ILA or support the union stand over here outside the docks. And all those that are not, go inside. That's the way we have an election; that's the kind of election we want."

Now, the biggest anti-union and pro-company union outfit at that time was Matson Navigation Company. The key issue there was whether we had to belong to the company union or not to go to work. Matson insisted that nobody could work there unless they were members of the company union. The NRA board had ruled that the company union was a legitimate union, but at the same time they had had to rule that we had a right to be joining the ILA.

So when Matson fired four guys for not being company union members, our rank-and-file group tied them up for five days. We were trying to spread the strike all over the waterfront. The NRA had to move in then and try to arbitrate it, and we got the four guys reinstated.

This battle really got us off the dime. We'd shut down Matson and won our right to have the ILA there. This killed Matson's idea that you'd have to be a member of the company union—the Blue Book—to work there. Piss on that. So in no time at all, as a result of this battle, everybody that worked in Matson was a member of the ILA.

After the Matson victory, the general line was to give credit to me, and not only me, but to a whole group, our rank-and-file group that had a rank-and-file program. This was a program of action on the docks, with dock stewards and dock committees, see?

I was working at this time in a steady gang, that crack gang down at the American-Hawaiian Steamship Company at Pier 26. American-Hawaiian used to have a big fleet of intercoastal ships. Pier 26 was the first pier we had completely organized. One day we set aside, everybody would wear their union button on their hat. So one day, we marched in there, and the company didn't say boo. They didn't dare. This was after, I think, the tie-up in Matson.

One big thing a little before the Matson shutdown was to insist on the adoption of a set of bylaws and the election of officers for ILA 38–79. Lee J. Holman and a bunch of others who had applied for the ILA charter from the International in New York had set themselves up as temporary officers.

Holman and his people were the conservatives who were putting all their faith in the new NRA code. Instead, we'd put together our rank-and-file group, the Committee of 500. When the elections were held, I was elected to the ILA 38–79 executive board. The majority of the board members elected came from the Committee of 500. Lee Holman made it as president. We had three business agents—two were guys we were supporting.

At this point I spent all my time working and at union meetings. I went home to sleep, and that was just about all. So, home and family—they were just forgotten. I remember that. I'm saying it the way it was.

Just before the end of '33, we started a campaign at our local. We would call a rank-and-file convention of the whole coast, see? When I laid out the program, they—the rank-and-file group I was working with—thought I was crazy. This was way beyond what they were suggesting. They didn't understand the potential there.

So we had a local meeting here in San Francisco, and we all showed up. We used to organize for the meetings to make motions and vote and so forth. We advanced our plan to have a coastwide rank-and-file convention. That was adopted. Two of us were elected to travel up and down the coast to line up the other locals. I was elected with Dutch Dietrich, who was another rank-and-file guy at that time, although later on he testified against me at a deportation hearing.

This trip was the first time I'd stepped forward and made public speeches outside of the San Francisco waterfront. We started off on the train. What we were paid was a day's pay, $6.80. That's all we got to pay our fare, the hotel rooms, and everything. We had a meeting in Portland. They agreed to go along with the scheme. We went to Seattle, spoke at the regular union meeting, and got support.

We finally went to Tacoma, Washington. The ILA local up in Tacoma had kept going all the years since 1919. Tacoma was a union port where they had a union hiring hall. By now we were making headway, and Tacoma's leader, Paddy Morris, had the reports. So he's a conservative, but he's a smart guy; he went along with it. We went down south to San Pedro, too. The convention date was set for February 1934.

We went to our rank-and-file convention that February, right in the Building Trades Temple in San Francisco.[9] We drew up a set of demands and came out with a program to set up committees, to negotiate, and, if necessary, to strike.

Our demands were for a six-hour day, a wage increase, and union hiring halls.[10] We were pretty unanimous on that. There was no argument. Paddy Morris and the more conservative guys were smart, because they were all for these things. It was a matter of trade unionism, you see? So, we come out with a program, and then we set up a negotiating committee.

Bill Lewis, who was elected president of the Pacific Coast District, ILA, at the convention, was the head of the team to negotiate a contract. But the way Lewis's team did it, the owners agreed to meet with us, but only in San Francisco. The owners took the position that there was no coastwise organization of steamship companies. There was only port by port, see? And they refused to sit down with us on an industry-wide basis.

I was the one that drove the number one demand: We'd deal only as a district. That was the way we put it, but it meant we'd want one coastwise contract covering all the ports with the same wages set in, because wages and working conditions were different in each port. Like Pedro, wages for some were a dime an hour less.

I had also studied the background of the 1916 and 1919 longshore strikes, and one of the things that broke the strikes was the ability of the employers to play one port against the other. Ships are moving plants or warehouses that can pack the goods from one port to the other. It stands to reason that when one port is on strike, and the ship can move a few miles away and be worked by members of the same union, it's ridiculous.

So, it's a very simple thing, and I can remember one of our slogans: "One port down, all down." If we had to strike, strike all the ports at one time and all the ships at one time. That's why we wanted to have an agreement covering all ports.

The employers' position was they'd make an agreement for San Francisco and then urge the other employer associations to adopt it. That gave the other employer associations of the various ports like Portland, Seattle, and Pedro the right to reject it or to accept it with some exceptions. Now, we knew they were going to have certain exceptions, see?

So when the employers came out with this proposal for San Francisco, we said, "We don't want any part of that." We dumped that and set a strike date. By this time, we'd been fighting Bill Lewis and our negotiating committee, too, for considering the employers' San Francisco proposal. We said they came up with a lousy program.

Then we got a telegraph from the White House urging postponement of the strike date so the government could do something. Well, the strike date was postponed from March the 23rd, the original date. They set up a federal mediation board at that time, and negotiations went on.

When we finally went on strike, May 9, 1934, we had four demands. I've got it written down on a telegraph form. We'd deal only as a district. We wanted a six-hour day, a thirty-hour week, one dollar an hour, and the union hiring hall. We wanted the union hiring hall because of the shape-up.

Newly emergent strike leader Harry Bridges talking to reporters, San Francisco, 1934. ILWU Library.

When the strike started, we just worked day and night to get things in shape. The main thing was to get everybody out. The other side was all prepared, and they started to recruit strikebreakers. They had big ads. And "Navy" Bill Ingram, the football coach at Cal, organized all the young men. He said he'd train the football team workin' on the waterfront. Cal was one place they went for scabs, see? They recruited not just from the football team but from the student body as a whole, and from other places.

The shipowners had a big boat tied up down near Pier 18 in San Francisco. That's where the scabs used to live, on there. Our guys patrolled, 'cause the strikebreakers used to sneak ashore, get off the docks, and come uptown. We had squads that used to lay in wait for them. They'd find 'em uptown and dump 'em and roll 'em.

We had a hell of a time because picketing was illegal. One of the reasons is the waterfront was state property. We'd get out there with our flag, our union banner, and I think we had a couple of drums to march along. Then the cops would move in and beat the shit out of us.

The first big battle with the cops was May 28. But before that, a few days after we was on strike, we fought over the so-called longshore hiring hall of the waterfront employers. It was right down there on Mission Street just a couple of blocks from the waterfront. We marched up there and raided that place. And of course the cops were there. That was our first clash with the cops. It was very small.

The big battle of May 28 started when we had a long mass demonstration parade from the Ferry Building down toward Pier 46. We had it all fixed to break into Pier 38 where the employers were collecting scab products. Somehow I think the word got out to the cops. We marched along in front of Piers 18 and 20. There was maybe one thousand of us in a long line, three or four abreast, marching with our flags and everything.

In the middle of the parade was me and a handful of guys, and on the end was another bunch of guys. Now the scheme was that as we marched past Pier 38, the middle of us would charge into the dock, kick the doors down, and scramble over the dock. Then both ends would close in and follow us in, see?

I'm in the middle of the parade to lead the break-in. When we get down to Pier 18, the cops get out in front of us and utter an order, "Stop, no further." So the guys in front sent word—John Schomaker was in command in front—asking, "What do we do?" I said, "Let's go, move. Just ignore them. No trouble, keep on marching, go right ahead."

When we started up, then the cops charged us and started to beat us up and dump us. That was the first real brawl on the waterfront.

In June of '34, with the strike a month old, Joe Ryan from New York seized his authority as the ILA International president to meet with the shipping companies and the mayor of San Francisco. He tried to settle the strike by himself. Ryan was a conservative union leader who became a prisoner of the mob. In terms of money sellouts, he got certain payoffs in one way or another.

Ryan signed an agreement in the office of the mayor, Angelo Rossi, known as the June 16 agreement. It was supposed to settle for the longshoremen only. If the agreement was adopted, we'd all go back to work and leave the other maritime unions that struck with us behind. So that would've meant breaking our agreement with the other unions to all stick together and win the strike. This essentially was the reason that the terms of the agreement were made fairly attractive, like acceptable wages, a joint hiring hall, and the discharge of scabs.

Ryan went to a special meeting we called in San Francisco on June 17. It

Pickets parading along the San Francisco waterfront, 1934 strike. Bridges, in cap, is to the left and rear of the "We Want Full Recognition" sign. ILWU Library.

was at the Eagles' Hall on Golden Gate Avenue. I was chairman of the meeting, and I had a hell of a struggle. I insisted upon Ryan's right as International president to be heard, saying it wasn't a question of whether we agree with him or not, it was the fact that he was the International president of the union. We at least owed him the courtesy of letting him have the floor.

So Ryan took the deck. He droned on and on—he had a way of talking endlessly. And the longer he talked, why, the worse things got. Guys kept running up to me on the platform to complain. Sam Kagel, our economics consultant, said, "How long are you going to let this go on?" I kept on gaveling the guys down. Then, of course, an uproar would break out in the membership, with hootin' an' hollerin'. I'd have to gavel 'em to silence and say, "Look, fellas, the president's gonna have his say."

The meeting ran to a close and a vote was taken. I insisted upon a secret ballot but my proposal was rejected by an overwhelming vote. Everyone then voted on the June 16 agreement. I think there was something like twenty-four hundred opposed and a couple of hundred fors.[11] Coastwise, the June 16 agreement was rejected in all ports except one. That was Los Angeles, or the port of San Pedro. They voted for it, in a referendum, by a small margin.

Practically all the locals outside of San Pedro voted the June 16 agreement down in special meetings by refusing to take a referendum. They said it was so lousy they wouldn't waste the time and the money. Anyway, this killed the famous June 16 agreement. That was when Ryan left San Francisco. He left town with a blast, too, saying that the Commies had taken over the strike.

Right after Ryan left town, we set up the Joint Marine Strike Committee [JMSC] for the twelve unions on strike. I was elected chairman. With the June 16 agreement repudiated, we served notice on the employers that they'd have to meet with us and negotiate. So then we took over the negotiations. I was the chief spokesman.

HARRY BRIDGES: VICTORY IN 1934

Bridges now describes the latter stages of the maritime confrontation. The walkout culminated with the San Francisco general strike of July 16–19, called to protest the killing of two workers, Howard S. Sperry and Nick Bordoise, who were shot in the back by police, and the wounding of scores of others on Bloody Thursday, July 5. Bordoise, whose name was originally George Counderakis, was known on the waterfront as Nick Bordoise, his Communist Party name.

In general strikes, all regional workers boycott their jobs. Such strikes are not very common in U.S. history and are usually short, as in this case. Ultimately, the longshore strike was settled through arbitration by Roosevelt's National Longshoremen's Board, which called for jointly run employer-union hiring halls in each port staffed by ILA dispatchers. This guaranteed an end to hiring abuses and an ILA victory that inspired an upsurge of unionism in a multitude of West Coast industries.

Harry Bridges

The JMSC used to meet every morning for an hour. Then, right across the street from where the San Francisco Post Office Annex is now, not far from the

Embarcadero, there was a vacant lot. So we called the lines together there, and I'd get up on the soapbox and make a report to our guys before they scattered and went on picket duty along the waterfront. Maybe I'd take five minutes, a half hour, whatever it was, and give 'em a day-by-day report from the strike committee.

Of course, by this time, the whole idea of us being a Communist group and the whole thing being a Communist revolution was being picked up by the press. Then the strike committee, over my objections, would draw up—this is some of the reactionary guys on the committee—a resolution condemning Communism. This would then be introduced into the San Francisco Labor Council, again over my objections. As soon as it was adopted, that was a good sign that the cops would move in and beat the shit out of us again.

I tried to tell the guys; I said, "Look, fellas, you're asking for it." I didn't know too much. I wasn't too politically apt, you see? But I knew damn well to avoid tryin' to appease the fucking press. The worst outfit then was the *San Francisco Chronicle*. And sure enough, as soon as we passed one of those resolutions and it was in the paper, the cops would come in and beat the shit out of us.

By and large, we were all greenhorn amateurs. The one who had a little actual past union experience was me. One time, we were marching, and the attitude of the guys was the cops would never shoot us. I couldn't convince them otherwise, because they knew all the cops. Then they took all the old cops off the waterfront and sent some new ones down.

Suddenly, shots rang out. One of our guys falls right down, and he's squirting blood. And of course, my partner, who was a real anti-Communist guy, said, "Hey, he's been shot!" I said, "Of course he's been fucking well shot. I've been trying to tell you that."

Then my partner wakes up and says, "Let's go!" We break away and run across the vacant lot and around the corner. Just when we turned the corner, we heard shots go through the corner of the building. One missed us by about six inches. Just got around the corner. Then I was looking around over my shoulder and I could see the cop with the gun.

There were a lot of mounted cops back then, too. But we had a few tricks ourselves. One of our maneuvers was that when we had enough dried peas or marbles, we'd scatter them around so that the horses would fall over. There was the horses scattering in every direction.

Of course, once that happened to a horse, he got extremely nervous, and

A San Francisco policeman taking an injured 1934 striker into custody as a mounted officer arrives on the scene. ILWU Library.

he was scared to move. We also had something—I forget what it was—to hit the horse's belly with, and especially his prick if it was a male. They had geldings, see? So that's how we disarmed the horses.

We also developed a way of handling tear-gas bombs. At first, the cops didn't have tear-gas guns like they had later. They threw round tear-gas bombs that were glass. They'd break, and the tear gas would come out. So we got brooms like you'd sweep the floor with. We was out there like a bunch of baseball players. When the bombs came, we'd smack them and hit them right back into the middle of the cops.

Hitting the glass tear-gas bombs with the brooms didn't break them. But when they hit the deck, they broke. We also had buckets of water, so that when the bombs fell and broke on the cobblestones near us, we threw water on them. I don't know what good that did!

San Francisco police violence injured scores of strikers in 1934. ILWU Library.

There was another thing we did. Right down there across from Pier 46, they had torn down a building. A big vacant lot was being built up there. There was small stacks of bricks all over this vacant lot.

It was just perfect, because you got in there, and then the cops couldn't charge. The horses couldn't come in. We were there with a ready-made load of ammunition if we had to make a stand. It was made to order, you know? You didn't have to have many fuckin' brains to figure out how to handle that.

When we buried Nick Bordoise, the cook that got killed on Bloody Thursday, Sam Darcy made a fighting speech. I liked his tone. Darcy was the regional head of the Communist Party. He said, "We didn't come out here to cry, and Nick wouldn't want us to cry. What Nick wants is 'The fight must go on. We're just gettin' started.'"

This was Darcy's line. You bet your life. He said, "These are casualties, sure. But what Nick wants is 'No more casualties; we only want the casualties from the bosses, not from us anymore.'" That was no goddamn speech of "Here we're burying a martyr, and we start saying prayers." Bullshit, no.

You see, in a small way, temporarily a strike is a small revolution. A strike

Two of the workers shot by the San Francisco police, Bloody Thursday, July 5, 1934.
Charles Olsen (*left*) recovered, but Howard Sperry died. Nick Bordoise, found a block
away, was also killed by police gunfire that day. ILWU Library.

is a very serious thing. The strike weapon should never be used except as a last
desperate resort, when there's no way out. It simply means a form of revolution
because you take over an industry or a plant owned by the capitalists and temporarily you seize it. Temporarily you take it away.

That's another way of saying to an employer or an industry—in this case,
we said it to the shipowners of the whole world—"You might be worth millions
or billions; we don't say you own this until we tell you to operate." But never
do that unless you're sure you're able to do it. Therefore, we approach a strike,
at least I do, as a very serious thing. I approach it from the point of it being a
small revolution, and takin' over that industry or plant, we own it the while.
We seize it until we get our price.

In late June of 1934, the National Longshoremen's Board was set up by
President Roosevelt to mediate the strike, and then later on to arbitrate it. That's
what they eventually did. We fought arbitration all the way down the line,

'cause one of our demands was that we shall not arbitrate. But the San Francisco general strike was settled with arbitration.

We went back to work at the end of July. The arbitration hearings took place, and the decision came down on October 12, which was a big resounding victory. The union-controlled hiring hall we won officially went into effect around the spring.

We were the first union that called things together and took the position that nobody would shape up at the docks anymore. Of course, at first we didn't have a hiring hall, but by taking action, we forced hiring through the union hall near Mission Street and the Embarcadero.

After we returned to work, there was an awful lot of activity. Half the time we'd be taking job actions [short, spontaneous strikes] over conditions and tying up ships to get scab seamen off.

All longshore strikebreakers had to be laid off, fired, but there was a distinction. Longshoremen that had been working before and didn't go on strike were called "loyal employees," and the order did not apply to them. They were officially longshoremen on the waterfront. The other guys were just called scabs.

I thought the loyal employees deserved another chance. I went and appeared before the gang bosses in San Francisco who'd stayed on the job and said, "You should be judged from what you do from here on in. You didn't understand, we weren't able to get to you the right way. Now, join the union and fly right from here on in. Everybody's welcome."

I went on, "You weren't the guys who actually came to break the strike. All the scabs were fired. At least you guys were already here. After this, we all work together. That's the name of the game from here on in." But I also told them, "Now, if we want to get rid of you guys, we can. We can hard-time you. So straighten up and fly right." Then I went and fought it out with the membership and got their agreement. And most of those guys turned out to be the best union men we ever had.

Same old principle—you're going to make mistakes. We can all make mistakes. We're not better than that. It was the same with the San Francisco black guys who were loyal employees and stayed in, except I had a tougher time settling the membership thing.

I had to go into the whole question of blacks. I said, "Look, fellas, the only way these guys ever got a job was as scabs. The bosses saw to that. Let's right now say, 'You've got a job as a working stiff. No discrimination.'" Same thing, see?

The way we integrated our local was we had some black gangs that we pulled out in the middle of the strike. So we started off with a small number and built it up as we went along.

When the strike started, all the black gangs at certain docks stayed in. They didn't come out. Luckenbach dock and the Grace Line dock were the two main black docks. These black guys had been imported to break the 1919 longshore strike. That's how they come onto the docks in the first place.

So in 1934, we concentrated on getting them out. After we'd been on strike about a month, they'd come out. Some of them, not all of them. But by the end of the strike, I think we had all the black gangs out.

It was the same thing with many of the guys we organized later. Some licensed officers sailed all during the strike. When we set up the Maritime Federation of the Pacific [MFP] in 1935 to get all the marine unions united, we had to say, "Look, we gotta count them in." That's how we put together the federation. We said, "Forget what they did do from here on in."

That's why, in 1936, when the maritime unions struck again, it was solid as a rock. No trouble at all. It was the end for the employers. After '34, they never, never tried to use scabs again.

So after '34, this thing paid off. Giving those guys a chance meant they closed ranks and just served notice on the employers that they didn't dare operate in 1936. They couldn't get scabs in the area anymore either. We made the rounds of the colleges and the unemployed down on the Skid Row and said, "Don't scab." We covered all those places, and we lined up the labor movement.

Don't forget, thirty-five thousand workers joined the union movement during the four days of the San Francisco general strike in '34. And we organized the city's streetcar lines. There was the municipal line, and then there was a private Market Street railway. That was a line with a bad record, too. It was tough to organize, but we organized it.

We were organizing during the '34 strike and afterwards. The guys used to take time off to go into restaurants and organize, and into all kinds of places all over the waterfront. They used to ask, "Where's your union card?" at a bar, or at this, that, or the other plant, like the American Can plant and various places like that.

We're the ones that organized and shut down the big store at Fifth and Market Streets in San Francisco. That was Hale's back then. We were working with other unions and the Labor Council.

After the '34 strike, we also held anti-fascist, anti-Nazi demonstrations. We started on the scrap iron beef where we boycotted exports to fascist Japan.

By this time, the Nazis had taken over in Germany. A new German cargo ship came to Oakland. On every German ship there was a couple of storm troopers, and they really run the ship. Now a lot of the crews were Communists on the q.t. So, I forget the ship's name, but she sunk over there in Oakland. She was fully loaded, and after we finished the job and got all our people off, she quietly went down alongside of the dock. She was a brand-new ship on her maiden voyage. Fritz Wiedemann was head of the German consul in San Francisco. He screamed that we deliberately sabotaged her. We called it a complete accident!

My last time working on the waterfront was just before the '34 strike. When the strike was over, as chairman of the strike committee, I didn't go back to work. I stayed on negotiating, and elections took place, and I was elected president of the San Francisco longshore local.

In office, I always felt that the ones that direct everything is the rank and file. And I'm its spokesman, that's all. The rank and file is the power of the union, see? They're the ones that can shut things down.

Everybody was pulling together in 1934. We had across-the-board unity of all kinds of guys that later on turned vicious and red-baiting and so forth, but not then. We had a beautiful united front.

SAM KAGEL: UNION ADVOCATE, 1934

Sam Kagel retired as coast arbitrator, or impartial judge in contract disagreements, for the longshore industry in 2002 after fifty-four years on the job. But Kagel started his career seven decades earlier as a union advocate for the Pacific Coast Labor Bureau, a consulting firm that represented organized workers in negotiations, mediations, and arbitrations.

The PCLB was new when the twenty-three-year-old Kagel joined it in 1932. Once the 1934 strike began, he worked with Bridges daily. After the strike, Kagel represented the union through the rest of the 1930s.

Sam Kagel

About 1906, my father, Hyman Kagel, came to San Francisco to avoid the czar's army and to get his butt out of rural Russia, where the Jews were being slaughtered. He knew my mother, Zelda, who was from a Russian village some miles from his. When she first got to this country, my mother worked in the Triangle Shirtwaist Company in New York. That was where they had the huge fire in 1911 that killed so many women who had been locked inside by the factory owners. Fortunately, my mother left for San Francisco way before that happened.

I was born in San Francisco in 1909. When I was about five, we moved to the East Bay and settled in Oakland, where my parents bought into a small grocery store at the corner of Fourth and Harrison. That was part of a poor working-class neighborhood then. When I was in the sixth grade at the Harrison Street School, I used to collect stale bread from a local sandwich maker so we could feed the kindergarten kids.

At our house, we had a little shed where my father piled newspapers to sell. My chore was to bundle them. I became a speed-reader by racing through the comic strips. Even before high school, I read Jack London, who was from our Oakland neighborhood. Eventually I got to Frank Norris, Emile Zola, Anatole France, and Upton Sinclair. Those guys were basically sociologists who turned out to be great writers. Zola wrote a fantastic story about coal miners. He also opposed discrimination in France during the famous Dreyfus case.

As a kid, I worked loading watermelons into horse-drawn wagons for the local fruit sellers. My father drove one of those wagons. We had a fruit stand in the produce market. When the watermelons came into Oakland on trains, I would drop a few off for the Wobblies who rode the rods. The Wobblies, as they were known, were members of the radical IWW.

The Wobblies would talk with me generally in their economic terms, although we never had any great or long conversations. I knew about them though. Six blocks from our house there was an IWW reading room. About 1923, I saw a bunch of guys dressed in army uniforms trash the place. They threw the Wobblies' typewriters, furniture, and books out into the street. This was part of the post–World War I red scare of the early 1920s.

I also remember a couple of guys coming to our house around the same time. They wanted my mother to turn the minutes of the Workingman's Circle over to them. She was the secretary of that group, which was an organization of Jewish people whose primary interest was supporting strikers. My mother wouldn't give these guys the minutes. She was not even an American citizen at the time. I thought that was very brave of her.

In the mid-1920s, I went to the University of California, Berkeley. I paid my way working in the produce markets and passing out towels in the Harmon Gym. My senior year I was hired to read examination papers in economics. I graduated in 1929 and became an economics graduate student and a teaching fellow. Then I met Paul S. Taylor, the labor economist, who was at Cal. He got me a job with the PCLB.

I took the PCLB job on a temporary basis in 1932 and stayed for ten years. The Labor Bureau was part of a New York outfit. Our Pacific Coast office was set up in San Francisco by Henry Melnikow, who had been representing the typographical union in negotiations and arbitrations for a year or two when he hired me as an assistant. Melnikow was a brilliant statistician and economist. He really knew how to present witnesses and how to cross-examine, too.

I couldn't have gotten a better teacher than Melnikow. When he had an arbitration case, I would do the research and help put together the exhibits. Remember, this was the Great Depression that started in 1929, and the employers were cutting wages. Usually the question was how small the cut was going to be. In increases, you were talking about two or three cents an hour. When we got that, we'd go out and get drunk.

Of course, nobody knew what was going to happen during the following nine or ten years. Between '32 and '41 or '42, we had what I would consider fifty years of labor experiences all smashed into this short period.

When the unions began to stir in the 1930s, the Labor Bureau was the only place they could come to. Lawyers were not in the collective bargaining field yet. We only used lawyers when we got arrested. Generally the lawyers didn't get into collective bargaining until the U.S. got into World War II in the early 1940s. When the War Labor Board [WLB] was set up with millions of regulations, then the unions got the shit in their neck [had trouble], as we said on the waterfront, and the employers likewise. Then we all ran to our lawyers

In 1932, the PCLB had a small office in Room C on the mezzanine of San Francisco's Ferry Building. The Ferryboatmen's Union, the Masters, Mates, and Pilots [MMP], and the Marine Engineers' Beneficial Association [MEBA] were all in the Ferry Building, too. Our office had glass windows facing the bay. I saw the Bay Bridge being built from the first hole to the weaving of the last cables.

I started to get acquainted with the longshoremen around 1932. That's about when I met Harry Bridges. This was before the San Francisco longshore local was actually set up. On occasion, the longshoremen would come around and talk with Clyde Deal of the Ferryboatmen's Union. Then they would talk with us or with me, particularly because that's what I was assigned to do. Harry wasn't a big name with us at first. He was just another longshoreman among several who wanted to get rid of the company-dominated Blue Book union.

Once section 7A of the National Industrial Recovery Act passed in 1933, things changed. Section 7A said workers could join real unions, although there wasn't statutory enforcement until the Wagner Act passed two years later. Still, under section 7A, Matson Navigation had to rehire longshoremen they had fired for union activity. That was a big deal. As Harry said, that was the end of the Blue Book.[12]

Our Labor Bureau office developed a union petition and gave copies to the active longshoremen. They went up and down the waterfront signing everybody into the Pacific Coast District of the ILA.

In 1934, the longshoremen demanded a coastwide agreement, a union hiring hall that would get rid of the fink halls at the other ports and the morning shape-up for jobs in San Francisco, a six-hour day to spread employment around, and some increase in wages. Once the '34 strike began and the other maritime unions went out, too, the longshoremen expanded their original demands to include the requirement of a settlement for everyone.

I discussed all these things continually with Harry. These demands were solely what the longshoremen up and down the coast said they wanted. They were all pure pork chop issues. They were not designed politically by Communists, Republicans, Democrats, or anybody else, despite the employer charges at the time that the '34 strike was a Communist uprising.

Five weeks into the strike, Harry became chairman of the Joint Marine Strike Committee set up then by all the maritime unions. For all intents and purposes, he was the committee. There were other outstanding guys on the JMSC, like Randolph Meriwether, who headed the MEBA, but Merry did whatever Harry wanted to do and whatever I advised.

I actually became a member of the JMSC because of Meriwether. I represented his union and worked with him on everything. We became close friends. When they said to pick guys to represent the MEBA on the JMSC, Merry said he wanted me as one, even though I was not a member of his union per se. But I was made an honorary member in June 1934.

It was all very exciting. Here I was, for God's sake, a young guy in the midst of an event I knew was of major concern. I knew that because I already had

Harry Bridges (*left*) and Sam Kagel conferring in 1934. Henry Melnikow is visible on the right, and Matt Meehan is at the upper left. ILWU Library.

this background in labor economics and history. I was full of piss and vinegar, too. Hours and days meant nothing to me. We would go day and night, weekends included. There was no such thing as regular hours.

I lived in Berkeley but could get to San Francisco easily because the ferryboats were not on strike. Sometimes, when it got late, I would stay overnight in this wonderful old hotel near the waterfront. It was right across from the Southern Pacific Building. I think it was called the Terminal Hotel. They charged a dollar a night. Sometimes, when it got very late, I just slept on my desk at the Labor Bureau. But I never felt put upon. This was part of the job. I was representing unions, and I was a member of the JMSC. I wasn't there for the fun of it.

Then came the battle on Bloody Thursday, July 5, when the employers tried to force open the port. I saw a lot, although, thank God, I didn't see the guys getting shot in the back. I was in my office in the Ferry Building when everything started. You could smell the fumes from the gas and from whatever else the police were shooting, and you could hear shots. I left my office and watched the battle as it moved up and down the waterfront. The mounted cops tried to break up the crowds of strikers by using their horses' rumps to move in and separate people. And I saw guys getting clubbed.

During the middle of Bloody Thursday, Archbishop Edward J. Hanna, who later served on the board that arbitrated the strike, got me on the telephone. He wanted to meet with people from the JMSC. The only other member I could get at that moment was Ed O'Grady of the MMP. We went to see the archbishop. He wanted us to do something to stop the rioting. He was very worried about it. I said, "Hey, so is everybody else. People are getting killed!" I pointed out to the archbishop that what was going on was beyond our control. It was the police who were using tear gas and live ammunition.

Despite the violence, federal mediation hearings were ongoing during the strike. I had to testify for the MEBA on July 9, the day of the great funeral march up Market Street for the two workers the police killed on Bloody Thursday. I cut the mediation proceedings off at the end so I could join the funeral procession. Nobody said anything while we marched. Except for the low music and the shuffling of shoes, there wasn't a single sound. We just got in line and walked.

I can still see the San Francisco general strike of July 16–19 held to protest the killings. I can still see it and feel it. It was an exhilarating moment at the beginning. I looked up Market Street and there was nothing moving. It was like in the movies, where something happens and all of a sudden the film shows blank. But it was short-lived, as it had to be. It was really a sympathy strike that was ended before it could completely unravel.

We had Harry testify before the National Longshoremen's Board set up by President Roosevelt to arbitrate the longshore strike. Harry had been on the waterfront for years, had worked all types of cargo, and had been a member of a star gang, which was a kind of pre-strike steady gang that was really a form of favoritism. We knew he was articulate because we had been dealing with him, and his name was "the name" in this event. So what better witness do you want to describe the conditions on the waterfront? Harry was made to order.[13]

We didn't want to put on a lot of witnesses. There was no point to that. So we used Harry. I worked with him for hours getting him prepared for the testimony. He and I used to sit in our office at the Labor Bureau, work hard, and drink Old Quaker, which was one of the earliest whiskeys that came out after Prohibition ended in 1933.

I remember how Harry spoke publicly in those days, and afterwards as well. He wasn't given to impassioned speeches. He just explained what the situation was on the waterfront, what the longshoremen wanted and why they wanted it. He never got excited when we met with the JMSC or the federal mediators or when he appeared as a witness in the arbitration proceedings. Harry just knew where he wanted to go and how he was going to get there, and it was no big excitement.

Harry's testimony to the National Longshoremen's Board was outstanding, and the union got its basic demands satisfied in the '34 strike arbitration award. One thing the award did not cover was conditions like sling load limits. In those pre-container days, the hand-worked cargo was moved to and from ships in slings. Before 1934, the loads were too heavy and were dangerous. So once the longshoremen were back to work, they undertook by job action, or quickie strike, to cut down on the size of the loads. The employers screamed bloody murder about these work stoppages.

There was an arbitration system set up after the '34 strike under which the secretary of labor selected arbitrators for the longshore industry. The first arbitrator, Judge Max C. Sloss, who had been on the California Supreme Court, decided some early cases against the union, including these work stoppage beefs. He called me at least twice to complain since Melnikow and I were representing the union. Sloss said the longshoremen were not obeying his work-stoppage decrees.

I told Harry about this. He said, "Look, I tell the guys to cut it out. That's the best I can do." Finally he went to his membership. They took a vote and decided to seriously observe the Sloss awards. But in the meantime, the sling loads were reduced in practice. There was some slowing of the cargo hook as well, which meant that the pre-strike speed-up was eliminated.

Looking back, Harry's great achievement was in setting up a democratic union that was exactly the opposite of the kind of autocratic union then in existence on the East Coast under ILA president Joe Ryan. Harry was the guy, there's no question about it, and it wasn't the Communists who did it. Harry was accused of copying the Communist line, which is crap. Of course, the Communists were very active in the 1930s, and they were looking for credit wherever they could get it, but they didn't have anything really important to do with running the '34 strike or Bridges.

BILL CHESTER: CIVIL RIGHTS LEADER

Bill Chester joined the ILWU in the late 1930s. He was appointed northern California regional director by Bridges in 1951 and was elected ILWU International vice president in 1969. He was the union's first black International officer. Throughout his career, he was associated with the ILWU's use of its power to fight discrimination on the job and in the wider San Francisco community.

Bill Chester

I'm the son of a railroad worker. I was born in Shreveport, Louisiana, in 1914. My early school days were spent in Kansas City, Missouri. After high school, I went to Western College in Kansas for two years. My father died when I was eleven years old. I had no sisters or brothers, but my mother and I were like pals in the early ages coming through the Depression of the 1930s.

Because of the Depression, I had to interrupt my education. I enlisted in the Twenty-fifth Infantry Regiment of the U.S. Army and was stationed for three years at Fort Huachuca, Arizona. We were an all-Negro unit.[14] This was before integration took place in the army. There were only two Negroes in official capacity at that time, the chaplain and a warrant officer. I was dissatisfied that there were no Negro line officers. It was at that point that I started thinking about the social evils of our country. That was the very beginning of my thinking about civil rights.

Some people who were visiting the fort told me about San Francisco. I had read a little about it, and my company commander was from that city. There was something that struck me about the way they spoke about the town. When I was discharged—this was in the late 1930s, prior to World War II—I decided to travel to California to take a look.

When I arrived in San Francisco, I had the names and addresses of a couple of friends who were shipping out in the old Marine Cooks and Stewards Association [MCS]. When I got there, they were at sea, so I took a room at the YMCA. It happened that about a block away, on the Embarcadero, was the hiring hall of the longshoremen's union. Being out of a job, I was told they hired there. So I went up, stood in line, and got work. That was the start of my employment in the maritime industry.

When I first entered the labor movement on the San Francisco waterfront, there were only seventy-five blacks in the longshore local. They weren't very active. Most of them were blacks who had originally been brought out by the Luckenbach Steamship Company for the purpose of strikebreaking. But our International president at that time, Harry Bridges, told me he went down and talked with these workers and persuaded them to join the 1934 strike and come into the union. Most of these workers were well-meaning men who made a contribution in the union to the best of their abilities.

I continued in employment in the maritime industry around San Francisco from 1938 until World War II in the early 1940s. I was called back into the service then and stayed there until the war ended in 1945. When I came back to San Francisco, I was reinstated to ILWU membership. I've been here ever since.

The great influx of blacks into the maritime industry on the West Coast started during World War II. There was a great shortage of manpower in the longshore industry because of the many ships that had to be loaded. The longshore workforce in the San Francisco area went from about 3,200 to 10,000. It was then that blacks who were working in some closed Gulf Coast ports migrated to California. The ILWU on the waterfront was one of the few unions in San Francisco where they could get a job without discrimination.

On the other hand, policies of discrimination existed in the ILWU on the West Coast, although the union's International constitution forbade it. The Portland longshore local excluded Negroes for a number of years. To bring about equality and truly eliminate discrimination, a group of us San Francisco area blacks formed ourselves into what nowadays you'd call a black caucus. But in those days, in the 1940s, we just called it "getting the boys together to talk over a problem."

It was really about five or six of us at the beginning. We would get together and talk about what should be done to eliminate visual discrimination. We felt that the number one job was that blacks had to prove that they were just as good if not better union men than the whites. Their performance on the job and at meetings had to be outstanding in going along with policies that were constructive and opposing policies that we felt were destructive.

From that basis, we felt that any time there were new members to be admitted to the union, representation of all the races in the community should be there. This policy succeeded to the extent that we've come from seventy-five black members in 1940 to the point where now [1969] about 51 percent of the longshore membership in the Port of San Francisco is black.

Longshore Local 10 hiring hall, San Francisco, 1946. ILWU Library.

We were fortunate in the beginning, too, to find a group of well-meaning "progressive whites," as we called them, who would work with us. They were not in our caucus, but they knew what we were doing. At membership meetings, as we presented our program, we more or less had their unqualified support. Most of them were somewhat older men. Many have been pensioned off or have passed on. They were a fine coalition of progressive whites that gave us every bit of help that we needed.

The first leadership job I had within the union in San Francisco was as shop steward of the gang on the ship that I worked in. Then I was elected chairman of the local's investigating committee, which evaluates men for promotions to different job categories. It also investigates potential new members. I suppose that where I became more known was during the 1948 longshore strike, when I was elected chairman of the publicity committee. In those days, there was a white majority, but I got enough white support to get elected.

As far as jobs are concerned, today we have a longshore union membership committee of four. I'm the chairman. The employers also have four people. Since 1959, this joint committee's been intact. All the workers who have been admitted to the longshore industry in the Port of San Francisco have been approved by this joint committee.

The committee on the union's side has had progressive-minded, thinking whites. The strangest thing is that we've educated the employers, too. When we get ready to register men now, the employers will say, "Bill, did you make sure you got some black people from Hunter's Point in San Francisco? Did you take care of the black people from West Oakland?"

For some of this progress you have to give credit to the people from Hunter's Point and West Oakland, because they made their wishes known with a loud, clear voice. Well, each time we've admitted men, our joint committee's been lucky enough. I put it this way since at least 50 percent of all the new people registered have been black.

Later this year, we're going to register six hundred new men. We're processing applications now. In selecting the six hundred, we gave representation to the black community, to the brown community, to the yellow community, and to the white community, too, where that's located in poverty areas.

In 1951, I was appointed by International President Harry Bridges as the ILWU northern California regional director for the territory covering Fresno to the Oregon border. I served as regional director for eighteen years.

This year, I was elected International vice president. Jack Hall, our great Hawaii regional director who organized the Islands, wanted to run for the job. The blacks, Mexican Americans, and liberal whites felt it was necessary for me to make a race for the job, too, because our union couldn't be one step behind the times. We took the position that with the people in the South on the move, as liberal as our whites were at the International level, it was about time some black made a contest for that job.

Our union was so broad-minded that the members amended the International constitution and added another vice president. So Jack got elected vice president and so did I. People felt confrontation might tend to destroy black and white unity. After evaluating things, they decided there was a need for another vice president. We'd had one in the past and we had eliminated it. Since that time we had increased our membership, so we added one back.

Once the blacks in the ILWU started making the move for full equality, change filtered throughout the entire maritime industry. When I first started, there wasn't a black girl working in the office. Since then, we've had three black office managers. Some eleven years ago, I was asked by the employers' group, the Pacific Maritime Association, to recommend a black for the job of port captain. I recommended a member of our union who is still the port captain for Pacific Far East Lines.

Unions in the industry like the Marine Firemen, Oilers, Watertenders, and Wipers Association [MFOW] once had a policy of exclusion of blacks. But because of the appearance of blacks in the ILWU, we got blacks into the MFOW. We were also able to break down the lily-white structure in the Sailors' Union of the Pacific. In all of the various branches of the maritime industry, including the organizations of ships' officers, we've caused the other unions to take notice and break down discrimination.

We also went outside of the labor movement to bring our union programs to the wider community. This is something we discussed years ago. We found that, in a sense, the union is the community. Therefore, a labor leader in modern times could no longer confine all of his activities just to collective bargaining and not take the responsibility of following that worker to his community to see that he had the same protection there that he had on the job.

We found that many members of our union—practically all of the blacks— were members of the National Association for the Advancement of Colored People [NAACP]. Some were chairmen of the boards of trustees at Baptist and Methodist churches. So as black leaders in the trade union movement, we worked collectively with the Baptist ministers group, or any other religious or civic organization.

Our first alliances were with ministers with churches about the size of this living room. Later, the more sophisticated minister came along. I have attended many of the Baptist ministers' meetings that they hold on the ministerial alliance level. I have always been made welcome because I've always gone there to talk about unity between the clergy, the rest of the community, and the trade union movement.

One of the ministers I work closely with now is Dr. Hamilton Boswell. He impressed me greatly with his theory that he didn't believe in telling people how they were going to live in heaven if he couldn't help them live well here on earth.

If a church needed some money to buy a bus to bring kids to Sunday school,

Dr. Martin Luther King Jr. visiting longshore Local 10 in 1967. During this visit, Local 10 made King an honorary member of the ILWU. *Left to right*: Curtis McClain (ILWU); Reverend King; Albert James (ILWU); Bill Chester (ILWU), who arranged Dr. King's visit; LeRoy King (ILWU); Reverend Ralph Abernathy; Dr. Gus White; Reverend Edward Stovall; and Revels Cayton (ILWU). ILWU Library.

we took the lead in the union in saying, "We're going to donate $250 toward that bus." Every year, we bought a $500 membership in the NAACP. We sponsored St. Francis Square, a low-cost housing project in San Francisco's Western Addition that opened in 1963.

We went into every aspect of community life. We encouraged our black members to deposit with savings and loan associations run by blacks. The union did business with Kaiser Hospital, so we met with Edgar Kaiser and said, "We want some black interns and black physicians on the staff." Everywhere we could, we made the union's weight felt. Not only did we do that for the black community, we did it for the brown community, too.

We went to city hall in San Francisco and told the mayor, "There's not a black supervisor up there. We don't feel the city right now is sophisticated enough to elect one, but you appoint one, and we'll elect him next time." We were successful in getting Terry Francois appointed as the first black supervisor. We followed that up by getting the first Mexican American appointed, and we're working now on getting a Chinese person appointed. Then we'll fight for their reelection. We were successful in electing Willie Brown as assemblyman for the Eighteenth Assembly District, too.[15]

We've also used the union's strength to get blacks hired in private industry. For example, we got $60 million of pension fund money in the Bank of America. I am one of the trustees. So I told the bank officials, "You are using my door and my money and my members. I'd like to see some black girls and boys around here in some of these banks." This is the way you have to be to get the job done.

Because of the way San Francisco blacks in the longshore industry have gotten along with their white allies and been able to utilize their union strength in the community, they have also served to break down racial discrimination in most of the other trade unions in town. San Francisco is one of the most unionized cities in the United States. But for a number of years, we didn't have black plumbers or electricians. There was nothing in the building trades. Yet as a result of community pressure, and of showing that it can be done and can work, we've been able to crack through in some of the building trades locals. We're beginning to make overall progress.

Here's another example of the kinds of things we've done. In 1945 we had a Negro named Audry Cole. He passed the San Francisco civil service exam to drive streetcars for the city. He took his first car out and drove it to the beach. Some whites pulled him off the car and whipped him. They didn't want Negroes to drive streetcars.

We said, "Cole, you're going to drive that car." Then guys in our union— there were always four or five of us—would ride the streetcar whenever he was driving. We rode in shifts, putting in two hours apiece. He didn't have any more trouble. As a result, today 55 percent of all the people who drive buses and streetcars in San Francisco are Negroes.

Around 1951, I was appointed West Coast regional director for the old National Negro Labor Council. I remember when we had a delegation that went into Sears and Roebuck and demanded that Negro salesgirls be employed. We were politely told that they didn't think the public would accept it. Besides, they said this was a policy matter that would have to go to the national officials of the firm in the East.

So we promptly put up a picket line where a new Sears and Roebuck facility was under construction. We used ILWU signs and banners along with National Negro Labor Council signs. We knew that even though you might catch a local union where their own policies were discriminatory, if you had what they considered a bona fide picket line in front of any establishment, they wouldn't cross it.

Well, the Teamsters wouldn't deliver. The building trades people wouldn't work. Construction stopped. So the company officials came out from Chicago and assured us that when the store opened, all people would be hired regardless of race. If you go to Sears and Roebuck now, you'll find black buyers, salesgirls, and everything else.

We were pretty well established by the 1950s as a group of workers who didn't just look at their own selfish points of view as far as what they had economically. We were willing to participate and spread the experience that we had learned in the trade union movement. In my experience, the best avenue of success is proper organization. And I found that the black community had all of the potentials. It was just a question of organizing and putting it together to where they could collectively go down and talk with the power structure to get some benefits from it.

CLEOPHAS WILLIAMS: AFRICAN AMERICAN PRESIDENT

In 1967 Cleophas (Bill) Williams became the first black worker elected president of San Francisco Bay longshore Local 10. The union membership reelected him president three times during a long and distinguished career with the ILWU that spanned the years 1944–81.

Cleophas Williams

I was born in 1923 in Camden, Arkansas, a little place about seven miles from the Ouachita River. My father, John Henry Williams, was principal of a school for black children. My mother, Bertha, was a schoolteacher also, but she died when I was three and a half. Later, my father married a wonderful lady named Ardella, who was a very caring, meticulous, and loving mother. She taught me my ABCs and my first numbers. She's still alive today [1998] in L.A. at ninety-four years.

My father was feared by local whites because he was very courageous. When he went to the country store in Lester, Arkansas, certain deferences were expected of him that he didn't offer. And when whites would come to the house for some reason, they would come in twos and threes, never one on one.

In 1929, when the stock market crash occurred, my father was teaching school as principal in Chidester, Arkansas, for a hundred dollars a month. When he got his next assignment, his wages came down to ninety dollars. He decided to pull his money and buy a truck farm, twelve or fifteen acres. He planted corn. When the crop came in, a group of night riders, or Klansmen, tore the fence down, rode up and down the roads screaming and hollering, and totally destroyed the corn.

The night-rider attack wiped us out, so my father went to Ashdown, Arkansas, to teach school. His wages there were down to thirty-five dollars a month. Then we moved to Hope, Arkansas, but things were still very difficult.

In Hope, there were always white families who would come to our house asking for food. Dad would never refuse them. Our food was just basic getting-by food, but whatever we had, we shared. These white migrants would get off the train at this little whistle-stop and knock on our door. They never expressed the antagonism we often saw displayed in other places.

My sisters and I tried to pick cotton so we could get shoes and school clothes. It was tough to go out there with people who had experience with these long canvas cotton bags. At the end of a week, I hadn't earned enough for a pair of shoes. Finally, my father and mother decided to teach us at home that year. They made sure we were well educated. We were poor, but we had good books and an encyclopedia.

The only white kids we saw were on the street or in the store. The lines were clearly defined. Black and white were segregated, including when we went back to elementary school in Hope. Later, I went to Booker T. Washington High School in Texarkana. It was an all-black school, too. We have an alumni association now from that school. I'm the secretary of the northern California chapter.

I was at another segregated school, Arkansas Agricultural, Mechanical, and Normal College in Pine Bluff, when the draft board got on me in 1942. Before I went into the army, I came out to California to work at Moore's Shipyard in Oakland as an electrician's helper. I'd made a dollar and a half a day as an assistant maintenance man in a hotel in Texarkana. At that time it was the best job I'd ever had, and the white engineer there taught me a great deal about electricity.

When I got to California, I went to the employment office and told them I had done electrical work. They sent me to Local 595 of the International Brotherhood of Electrical Workers [IBEW] for some kind of clearance as a union person to work at Moore's. That was the first time I'd ever been in a union hall. I made ninety cents an hour working on these Victory and Liberty Ship freighters.

There was discrimination, of course, but things were so much better than where I had come from that I appreciated the improvement. The money seemed astronomical at close to fifty dollars a week. The IBEW took my dues money and gave me the right to work on a permit. But they didn't invite me to any union meetings, and I didn't go to any.

I was drafted into the army during 1942–43, got discharged because of a knee injury, and returned to Moore's. But contracts were getting slimmer and slimmer for Moore. I heard a fellow talking in a barbershop about longshoring. There was a surplus of longshore work in those days. I looked into it and got referred down to the waterfront for processing on February 15, 1944. That was the date I was hired.

The next day, I went to work at Pier 23 in the hold of a ship discharging coffee. That first job was with "Goat" Labin's gang. The work—it was all break bulk then—was very hard because I didn't know what I was doing. The old-timers would let you fail for a while and enjoy the comedy. Then they'd come over and show you how to do the work.

There was a lot of hard work, too. Sugar in one-hundred-pound sacks, for example, was stored in very tight. The sweat from the ship or any moisture would cause it to become compacted, and you had to break it loose with your hook. We had special sugar hooks that were different from regular cargo hooks. We tried to make slides to take advantage of gravity to bring the sugar down, but when it got low, we had to muscle it.

Back then, more white fellows worked in San Francisco than in the East Bay. When I got on the East Bay side, I ran across lots of black longshoremen from the Gulf Coast who had had experience. They'd heard there was plenty of work here, and longshoring was kind of short on the Gulf. They taught me lots about the work.

I didn't feel any hostility from the white longshoremen, although some were very indifferent. You were kind of a nonperson to them. They'd walk by and wouldn't speak to you. Those who were more active in expressing concern, I later found out, were considered to be left-wingers. They were the ones that would come over and speak to you and ask you about your housing and your transportation.

In '45, when the war wound down, work reached a point where they didn't need all the men who were here. They had to lay off about eight hundred, and they were just about all recently hired black fellows. But because of seniority of hiring, that was understood. We were used to being hired last and fired first. The first group of fellows who were knocked off were given the impression that if work ever improved, they'd get back on. That never did happen. I survived because my registration predated theirs.

There was antagonism between some whites and blacks then because the new black leaders articulated our vision and our hopes very well. Albert James from the Gulf and Johnny Walker from New Orleans were the most vocal. They brought their labor background here from their history with the ILA in the Gulf. They transferred their skills to the union combats here.

James was so fluent he could take an idea and make it visible. Walker was very courageous, and Bill Chester, a new leader then, too, was very methodical. I was still very young; I listened. I didn't even understand how you made a motion on the union floor. I had to learn totally from scratch. But I learned from them and from others.

In the meantime, Harry Bridges talked at most meetings. He made one remark that took him off the fence completely and put him on the blacks' side. He said that if things reached a point where only two men were left on the waterfront, if he had anything to say about it, one would be a black man. So that was very clear where he stood. No vacillating at all.

After that, the hounds were really at his tail. There was an element in the union that constantly vilified him at meetings. The comments might not be directly racial, but you didn't have to be very brilliant to understand that one of the reasons for these attacks upon Harry was his stand on race. Bridges was not a personal friend of mine, but I don't know anybody I admired more. Some of the things he did were just incredible for the time.[16]

Around this same period, in the mid-'40s, I attended the California Labor School [CLS]. The ILWU backed it, and many of its teachers were identified with the Left. The first time, I went in order to get my union book. I was forced to go then. Later on, I chose to go. I took history, sociology, and economics. These classes expanded my mind. This was the first time I had ever gone to an integrated school. I was curious. I wanted to know. And what I wanted to know, the CLS taught.[17]

In 1950, the McCarthy era and the waterfront screening program came along almost simultaneously. The Korean War brought on the screening. It was devastating for all of us, black and white, because many of the fellows who had flirted with the CP [Communist Party] were screened out and couldn't get cleared for navy or army work. Just being on the waterfront, it seemed, we were suspect.

I'd gone to the CLS, I was in all the marches, I subscribed to the Party's paper, *The People's World*, and still I got my government work pass. Somebody else did less than I and didn't get in. I had friends that wanted to know why I was cleared. I don't know, but I do know I never put my name on any paper. I had a heartbeat for what the Party was doing in many areas, because it chose to do things that nobody else would touch, like speak out for black people. But that didn't mean I cared to be a member. I had an interpretation of what their agenda was, so that was that.

I'd been involved in the NAACP since 1949, but after 1955, during the early stages of the integration movement in the South, I took membership cards and began to solicit members on the waterfront. This was whites and blacks. Most of them said "yes." Doing this, I learned many names that I never knew before. One good thing that happened from this was that years later, when I began to run for union office, a trail of men would come by and I could call them almost all by name.

No new longshoremen were hired in numbers after World War II until the '59 B-list men came in. These B-men worked on the waterfront on a probationary basis.[18] With that program, here again Harry defined his social consciousness—in conjunction with Bill Chester, who later became an International officer—because Bridges had to take on the conservatives of the local's Democratic Club and Fathers' and Sons' Club.

The conservatives argued, "These jobs are ours, and our sons have a right to them." But Harry said, "Jobs are not a trust of the workers—jobs belong to all people, and we are going to have an open sign-up." The B-list committee then solicited new workers from black communities with high unemployment rates. Most of them became good union men.

Around 1959, Odell Franklin and I joined the Longshore 56 Club started by Eddie Parker, a gang boss from Gang 56. The group started as a welfare club, but I suggested that we broaden the agenda to include financial investment. Then we petitioned that we didn't have any black walking bosses or ship's clerks on the waterfront. I became the secretary and did lots of writing and agitating for the group. The club only had twelve members, but out of the club, Odell Franklin became a Local 10 business agent and secretary-treasurer, Parker became a walking boss, and I became a dispatcher and president of the local. The club lasted until maybe '68.

My wife urged me to get involved in union politics. She said, "Those who have been better educated and better exposed have a responsibility to the rest of the people. You cannot afford to sit on the sidelines." It was Odell Franklin who encouraged me to run for dispatcher in '64. I ran ninth out of the nine dispatchers elected that year, but I was elected.

I was also the most vocal of the dispatchers when it came to taking on the hierarchy under James Kearney, the local's conservative president. At that time, I just didn't believe a circle saw would cut me. I defended a white guy named Richard O'Toole who was deregistered; I took on Kearney because he did nothing to help O'Toole or two black guys who had been in trouble a bit earlier. That lifted me above and made me visible. A little later, I ran for dispatcher again, ran second that time around, and became assistant chief dispatcher. I was elected president of the local for the first time in '67.

In late '71, I was elected president during the 1971–72 longshore strike. I solicited support for the union from my church and from the black community, and I was very well-received. I had worked previously for the NAACP, so when I carried the banner for the union, I had credibility. Getting support wasn't so difficult because people knew where I stood.

When I was elected president in the mid-1970s, there was a crisis I had to deal with. The local had this huge deficit that people did not want to face. I went home and read the constitution. This particular article stated that when the longshore caucus and convention funds reached a certain low, the membership should be automatically assessed.

At the next union meeting, I told the members, "As of tomorrow morning, we are running this union out of the caucus and convention fund, and every member is assessed sixty dollar for six months." For the first and only time in my life as a member of Local 10, members came up on the stage and picked me up as you would pick up the Super Bowl coach who had won the big game. They said, "We like you because you have guts." George Kaye, our secretary-treasurer, who backed me up, the staff, and I went on a thirty-six-hour instead of a forty-hour week, too. Soon that deficit was gone.

Just before we went out of office, George Kaye and I decided, "We shored up the finances, now we're going to shore up the dispatch system." We instituted a new sophisticated rotary dispatch system, which limited every man from the hall to one shift only. Jobs came into the hiring hall that hadn't ever been in the hall before. It was everybody back to the hall unless you had official status as steadily employed men. So we eliminated the preferred list where jobs weren't shared.

I was going out of office, as I said, but I had made up my mind that there were some things I intended to do as part of what I felt was right. My parents had taught me about sharing, and I'd broken into fair play and the sharing of jobs in 1944 at our old Clay Street hall in San Francisco. That hall is still dear to my heart, and so are its standards.

When I first came on the waterfront, many black workers felt that Local 10 was a utopia. Even the level of struggle we faced in Local 10 was something so high above what most of us had experienced in Arkansas, Texas, and other places in the South that we were willing to get involved and take our chances at the results. We're talking about a union that gave you a chance to be somebody, to hold your head high.

Local 10 was the most democratic organization I've ever belonged to. If you wanted to go out there and face that membership and campaign and work with them and relate to them, that was your challenge, and you won and you lost. When it came to the hiring hall, the boards were controlled democratically by seniority. Favoritism was minimized.

This union was the greatest thing in my life, other than my family. In terms of economics and social growth, this union was a platform on which I made my stand and found a place in the sun. I was political and became president, but when I was out of office and working, I was even more proud. I had the most prized thing on the waterfront, a longshore registration, and I didn't mind working. Some called this arrogance, but it wasn't arrogance. It was pride.

WHITEY KELM: RED-HOT UNION MAN

Ted "Whitey" Kelm was a dedicated unionist from his employment as a sixteen-year-old merchant seaman during World War II until his death in 2008. Screened, or barred from American merchant ships in the McCarthy era, Kelm became a longshore worker and an ILWU stalwart in the 1960s. In many ways, he personified a generation of ILWU rank-and-file members who experienced

Longshore Local 10 drill team members leading a May Day protest march against the war in Iraq, San Francisco, 2008. *Left to right:* Jimmy George, Ed Thomas, and drill team captain Josh Williams. Photo by Delores Lemon-Thomas. ILWU Library.

World War II, worked on the waterfront afterward, sometimes encountered McCarthyism personally, and fought for unionism throughout their lives.

Whitey Kelm

I was born in New Jersey in 1928 and lived there until I went to sea in 1944. My mother's parents were born in Finland and my father's in Germany, so I'm second-generation American-born. I had two brothers. My father died when I was eight, and we had a struggle. This was during the Depression, and here we were, a fatherless family. My mother used to put lard on our bread and flavor it with salt to substitute for butter.

I couldn't get into World War II fast enough. I jockeyed my birth certificate so I could jump the gun and get in there. By the time they found out about it, I was past sixteen and already sailing. My first voyage was through the old CIO

Marine Cooks and Stewards Union [MCS]. I washed dishes all through the Mediterranean. When I got back, I transferred into the CIO National Maritime Union (NMU) and worked my way up to able-bodied seaman.

We had general quarters at sea often because of German submarines. I saw one ship go down, but I got lucky and made it through. I also consider myself lucky because I had shipmates who were charter members of the NMU. They had experienced the strikes in the 1930s. I had shipmates who had been in the '34 strike on the West Coast and who had fought the fascists in Spain. They just hammered me over the head with unionism. I soaked it up like a sponge. So I emerged from World War II a red-hot union man.

In 1946, the year after the war ended, the CIO marine unions set up a Committee for Maritime Unity [CMU], which to me was the greatest. Harry Bridges was the prime mover behind CMU. This was when the AFL and the CIO were still separate. Our seven CIO unions included the MCS, the East Coast–based NMU, the ILWU, and four other marine crafts. The idea was that we would negotiate as one, strike as one, and settle and return to work as one.[19]

I was back on the East Coast when the CMU got going. We were primed to strike on June 15, 1946. Our big goal was one national agreement date. There was a strike rally in New York City. This was the first time I heard Bridges speak. I remember thinking, "That's what I want to hear." Then President Truman announced, "You strike and we'll send in the army, navy, marines and coast guard to load and sail the ships." With the kind of unity and spunk we had in those days, we told him, "Go ahead and try it."

Harry contacted longshore unions the world over. Telegrams poured into Truman's office. They all said, "Load a ship and sail it with scabs and it will not be unloaded in this country. It will sit until it rots." Truman threw up his hands and said, "Okay, boys, go ahead, have your strike." So on June 15, we walked. I was still a kid. This was my first time with a picket sign. I'll never forget it. The strike lasted two hours, 'cause we were so strong. We got a contract and went back to work.

Unfortunately, before long, McCarthyism raised its ugly head. Joe Curran, who led the NMU, sabotaged the CMU. He joined the ranks of the red-baiters. Harry, of course, was the main target. Curran got everybody to vote to leave the CMU, including the members of his own union. So the CMU lost all its power.

At the same time, the NMU took a right turn internally. Those of us who had been in the union a while fought it. But I'd be sitting in a union meeting in

New York and I'd have six paid goons standing around me, waiting to beat the crap out of me if I raised a point of order. I felt marked, like a pink elephant. So in 1950, I went "schooner rig" with a little zipper bag, stuck my thumb out, and hitchhiked to the West Coast. I prolonged my membership in the NMU by eighteen months doing that.

Around the same time [1950], the Teamsters raided the ILWU warehouse local in San Francisco. This was when the CIO kicked the ILWU out for being left-wing. The Teamsters tried to take advantage. Some NMU guys and I wanted to support the ILWU. The Teamsters put a picket line in front of an ILWU warehouse to keep the ILWU people out. In response, the ILWU organized a caravan to break up the Teamster line. We went along to help. We ran the Teamsters off, too.

This was also when the Korean War [1950–53] got going, and the government began to screen seamen off the ships. You'd go on board, but you'd get a notice that said, "Your presence aboard this ship is inimical to the security of the United States." So you couldn't sign on. I made six attempts to ship through the NMU, and the same thing happened every time. Never was I able to face my accuser. I'd gone away to World War II a real patriot, but now I couldn't escape feeling like a pariah.

At length, I went back to New York, where all us guys on the East Coast who had been screened got together and formed a Seamen's Defense Committee. Nineteen of us sued the steamship owners, the NMU, the government, and the Coast Guard. It took eight or nine years, but we won. We didn't take the NMU membership's money though. We just used the suit for leverage. After we won the case, I went back to sea for a year, just to show 'em I could.

In 1959, I heard there was a chance of becoming an ILWU longshoreman, so I came back to the West Coast. There was still break bulk cargo work to be had then, and I knew everybody in the union. Besides, I'd put my ass on the line for the ILWU at that warehouse. I thought, "If anybody's going to get on that B list, I'd better by one of 'em." Well, I waited for longshore to open up, and in '63 it did. That's when I made the B list.

Strangely, I liked unloading coffee ships. Two of you would work these 150-, 160–pound sacks. Pump on them all day and you'll know it. I also liked loading canned goods. You'd start on the bottom deck, build canned goods up, floor off with walking boards, and work back in the ship's wings with a four-wheeler, stacking more canned goods.

What I disliked was black sand. The sacks were small, but they weighed 150 pounds. It took two guys to pick 'em up. When you bent down, you had to have signals with your partner or you'd bump heads, 'cause the damned package was so small. It was a real awkward situation.

When I was a B-man, Harry used to pop into the hiring hall. We'd become friends, but he liked to argue, and he'd provoke it. In the main it was over the steady-man issue, clause 9.43 in the longshore contract.[20] That was Harry's thing, and I didn't like it. My point was that nothing should bypass the hiring hall.

In the mid-1960s there was a civil rights drive on the hotel industry in San Francisco. The goal was to end employment discrimination. There was a demonstration at the Sheraton Palace Hotel. The ILWU endorsed it. That was all I needed. I went over there with some other Local 10 guys. We picketed, then entered the building and sat down on the floor. Four or five of us longshoremen linked arms. The cops arrested us, but the union lawyer got us acquitted.

One time in the 1960s or early 1970s, word got around that our warehouse local needed people to picket this plant in San Francisco. I volunteered. Pretty soon here come a crowd of twenty scabs. Leading 'em was this big bastard. I said to him, "That's far enough, scab." Next thing I know, I'm being restrained by the cops. They wanted to put one of the scabs into a police car with me, but I said, "I'm not riding with no damn scab." So they put me in a paddy wagon by myself and drove me to the Green Light Hotel. I ended up with a one-hundred-day suspended sentence.

By the early 1970s, I'd worked as an extra in some films. Finally I got a speaking role and got into the Screen Actors Guild. I went to Hollywood in 1975 to act in TV and films and still work on the waterfront out of L.A. longshore Local 13. My best acting job was in the classic labor film *Norma Rae*. It was about a cotton-mill union, and I wasn't about to turn that down. I played the part of a factory plant boss.

After I retired in 1990, I moved to the Rocky Mountains. There are conservative people around here, but I don't care. I tell 'em, "I'm union. I had a hernia operation. Know what it cost me? Seven bucks!" They can't believe it, you know?[21]

SAM KAGEL: COAST ARBITRATOR, 1948–1999

During World War II, Kagel left union advocacy and became northern California director of the federal War Manpower Commission (WMC). After the war, he attended law school. In 1948 he returned to the waterfront as the arbitrator for the West Coast longshore industry. Kagel held that post until 2002. A legendary waterfront figure, he was still in office in 1999 when he explored the origins of the industry's sophisticated arbitration system.

Sam Kagel

The 1948 longshore strike was ending about the time I finished law school at Boalt Hall of the University of California, Berkeley. Longshoremen had gotten the union-controlled hiring hall the hard way in 1934. The employers tried unsuccessfully to get rid of it in '48. It took a strike to say "You can't do that."

When the strike was settled, the employers installed a new bargaining agency, the PMA [Pacific Maritime Association]. The ILWU and the PMA established a fresh grievance procedure and decided that they were going to pick the arbitrators. Before this, the arbitrators were always selected by the secretary of labor.

The employers knew about my activities with the WMC. I was now kosher with them. So both parties, the ILWU and the PMA, asked me if I would be their coast arbitrator.[22] He would be the guy to whom regional or area arbitration decisions could be appealed. I took the job.

Under the new ILWU-PMA setup, we established a process called "instant arbitration," with area arbitrators available twenty-four hours, seven days a week. I can't say that somebody sat down and came up with the idea of instant arbitration. It occurred to me, but I'm sure it occurred to everybody else because it was so obvious.

At one point I said to the ILWU guys and the employers, "Look, you picked me as coast arbitrator because I had a background representing unions and presumably I know something about the longshore industry. So why don't we do the same thing with the area arbitrators? You're going to have four of them. Pick two from the union and two from the employers. You have the right to cancel 'em at any time." They thought that was a great idea.

We knew the locations for the four area arbitrators—San Pedro, northern California, Oregon, and Washington. Now [1999] we're in our fifty-first year. At no time was any area arbitrator discharged by either side. That's not to say that there haven't been complaints. But Harry had a firm position on that when he was ILWU president. Locals would complain about an area arbitrator, and Harry would say, "That's it. We're not going to start changing arbitrators. Let 'em die or let 'em retire." And that's what's been done.

Before that, they had revolving arbitrators. Up to 1948, they had over two hundred arbitration awards from different arbitrators at different ports. One of the things done in the '48 strike aftermath was to wipe them all out. Then we started out anew.

I mentioned the concept of instant arbitration. In practice it functions like this. If any work stoppage occurs, the area arbitrator goes right down there. The longshoremen are not supposed to strike, but they can stop work if they think a job is unsafe. The arbitrators go down there to check it out. We're talking about people selected from within the industry, too. We're not talking about a professor who wrote a book. So they know something about the longshore industry.

The area arbitrator can order a correction of an unsafe condition, or say to the longshoremen, "That's not a safety beef." If the area arbitrator finds that it is a real safety beef, he tells the employer to correct it. The longshoremen can work somewhere else on the ship, and they get paid for their time standing by.

If, on the other hand, the area arbitrator finds that it was not a real beef, the longshoremen go back to work and don't get paid stand-by time. There used to be other claims we don't see often now because of containers. Sometimes cargo was stinking or in need of repair, for which there were penalties, and this would cause work stoppages.

The first safety beef involved a load of lumber that had disintegrated. The longshoremen claimed this was an unsafe condition. They turned out to be right, too. The answer was to go down there and look at it, not sit around and wait until there was a hearing up at PMA headquarters with the ship standing by.

The idea was to get the ships out because there were crew, interest, and other expenses to pay for, and if the longshoremen were not working, they were not getting paid. So instant arbitration was just a matter of common sense. Now, after a dispute has been settled on the dock, if you still want a formal hearing, you can have it. As noted, the resulting decision by the area arbitrator can then be appealed to the coast arbitrator.

I mediated the end of the 1971 West Coast longshore strike. It had been going on for over one hundred days. Under President Richard Nixon's direction,

Mediator Sam Kagel announcing the settlement of the 1971–72 longshore strike. All those identified are ILWU people except for Kagel, PMA president Ed Flynn, and PMA official Ben Goodenough. *Front row, left to right:* Harry Bridges, Kagel, Flynn, Goodenough, Evelyn Wakefield, Mel Banister, and unidentified. *Second row, left to right:* M. Tony Garcia, Chester Nelson, Jimmy Herman, Cleophas Williams, Terry Sweeney, Robert Rohatch, Don Garcia, and unidentified. Photo by Luis Carballar. ILWU Library.

Congress was entertaining the idea of a statute providing for compulsory arbitration. Of course, Harry didn't want that, since it would take away the union's main weapon, the strike. So there's no doubt that this was part of the pressure on Harry to meet with the employers.[23] That's when I was called in, and even though I was the coast arbitrator, they called me in as mediator.

We met for seven days and eight nights and came to an agreement. That ended the '71 strike. There were five, six, or eight issues involving what we call "steady men," or workers who are employed directly by stevedore companies rather than through the union-controlled hiring hall. These matters were not settled at the time. I said to Harry, "How the hell are we going to settle the strike with these issues unresolved?" He replied, "You and Rudy Rubio will work 'em out." And that's what happened.[24]

As to Bridges and the ILWU, I'd say that Harry had an integrity that was recognized by the workers. He was interested in having a democratically run union, and he never lost touch with the rank and file. If you have integrity, are honest and straightforward, take firm positions—even when you're wrong but are representing the interests of the people you're supposed to represent in a democratic fashion with no discrimination—what else do you want? In my book, Harry had all those characteristics.

The union itself truly works in a democratic manner and is responsive to its membership. You don't have any dictators. Everything is submitted to a vote. The drafting of proposals is done by a caucus of elected officials. Negotiations are carried on by an elected negotiating committee. During the life of the longshore contract, you have an elected coast committee, which represents the workers in enforcing the agreement.

These characteristics, while not rare, are not common in most unions. They are certainly completely rare insofar as employer groups or corporations are concerned. And while the ILWU gets the best conditions it can, and has one of the best longshore contracts in the world, it nevertheless has been willing to take positions on social issues. The union took positions condemning discrimination. It was not always successful with all of its own people, but it still did this. That's why I think the ILWU is a different union and an outstanding operation.

HERB MILLS: THE ASBESTOS WAR, 1972–1978

Retired longshore worker Herb Mills is a former Local 10 secretary-treasurer. In that office in the late 1970s and early 1980s, he orchestrated boycotts of military cargo ordered by Latin American dictators. This story of his 1970s struggle to eliminate the cancer-causing agent asbestos from the San Francisco waterfront depicts the union's on-the-job militancy and concern for safety. It also illustrates in practice the arbitration system described by Kagel.

Herb Mills

I was a longshore Local 10 business agent during 1972–74, when asbestos began to be a real issue in the media. After a while, it seemed as though every other day there'd be an article in the *San Francisco Chronicle* on asbestos and the health hazards that it posed. I was like everybody else in Local 10 then—I didn't know beans about asbestos. In past years we'd be loading or unloading asbestos, and, Lord, it seemed like you'd be wading around in it ankle deep, bucking it up over your head, and breathing the fibers.

So I began to say, "Holy smoke, this stuff's bad!" First of all, I was trying to get educated myself. Then, because of being an officer, I had access to the Local 10 bulletin. I began to submit items to the bulletin on asbestos, just telling people, "Hey, read the morning paper, man." We then had a couple of workshops on asbestos courtesy of the stewards' council.

In the meanwhile, I had learned that there was a doctor in Berkeley named Phil Polakoff at Herrick Hospital who had studied under Dr. Irving Selikoff at Columbia or someplace. Selikoff was one of the country's leading experts on asbestosis. Polakoff was beginning to be an authority on asbestosis and related ailments himself. I got ahold of him. He turned out to be a real live wire. By then he was working with the Asbestos Workers and other people like the Mare Island shipyard employees in Vallejo. He was trying to get unions involved in a health committee around asbestos. So we had several meetings about this at Local 10.

By '75, I was out of office and was the steward of a gang working a ship at Pier 32. There was what we thought were asbestos fibers scattered in the structural members of the hold. It turned out that three voyages before, there'd been asbestos down there. Prior to that, we had talked to the Occupational Safety and Health Administration [OSHA] people in Washington, D.C., about asbestos and been told, "Oh yeah, that's bad stuff." We'd then said, "We're on the West Coast, and we've got a contract that says we don't have to work if it's unsafe. Are you ready to say that over a phone if somebody calls you about it?" They said, "Yeah, sure."

So I got ahold of Dick Austin, who was the business agent then, and told him, "We got asbestos down here." Dick shows up and we stop work and come out of the hatch. The employer says, "What the hell's wrong now?" We said, "Well, they got asbestos here." He says, "There ain't no asbestos down there." We said, "Yeah, it's fibers all over the place." He says, "Fibers all over the place? What are you, out of your mind?"

Well, the so-called safety man for the PMA came down, and so did the arbitrator. We said, "Just call OSHA back in Washington and tell 'em what you got here." The OSHA official says, "You ought to shut that hatch down, get the people all suited up, and vacuum the damn thing out. Then somebody can go back to work down there."

This went to arbitration, which of course we won. We had several other work stoppages, but because of that arbitration, which was the first of its kind on the West Coast, that was the end of that. They'd just take the goddamn asbestos off the dock and take it back to wherever it came from. Presently, they ended up totally doing it a different way, or going out the Gulf Coast, or I don't know what the hell they were doing with it. It probably ended up in containers, and nobody ever handled it again.

At that point, we had the job end of the thing under control. That arbitration went up and down the West Coast, and pretty much the same thing happened elsewhere. Now the problem became what to do about this. Since I'd been a business agent, I'd had this concern: How do you hold somebody liable for this? Then I found out that the incubation period is twenty-five years. The employers were saying, "You gotta say what ship, what date, and who was the stevedore company." So I knew real early on that we had to be moving toward a black lung type of thing where there was industry-wide liability.

We ended up running a survey in Local 10 asking "When and where in years past did you work asbestos?" We got two or three hundred of them filled out. It told us a little bit. Some guys would actually have a time book that would go back, but for every guy that's got a time book that goes back twenty-five years, you've got four hundred guys that ain't got it.

Out of this, in discussion with several attorneys, and from these kind of seminars that we had about how to proceed, it turned out that the best thing would be to focus on the manufacturer and the shipper rather than on the mode of transportation or the stevedore company. That's pretty much where it was left. Asbestosis did get covered under state workmen's compensation, and, of course, the men were no longer being exposed to asbestos at work.

We did have an X-ray screening of anybody in Local 10 who wanted an X-ray. The screening was set up by Dr. Polakoff. This was in 1978, when I was the Local 10 secretary-treasurer. Polakoff had specialized X-rays taken from a unique angle required to reveal the disease. The X-rays were then read by radiologists trained in detecting asbestosis and related medical problems, like cancer. Well, that was really something!

We ended up on *60 Minutes* or 20–20 or one of them programs. It was good coverage. There was a big X-ray van parked right outside our hall. There was coverage in the *San Francisco Chronicle*. We were trying to encourage other unions to push on this thing as well. "Hey, goddamn it," we were saying, "get a fucking van, too."

All this suggests that increasingly safety can be a worker education problem. Like with asbestos—for Christ's sake, who knew about asbestos? It's the same with really hazardous cargoes, where you can get a drop on your skin and you'll be a vegetable in five minutes. People don't think about absorbing poisons and toxins through their skin. They just think about smelling or swallowing stuff.

When they began to ban insecticides and pesticides in the United States, who do you suppose was working them to export them to the Third World? Us. There was a rash of that stuff. Somehow or other it was all right to send it off to India.

Well, then I was insisting on special bridles.[25] I wanted an ambulance right on the dock. You was always getting undercut, but that was not an outrageous demand. I felt we should say to the employer, "You got six barrels of this stuff? Don't even think about moving it until you got a medical team on the dock with atropine." I was quite serious about this. What are you gonna do if you drop one of them things? Go get somebody in public services from San Francisco General Hospital?

My point is that we got a longshore contract that says, "Damn it, you stop work when it's unsafe." It also says that our Pacific Coast Maritime Safety Code is the minimum—there ain't no maximum. The maximum is whatever is unsafe. It don't have to be in the safety code. So worker education is really key. You want the guys to be alert to safety—not just when you're there as the business agent, but so they'll see it on their own and give you a call.

2

LONGSHORE

THE LOS ANGELES AND LONG BEACH HARBORS

LOS ANGELES AND LONG BEACH HARBORS HAVE THEIR OWN HISTORY OF events surrounding 1934. Hiring in the 1920s, for example, differed from that in the Bay Area. San Francisco–style dock shape-ups persisted in Los Angeles. But the region was more widely known for its employer-run fink hall hiring system, which was notorious for favoritism, discrimination, and corruption.

In contrast to San Francisco and the Northwest ports, too, where the great majority of waterfront workers were of European backgrounds, many Mexican Americans labored at the Los Angeles Harbor during the nonunion years. Most were segregated into onerous work categories, including lumber handling, then a dangerously fast-paced job, cleaning ships' boilers, always a noxious task, and shoveling irritants like sulfur, ore, and coke.

During the early 1920s, a strong IWW tradition existed in the southern California waterfront towns of San Pedro and Wilmington, as in the Northwest. But the IWW foundered when it lost a longshore strike in 1923. Subsequently, the local Ku Klux Klan (KKK) terrorized area workers and their families for months.[1]

ROUGH CONDITIONS BEFORE THE UNION, 1923–1934

John Rodin and Frank Sundstedt, two ILWU longshore Local 13 veterans, recall a brutal 1924 KKK attack. Sundstedt and fellow Local 13 members Henry

Gaitan, Elmer Mevert, and Ed Thayne describe working on the waterfront during the nonunion decade after the Wobbly strike.

John Rodin

Before the 1934 strike, my father was blackballed on the waterfront on account of the Wobblies. He wasn't no Wobbly, but he sympathized with them. He was a union man; he believed in them. In 1924 the KKK raided the IWW hall across from my mother's house in San Pedro. The meeting was supposed to be an IWW party for the working people.

The KKK come in there and they busted out the window and kicked the people around. We went out the back door where they were cooking coffee, and I was pushed in. I still got the scars from here to here. I was nine years old. I remember going home and telling my mother I got burned. Frank Sundstedt's sister was burned there, too. She was also just a kid. We was in the hospital together. The Wobblies paid for the hospital bill. I guess they got donations.

The KKK wanted my father. They knocked on his door, and when he opened it, they busted him over the head. My father was bleeding and they had a gun on him. That's what I remember when I come back from being burned. They thought my father's house was an arsenal for the Wobblies; that's what they said. He was just a sympathizer. He figured the Wobblies might do something for the unions.

Frank Sundstedt

I remember the KKK burning crosses on the hillsides and in front of people's homes. They were out after the foreign-born and the Catholics. A number of longshoremen were taken out by the KKK into the Santa Ana Canyon and tarred and feathered just for being trade unionists.

In 1924 the Wobblies and their families were having a social. All of a sudden these KKKs threw pipes and broke the glass at the doors and came in and started tossing chairs around. They went into the kitchen and dumped this hot coffee on my sister and Johnny Rodin. My sister had to learn to walk all over again. She was hospitalized for three weeks. Then they brought her home, but she was bed-ridden for months.

In the 1920s they had a shape-up system down here. You just showed up at the dock where the ship was coming in. If they needed you, they'd hire you. If they didn't know you or didn't like you, they wouldn't. They had all kinds of little systems. For example, the old-timers would wear matches stuck in their hat bands. Three matches was a code. Maybe it meant a duck to the boss, or a chicken, or a turkey, or a bottle of wine or whiskey. It was a signal that the longshoreman would take care of the boss if he'd give him a job.

Where they had to break bulk cargo, they worked the men until the ship was done. Often a man would catch his job out of the employer-run fink hall, and then he'd work until the ship left. The fink hall wasn't much of a hall. You'd just show up down on Seventh Street between Center and Palos Verdes. The guy that ran the fink hall would come out with sheets of paper indicating where the jobs were.

They also had what were known as star gangs. A star gang was one they knew would pump, would put out more tonnage than another gang. So if you were a member of a star gang, you were assured of regular work.

Henry Gaitan

If a ship was going to sail that day, you kept on working until it left. The longest shift I ever worked was thirty-two hours. On one long jitney-driving job, I done pretty good until midnight, when I started going to sleep. I was pulling this ore. They had a steel bucket that landed on the four-wheeler. I had to take it off the hook. So when the guys seen me sleep, they hit the side of the bucket to wake me up. Boy, was I glad when I was through. I had a bite to eat, laid down in my car, and completely passed out. I'd worked thirty hours. I was making sixty cents an hour, no overtime.

I had a lot of trouble because I was one of the first Mexicans to drive a lift. The company used to hire Italians over here, then a group of Mexicans over here, then a group of something else, and then they'd say, "Look, those guys can do better than you guys." And at that time the winch drivers had to be Scandinavian or German. As a Mexican, you weren't allowed on the winch handles.

If you had a nice-looking sister, and liquor, and a wife that would put out, you'd have a job. I seen it here on these docks before we had the union. There's one case where a guy was fired. He was drinking at somebody's house where they were bootlegging, and the guy wasn't buying, so the foreman fired him!

Elmer Mevert

Nitrate jobs were tough. I did that at Outer Harbor. They'd just hire enough guys. The higher the piles got—they'd go clear to the beams with sacks of nitrate—the more guys they'd have to hire to keep passing the sacks up.

It was just a continual operation, and your hands would bleed from that rough burlap. Packing bananas, your shoulders would swell up, your arches would break down. Sesame seed come in great round sacks, and they were slick as silk. You couldn't stack those things for love or money. And they weighed 100 kilos—that's 220 pounds. If you had a bum partner who didn't know how to handle them, you broke your goddamn neck.

You never worked fast enough. The boss would come around and he'd pressure you, "Hey, the hook's hanging." Jack Foster, one boss, would stand there by that port. He'd tap you on the shoulder: "Door six, door seven, door three." Once in a while he'd tap a little too hard. He was just a big, tough, gung-ho boss who was brought up in the old confrontation days of the post-Wobbly strike.

Ed Thayne

You had a lot more accidents in those days. The companies were so greedy and hoggish that they wanted to get every ounce of energy and blood out of you that they could. If you were hurt, it didn't mean anything to them. I got hurt several times myself. You'd go down in the hold—you never heard of a safety net before the 1934 strike. The boss just said, "There's the cargo—you work it." A lot of men got hurt because they didn't have something to protect them from falling, or to keep falling objects from hitting them.

Some of those bosses liked those huge big loads of pipe and steel. You bring out a load on a pipe truck, there's pipe falling off all the way from the hatch to the street. There'd be scattered pieces of pipe all up and down the waterfront. Then you've got to get down and straighten it out. They lost time by their overloading. They were stupid.

I know of favors that people done. I was working steady. It was about 1931 or '32. I was asked to come up on Sunday and paint the foreman's house. He says, "You be there, I've got a whole gang coming." I said, "I can't make it." I didn't go along, but I drove by and there was ten or fifteen guys with paint-brushes, all steady men.

On Monday morning I went back and stood by the jitney I'd usually been using. The foreman came down, looked us over, and said, "Spider, you come and take this jitney here." And he just left me standing there. I still waited, diligently stood by. He assigned five guys to hatches, and then he just looked at me and walked away.

When I first started to work on the waterfront, it was eighty cents for dock men and ninety cents for hold men. In a year or so, a notice come out in the papers: Longshoremen accepted a pay cut from eighty to seventy cents an hour. When I got my check that week, we found out, yeah, you guys got a cut. So then it wasn't very long—this was close to '34—until they put another ad in the paper: Longshoremen accept another pay cut from seventy to sixty-five cents an hour. And they never discussed that with anyone.

Well, when we fine-read the full gist of it, all dock work had been reduced to fifty cents an hour. Car loading and unloading had been reduced to fifty cents an hour, and no overtime. Well, that broke our back. I said, "Them sons of bitches, what else will they think of?" After they'd given us these cuts, why we figured it was just about time to go on strike. All they done is put it in the paper, so we thought we'd really give them something to write about!

CONFLICT AND TRIUMPH, 1934

In the 1930s, employers throughout the United States routinely used strikebreakers, armed guards, and outright violence to suppress labor unions. Usually the local police sided with the employers, as was the case at San Francisco in 1934. Sometimes workers met deadly force and oppressive odds with violence of their own.

A particularly tragic version of this historical dynamic occurred during the 1934 strike in southern California. Around midnight on May 14, five days into the dispute, a group of longshore workers raided an employer-sponsored "strikebreakers" compound. When hired gunmen guarding the scabs fired at the onrushing workers, longshoremen Dick Parker and John Knudsen were fatally wounded. Parker passed away in the early hours of May 15. Knudsen died a month later. They were the first union martyrs of the Big Strike.

There were many other examples of confrontation in 1934. Here Local 13 workers Pete Grassi, Corky Wilson, Archie (Jumbo) Royal, Al Langley, and Joe Stahl reflect on the coming of the strike, their own 1934 experiences, and the conflict's aftermath.

Pete Grassi

My dad was in that '23 strike they lost. He was a Wobbly, a member of the IWW. He used to talk to me about your rights to sell your labor, equalize the work, have a hiring hall, guys rotating instead of that steady stuff. In the '23 strike they couldn't get it. Then you had to suck ass to get jobs through the '20s all the way up to '34. What was wrong with the '23 strike was one port would be out, the other ports were working. So when the '34 strike came, you gotta give Harry credit, it was unified.

Between 1928, when I started hustling jobs off the docks, and 1933, there was union talk, but you couldn't say much. When the labor bill came out in 1933 [section 7a of the National Industrial Recovery Act], it gave you the rights to organize, to join a union to bargain. My father said, "The day is gonna come, you gonna have rights." He passed away in 1929. He didn't live to see it, but it came through.

When the '33 law came out, they started to organize strongly. Even guys who were working steady felt what the hell, you'll be left out lookin' in if you don't join. I got my union book from Joe Simons, an old Finn and a Wobbly. I was initiated July 26, 1933. Then I hustled, talked to guys: "Join, get a book; dollar to join and fifty cents a month dues; they've cut your wages; you know how you've been treated." We talked to a lot of them guys who were here during the '23 strike. When the '34 strike came off, 90 percent came out.

During the strike I got rousted around—that's kicked around by the law. If you was more than three persons, they'd roust ya, take you to "seventh heaven" at Seventh and Front in San Pedro. That used to be the jailhouse. Up the elevator to the top floor—they'd work you over.

After the strike I became active on the docks in job actions, quickie strikes over load limits. Before the '34 strike you was building loads two and three tons on the lift board. We cut it down to 2,100 pounds. Little by little, and after the '36–'37 strike, it was all written out what the load limit was.

How we broke the steady-gang system down here is we got the dispatch hall after the strike. Now we had the rights to elect our own dispatchers. We

Longshore Local 13 members lining up for a Labor Day march, San Pedro, late 1930s. ILWU Library.

set it up so if you wasn't working a steady gang, check in the hall. If there was work for them gangs, the dispatcher would send them out. So when the stevedoring companies would call over, "We'd like to have our gang back," the dispatcher would say, "They're working." He'd send a group out of the hall, using a rotating system. That broke it up in six months. Then our guys'd say, "Jesus, I never thought it'd be this good. You don't have to take no horseshit."

That union dispatch hall was the greatest thing that ever happened. If I didn't want to go to work, I replaced myself for one day. I didn't have to ask the boss. Before the union he'd say, "You can't take off. If you don't show up, somebody else'll be in your place."

Corky Wilson

During the strike I done my picket duty with the Sailors' Union of the Pacific. That's who I went on strike with. I had worked longshoring, but that wasn't my bread and butter until 1935. I was to go around these bars with a couple of other guys—longshoremen did the same thing—to where the sailors hung out. These broads on Beacon Street in San Pedro was working for us. They would get these imported strikebreakers, then get away to make a phone call to our headquarters: "I got three finks in here, come and get 'em."

Those women knew we made our bread and butter here. This was a workingman's town, and the strikebreakers was taking that away from us. If the scabs came ashore at the harbor, they got beat up. There's always one or two longshoremen and sailors around where anybody comes in on a boat. There's somebody there to tell somebody else because most everybody grew up together. San Pedro was a little town in 1934, about twenty-five thousand people. So anytime a guy come in here and took bread and butter away from somebody in this town—look out!

Archie (Jumbo) Royal

I was a miner in Colorado and then a longshoreman way before '34. During the strike I was watching for a guy who owned a taxi to bring a bunch of scab longshoremen by. This policeman come up—"What the hell you doing there, Jumbo?" They had a ball field there. I said, "We're going to play ball!" He said, "No, we know every move you make before you leave your hall." I asked, "You got the hall tapped?" He said, "I don't know, but you got stool pigeons."

We were to make a raid on the scab bull pen across the bay, and one at Pier 145. But the rumor was out. So we had a meeting at White Point out in the open so there won't be no wires. They agreed to attack the bull pen at eleven thirty at night, May 14. This guy who connected the lights at the harbor said, "I'll pull the switch."

We went down by the railroad track, facing the bull pen. No light went out. Then I said, "What the heck we standing here for? Come on, boys, they won't get all of us. Let's go." So we did, and hell turned loose then. There was tear-gas bombs and everything else. The guy who was supposed to throw the light switch never did. I don't know why. We never caught the stool pigeon, either.[2]

Al Langley

The day the strike was called, some guy from Bethlehelm Shipyards where I was working said, "Hey, you want a good job? Go longshoring." I asked, "Are you nuts? See them guys walking out there? Them is pickets. Go through there, you're gonna get your head knocked off. Besides, them are *union* men. You don't go through union pickets." He said, "I just thought you wanted a good job." I go, "Not that bad!"

After the longshoremen went on strike, we organized in the Bethlehem Shipyards. The president of the longshore local asked us for men for picket duty. I was with the first ones; there was ten of us went. In some places you would see the trucks come up with scabs. They would drive right through your picket line. If you was lucky and had some rocks, you'd throw at 'em. If you didn't get out of the way, you'd get run over. They had policemen, armed guards, and motorcycle cops with them all the time.

During the strike we used to go uptown to these employment offices. From there, the scabs would go to the steamship company office and get money to come down to the dock. We'd follow 'em, take that money away, and say, "There's a strike down there, don't you come down."

I seen one guy that came down and made the mistake of asking some of the guys where a certain ship was. They took every stitch of his clothes, beat him, hung his clothes on the trolly wire, and sent him down the street, naked. The cops picked him up, put a blanket around him, and took him uptown again. He never come back.

A year or so after the strike, I quit the shipyard. I worked out of the longshore permit hall from early '36 until I was initiated in August '38. All of my friends were longshoremen. In '34 I'd worked in the strikers' soup kitchen from five in the morning 'til noon. I used to wash dishes until my fingernails come off.

I wanted to be a longshoreman anyway, because after the strike there wasn't a job in the world to equal longshoring, although it was hard, hard work. Every job I had before, if I wasn't there, I was fired. As a longshoreman, you could work when you wanted to. You had freedom of choice of jobs. If you didn't like a job, you could get somebody else to take it. All this added up to my idea of freedom, of what a union actually meant to a group of people.

Joe Stahl

In '34 I was working steady, driving jitney for Banning Company, and I was never contacted to join the union. If I'd been around the fink hall, I'd probably have signed up. I worked nine days in that strike. I needed the money. I'd just got married not too long before that, and we had a baby boy.

After nine days Art Lawback and this other guy, Caldwell, come down and said, "Joe, when you get through tonight, you're gonna come out." I got to thinkin'—I'd sooner be out there with my friends than what I was doing. After I came out, Caldwell—he was a tough guy—Johnny Vassey, Tom Ressler, and Skipper said, "Joe, we're gonna take you over to the hall, and we're going to get you in the union."

I went to the union hall with these guys the next day, and all the longshoremen go, "There's that goddamn finky Joe Stahl," but they didn't tackle us 'cause I was with four tough guys. They took me in and said they were going to have a meeting in a couple of nights. "What are you willing to do, Joe?" they asked. I said, "I'll do anything, run down scabs, whatever. I want to get into the union." "Okay," they said, "we're going to put you in front of the meeting."

I had to get up in front of all those longshoremen. I told them what I'd do. The only way they'd take me in was if I'd help run down scabs. I said, "I want these four guys who are tough. I'll do the driving." We dumped twenty-three carloads of scabs in one night. We'd watch them come out of the bull pen to drive home, find a good spot, and just run them right into the curb.

I was down there when the longshoremen raided that big-tent bull pen the night of May 14, when Dick Parker was shot. They wounded another striker, John Knudsen, and he died later. You know, the police were for the scabs. The scabs could go in the bull pen with pick handles and everything else and come out with them in their cars. We got caught with them, and they put us right in jail. We had to go at 'em bare-handed.

After the '34 strike there were two full gangs of guys who had stayed in. So the longshoremen decided to run them off the waterfront. There were twenty guys to work over and fifty or sixty longshoremen to do it. I was with the union men, but I never touched one of those guys. I did the same thing they did, only they stayed in. They broke up the two gangs, and that was the end of those guys. Now, I could have been one of them, but I came out, and am I glad I came out, 'cause I made good on the waterfront, worked there all my life, and retired when I was sixty-three.

THE MEXICAN AMERICAN STRUGGLE, 1934–1960

Local 13 members Joe Uranga, Ray Salcido, Sr., Henry Gaitan, Ruben Negrete, and Elmer Gutierrez recall pre-union conditions and the 1934 strike. They also address discrimination against Mexican American and black workers on the southern California waterfront.

Joe Uranga

I was born in 1910 in Clifton, Arizona. My father worked in a smelter there.[3] He'd been a labor leader in Mexico. My mother died in the flu epidemic of 1918. Then my father and I left Clifton and came to live in San Pedro. He got a job at the Los Angeles Ship Yard, which is Todd Ship now [1983]. He became a longshoreman in the 1920s.

It was rough living with my dad alone. He used to buy me tickets to eat at the San Pedro Cafe. I'd get all my kid friends and we'd go through the tickets in two days, one day. Finally my dad said, "That's it. You gotta live on bread, pork and beans, and water. Go hustle your own meal."

Before the '34 strike, they had the employers' fink hall with the shape-up hiring system. There was a ramp, like a cow ramp, that ran from one end of the hall to the other. We'd go around there for extra work about 1928, 1930. The dispatchers would stand on top of this ramp, especially on "white boat" days. There were two white Matson Navigation Company ships, the *Yale* and the *Harvard*. You'd work about two to three hours at racehorse speed to unload.

Bob was the guy that used to come in to dispatch workers to the white boats. He'd have a stack of cards about so high. All the guys that worked over there steady used to anticipate where the cargo went. They were already there. But all the extra men he picked out of the fink hall. He'd come in and give you a card, give you a card, and give another card. Guys would cry, "Gee, Bob, hey, Bob, gimme a card!" You wanted his attention, the son of a bitch. Finally he'd get tired, and he'd take these cards and throw 'em out everywhere. Then if you didn't get a card, you'd get the streetcar to Pier 175 to see if you could pick work up there.

We used to call working the white boats "the racetrack." You'd come up there, you'd go to the hold. The guy was watching you, saying, "Come on, let's go; come on, let's go." You ran yourself wild. You tried to impress the bosses and Bob, so they'd think, "Hey, that guy's a good worker. He don't stop, he keeps on goin'." If Bob or one of the guys we called "pushers" on the white-boat dock wanted you back, you didn't have to go down to the fink hall the next day. He'd give you a card to come back.

Back then all the old-time longshoremen were Anglos—Swedes, Germans,

Joe Uranga, 1983. Photo by Daniel S. Beagle. ILWU Library.

Norwegians, and Italians. You had Italian gangs, Swedish gangs, Portuguese gangs, and things like that. They didn't have any Mexican gangs. The few Mexicans that worked were mostly on the fink hall's lumber list, like my father. It was a job that never stopped. They never loaded lumber here, but they took it out. They were always moving. It was a different kind of a job.

Lumber handling was just something the Mexicans got into. They had more Mexicans working lumber than on freight because freight jobs were a little more clannish with their Swedish and Norwegian gangs that worked steady for the stevedoring companies. If a steady gang needed somebody extra, or casual, you got him out of the fink hall. There were a few Mexicans that worked in steady gangs, but there was no Mexican gangs until after they organized. I had one of the first Mexican gangs—it was given to me around 1941, during the war, when we got all the influx of work.

In the pre-union years, the Mexicans also used to work as ship scalers, scraping off the barnacles underneath raised-up boats and painting the outside. We used to stand in line for that, too. The boss would pick you out. It was mostly Mexicans. We used to make fifty cents an hour.

For one scaling job they had what they called a "boiler gang." You'd go inside the hot boiler and clean all of the soot out of it. You'd go into the fire boxes. You'd wrap yourself up in a couple of suits of pants, wrap up real good, and go inside and scrape. You didn't last too long. You talk about lung asbestos now—well, that was worse. All those Mexicans did it. They had to get a job. Guys would last maybe five or six years doin' that. They're all dead now. You don't see any of those guys around anymore. Later we organized the scalers. I was a member and became a president and was quite active.

During the '34 strike the organization was quiet. What was going on wasn't publicized. We were the troops, the buck privates. We did the dirty work. They'd say, "We need somebody at a certain place." Well, okay, there we were, ten or fifteen of us—me, a lot of Mexican kids, and Anglos, too.

The struggle in '34 was something worth fighting for. I remembered the conditions of my dad. He didn't say much, but you could see them by going down to the fink hall and standing around.

What made me so loyal? Love for the people, for the organization, and my background of being poor, never having anything, and then going back to work and making some money and working with guys. After the strike three of us bought brand-new cars in 1937. Hey, this was it, man. This was just like throwing open new avenues and living.

Ray Salcido, Sr.

I was born in Chihuahua, Mexico, in 1899. I worked pick and shovel when I was young. My brother and I worked for American Smelting Company in Arizona and laid railroad track for Union Pacific in Nevada. After World War I, we came to San Pedro to stay with my uncle, Chuchu Salcido, who raised us. Chuchu was in the longshore union later.

In Arizona I'd been in a miners' strike when I was about fifteen. Quite a few of us strikers went to jail. We was doing everything we can to stop the strikebreakers, like throwing rocks. I was in jail for thirty days.[4]

In the 1920s I worked for Patton Blinn Lumber Company on the L.A. waterfront, where Chuchu was working. He helped me get the job. The workers were mostly Mexicans. You had to work hard there to keep up the pace. We separated and stacked lumber that came from the ships. I worked in the lumberyard for about nine years.

By 1934 I'd left the lumberyard and was working on the waterfront unloading lumber from ships. During the '34 strike, we stopped the strikebreakers. They wanted to start working, so we got sticks. Then the police came. We couldn't run fast enough because there was too many policemen. That's when they got us in jail.

I was with Dick Parker when he was killed. Him and I was together around the tent where they had the strikebreakers inside. He said, "Ray, I'm shot." Then I picked him up and got him out of the tent.

After the strike, they dispatched by hours. The ones that had the fewest hours went out to jobs first. There were dispatch boards for different categories after '34, too—jitney drivers, lumbermen, freight men, and shovel men that shoveled coke. I was on the lumber board, where most of the men were Mexicans.

Henry Gaitan

My parents came from Mexico, but part of my people are from Italy. I was born here in the U.S., in Missouri in 1914. My father was working for the railroad at that time. I was taken to California when I was three and a half. I grew up in San Pedro speaking Spanish.

I started working in 1931 sewing sacks at Long Beach Dispatch Company near the waterfront. I became a cooper. I could fix wooden barrels. I stayed at Long Beach Dispatch until 1934. But only very few times was there more work than a day and a half a week. So prior to the '34 strike, I also worked on the docks when they needed an extra hand. This would be about once a week.

I joined the ILA [International Longshoremen's Association] when it first started. When I wasn't working on the waterfront, I'd go to the fish market and give them a hand. Manuel Lopez was a fisherman there. He recruited me into the ILA. He was Spanish and belonged to a Spanish group in Wilmington, the one that organized the Abraham Lincoln Brigade that fought the fascists in Spain. He was always talking about unions and work conditions, and he induced me into getting in the longshore union.

As a young Mexican then, I was welcomed into the union because I paid my dues and I was one of the first to get in. I was sworn in at the very first meeting of the ILA. It was at Victoria Theater. During the '34 strike, I was a picket and got arrested twice.

In the beginning of the union, the Mexicans always got these jobs where the work was the hardest. The jobs they used to get the most were handling lumber and shoveling sulfur, ore, and coke. I got a couple of jobs working coke. They used to bury you, and then you had to work your way out. It would cover you. You would have to work to the escape hatch. At that time we didn't have the union we have now. We went through a lot of hell.

In the '30s, being Mexican would make an effect. If they was gonna let somebody off early, it would be somebody else besides you. If it would be an easy job, somebody else would get it. If there was a jitney job open, they wouldn't ask you, they would ask somebody else. About the only time they'd ask you was if they couldn't get nobody else.

I wanted to get into a ship gang, but you had to be twenty-one. When I got to be twenty-one in 1935, I went down to the ILA hall and worked in the hold. One day I caught Billy Walter's gang. It was the number one gang from Metropolitan Company. Walter spoke German, and I could understand a little bit of it. I'd worked up in San Pedro in a sort of a club with nothing but Germans. I got a few words. So when I went with him, he didn't mind. The guys in the hold didn't mind either, and I was the youngest one in the group, too. That's how come I learned how to handle steel and heavy stuff.

When World War II started and black workers came on the waterfront, white guys would say, "I don't want to work with that n——r." When the blacks started comin' in, even the Mexicans had a tendency to feel the same way. I said, "Wait a minute, what's the matter with you, damn fools? They're takin' the pressure off of our neck." By the end of World War II, the white longshoremen who hadn't liked Mexicans had changed their mind.

I felt the blacks were OK if they were willing to work or if they'd work together. One time there was a black guy and nobody wanted to work with him. I said, "I'll work with him." We had this wool coming from Australia. When I seen him load that wool, I knew he knew his business. So I listened to him. I come out of there at the end of the job and I wasn't as tired as I would have been otherwise.

And I'll tell you, some of those blacks has been better union men than some of these people we already had. I always say, "You gotta work with what you have. You gotta make the best." If you have a confrontation with people, you got something in between you that later on will backfire on you.

Ruben Negrete

My grandfather came here from Mexico way before the turn of the century. On my mother's side, they were merchants in Mexico. I was born right here in Long Beach and was raised in Los Angeles County. My father did truck gardening on the other side of Maywood. The depression hit us in '32 and made us go to work. My father lost everything. I was only sixteen or seventeen years old. In '35 I moved to Wilmington and started in the lumberyards near the waterfront. I worked like a mule there from '35 to '41.

I came down to the waterfront during the Second World War in '44. At that time, they wanted anybody. Most of the guys—what you call the Anglos—who had been working as longshoremen took off for jobs at the shipyards or went to sea. Before my time, prior to '41, I think there was 10 percent of the local that was Mexican. During the war, they were begging the Mexican people to come in. After the war, Art Almeida, one of our guys, looked into it. By 1960 there were 37 percent Mexican guys and 37 percent Anglos. The rest were blacks. It was something like that.

So before the war there wasn't many Mexicans, and you couldn't get on the winches, you couldn't go bossing, and you couldn't drive jitney. Me, I worked in the hold from '44, when I come in, 'til about seven years, and on and off after that. Later I was a jitney driver. After '51, more Mexicans got these better jobs. Before '51, they had a few, but you could count 'em on your hand. Also, after the war, some Mexican guys got to be dispatchers, and Mike Salcido became the first Mexican secretary of Local 13.

The first Mexican guy that was sponsored into the marine clerks local was in '52, '53, something like that. Sponsoring was where they put you down as sponsoring a guy into the local. It was supposed to be for sons and brothers.

The five hundred unemployed was a dirty trick.[5] In '46, we were gonna go on strike. They had too many guys. They said, "Well, we'll lay off five hundred of you guys so you can collect the unemployment, and you'll be the first ones taken in after work starts again." What they wanted to do was get rid of the guys, who were mostly blacks. There was a few whites and Mexicans, but mostly blacks. They were low-seniority guys. I was right on the edge of the five hundred unemployed. A few guys after I come in, that's when they stopped. There was a cutoff date. If you got your union book before that, you could stay.

When the time came to bring men in, around '47, '48, they had a bright idea of bringing in some of the sons and brothers. That's where the turmoil come in. Some guys who had never seen the waterfront got in because they were sons and brothers of longshoremen. And some of the local's politicians welshed on the deal with the five hundred. I was there when they told us, 'cause I thought I was gonna be one of the five hundred: "Work resumes, you'll be the first ones to come back." That's when some of these five hundred sued, which you couldn't blame the guys. The politicians were monkeying around with a guy's livelihood, depriving him of feeding his kids.

Later on I got three sons into the union by sponsorship. Different people sponsored them. Many Local 13 people are related. I got a lot of relations here—cousins, nephews, and the three boys. Nepotism? Where isn't there nepotism? The superintendents of these big oil companies get their kids in there. So, something like this, I don't see what's wrong about it. Here, it is like a family to a certain extent. All of us have lived in the harbor area all our lives. I was fifteen years on the sponsorship committee. I was chairman a few times. But eventually, they didn't have any more sponsorship.

Elmer Gutierrez

My folks were from Mexico. I was born in Fullerton, California, in 1917. I've lived in the harbor area all my life. My dad worked in the lumberyards. He died in 1925 when I was eight years old. We didn't know too much about having steaks every day. We were lucky to have a pair of shoes on.

I was in the first group of Mexicans that went into the longshore union early during the war, in 1942. They were desperate for help, but sponsorship was about the only way you could get in then. I had a charter member sponsor me. He worked in the lumber part of the longshore industry. He was a Mexican fellow named Marciano Lopez. By the end of the war, maybe 25 percent of the Local 13 members were Mexicans.

Ruben Negrete

I've had good feelings toward this union since I started. Even though we worked hard during the war, we knew we were doing something for the country. And the wages were good, better than the lumberyard, better than anything else. Another thing, after the war we were treated equal to anybody. Now if it wasn't for the ILWU, I think 99 percent of us wouldn't have what we have. Anything I can do for the ILWU, I'm willing to do.

Being in this union was a big education. I never had the opportunity of being in anything. All I do was mule train before—really work hard. After I joined here, a few years later I started getting active. The ILWU made life a lot easier and more interesting. You get to meet people from different places. Once they know you belong to the ILWU, they look up to it, all over the world. I was an ILWU overseas delegate to the Philippine Islands in 1975. Harry was looked up to. The ILWU was looked up to. People knew it wasn't a corrupt union, that it was a straight, working-stiff union.

WALTER WILLIAMS: FIGHTER FOR AFRICAN AMERICAN EQUALITY, 1943–1970

Local 13 member Walter Williams fought for years to end discrimination against black workers. He led the 1946–49 effort of five hundred mostly black, deregistered Local 13 men to regain their longshore jobs. Williams describes the "Unemployed 500" battle and his other pioneering activities on behalf of African Americans.

Walter Williams

I was born in Atlanta, Georgia, in 1918. My mother brought me out to California with my brother when I was a year old. I've spent practically all of my life in L.A. My mother was the sole breadwinner for the family. It was kind of rough. I had to see some of that depression, had to feel some of it. The Depression raged from '29 on. I got to be nine or ten years old, and I started delivering newspapers to help out. When I was about eleven, I'd go down to the produce industry to earn a few extra pennies or a buck or two. Young as I was, I was always kind of tall and strong, and I would unload and load trucks for the produce merchants.

I got to the place where I could drive the trucks even when I was thirteen or fourteen years old. After I became an adult, my brother got me a Teamster job driving for Ranch Market. I got a dose of what at least some of the trade unions were about, because in 1939, a month after I got the Ranch Market job, the Teamsters Union decided that it was too much to have two black guys operating trucks for this one market.

Walter Williams, 1984. Photo by Harvey Schwartz. ILWU Library.

So I lost the driving job and became a foundry worker at Magness Brass and Lead. In that foundry I began to see how broad race discrimination really was. The job didn't pay much—it was nonunion—and they made certain that black people understood that they were low on the totem pole. They had separate washrooms, locker rooms, and showers. Employment opportunities were very limited. But Mexicans and Filipinos immediately were observed to be semiskilled workers. They were molders, and that paid double what we laborers were making. And they were considered as Caucasian. They changed and showered with the whites.

I really got interested in unions after I got booted out of my job through the Teamsters, who were in the AFL. I heard that the new CIO was a union that didn't discriminate. I went to the headquarters for the Los Angeles Industrial Union Council, CIO, and talked to a few people. They said, "Do you think you can organize the foundry?" I said, "I'll sure as hell make an effort to organize it, because there's no job opportunities for blacks, and if we got the union in there, it would help."

Ultimately the foundry fired me for union activity. I had gotten all of the black guys signed up and had started signing up some of the white guys. A CIO official said, "How would you like to become an Industrial Union Council organizer?" Soon I was working under Slim Connelly, the CIO leader in L.A., and Ralph Dawson, the top CIO organizer. The International Union of Mine, Mill and Smelter Workers, CIO, finally organized Magness Brass and Lead. I didn't finish the job, because I went to work for CIO, but I helped. I worked for the CIO Council for about a year. Then I went into the defense industry.

I went to Cal Ship at San Pedro and learned how to weld. We're talkin' about '41–'42. We had trouble there because the AFL Boilermakers, who had jurisdiction, didn't want blacks in the union. They had a race restriction clause in their constitution, and they would not agree to let blacks become regular members. "If you want to work in the shipyards," they said, "you have to be a member of the auxiliary."

I never attended an auxiliary meeting. That was like paying to be discriminated against, or subscribing to it. A friend introduced me to a committee that was beginning to function and was interested in trying to remove the discriminatory practices. Before I knew it, I found myself at the head of the committee. We decided to organize a no-dues-paying campaign.

We took the position that we were not going to pay to be Jim Crowed. So we picketed the auxiliary to keep the blacks from paying their dues. "If you want your dues," we said, "you're going to have to give us a regular membership."

We petitioned President Roosevelt's Fair Employment Practices Committee [FEPC] for a hearing. FEPC came out to Los Angeles and held the first West Coast hearing that involved the Boilermakers and the shipyards. We charged them with discrimination because of race. The FEPC decision was that the union and the companies were not to approach us on the matter of paying dues, and they were not to disturb us on the job.

Later we had to go to court anyway because the union declared that they weren't paying any attention to the FEPC. We were just about to win a legal decision in L.A. when the Supreme Court ruled that the practice of the Boilermakers was discriminatory. As a result, they took us in. We were now accepted as regular members.

Soon I left Cal Ship and went to work for a short time for a steel company that was making military landing barges. Then I heard about longshore opening up. It was 1943. I said, "This is a damn good opportunity to become a long-shoreman. That holds more prospects for permanent work than making landing barges, because after the war, that's over." So me and a friend made a beeline to the longshore industry.

Local 13 and the employers already had things rigged up so we wouldn't stay too long. I remember signing a commitment to being terminated at the end of the war. I didn't like it, but you had to get your foot in the door. I observed quite a few black guys on the docks, but I found out that very few of 'em were regular longshoremen. Most of them were working extra like I was.

A large number of white people in the union didn't want blacks in. It was obvious we were resented. Some of the regular longshoremen would call for replacements rather than work with black guys. And there were fistfights all over the damn place.

One thing that kept battles going was that a lot of the white longshoremen insisted on calling the drum on the winch the "n——r head." It was painted black and had a little white or red dot in the center. I wound up going before the local executive board to tell them they should pass a motion that offensive terminology should be abandoned. I said more and more guys were going to get hurt, and that this sort of thing didn't do anything to help build unity in the union. They passed a motion saying the gangs were not to use that kind of ter-minology in trimming gear.

I don't know if this anti-black attitude stemmed from a Southern back-ground and feelings a lot of Southern people bore, or whether it was because the old-timers considered us invaders who weren't there in large numbers when the union first organized. There weren't a lot of black people living in San Pedro and Wilmington then.

After I was there for a while, I began to hear whites raise the question, "What are you guys going to do after the war? You've already signed the state-ment to allow yourself to be deregistered." Some were arrogant about it. "This union was lily-white before you guys came down here," they said, "and after the war it's going to be lily-white again." I told 'em, "Well, you know, a lot of things can happen. I plan to work down here."

I knew that if you worked on a job for over six months, you were establish-ing job rights. I had learned what unionism was about through my association with the CIO Industrial Union Council. So shortly after we were there for six months, we began to raise the cry that we wanted some kind of a membership. The local was collecting money. I said, "If you collect money, you're going to give us something. This is taxation without representation."

We began to organize among ourselves. We'd meet anywhere from once to four times a month. There was a real hard core of guys who would be least likely to be intimidated and could think real well. But we had the support of all of the black guys there. They knew we were organized. At one time we thought of putting out a bulletin, but we knew the racists in the union would accuse us of dual unionism. So we said we won't do that.

We agreed to try to keep aggressiveness down on the waterfront, because we knew that if we did succeed in staying there, nothing would be gained by acting big and bad. We had to try to win the friendship and confidence of the people we had to work with. So usually, when a battle got to raging between a black and a white guy, the black guy didn't start it. But we also made up our minds that we weren't going to be taking any blows without giving 'em back. As a result, I think we won the respect of most of the white guys down there.

After the war, there was a movement to deregister us. One of the local's officials referred to us in a union meeting as a "special interest group." I went down to the mike and said they could call us a special interest if they wanted, but our interests were basic interests. Recommending that five hundred guys be deregistered meant you were getting rid of about 90 percent of the black guys in the local, and to me it was discriminatory. "There was nothing," I said, "really special about anybody wanting to hold on to a job and not be made the object of race discrimination."

At the next meeting, they deregistered us. This was in 1946. L. B. Thomas was the proponent of the action. Bill Lawrence was the one white guy who stood up for us.[6] After the motion was passed, he spoke against it. It took guts to stand up in Wilmington Bowl and do that. Lawrence said he felt it was morally wrong and more than likely legally wrong, and that we could survive together. He urged them to reconsider, but it didn't do any good.

After we were deregistered, we took the name Afro-American Labor Protective Society [AALPS]. We had to consider legal action. Some wanted to make the employers and the union the targets of a joint suit for damages as well as reregistration. I proposed that if we sue, we sue for the jobs and to hell with the damages, because if you believe in the union, you're going to hurt it as little as possible.

We were split down the middle. So I told the guys I won't be joining any action to collect damages. A few guys did sue and collect money, but I wasn't one of them. I influenced most of the guys not to sue for damages. The idea, I felt, was to get back in the industry and to help build the union. I did sign up as part of a number of plaintiffs who filed a suit for the jobs.

From April 1946 to December 1949, when I was away from the waterfront, I wound up being a hod carrier. That was backbreaking work, but I didn't have much choice. I was on that job when I got notice that they were going to reregister us. It was sort of an out-of-court arrangement.

In the 1950s I learned how to operate winches. What got me into this was that I was standing in the ship's hold one afternoon and a white guy named Pelt taps me on the shoulder. We were good friends. He says, "You better not take a job in the hold. Somebody's going to drop something on your head." I said, "How do you know?" He said, "Don't worry, I know. Do anything except work in the hold."

Pelt had supported our struggle all the way during the deregistration. I sure don't want to paint the picture that it had been solidly a situation of black against white. There were a lot of white and Mexican guys, guys of all ethnic backgrounds, really, giving us good, solid support. My partner and I would be talking on the job, and they'd come out to us and say, "We realize you guys are in a fight, but hang in, you'll win. You guys aren't by yourself." This kind of thing kept a lot of us encouraged.

Pelt may have saved my life. I'll never know. But his warning prompted me to decide to operate winches so I'd be up out of the hold. I didn't know the first thing about them. I told the guys to stand clear, and it didn't take 'em long to know that I wasn't working safe! I just hung in until I learned. As time went by, guys would say, "I've got to give you an A for trying; I got to help you." So then white guys would come up and teach me. Ultimately I drove winches for a number of years before I started operating cranes.

Around 1960 we took a delegation up to San Francisco to talk to Harry Bridges. Blacks weren't being promoted when it came to making hatch bosses out of longshore gang members. They weren't paying any attention to seniority or anything. We wanted to find out where Harry stood, and whether we could expect any support. He said, "Go back. You got a local union back there. You got local autonomy. It's a democratic organization. Go back and do it in the local."

I was angry—I said to Bridges, "We're outnumbered twenty to one. How the hell do you expect us to do it?" He said, "You got to educate the guys." I said, "That takes too damn long. We're being cheated. As dues-paying members, we feel we're entitled to an equal opportunity on all levels." He says, "I'm just not going to upset Local 13 over the race question."

Harry was looking at trying to keep the whole damn ship afloat. There was pressure with L. B. Thomas on one side and Bill Lawrence on the other. They were at the meeting. It could have caused one hell of a rift. But things did change for the better. Maybe Bridges did some things behind the scenes to help.

I say this because I remember a time when I went to a longshore caucus in San Francisco. The Local 13 rank and file had said, "Send Williams up as a special delegate to raise the question of race discrimination." The local's leaders watered down the gesture by limiting my per diem. The question of race discrimination and Local 13 hadn't come up yet when my per diem ran out. Harry got wind of it. He says, "We're going to see about that."

Harry called a separate meeting with the Local 13 people and chewed out the president and the rest of the delegates. He said, "That's not the way we're supposed to operate, and you guys know it. If Williams comes up as a delegate, he's supposed to come up just like all the rest of the delegates. Give him his per diem, or the International's going to do it and you're going to pay us." He wasn't playing it political then—he just met 'em head-on. So maybe he did do some things to help us behind the scenes, too. By the way, the local did pay my per diem, and I did address the caucus.

In the 1960s, the struggle became getting blacks promoted to crane operator status. I went out on my own by taking volunteer crane jobs. They'd run out of regular crane operators, and anybody had an opportunity to try. All they could do if you couldn't operate was just call for your replacement. We had one black Local 13 crane driver, but he got sick. I figured there would be no black guys operating cranes. So I says, "I might as well start breaking in, and then maybe try to open up the way."

Although we cannot claim total credit for causing all the integration seen later in Local 13, I think our efforts were largely responsible for the changes that took place. Just our letting people know we were concerned, we weren't giving in, and we're going to continue to press the fight might have had nuisance value. It's a hell of a way to put it, but I think we won friends as we went along. We won respect. I could feel it.

I could see attitudes softening. On two occasions, different white brothers approached me. I don't know the names of either of these guys, but they knew who I was because I would get up at the mike and raise hell. Both of them said almost identically the same thing: "You know, Williams, I may never learn to like you, but somehow I respect you."

I think the whole damn thing was an educational process. The struggle, the tempers lost, the actual physical battles with people nursing their bruises made a few of 'em say, "Well, why shouldn't he get PO'd? I acted like I wanted to spit on him." I had one brush just before I left the waterfront in 1981. The guy was totally hostile before we had a run-in. After that, he was very friendly. I don't know what kind of phenomenon you would type that to be, but I guess it's just that certain things like that have to happen.

I hope all of this means that it will do the union some good. I hope all of the bad feelings we experienced one toward another because of race is water under the bridge. Things have improved in Local 13. I just hope we'll be a stronger union as a result. It would be tragic for these differences still to be made when some guys are Mexican and some other guy's a black man and somebody's something else, because we need each other. We're going to have to have the kind of unity we always used to talk about to survive.

TWO WHITE GUYS OPPOSE DISCRIMINATION, 1937–1949

During 1946–49, while Walter Williams led the Unemployed 500 in their attempt to get re-registered in Local 13, Loyd Seeliger and Jackson Newton, two white ILWU warehouse Local 26 activists at the L.A. port, helped the 500 obtain waterfront work. In doing so, Seeliger and Newton personified the union's traditional stance against discrimination.[7]

Loyd Seeliger

My father was German. My mother was German, Irish, and Scotch. They was farming people in the Territory of Oklahoma, where I was born in 1906. The family moved to Weiser, Idaho, when I was six months old. My father run a transfer business that moved freight from Weiser depot to the narrow-gauge railroad that went up to New Meadows. He hauled suitcases and trunks from the trains to the hotels. There was one black family in the little town we lived in. I didn't know anything about discrimination at that time.

I didn't know too much about black people 'til I come to southern California during the Depression. I was sitting on the S streetcar on San Pedro Street. We's coming into town. I was working for Union Terminal Warehouse. A pregnant black woman was standing in the aisle. I got up and said, "Take my seat." This guy alongside jumped out and says, "What are you doin' givin' a seat to a damn n——r?" One word brought on another. We got in a fight. The streetcar people stopped us and kicked us off. That's the first thing I knew about discrimination.

When I come to Los Angeles, as a kid, I was always for the underdog. I don't care who he was, if he was gettin' kicked around, I'd try to help him. I saw this with the Mexicans and the blacks in southern California—they was good people, but they wasn't getting a break in anything.

In 1937 I was hired to help recruit warehouse workers into the old ILA [International Longshoremen's Association] local that became warehouse Local 26, ILWU, later that year. In my organizational work, in going to warehouses and seeing how the blacks and the Mexicans was treated in the waste material industry, I couldn't believe my eyes. I just couldn't think that this could happen here in the U.S. That's the reason I got involved in startin' to pull people out of the mess they was in.

Jackson Newton

I was born in Texas in 1913. When I got out of high school in 1932, I played baseball for the Vernon Dusters. They took up a collection. People who wanted to pay did; people who didn't got in free. Then we split the money. I finally left Texas and came out to California in 1936. There was no work back there.

I had a friend who was working at the Santa Cruz Cement Company in Long Beach Harbor. He took me down there, and I went to work for fifty cents an hour. In less than a year, we organized the cement company into the old ILA; after that, we went into the ILWU. When the union came in, we was raised ten cents and started getting sixty cents an hour. I wrote my mother that I was makin' a whole penny a minute!

After the war, Loyd was elected warehouse Local 26 business agent for the harbor. I became the first chief steward at National Metals after Loyd organized the place in 1947. I'd had another Local 26 job, but I assisted Loyd in organizing National Metals and then became a crane driver there. That was a good job. I was also on the local's Harbor Executive Committee.

Loyd Seeliger

I was the business agent, dispatcher, organizer, negotiator, and everything in 1946, when I first got elected to office at the harbor. We built the local up by hundreds of members down there.

Jack was the only white guy who'd take the job on of breaking the blacks into crane driving back then. Bennie McDonald, a white longshore Local 13 crane driver, helped us out quite a bit. He claimed that some of our black guys could become crane operators. I got Jackson to go over to National Metals. He run a crane. Then we started trainin' all the black guys.

Jackson Newton

Felton Reese, a black guy, was the crane oiler. He said, "Would you show me how to operate this crane?" I said, "I sure will." One white guy said, "You mean to tell me that you're gonna learn those damn n——s how to run crane?" I said, "I sure as hell am."

I was willing to help the black guys because I thought, "What difference are they than I am? Shouldn't they do things the same as I, and have the same position that I had and become crane operators? Just because they was black doesn't mean they couldn't operate the crane." And Loyd Seeliger's influence helped bring me the truth.

This was around when longshore Local 13 deregistered them 500. The majority of them were black. They come into Local 26 for jobs. Local 13 didn't want anything to do with them because they was afraid they would demand to be in Local 13 if they started working back on the waterfront doing extra longshore jobs, even through Local 26.

Loyd Seeliger

Local 13 was afraid the 500 guys would build up hours and seniority. We picked 'em up in Local 26. We'd get them back onto the job. Finally we won out. It got to where Local 13 would hire 'em because there's several suits at that time in court.

But in '47 I had a hard time getting the blacks in Local 26 hired through the Local 13 hiring hall. They'd call the state unemployed hall before they'd call us, and we were their sister local. They'd call the state office to get guys out, and they wasn't union members.

Local 13 didn't turn the black guys back after we dispatched 'em. But they'd bypass us and go call the state employment office and other locals and different things to fill the job. Then the Local 13 dispatcher would call me up and say, "Loyd, we haven't got any more jobs. We might have 'em this afternoon."

I finally went over and talked to Bill Shoemaker, the guy who was head of the state employment office. He got to where he wouldn't fill the Local 13 order 'til he found out I was in the 26 dispatch hall and got all my men out first. Then he'd fill the orders from 13.

I had to tell Shoemaker, "Look, we're a sister local. We get the first preference. When they start callin' in the orders over here, you call me and see if I can fill all the men." So he'd call me and say, "I've got thirty jobs. Have all your men been dispatched?" That's how we broke it up.

About this time, Local 26 needed to fill jobs orders from National Metals, where they were cryin' for more burners. These were workers trained to break up scrap metal with cutting torches. We didn't have enough qualified men. I got a lot of black guys from the state unemployed hall, and we set up a school to teach 'em how to burn.

I'd call this fellow up and tell him I wanted some black guys. We set up a school at Banning High School. I even went to National Metals and had 'em haul a load of scrap over there so the guys could learn. After we taught these guys how to burn, we'd dispatch them over to National Metals. A lot of 'em was the Unemployed 500 longshoremen.

The reason I was askin' for these guys, see, was to keep 'em in the harbor. At the same time, there was a move to run the blacks out of San Pedro. The police chief was from Alabama, and he talked with that Southern Alabama talk. He was a vicious character, and there was a lot more like him on the San Pedro police department.

The black people had to walk around and not do anything a little off color or they'd land in jail. I was over there all the time gettin' somebody out. They'd pick 'em up and say they was drunk and throw 'em in the can, and they wasn't drunk.

There was a black guy called Little Hat. He run a café and bar in San Pedro. The police beat him up and threw him in jail. I went to his trial and said he was a member of Local 26, an honest, good-working guy. It got him off with just a little fine. They had him for resisting arrest or something like that.

They even tried to run the blacks out of the housing places. The real estate people wanted to get 'em out of the Banning project, tear it down, and build homes—which they did. We tried to get 'em in other places so they wouldn't be run out of Los Angeles.

There was quite a bit of racial prejudice in San Pedro at that time. I went with Percy Sanders and two or three blacks to a restaurant. These restaurants wouldn't serve you. You'd go in, all order, and they'd come and give me my order. I'd say, "What about my friends here?" They'd say, "We don't serve colored people." We'd just walk out. We kept that up 'til we'd notified everybody that they don't let blacks eat in that restaurant.

Jackson Newton

After they started hiring all the burners at National Metals, and the majority of them were black, the yard superintendent come to me. He says, "I don't understand this. Every morning we order some men, and I see a whole black cloud comin' over here to go to work."

Loyd Seeliger

That superintendent didn't know that I was on the other end organizing this thing and teachin' 'em to burn at the Banning High School. I'd send 'em over, and he couldn't figure out why he couldn't get just white burners, although we did have quite a few white and Mexican burners, too.

So we got all these people workin' at National Metals, including a lot of the Unemployed 500 longshoremen. Over the next couple of years, when the 500 guys got laid off at National Metals, they come back to the Local 26 hall, and we recycled them back to 13 through the hiring hall. This is where my friend in the state employment office would always check with me so my men was out before he'd send anybody to 13.

As for Local 26, we organized a lot of black people into the local from the 1930s on. There never was opposition in the local to organizing black workers that I can recall. Local 26 always seemed to be a very good group of people. We used to tell 'em in the general membership meeting, "If we're gonna have a solid union, we've gotta have everybody organized." We stressed the fact that if we didn't get everybody into the union—including blacks, Asians, and

An integrated warehouse Local 26 function, Los Angeles, 1951. The McCarran, Smith, and Magnuson Acts were all used to suppress labor, immigrant workers, and the Left during the McCarthy era. ILWU Library.

Mexicans—we would not have a solid union to fight an employer. We started out that way, and we never did have any opposition.

BILL WARD: SIXTY-FIVE YEARS WITH THE UNION

William T. (Bill) Ward was a longshore Local 13 officer and, between 1963 and 1983, an ILWU Coast Labor Relations Committee (CLRC) member. The elected members of this important committee protect the union's interests under the coastwide longshore contract. Ward covers a multitude of topics going back to 1934 that range from basic safety issues to the container revolution of the 1960s–70s. In retirement he remains active as president of San Francisco's Copra Crane Labor Landmark Association.[8]

Bill Ward

My dad, Fred Ward, identified himself in support of the IWW. He was never a member, but he had great respect for their organization. He was raised in Kentucky in a miners' locale, left there just prior to World War I, and hitchhiked and rode the rails around the country.

I was born in 1927. My recollections come in about 1933. We were living in Compton, California. My dad got a fill-in job on the Pacific Electric, a commuter railroad in L.A. He also got waterfront jobs on the shape-up for American-Hawaiian Steamship Company. Their berths were close to one of the railroad's maintenance stops. By early 1933 he was in the longshore union, the old ILA Local 38–82 that is now ILWU Local 13.

My dad got into a Dollar Line gang and stayed with it into the latter part of 1933. He also sometimes was a floor runner. That's what they called a clerk who did the tallying work on the docks. A group of people in the ILA longshore local then were organizing the clerical workers. My dad supported them, preaching unionism and organization. Since he was one of their first organizers, when the marine clerks got their ILWU charter later as Local 63, they gave him Book No. 1.

Before the 1934 strike, longshoring was all heavy, hand-handled work, and the men were fighting the speed-up at every turn. After those twelve- and eighteen-hour shifts, some longshoremen would go to the Robel Inn, a transit hotel in San Pedro where I used to deliver papers. They'd be completely exhausted. They'd sleep eight, ten, twelve hours. It was usually a day and a half or two before they were ready to go again. One time I went down there to deliver my papers, and five or six longshoremen were getting rubdowns. They had hot steam towels they'd wring out and put on. Their legs were all sore and bruised.

In December of '33, we moved to Wilmington. We went through the '34 strike and got a house in San Pedro late that year. During the strike I used to sell papers at the scab compound, hear things the scabs were talkin' about, and tell my father where I thought these people were gonna be the next day. This allowed the union to know where to demonstrate with a great amount of vigor. One day the scabs or the Pinkertons started giving me false information. So my cover was blown. Finally they wouldn't let me back in there anymore.

I really didn't realize what the hell was going on until after the shock of the killing of longshoremen during the 1934 strike. That was a clear recollection I

Bill Ward at one of the ILWU's annual coastwide memorials to the martyrs of Bloody Thursday, San Francisco, July 5, 2004. Photo by Harvey Schwartz. ILWU Library.

could identify with. I knew many longshoremen. Their kids were in my age group, and we hung around together. So that was an impact that really started me to be aware of what my father was up against.

My dad was a marine clerks' local officer through the 1930s and 1940s. When World War II came, he got me a couple of jobs on the waterfront, but I was in the navy for most of the war. From 1948 to '50, I was a marine clerk. During the 1948 longshore strike, we had a committee for procuring food. We used a boat I had to catch fresh fish that we distributed through Local 13's food distribution service.

President Truman stopped the '48 strike under the new Taft-Hartley Act. During the injunction period, you did just enough to stay on the payroll.[9] The discipline in the ranks was such that a dock gang of six men would load these old-time plaster boards. A jitney driver would pull these three boards on three trailers from the dock or out of a boxcar to the ship's gear. The cargo would be hoisted. Then that jitney driver would bring those empty boards back to the dockside for more cargo—and only three loads an hour would be hoisted. The trick was to pull that all day and stay on the payroll.

The '48 strike had historic significance that nobody realizes yet. We won, and we went back to work with a dignity and a pride that we'd taken on this shipowners' industry and beat 'em. Our dispatch hall—the employers had attacked it—was intact. Now we could prove to 'em how good we were. We kept tellin' the employers that come 1951, we're gonna get what we didn't get in '48 and more. That wasn't just common to L.A. either. That was happening in San Francisco, Seattle, Portland, Coos Bay, and everywhere else.

In '51 the employers rolled over on us. They tried to hide behind the flag and the Korean War, but in '51 we got added holidays, more vacation, a real benefit in the pension plan, and a welfare plan that was vastly expanded over the original one that came about in the '40s.

By 1950 I'd discovered I wasn't interested in the pencil side of the industry as much as the physical side. So I transferred to the longshore local. From 1950 until I became a CLRC member in '63, I was a Local 13 longshoreman. In those years, everything was break bulk cargo.

Borax sacks, for example, came in one-hundred-pound units. That was tough work, because you were picking up a dead weight confined in a very small area. Two of you would have to throw that thing anywhere from three to six or eight feet to get it stowed properly. You'd put in eight or ten hours; in those days, there was a ten-hour and then it went to a nine-hour shift. You knew you'd put in a day's work. You didn't have any trouble sleeping either.

The days of loading hand-stowed cargo were a lot harder or a lot more detailed than what the words "hand-stowed" say. Visualize a Grace Lines vessel going to South America. They had upward of twenty-six ports of call on every voyage. There had to be block stowage of cargos for twenty-six different ports. That means the cargo has to be stowed to make the ship seaworthy, but at the same time you had to have that cargo available for discharge when you reach each port.

The second thing that went into hand-handling of cargo was the art of building bulkheads—corners, so to speak—of cargo that were masterpieces of work that longshoremen learned through experience. Whether it was cartons, bags, sacks, loads of lumber, whatever, you learned how to intermingle the ends or the corners of those loads so that while the ship rolls at sea, that cargo's not going to shift.

The bulkhead and the face that you built would look much like the pattern of a brick building. Then there were longshore carpenters who would put a wooden barrier up all the way to the upper deck. It would be nailed and wired into place sometimes with cables that reached to the ribs of the ship and were held in place by sea clamps. You'd tighten that up with a turn buckle after you put up a wood fence.

So the hand-stowing of cargo was a lot more than just picking the cargo off

Break bulk cargo handling, winch drivers in the background, Port of Long Beach, 1963. Photo by Otto Hagel. Copyright 1998 Center for Creative Photography, University of Arizona Foundation.

a pallet board and putting it on the skin of the ship. All this changed with the coming of containerization and the Mechanization and Modernization [M & M] Agreement of 1960, where we allowed the employer to introduce new labor-saving machinery in exchange for security for our members. We said we're not going to lose a member in this transition. Everybody's going to be taken care of. As it worked out, everyone was taken care of, and some of those guys are still living on pensions today.

Matson Navigation Company, with its vessel *Hawaiian Citizen*, set the stage for change. They introduced their operation in 1959. It gave the longshore worker an opportunity to see what mechanization was all about, even in the crude way it was done then, taking an existing vessel and raising the gear off so you'd have room to put nothing but containers on deck. There were specialized cranes that were built specifically for Matson's operation. Well, after the worker saw that, or read about it in *The Dispatcher*, it didn't take long to sink in that this was the coming way the cargo was going to be moved.

I voted against the first M & M Agreement in 1960 along with nine of the ten longshore caucus delegates from Local 13, and went down and talked against it on the basis that I wasn't opposed to the concept, but I was opposed to the amounts that were settled upon. After I got over my mad at not having enough money, I went to work on the basis that we needed this type of a contract to survive and grow, and that whether we kept the old contract or got this new one, the changes were going to come on the waterfront rather rapidly.

There were a lot of people in the local caucus level that wanted the status quo to continue. There was good reasoning for that, with a sling-load limit and the make-work practices that had developed up and down the coast as a means of security. All that was going to be wiped out.

Some people were leery that there wasn't enough protection in the agreement as presented at the coast caucus level to preserve those long-standing conditions we'd gained that were based on informal "hip pocket rules." But by and large, the ranks had accepted the idea, and that showed up in the vote even in the first M & M Agreement that Local 13 turned down. The rest of the locals, or the majority of the workers, passed it.

Probably the biggest objection to both the 1960 and the 1966 M & M Agreements came when we had not really done our homework on the safety end. That's when we finally got around to putting in the onerous workload safeguard and the contract language that said, in effect, that you don't have to work when you, the worker, believe it's not safe, and there would be no penalty.

A few years before M & M, in 1957 and '58, I'd been elected Local 13 business agent. You could only serve two years, so I wound up my term in '59 and immediately got put on the local's Labor Relations Committee [LRC], which negotiated all the local contracts we had and also took care of members' disputes with the employers. In '63 I was elected to Longshore Division office as a CLRC member. The ILWU International office is in San Francisco, so I moved there.

As part of the job duties assigned to me as a coast committee member, I became administrative trustee for the ILWU-PMA Pension Trust and Welfare Fund.

When you are an administrative trustee, there's certain things that come up over a period of time that you just can't cover in writing out a trust agreement. The philosophy of the parties in the ILWU and the employers' organization, the PMA, was that everyone who had qualifications—and these were very lenient, by the way—was entitled to a pension. Now, PMA and the waterfront employers didn't have any records that went back through World War II even. Various companies had some records, but a lot of them had none at all. So we had a job there of verifying that certain longshoremen were here in those years.

What the parties had agreed to was that if longshoremen could prove they worked in the industry in those years prior to . . . I think it was 1942, then that was enough to grant them credit. Pension payments were made for the first time in 1951. All those people who qualified with twenty years went back to '31. So quite a few of 'em had to have sworn statements that were notarized that said, "Yes, I remember John Doe. He was here in 1932 or '33 or whatever."

We went to a great deal of trouble to make sure that all these longshoremen had their day in court, and when you look back on our track record of that original charter member pension plan, 99 percent of the people entitled to a pension got one. That included people who were still retiring in 1963 and all the way up into the '70s where they had to have credit for years that were way back prior to World War II. As for the 1 percent, the reason we never got them was because they never raised the issue—we never heard from them.

Now, as to welfare coverage, the goal of the Longshore Division has always been to have absolutely no out-of-pocket expenses for members in health plans. We pretty much achieved that. We've cut down on a lot of the out-of-pocket expenses for the optional program. Our main thrust has always been that we have a program that makes the longshoreman's wages truly his income, meaning that he's not going to have to put out money for dentists and doctors. It's still the union's goal to have those costs completely taken care of.

By 1971 we hadn't had a confrontation where we faced down the employer since 1948. The '48 strike was on a principle of saving the dispatch hall. Wages weren't a problem. But in 1971 we had just gone through two five-year M & M Agreements that changed the whole atmosphere of longshoring on the West Coast. A lot of people did not think the employer was giving them enough on the bargaining table. In the minds of the majority of the workers, even though we'd had a good contract offered to us, there was more there and let's get more.

For any strike I'd been involved with in the ILWU before '71, we always wanted something that was going to be a permanent part of an agreement. The '48 strike and the efforts made prior to World War II sought to build in certain safety precautions. In 1971 there was a departure from that. There were several issues—the steady-man question existed, but it wasn't the catalyst. The prime emphasis was more money, not some condition that was going to be an integral part of upcoming contracts. A lot of us found that to be a flaw in the thinking of the people advocating the strike. So when the strike was over, in effect, what we had done is go out for 134 days for ten cents.

In 1974 I was appointed to the committee that was formed by the Department of Labor in Washington, D.C., to put together safety standards for marine terminals. I served about nine months. There were two people from the ILA. I was the only one from the ILWU. There were employers from the East, West, and Gulf Coasts and some representatives of the public.

The employers were quite apprehensive of any changes. The first four months of sessions were taken up with the representatives of labor and the public lobbying the employer members to loosen up. We said, "There's no tragedy in some of these regulations, like having marked thoroughfares for vehicles on docks, having guard rails adjacent to cranes where they are run on a track so that people can't walk into 'em, and having marine-type stretchers available and safety things that we've had on the West Coast for ages." But in a lot of places in the Gulf and the South Atlantic, that was pretty foreign to most of those employers.

To be fair, there were a few times we introduced things that were in the Pacific Coast Maritime Code that we had been enforcing out on the West Coast and in Hawaii for years. But trying to have that put into the national code wasn't something those employers were prepared to do. A lot of times that meant modifying our position to get something into the OSHA [Occupational Safety and Health Administration] standard code. But this didn't usurp our protection because that is covered under the ILWU-PMA longshore contract. We still have our marine code here on the West Coast. It is better than OSHA's in some instances.

The terminal safety code that resulted wasn't complete by any means, but it was a great improvement. There had been some very unsafe practices, especially in bulk-loading terminals where machinery was antiquated and not electric-proofed and there were sparks on practically a daily basis. Once you got enough dust in the elevators, with the right amount of cool air or hot air as the case may be, you had an explosion. So that was taken care of because all these elevators had to change over to spark-proof machinery.

I stepped down from the Coast Committee in 1983, went back to longshore clerking where I started, and then served briefly as interim CLR committeeman in 1990. Today [1998] I can look back and compare things to when I came on the docks the first time in 1943 as a high school student. The only thing I took home was a straight-time wage, with overtime after six hours.

Now when registered longshoremen leave the docks after a day's work, they take home a very high wage and benefit credits toward pensions, holidays, vacations, and medical coverage for them and their families. They have a fair dispatch system. They have the freedom of a forty-hour week. They can make themselves available for work just one day a month if they wish—that doesn't guarantee 'em the benefits, but it does guarantee 'em a job. Is that a great union or what?

3

LONGSHORE, SHIPBOARD, AND BOOKSTORES
THE PACIFIC NORTHWEST AND CANADA

THE ILWU IN THE PACIFIC NORTHWEST AND CANADA HAS ITS OWN HISTORY. As at the L.A. Harbor, there was a powerful Wobbly tradition in this region in the early twentieth century. Many Northwest timber workers joined the IWW, and so did waterfront lumber handlers in places like the port at Coos Bay, Oregon.

Seattle's militant tradition led to a general strike in 1919. Among the few well-remembered general strikes in U.S. history, besides San Francisco's, it was lost just as the country entered the conservative post–World War I era, although it did leave a powerful memory of labor solidarity.

One unique aspect of the Northwest is that it was home to the only Pacific Coast ILA local that survived intact during the 1920s. In Tacoma, Washington, ILA workers preserved their organization into the 1930s and beyond. More conservative than the coast's other major locals and the new ILWU of 1937, the Tacoma longshore local stayed out of the ILWU for twenty-one years.

When the Big Strike of 1934 came, the Northwest had its own martyrs, Shelvy Daffron and Olaf Helland of Seattle. In Portland, no one died, but there were battles and serious injuries at all the major ports. (Besides the six unionists who died in U.S. West Coast ports, a seventh, Bruce Lindberg, was killed by a scab in Hong Kong. Lindberg was a seaman who had shipped out from Seattle.)[1]

In Canada, longshore workers struck against exploitative conditions in 1935. They lost and labored under a company union for nine years before going ILWU. Forty-five years later, the ILWU acquired a shipboard jurisdiction when the Inlandboatmen's Union of the Pacific (IBU) affiliated with the ILWU following an important Washington State Ferries workers' strike. In 2000 Portland booksellers joined the ILWU, too.

MARVIN RICKS: THE 1934 STRIKE IN PORTLAND

Portland longshore Local 8 veteran Marvin Ricks recalls the Big Strike in the Columbia River city. He vividly depicts pre-strike working conditions, the strike itself, and his ordeal as one of twenty-eight workers unjustly charged with the murder of a scab who was killed shortly after the strike.

Marvin Ricks

I was born October 22, 1911, in Newberg, Oregon. When I was four, my parents moved to north-central Washington, where my father had been a wheat farmer. In the spring of 1929, we moved to Ethel, Washington, ten miles out of Centralia. We were going to start a dairy farm. Dad bought a bunch of cows. I bought a bunch of heifer calves. I figured I would have to milk for ten years—then I could hire the work done.

The crash and the Depression came in the fall of '29. Milk that had sold for $2.20 for X amount dropped to $1.10. So in 1931 we sold the cattle. We got just half of what we paid for them two years before. Next we moved to Portland, although I would go back to north-central Washington and work in the apples, picking and spraying.

Over the winter of '31–'32, I cut cord wood in the Portland area. I was getting one dollar a cord, all split and piled four-foot wood. On a good day I could make two cords. That gave me two dollars a day. I had to take my saw over to the neighbor's to file and set it—he had a vise. His name was Neal Dagen. He also happened to be a longshoreman.

Dagen was working steadily, as much work as there was in those days. When I turned twenty-one, he says, "Hey, kid, be over at the house in the morning and I'll take you down to the hiring hall and get you a day or two's work." We didn't have a union-controlled hall then. The hall was run by the employers. The first day I was there, Dagen got me a job. We worked from eight in the morning until midnight. Basic pay was seventy-five cents an hour, no overtime. I still made more in one long day than I made in any week cutting cord wood.

Neal Dagen introduced me to a man who had a gang that worked shoveling sulfur two days a month. Nobody making any money at all wanted to shovel sulfur, but there were two days every month that I did it. Another man had a gang that loaded green hides once in a while. I got a day or two's work there.

A green hide was a complete cowhide that made a bundle two feet long, a foot and a half wide, and six or eight inches high. In August, if those uncured hides had sat for a month, you can imagine the smell. They would keep the doors on the docks open about six or eight inches so the air could blow through a little, but it didn't do much. If you got on a streetcar after work, everybody got as far away from you as they could.

Hides paid a ten-cent penalty, so you made eighty-five cents an hour. Making any money when I first started was good. I have sat in the employer-controlled hiring hall for fourteen days and gotten two hours' work, what we called "noon relief." They would hire a complete gang of men for eleven o'clock and have them relieve one hatch between eleven and twelve while that gang went to dinner. Then you relieved the second hatch between twelve and one. At seventy-five cents an hour, you made a dollar fifty.

I was also introduced to a fellow who occasionally ran a job lining a ship, which meant building a wood centerline down the middle of the vessel so that bulk wheat would not roll when the ship rolled. You didn't want all the wheat to get on one side and capsize the ship. So sometimes I got a job doing that.

After we got a union and won the '34 strike, of course, the work was evenly divided. We used the same hall. We just had different people running it, and we moved the loan shark and beer joint out of there. But before the union, we had fifty-five gangs working out of the employer-run hiring hall, thirteen men to a gang. Usually those gangs were full. All the other workers, myself included, were called "extra men." They did the less organized jobs, like lining ships for bulk grain and working on the docks where there were no regular gangs.

I always refused to pay for a job, which back then kept me from getting a certain amount of work. One fellow said, "My brother is taking out an extra gang this afternoon, do you want to work?" I says, "Certainly." In an hour, he came back and said, "I need one dollar." I says, "Certainly, I'll loan you one dollar." Come payday, he didn't pay me. The second payday, I said, "Hey, where's my one dollar?" He says, "Didn't you work for my brother?" I said, "I still want my one dollar." I got my one dollar back, but I never worked for his brother again.

There was one gang boss who raffled off a radio. He had twelve men in his gang. Every week everybody in the gang bought a chance on the radio for a dollar. I don't know how many years this went on, but there was never a drawing. If you're only making twenty-five or thirty dollars a week, twelve dollars is quite a little addition. In other cases—remember, under Prohibition, liquor was illegal until 1933—a bottle of moonshine whiskey passed to a gang boss bought a job.

The employers cared little about safety then. If it slowed the work down, to hell with safety. We killed five or six men a year in Portland from waterfront accidents. Any way you could think of to kill a man, we managed to do it. My friend, Dagen, who took me down to the waterfront, was killed just a few years afterwards. They dropped a load of scrap iron that hit a piece of pipe laying in the shelter deck with one end sticking out over the open hatch. Dagen was tending that hatch ten feet above and twenty-five feet across. The pipe hit him in the head and killed him.

You didn't have safety nets or anything. Fellas would slip off the dock and fall into the river. In those days you had a log around the dock to keep the ship from rubbing the piling. If you fell in, you landed on top of a log twenty-five or thirty feet down, and that was the end.

One day Howard Bodine came around when I was at the hall and says, "Hey, Marvin, you wanna join the union?" I said, "What's a union?" I was from inland, I'd never heard of one. I'd heard of Communists, but I'd never heard of a union. He started explaining, and I told him, "Can I wait 'til tomorrow to give you an answer? I'll talk to a couple of my good friends."

Well, Dagen and his best friend both says, "Yes, we plan on joining, and we think you should, too. We don't think the union will last over a year before they break us, but it'll give you a chance to get better acquainted." I forget whether it was one dollar or two dollars—some outrageous sum—to join. Dues were one dollar a month.

We all got a button when we joined the union, but nobody dared to wear one before the strike. Your gang boss might have joined the union, too, but if he showed up with a bunch of men with buttons on their hats, the walking boss, if he was a good company man, was not going to hire that gang. So there was kind of a blacklisting, but not as such.

Several ships were still working the morning the '34 strike started. One of my first jobs was to go around with a bunch of men to every ship in the harbor that was working and tell the gangs that everybody was out and they'd better get off the ship right now. We talked most of them into leaving. Some gangs

Picketing during the first day of the 1934 strike, Portland waterfront. Oregon Historical Society, OrHi 81702.

didn't quit, but we did nothing at the time because we were just four men per group making the rounds. As the strike got going, the things we did were considerably different.

When we got organized, then those guys who were working the ships had been warned. That's why the employers kept the strikebreakers on board ship, or on the grain docks, or out at Terminal 4. That way, those men didn't have to come back and forth, because they had a little problem getting back and forth.

One night the phone rang. It was the fellow that ran the beer joint up on Twenty-third and Burnside. He says, "Hey, I've got two guys in here that sound like scabs." We said, "Okay, we'll be there." We walked in. Here are two fellas sitting down, drinking. We knew them both.

We said, "Well, hi, fellas. We know you're too drunk to drive home. We'll see you get home safe." Meanwhile, you have a wristlock on each one, so if they make a sound, you could break their arm. We led 'em out. You go as good pals, you're helping the two drunks. We got 'em outside, talked to 'em by hand a little while, and turned 'em loose.

You might say I was in a flying squad—we called it a "riot squad." These were squads made up of football players, boxers, or wrestlers, the single men that didn't have much to lose. There were four squads of us on the shift I was on. If there was trouble at a dock, they called for us, and here come forty men down there in a hurry. Throughout the strike we kept ten pickets at every gate, at every dock on the waterfront. We kept them twelve hours a day, seven days a week. Well then, we had these forty men that could go anywhere at any time to reinforce. And we did make a difference.

They did capture our navy though. One of our fellas had a fishing boat that we used for a patrol boat. At Terminal 4, these scabs were working a ship. We made slingshots and pulled up to the ship and started shooting at the winch driver and hatch bosses. They were throwing shackles at us, or whatever they could find. I don't think anybody hit anybody. But they swore out John Doe warrants for the four or six of us in the boat. Then the harbor patrol confiscated our navy—they took our boat away and tied it up.

When the strike started, nearly all the regular police were our friends. They were working men. Then, pretty soon, you found all the good guys uptown, directing traffic, and you had every bad one on the waterfront, plus a bunch of special police they stationed at Terminal 4. The July 11 tragedy, when the police opened up shooting near Terminal 4, was completely unnecessary. They claimed they only used riot guns, but Elmus "Buster" Beatty had a .45 slug in his neck and was off for a year. Four pickets were shot that day, two critically.

We did have someone in the police department who sent us a list every week of all the special police that were hired, including addresses. So there were specials who happened to run into unfriendly people in the streets. Then we had this detective who used to tell us this and that. Once he says, "They're moving a bunch of scabs in the morning. We have orders to take them to point X. At point Y, the harbor patrol is to pick them up and guard them the rest of the way. Somebody forgot there was one block in between those two points."

"I will see to it that we protect them only to the point that we were told," the detective said, "and that none of the harbor patrol go beyond that point." So there was quite a bit of monkey business out in the street that morning in that one block. There were police on both ends, but none made a move because they hadn't any orders. That is what you call having friends.

We had other friends, too. The local prostitutes made us sandwiches, which were wrapped up real nicely with the girls' cards inside. Broadway Cab delivered the sandwiches for free. One night a week, everybody on the picket line, two or three hundred men, got sandwiches. Another thing, being times were tough, the madams donated rooms. They would put four to six men in a room for the duration of the strike. A lot of the area farmers were liberal, too, and donated produce to us.

I was on the soup-bumming detail for a while. One of my duties was to go up to the Good Eats Cafe on Burnside at ten o'clock at night when they closed. They gave us whatever coffee and soup they had left over. We had bumming committees for rooms, food, produce, and everything, because you couldn't get much help from other unions. In '34, what unions you had were very weak. We were what got unions going.

After the strike, the work paid $.95 an hour. I made $210 the first twenty-one days. That's $10 a day. I was working pretty steady. I remember twenty-one days because on the twenty-second day I got arrested. What happened was that a bunch of our men who were provoked by an employer agent raided this company union scab hall.[2] A shot was fired, and a scab named James Connor was killed.

When I got arrested, I said, "What for?" They says, "Murder." I thought, "Ah, what a relief." This might have been for assault and battery, kidnapping or sabotage, but when they said murder, I knew I didn't do it. I wasn't there. I'd gone to the dentist that day. He was late, and I was waiting alone at his office when the shooting took place. But I couldn't prove it. He had no secretary. In the '30s you did well to support yourself, let alone a secretary. Anyway, they picked up everybody that any of the scabs saw or thought they saw.

I was taken to jail. You weren't allowed to call out for twenty-four hours. I disappear, wiped off the face of the earth. When they questioned me, there was the assistant district attorney, "Big Bill" Browne, the head of the police "Red Squad," two policemen, and two detectives. You're this scared twenty-two-year-old kid with six people throwing questions at ya, and you haven't even been allowed to call out. Well, one thing, being as I hadn't been there, I could tell the truth. I didn't get confused in my story.

They took us down to the city jail and threw us into the bull pen where the drunks had been heaving their guts out. It was horrible. They were picking up two, three, four longshoremen a day. We got watery mush for breakfast with two slices of moldy bread and a little thin soup at lunch and dinner. The only thing you could buy was Milky Way candy bars. It took me twenty years before I could eat another one. After a week they moved us to the county jail, where the food was good, and they let the union or your wives or friends bring food in to you.

There were twenty-eight of us charged. A quirk in the law let them charge us all. Once there were thirty-two, but we proved that four of us weren't there.

When we started having our preliminary hearings at city hall, they hauled us down and back in the Black Maria. They'd take us out ten at a time on a chain. We only shaved on shave day, so the public got to see these ten unshaven, rough-looking characters on the chain.

In a while, some kid that had scabbed broke down and told the police he'd seen another scab, Carl Grammer, shoot Conner. The cops found the gun, too. It matched, and they had proof that Grammer did it. So we finally got turned loose.

After the strike, we had our names in rotation on the dispatch board. We had to take in some scabs, including "Big Nose" Riley, who was right next to me on the list. So I got him often. I managed to work with that man for over two years, not steadily, but quite a bit, without ever speaking to him. And neither, as far as I know, did anybody else in the gangs.

When the strike was over, I was happy to have a little money to spend, which before I didn't have. I owed the kid at the service station two dollars and I could pay that off. Today, *The Oregonian* says we are upper middle class on account of our good wages. Years ago we were looked down upon and called "Communistic bums." I do recall that Matt Meehan, one of our '34 leaders, was a Wobbly, a member of the radical Industrial Workers of the World, the IWW. I used to be against the idea of Wobblies, and against Communism, but now I think they did more for the union and getting organized than anyone.

You have to have a radical. The rest of you may hate your conditions, but you go along, whereas you need some no-good so-and-so to stir it up and get you going. I think nearly all of our early top leadership was a little bit on the Wobbly side, whether you could prove it or not. Now I don't know about Harry Bridges, but it takes someone like him to get out and do the job.

I also feel we have to organize to stay alive. You just can't stand alone. You need people to back you when you have trouble. Taking in the salespeople at Powell's Books, which we did recently in the new Local 5, hits my sense of humor as a good thing. It was getting two completely opposite types of workers together.

UNION STRUGGLES IN NORTH BEND AND COOS BAY, OREGON, 1920–1940

Longshore Local 12 is an affiliate of the ILWU from the small port at Coos Bay. In the 1920s and 1930s, Coos Bay longshore workers handled logs and lumber bound for California and Asia. This was decades before the collapse of the Northwest timber industry in the late twentieth century.[3] *Henry Hansen and Don Brown, veterans of the 1934 strike, recall early days at the port.*

Henry Hansen

I'm the son of a Coos Bay longshoreman. Dad would allow me to work with him sometimes when I was going to high school in the mid-1920s. Then, the port of Coos Bay was serviced mainly from San Francisco for groceries, building materials, and machinery. It all came up by steam schooners—small, maybe 150-foot crafts. The trucking industry put the steam schooners out of business. The last ones to go were a couple of package-loading operations that existed for a few years until World War II.

In 1920 an important phenomenon took place on the West Coast. This was the beginning of the export of raw logs and timbers in large quantities to Asia. Everything was loaded piece by piece, by hand. We used a special instrument for loading logs. It had a wooden handle, steel point, and a small hook you could use to roll timber or logs, or you could spike and pry.

When we loaded lumber in the hatches, which were usually small, half the time it would come down in slings using the ship's gear. You'd have to stow that cargo floor by floor, twelve inches to a floor—twelve inches because that was the dimension you could usually work out with lumber. To maintain that floor and handle the cargo with the speed the shipowner demanded took a hell of a lot of skill and hard work.

In the early days, logs were worked from the offshore side, the water side. Logs were rafted and floated down to the ship. You wore cork shoes—that kept you from slipping, usually. Bark would break off, and you'd go in the water occasionally, but there'd be months you wouldn't fall overboard. You learned that. The boom stick that surrounded the raft of logs had no bark at all. So you learned to walk on that, or you didn't work on the waterfront. In later years, with the advent of the truck, they had sorting yards, and they'd bring the logs out to the ship's side loading from the dock side rather than from the water side.

There was no limit on hours before '34. Say it's going to take three days, like a steam schooner—the first day you might work from seven in the morning until twelve that night. Then you'd be back at seven or eight the next day. You'd go back, too, or there'd be a man in your place. The longest I ever worked was twenty-seven hours without a break.

Northwest longshoremen moving huge timbers called "fletchers," ship's hold, 1963. This hard work looked much the same thirty years earlier. Photo by Otto Hagel. Courtesy Labor Archives and Research Center, San Francisco State University. Copyright 1998 Center for Creative Photography, University of Arizona Foundation.

In the early days I was fired lots of times. Maybe somebody's brother-in-law or some outstanding athlete wanted a job. That's the way it went. Or you might want better wire put in the winches, or you might think a boom was too rotten. You could object, all right, but you usually went off the ship—your job was done. Hell, Frank Shaw, who ran the Independent Stevedore Company—the only stevedoring outfit in Coos Bay—could put you on the beach for six months or a year or forever if he wanted to, because there was no union. All your work and your livelihood was always in jeopardy.

In the 1920s there was no longshore union because the old organization had been broken in 1919. You got your employment from the employers directly. That filtered down through the walking bosses, and finally they developed the system of gang bosses. You had that one-two-three step of hiring. It was the same thing as the shape-up.

But the old-timers knew what unions were, you bet. There'd been a strong labor movement known as the IWW before World War I. They stayed until the early '20s, when they were broken up. Few Coos Bay longshoremen carried IWW red cards, though, because at one time the "good citizens" of the community had deported everyone who was a member of the IWW or was suspected of being an IWW. They'd moved them out to the beach, and if they'd had their way, they'd have put them on a barge and sunk 'em.

The waterfront got organized again in 1933, and in 1934 the people in the longshore union knew what the story was. They knew what was coming. Job security—that was why the '34 strike was supported. There were a couple of ships the employers tried to load. One thing here—we stayed away, at least openly, from any vicious attack on strikebreakers. We turned over one bus of strikebreakers in a little town down near Empire, and after dark there was lots of things, but on the picket line it was pretty well controlled. We didn't let it get to where the state could come in with the National Guard.

There were people—longshoremen, too—that thought we were going a little too far in demanding a union-controlled hiring hall in 1934. But after the strike they set up the [ILA-controlled] hiring hall. The way the hiring hall was set up, we had one neutral person in there under the terms of the '34 strike arbitration agreement. He was an old fella, a retired businessman from town. The union, though, elected the dispatcher. Charlie Smith was the first one. The old fella was put in there with him, but our guy did most of the work. Everybody—all the longshoremen—liked it fine.

After '34 a few of us went out on committees to organize. We got the woodworkers started. We talked to them, visited them, went out to their camps. We recognized the importance of surrounding ourselves with friendly people, people we could depend on, people who would recognize an obligation. If you don't better that guy's condition and bring it up to your level, he'll tear yours down, you can bet your bottom dollar on that.

Don Brown

Times was bad in the Depression, I'll tell you that. Once I left Florence, Oregon, where my parents were, looking for a job. I thought I'd go down to California riding the freight cars. I just got "vagged," thrown in jail for looking for work. Later I got a call to go to Reedsport, Oregon, north of Coos Bay, to play minor league baseball. I ended up playing ball and longshoring on weekends. Then the '34 strike came up.

They wanted us to scab. I went down and joined the picket line instead. I was a casual longshoreman, but to me it was just instinct. These people were down there trying to get some improvement on their way of life, which was horrible. I didn't like the way they could fire people, and I didn't like the dangerous, unsafe attitude of the mates on the steam schooners.

On the second ship I ever worked, they were loading big slingloads of random lumber, and not too good gear, into the hold. You'd be working away, and all of a sudden they'd holler, "Heads up," and here'd go a load of lumber over your head if you didn't run the hell out of the way.

Not long after the strike we got equalization of earnings, which became a principle. Everybody watched it like a hawk. Gangs went out by gang earnings. Another struggle was getting the size of sling loads down. We never did get it down like they did in some ports, where it was a standard sling load. But we got 'em reduced. Shaw would say no reduction, so we'd pick certain gangs and put a slowdown on. Everybody would be workin', but they wouldn't seem to get anything done. Naturally, he got the message.

In 1936 there was another strike. I was in Coos Bay by that time. The shipowners was depending on being able to starve the longshoremen out. I survived by hunting and fishing, and in '36 I paid nine dollars a month for our little apartment. Barb, my wife, had a job in a restaurant. The longshoremen helped one another. We had work parties. And it wasn't only during troubles. If a guy wanted to build a home, there'd be eighteen, twenty, maybe twenty-five people—all would pitch in, help lay a foundation, and throw up a house in nothin' flat.

I was still a rank and filer in 1940. I sat through the whole ILWU International convention they had in North Bend that year. It was quite evident there was a split between various factions. There was Bridges on one philosophical side of what trade unions should be and what could be done, and there was a conservative element of good, honest trade unionists working within the framework of what their thinking was. There was another faction which was out just to disrupt. But I was terribly impressed at how it was run. It was sure as hell democratic.

VALERIE TAYLOR: AUXILIARY PRESIDENT, 1949–1973

A dedicated union stalwart from a family of Northwest woodworkers and longshoremen, Valerie Taylor served as president of the ILWU Women's Federated Auxiliaries from 1949 to 1973. As organizations of wives and sisters of members, women's auxiliaries do important support work on behalf of unions. Taylor's testimony covers her life as an activist as well as the contributions of the ILWU women's auxiliary to the union and the wider community.

Valerie Taylor

I was born Valerie Wyatt in Morton, Washington, in 1913. My father was working as a logger back in those days around Aberdeen and the Grays Harbor area. The bosses then always had the philosophy "Well, if you don't like it, if you don't roll out, you can roll 'em up," you know, and get out. That kind of thing I remember my dad talking about. I can also remember my folks talking about the Wesley Everest killing right after World War I.[4]

We moved to North Bend, Oregon, in 1923. After we came down here, my dad went into carpentry and joined the Carpenters Union. In the early 1930s he belonged to the Unemployed Council. That was an organization of people who were trying to figure out ways to get better jobs.

My parents had a large family. I've always had lots of brothers, sisters, nephews, and other relatives living around here. My brothers worked in the woods. Later on they went longshoring and became ILWU Local 12 members.

In 1934 it seemed like every radio program would have things about the Big Strike, how it was coming along, and then finally wound up a general strike in San Francisco that just about shut everything down. My family and our friends were all on the side of the working people. We followed what was going on, and we knew the longshoremen were right.

About every evening the family and our friends would gather around our house and talk politics. These were the Depression years when no one hardly had any work, and we had lots of time to think about these things. We read all about Harry Bridges and heard about him on the radio.

This is all when Franklin D. Roosevelt was president. I remember one evening when a bunch of us were sitting there playing cards and talking politics. My nephew was about five years old. He was standing around the table. Pretty soon he says, "I know who the president is." So somebody says, "Well, who?" He says, "Harry Bridges!"

Of course, we did feel the Depression. When I was going to high school, a lot of us cut out cardboard and put it in the bottom of our worn shoes. Then my dad would cut leather out and put some hack soles on or heels or whatever we needed. We lived over on Maple Street and had a big house there, but we couldn't pay our taxes, so we lost the house and moved into a houseboat and lived down on the bay.

Still, our family didn't go hungry. We always put in a little garden, and the guys did a lot of hunting, so we had venison. We'd get clams and crabs, and we'd fish for perch. We'd go out across the bay in rowboats. We never had outboard motors, but after you got a little bill in your pocket, you could buy a rower.

We were a pretty close-knit family, so there were some good times. My sister and her husband lived close by. We didn't need to call on too many outsiders for a hand of pinochle. We had it right there all the time. But we were conscious of other people going hungry. We felt we were lucky living more or less out in the country instead of being in a big city.

My brother, Ronald Wyatt, his wife, Norma, who worked with me as an officer in the ILWU federated auxiliaries in later years, and I were in the Workers Alliance about 1936, '37.[5] I think my sister, Kate Skinner, and her husband, Jasper, were members, too. There were monthly meetings, and we had dues. We used to meet in the old Peter Logan Building.

The Workers Alliance was supposed to be for those people who didn't have a job. Some members were working on low-paid New Deal Works Progress Administration jobs and thought they weren't getting enough wages for cutting trails, building bridges, and working out in the woods. I didn't get out on those jobs, but we felt they weren't getting a fair shake, so we held a demonstration.

Around 1937 someone said, "Why don't you get into the CIO International Woodworkers of America [IWA] Auxiliary?" I could, because of my connections with my brothers working in the woods. So I joined the IWA Auxiliary, and from that I became a delegate to the old Coos Bay Area Industrial Union Council, CIO.

We had everybody on the CIO council, including the fishermen, the electrical workers, and even representatives of the Workers Alliance. The first thing they gave me was a job in the council as a treasurer. Later on I was elected secretary of the council. I served in that role for several years.

Unionists calling for a boycott of scrap iron bound for Imperial Japan, Coos Bay, Oregon, 1939. Photo by Harbor Photo. Courtesy of Nathan Douthit. Taylor Family Collection.

In 1939 there was a ship in port to load scrap iron bound for fascist Japan. The Japanese military wanted to use the scrap iron to kill the Chinese. My family, friends, and some IWA people got word that it might be a good idea to have a picket line on that ship. I didn't think the idea up, but I went along with it. The more forward leaders in ILWU longshore Local 12 supported us.

The guy who had the scrap iron wanted to see it loaded, of course. He got me arguing. He was about ready to slug one of our men, and I said, "Oh, here come the cops!" So this guy dropped everything and took off.

When World War II started, my husband, Forrest Taylor, went into the service. I took aircraft training in Coos Bay to become a riveter. Then I went to Portland to work in an aircraft company on the waterfront up there. My partner was actually named Rosie. She was a real little old riveter, too. We worked together quite a bit. So, yes, we really were Rosie the Riveters.

We needed someone for machinists union shop steward who we thought would be effective. It seemed like I wasn't too afraid to speak out back in those days, so I became shop steward and a delegate to the AFL Central Labor Council. The machinists were in the AFL, which was still separate from the newer

CIO then. Boy, sitting there with some of those old AFL conservatives, it was really quite an experience. But I managed to get by all right. Then I was elected as one of three women to the Tri-State Convention of the Machinists.

When I first joined the machinists union, you took an oath that said, "I will not knowingly advocate for membership in this organization any other than a competent white person." Now wasn't that cute! It wasn't very long before we got rid of that thing. Imagine, we had all kinds of people working in the aircraft plant. One of the women who was one of the inspectors of parts was Chinese. So we pointed that out, and there was hardly any fight over getting rid of the clause.

I was also one of the ones who sold war bonds. That was the thing to do. I think I came out with second prize or something like that. I won a one-hundred-dollar war bond. I still have a poster with big letters in there that says "That's to defeat Hitler."

When the war ended in 1945 and Forrest came back from the service, we moved back to Coos Bay. In 1947 I went to the ILWU convention held in San Francisco. Forrest was a member of ILWU Local 12. The ILWU federated auxiliaries used to have their convention at the same time as the regular ILWU convention, so we had a meeting. I was the delegate from North Bend ILWU Auxiliary No. 1. As a result of that first meeting—it was my first federated auxiliaries convention, but the third one that had been held since 1941—I became Oregon vice president.

Then in 1949 I was elected president of the ILWU federated auxiliaries. I held that job for twenty-four years. The business of the auxiliary was that once the union came up with a program, we tried to carry out those policies. After I got to be the president of the auxiliary, I attended every ILWU convention so that I would know what the ILWU policy was and I'd be sure that the rest of us carried it out at the auxiliary convention.

When I first went down to the federated auxiliaries convention in 1947, I really wasn't looking for any job. I thought it wouldn't be so interesting working with women, but I soon found out differently. The women's thinking was just the same as the guys'. I thought it was a good program that the ILWU was proposing. Then I found out that it took all of us putting our heads together to figure out how we could best carry the program out. So it was interesting working with women.

The women could do a lot of things that the men couldn't. The men were talking wages, hours, and conditions, but the women could lend support in many different ways. I think probably we did more letter writing to our congressmen than the ILWU president did. We were constantly bombarding Washington with letters from the perspective of the policy of the ILWU.

We would always go back in the kitchen, of course, serving. That was important sometimes, too, like at meetings where the guys didn't have to recess to go out and eat. We figured that helped some. But I felt that we should have more than just sewing circles. That went along with it, but that wasn't the predominant thing. We were most concerned, most all of 'em, with frame-up cases and things like that that we wrote about. We were on a lot of picket lines, too.

Our North Bend auxiliary had public meetings in the Local 12 Longshore Hall to support various people involved in legal cases, and we took up collections and circulated petitions for a great many causes. Some of our members circulated a petition for Angela Davis, the famous American Communist Party activist who was tried around 1970.

The auxiliary also did various work in the community like supporting bloodmobile drives, registering voters, and helping with just an endless amount of things. Whatever kind of community work there was, why, we were usually into it. I think we were pretty highly respected for these activities, too. I even worked to help Henry Hansen of Local 12 on the petitions to get a community college here, and we're proud of that. So we weren't just out in left field all the time.

It was still in the 1940s that some of us helped organize a big mill near Coos Bay. I was interested in seeing that the leaflets the woodworkers union was putting out were being distributed. So I volunteered to help. I went out to the logging camps, too, with some of the organizers.

I supported the Progressive Party ticket in 1948. The Progressive Party opposed the coming of the Cold War and put up Henry Wallace for president. The longshoremen sponsored Wallace when he came to our community.

In '50 I ran for the Oregon State legislature on the Democratic Party ticket. It was mostly union people who suggested that we run somebody. I didn't have much of an idea that I'd win my election bid, but we just thought we needed somebody out there to put programs before the people to give them some kind of a choice.

When Bridges got stuck in the can in 1950 for opposing the Korean War,[6] I wrote a letter in support of him. It was a group decision of the auxiliary to write to the president that we thought the war was immoral. I got put on the carpet by the right-wing faction's leader in Local 12. The local was split right down the middle then. But I only got into difficulty that one time. Usually we got along pretty good.

Around 1950 some people started calling us "reds," but that was something you had to kind of get used to, because if you let that stop you, you wouldn't be doing anything. The FBI knocked on your door every few months, it seemed like, but we never got very friendly with them. I did have to go before the House Un-American Activities Committee in Seattle.[7]

It's the same like I thought about Harry Bridges: If that man had been just an ordinary worker down in the hold of a ship and never said anything, there would have been no attempt to deport the guy. We felt that we were kind of getting the same kind of flak. And, my God, you can't let that stop you.

Once an immigration officer came to our house and knocked on our door. He wanted information about several people. Of course, I didn't give him any. I finally wound up telling him, "You've got a hell of a job to perform. I think you ought to be ashamed of yourself." I thought, "He must be one of those SOB kind of guys, trying to get information about these poor people that's trying to make a living."

The name "left-winger" stayed attached to me around this area, I think, because I was on all the picket lines. Whenever I'm around town, I still join 'em. Not long ago, we were on one at a clothing store in Coos Bay called the Hub. We walked that one for days. So the strike got over, and I met the owner one day on the street. I said, "Oh, I'm going into your store to get myself a new pair of shoes. I wore mine out walking your picket line!" He couldn't do anything but laugh.

Somebody has to do these things. I certainly was never by myself. We never were a large organization in North Bend, probably thirty or forty gals in the auxiliary, but that's not too bad. Still, my father used to say, "They'll probably take you out to the nearest tree and hang you someday." He was just kidding, of course.

I just did what I thought was necessary. I didn't feel like I was doing anything more advanced than anybody else, but somebody had to speak out. What's that saying about being ashamed to die if you haven't done some good for humanity or some such thing like that? I kept that in the back of my mind. Working to make this a better world for having lived in it has been my philosophy. All my life it seems like I've been circulating some sort of a petition. My sister says, "You're going to die with a petition in your hand." I'm circulating one right now.

JERRY TYLER: SEATTLE ACTIVIST

Seattle's longshore Local 19 veteran Jerry Tyler had a career that resembled those of many dedicated mid-twentieth-century ILWU activists. He lived on the road and worked survival jobs in the 1930s, went to sea during World War II, and found being an ILWU longshore worker a lifesaver in later years.

Jerry Tyler

I was born 11–11–11. That's a birthday you can't forget. I was born in Shenandoah, Iowa, a little country town. When the Depression hit in the '30s, we didn't even know there was a depression, 'cause we thought everybody had a tough life all the time. Dirt farmer, small farmer, he didn't have a very easy time between the bank, the mortgage, the thunderstorms, the hailstorms, and every damn thing you can think of that could go wrong on a farm.

Although I grew up a farm kid, after a while we moved into Shenandoah. They had two of the country's biggest nurseries there, and I worked as what's called a "nursery rat," pruning, sanding, doing stoop labor. Then I got a job in a clothing store. I also worked in a vegetable cannery over in Nebraska City.

I tried fighting, but I didn't make much money at that. This was in the late 1920s when I was sixteen, seventeen, eighteen. I had a good trainer and didn't do too bad. I started out as a bantamweight; I was a little wart then. But when I gained weight—I ended up a lightweight—that slowed me down a bit. They started tagging me. We discovered I had a glass chin. There's only one cure for that—that's don't take punches. So I got the hell out before I was brain damaged. Well, I think I did, anyhow!

My mother always wanted me to go to college, and they had one over in Lamoni, Iowa, so I went there for a year. But I knew my parents couldn't afford it, because this was in 1929, '30, '31. There was no work to be had anywhere, and they had other kids. So I just took off. Grabbed myself an armload of boxcars and headed west, like everybody else.

It was a crowded existence. There were a lot of guys on the trains. You'd be coming north out of L.A., headin' to Portland or up to Washington to work the apples. And here would be a bunch of guys going the other direction. They'd say, "Where are you going?" You'd answer, "Up to Wenatchee, over in there, to pick apples." They'd say, "Hell, man, there's a picker for every apple." You'd look at the guy and think, "Aw, you dummy, you wouldn't know a job if it bit you on the ass," and you'd find out you were both right. You're just traveling, hoping you'd find something.

Getting something to eat, that was a little tough. It took a long time for me to get up enough nerve to hit a back door. That was in the little town of Turlock, California. There was a black gal out in the back yard, splittin' wood. I said, "Hey, lady, I'd be glad to split some wood for somethin' to eat." She said, "Get on it." So I split wood. Then she called me in. I discovered I'd been at the back door of a whorehouse.

All the gals are sittin' around in their bathrobes. And boy, they fed me good! When I left, them gals all laid a half a buck or so on me and wished me good luck. So I've got a soft spot in my heart for prostitutes, people that are down on their luck and got a rough way to go.

I got one job on the Oregon shortline out of Salt Lake City. This was as a waterboy for the D&RGW, the Denver and Rio Grande Western railroad. They were laying new steel. "Waterboy." They misnamed that. You were a mule. First thing I had to do, before anybody was up, was uncover the ice, wash it off, bust it up, and put it in the keg on a pushwagon.

Then I'd go eat breakfast in the mess car, and the day would start. I'd push that damned wagon about a half mile, and finally move it off on a siding made especially for it. Then I'd start walkin' with a yoke around me that had two great big water buckets with tin cups hanging off it. This is out in the desert—god, it was hot! I'm yelling "*agua*," because most of the workers were Mexican, and I'd walk up and down with that goddamned thing—oh, I was tough then.

I landed in Modesto, California, where I got a job on a fruit ranch. Then I worked as a roadhouse waiter. A roadhouse was a nightclub. This was in 1933, when liquor came back, after Prohibition ended. If times were bad, I'd get laid off from the roadhouse and work at whatever I could get.

Well, the cooks in this one Modesto joint where I got hired were in the culinary workers union, which I joined. One time they said, "The waitresses over at the Greek's are not unionized." So they pulled a sit-in. We went over there just before noon, took all the stools and tables, sat down, and had a cup of coffee. We stayed all during lunch. The management decided, "I guess we'd better talk to these guys." That's how we organized that place. It was my first experience with a union, and it opened my eyes quite a ways.

When the 1934 strike happened, I was still in Modesto. Rent was four dollars a week. I'd joined the National Guard with my roommate, Clancy Johnson. We got two bucks a week for drills, so that paid the rent. They wanted to take the Modesto National Guard to Stockton for strike duty. I went to Cap Freeman and said, "Cap, I can't do that. My old man was a working stiff and I'm a working stiff, and here I'm going to go over there and stick a bayonet in some other poor working stiff? I can't do it." He said, "Okay, we'll put you down as if you're leaving the state. No problem." So I didn't go.

I went to San Francisco and got a job as a waiter at Goman's Gay '90s, an old place at Fillmore and Geary Streets. It was then that I sold my first fiction story. They called it "The Coward Who Had Killer Fists." I'd been writing all the time, trying to write for the pulps. In Modesto, when I'd worked in the roadhouse, I'd write during the day and go to work at night. A junior college teacher—I took some classes—told me who to contact, and I sent stuff off. After that first check, I couldn't write a thing for about two months! Then I started whacking them out while I was working at Goman's.

In December 1941, when we got into World War II, I was still at Goman's Gay '90s. I'd wanted to go to sea since I was a kid. For a farm boy, going to sea was romantic as hell. So when the war broke out, I got my chance. They needed people. I registered, got a trip card, and started shipping out of San Francisco in the old MCS [Marine Cooks and Stewards Association of the Pacific Coast, CIO].[8] I'd been a waiter, so I got a mess job. I even sold a couple of stories while I was going to sea, but there was a paper shortage, the pulps went to hell, and the short story market just died.

One night while I was working on a troop ship, a torpedo just missed us. I used to like to sleep out on deck back on the fantail. There was a gun tub right over me. I woke up in the early morning, and all these guys are tense. Everybody's at general quarters. I said, "What's going on?" A sailor answered, "A torpedo come by and passed just to stern of us. The guy on watch saw it." So that kind of put an ice cube up my rear end.

I'd been in Local 30 of the culinary workers at Goman's, but when I went to sea was when I really got introduced to unionism. At my first MCS meeting, I thought, "These guys mean business." They had a rank-and-file-operated union. I popped my mouth off over some deal, and that kind of set things in motion. They heard I could write, and they accepted me, babied me along, and got me involved. They asked me to write some stuff, and I wrote a stewards department newsletter for my ship. They put it up on the bulkhead in the mess room.

During the war I went on the old *Matsonia*. She was a trooper with a big stewards department. That was when the CP first approached me. I knew there'd been something wrong with our system, our economy. I'd heard all about these Commies and all that stuff, but pretty soon it seemed like they were the only people talking anything that made sense to a working man. So when they invited me to join, I said, "Sure, what the hell." I stayed in for quite a while after the war. I left the Party in the 1950s when I felt there was too much power at the top, that if you didn't agree with the top, the democracy wasn't there.

I came up to Seattle to ship out after I married a Seattle gal. Then I took port jobs when the act screening workers off the waterfront came in. This was during the McCarthy period after the war. Later I bumped into Senator Warren Magnuson, who'd backed screening. He was supposed to be liberal. I said, "What did you do that for? You know what you did to us? If you were a member of the Party, you got screened. But if you were even sympathetic or if you were a damned good union man, you got it, too. Didn't have to prove nothing." He said, "I never thought they'd use it that way." I thought, "You stupid son of a bitch, and you're a U.S. senator."

I became a MCS patrolman—that's like a business agent—in Seattle and was publicity chair for the union. I also got elected secretary of the CIO Industrial Union Council. We decided to have a CIO radio program. The Joint Action Committee pointed the finger at me. This was by 1948. After my first broadcast, I couldn't go anyplace on the waterfront without guys saying, "That was good, man, you gave it to them. My neighbors listened, too." Which was what it was for. On the day the 1948 longshore strike ended, I interviewed MCS and ILWU guys at a meeting and put that tape on the air.

When I was secretary of the CIO council and had the radio show, our local CIO didn't have any money. So I went down to the executive board meeting of ILWU longshore Local 19 and said, "It's important to keep this council moving. I would like to come down to the dispatch hall, and after everybody is gone, before you go outside to get casuals, I'd like to get a job. Anything I earn will be deducted from what the council was supposed to pay me." They said, "Yeah," and that's when I started longshoring. Soon, of course, with the McCarthy period on, station time got hard to get, and we had to fold the radio show.

When Local 19 opened the pool—we called ourselves "poolies," it was a B list—I applied. They took me in. We used to get all the crap jobs, stuff the regulars didn't want. Regulars we called "buttonheads" since they wore their union

Longshore operations, Seattle, 1963. Photo by Otto Hagel. Courtesy ILWU Library. Copyright 1998 Center for Creative Photography, University of Arizona Foundation.

buttons on their caps. We got the jobs working green hides, bananas, pig iron, fish meal, and all that good stuff. When you worked hides, you muscled every one by hand. They'd stink and have lots of maggots. They were hell to stow because they were slippery. There was nothing worse than having a tier of hides silently melt and fall all over, making you rebuild.

Actually, I started longshoring at the best time. I saw the whole revolution of cargo handling. When I started, there was no packaged cargo. You stowed everything by hand. Then you began getting packaged cargo, cribs, robots, and containers. If anybody told us ten years before this started that it was going to happen, we would've thought they were reading science fiction. But Harry was smart; he saw it coming.

Bridges attended some Local 19 membership meetings in Seattle. He said, "We can fight the employers on this container issue, and we can cost them millions of dollars. But we're going to lose. You cannot fight progress. So here's what I propose." That's when he come up with the M & M [Mechanization and Modernization Agreement] idea in the late 1950s of trading no opposition to containers for better health and welfare, early retirement, and nobody loses a job.

A lot of guys thought, "Bridges is crazy." I says, "That's what you said when he started in about pensions, and now you're glad that happened. So the crazy old son of a bitch must know something." He sold us on it, and I still think that was the best thing. There's a lot of guys that still say, "No, we should have fought it." Well, how are you going to fight the inevitable? We got a good deal out of it.

In the mid-1950s I made regular membership in the local. They'd had meetings for pool members, and I used to speak. And I'd been active in MCS. So it wasn't too long before I ran for Local 19 executive board and got elected. I was vice president of the local in the mid-1960s. Around the same time I became editor of the Local 19 newsletter, *The Hook*. George Olden, our secretary, talked me into it. He said, "We got some things we got to get out to the membership." So I had to do it. We always had a "safety first" bit, because longshoring then was neck and neck with hard-rock mining for danger.

Still, I says, "They want a hook, I'll give 'em a hook." So I burlesqued it, made it funnier than hell. I adopted the pen name Stevie Adoree, after "stevedore." It was a takeoff on the advice columnist Ann Landers. I wrote about guys who'd throw their old beat-up gloves and socks around, crap like that. "If they did that at home," I said, "their old ladies would beat their brains out."

Soon we had to reprint and make more copies. After a few months we found out it was the wives who wanted the paper. "Where's *The Hook*? Bring *The Hook*," the auxiliary told us. The women at home didn't hear what's going on, the men wouldn't tell 'em anything. So they'd go for *The Hook*. It got real popular. I'd write about the guys, using lots of names. "So-and-so's wife had twins," I'd say, "so we know he's gonna work a lot of overtime." Now, I was very careful and didn't go too far or insult a guy unfairly.

Then we had what we called "the big lump." That was when they disbanded the strike committee, which I thought was a shame, and paid back the strike fund. We also had a Social Security overpayment we called "the little lump." I wrote in *The Hook* that the little lump would be paid out on so-and-so date. I caught hell for that one! "Damn you," guys said, "that was my hold-out money. My old lady never knew anything." I almost had to take a vacation!

I retired the first day of 1974, when I was sixty-two. I took all my work clothes, boots and all, to the laundromat, washed them, and put a sign up—"I'm retired. If you can use this stuff, it's yours." Soon there was a check in the mail from Social Security and a check from the union.

"Damn," I thought, "this is going to happen for the rest of my life." My kids were all grown up then, I was single, I didn't own anything, and I didn't owe anything. Two weeks later I was in Cairo, Egypt, and I just kept rolling, traveling around. In 1981, when I was back in Seattle, I did start a newsletter for the pensioners that I called *The Rusty Hook*. I put out one issue and left to travel again.

I guess I was one of the luckiest guys that ever pulled on a pair of pants when I joined the ILWU. I just hit it lucky when I got in the pool. If it wasn't for that, I don't know where I'd be. When they run the pension checks off in Frisco, they must say, "Is that old bastard still alive?"

Every time I go to the hospital, or up to the clinic, or have to get some medicine, I think, "Thank God for Harry Bridges and the ILWU." I see other guys from other trades, retired and living on nothing but Social Security and Medicare, and I think, "You poor devil, you should've been a longshoreman." I remember when Frank Jenkins said he was talking to some guys uptown and telling 'em what we had. They kept asking questions. Finally Frank says, "Yeah, when you guys were calling us Commies, here we were, getting these good wages and conditions."

PHIL LELLI: LONGTIME TACOMA LEADER

After the defeat of the West Coast longshore strikes of 1916–23, only the Tacoma ILA [International Longshoremen's Association] local maintained a genuine union presence over the next decade. But when the rejuvenated Pacific Coast District ILA became the ILWU in 1937, Tacoma was the one major port that spurned the militant new organization. Tacoma joined small units at Anacortes and Port Angeles in staying ILA. The Tacoma local, which had a uniquely entrepreneurial approach to labor relations, remained out of the ILWU until 1958.

Phil Lelli acted as president of Tacoma ILWU longshore Local 23 almost continuously between 1966 and 1985.⁹ He recalls Tacoma's ILA years and the local's adjustment to the ILWU.

Phil Lelli

My father's parents came from Italy, my mother's from Germany. I was born near Tacoma in 1929, when the ethnic groups were all still divided—the Italians in one section of town, the Germans in another. It was remarkable that my parents ever got married. They were both Catholics. That kind of brought them together.

My German grandfather was a blacksmith. He came west to Tacoma with the railroad. When he was seventy-five, he dropped dead at his forge. That's the reward you got for working a lifetime for somebody in those days. My Italian great-grandfather came to this country as an indentured worker bound to the coal mines of southern Illinois. After his indenture time ended, he came out here.

My folks lived in a little farm town near Tacoma called Edgewood. Dad formed a small grocery store in 1931, during the Depression. He was kind of the caretaker of the community. He had credit on his books and tried to live his life treating people as they needed to be treated to live.

A lot of the longshoremen from Tacoma could not make a good living during the Depression. They migrated to little farm areas like Edgewood, worked one or two days a month as longshoremen, and tried to raise a cow and a few chickens as supplements. There were quite a few of these longshoremen in Edgewood, and I grew up with their kids. Since my dad had the grocery store, he knew most of the longshoremen and their families.

I graduated from Fife High School in 1947, worked on the railroad for three years, and played a season of football on a scholarship at Pacific Lutheran College. Then I became a union asbestos worker. But I'd gotten married, didn't like the travel, and started hearing stories about how unhealthy asbestos was. I also didn't appreciate the competitiveness in the building trades, where the guy you were working with didn't care if you got fired or not.

In 1955 this longshoreman friend of my dad's asked me, "Do you want to try longshoring?" I said, "Yes." I'd already worked a few times as an extra longshoreman. It was kind of a macho job at that time. You picked up heavy sacks and timbers. There was no automation whatsoever. But I was big and strong, so the work that was hard for one guy was easy for me.

Phil Lelli, 1987. ILWU Library.

My first waterfront job was with Roy Johnson's gang in 1948. It was carrying 180–pound wheat sacks down at Sperry's dock. At first it was tough even for me to carry those things, but as soon as I learned how to handle them I was pretty good at it.

I used to show how strong I was by carrying one sack on top of the other. That's 360 pounds. There weren't many guys who could do that. The longshoremen admired people that were strong. When they saw a strong young kid, they treated him differently than they would a guy they thought they might have to carry. I was well accepted in 1955 as what we then called a "permit man." A year later I got my full union book.

Doing your share of the work was something to those longshoremen. The guys that were heroes on the Tacoma waterfront were the hard workers. I'll tell you where I think that attitude came from. In 1916 the Tacoma longshoremen went on strike and lost. They didn't lose their union, but they lost control of dispatching. The union men thought, "The only way we're going to get our control back is to outwork the finks." Those were the strikebreakers who were getting dispatched to lots of jobs. The union men did outwork those guys, and the employers couldn't pass up the fact that they got more tons a day out of the union members.

After a year or so, the union men captured their work back. Now the productive gangs the employers wanted had all union guys in them. From the early 1920s until the 1934 strike, we were the only ones that had union-controlled dispatching on the West Coast. All the later West Coast union dispatch halls took Tacoma as the example.

In 1961 I became a steady gear-locker man. Longshore work was intermittent. I had four children. It made it difficult to budget your money on a day or two's work a week. One day I was down on the waterfront welding up my old boat trailer. This guy said, "Do you know how to weld?" I'd taken welding in high school. I said, "Yeah." He says, "Would you like to come in here for a couple of days?" I said, "Sure." I ended up staying as a gear-locker man for thirty-one years.

As a gearman before containers, you built the hoisting equipment. You decided what kinds of slings you needed. To some degree, you were a rigger. You did the splicing and a little welding. You do less of that stuff today because it doesn't take much of a guy to rig a container. Sometimes I spent every day for a week splicing cable just to keep up with what the longshoremen were doing.

During the mid-1950s, before we were in the ILWU, the ILWU locals around us in Seattle and Olympia let us travel to them for jobs. This was important because at the time there wasn't a lot of work in Tacoma. Then the ILWU cut us off. They said, "If you come into the ILWU, you'll still be able to travel."

We were then affiliated with a new AFL group called the International Brotherhood of Longshoremen [IBL]. This dated from 1953, when our old group, the ILA, got kicked out of the AFL for being ridden with gangsters. Well, there was a larger faction all the time in Tacoma that wanted to work through the ILWU. They were willing to sacrifice the IBL and did so in 1957 when they cut off paying the IBL per capita tax. Now there had to be a vote, and the majority by far voted to join the ILWU, which we did in January 1958.[10]

There were some guys that never came back to union meetings after that. They said, "I'm not admitting that we should have been in the ILWU." Some resisted because Bridges was branded a communist. We'd been here all by ourselves, too, with this Paddy Morris syndrome.[11] I certainly didn't quit going to union meetings or anything, although I voted for us to be independent. I'd seen how the AFL worked through the building trades, and I didn't want a centralized union telling me what to do.

I thought being independent we could achieve the best of everything. I would have said to the ILWU, "We want to travel, and we'll give you benefits if you want an alliance with us. If you have a problem, we won't work your ships." We'd be kind of an empire of our own.

That really is the way Tacoma was. Even though we'd been in the IBL, the AFL, and the ILA, we were still independent because we were so far from them. After we got in the ILWU, we didn't look to San Francisco either. When George Ginnis and I were in charge of the local for twenty years, we made our own decisions. I was usually the president. George was the business agent. We told the Bridges faction, or whatever you want to call them, what we thought was best for Tacoma and how we wanted to operate.

Actually, I think Bridges endorsed us. This was because, like us, he had a fair work ethic. I was told by people who knew him when he was young that he was a good worker himself.

In line with our own work ethic, George and I did something in Tacoma that nobody else did. We put together a package where we wouldn't draw money under the Pay Guarantee Plan [PGP] set up after the 1971 strike.[12] We passed a rule in the 1980s saying if there was any work in Tacoma, you had to take it or you couldn't qualify for the PGP wage guarantee. Since there was always grunt work, the guy who wouldn't do any had as his penalty that he couldn't sign up for PGP.

This was one way we retained the Tacoma work ethic that existed when I came here. If you were a crane driver today, tomorrow if there was just shoveling ore in the hold of a ship, that's the job you took. You weren't on top of no mountain anyplace. One day you were the guy in the hold, the next day you might be driving winch, and the following day you might be humping sacks in the warehouse.

George Ginnis was probably the hardest-working guy the Tacoma waterfront has ever seen. His basic philosophy was the same as mine: Work hard, get a lot of work into Tacoma, and we'll produce more opportunity for ourselves. We carried that to the employer, too. We had a unique situation in Tacoma. The port was entirely owned by Pierce County. It turned out that you could work with the people who ran the port to try to get more cargo and more opportunity onto our waterfront.

George ran the local on a day-to-day basis. I was more involved with the port as a political thing. I was never a full-time paid president, although I was offered the job several times. I always opposed the idea. Instead, I had my own little domain over at the gear locker. There was more union stuff in that gear locker than there was gear-locker stuff.

The company I worked for [Jones-Rothschild Stevedore] never said anything to me though. I ran the show the way I wanted. For example, Tiny Thronson, who was a 1934 strike veteran, used to sit me in the corner of the gear locker and talk the philosophy of the union to me at length. "Do a hard day's work," he always preached, "and you'll get rewarded with more opportunity." Tiny became a stevedore company manager, but his heart was truly with the working guy.

I'll tell you the kind of man Tiny was. The day the Tacoma longshoremen cleaned the scabs off the Seattle waterfront in '34, Tiny went in on the first dock. At the bottom of the gangplank, the mate shoved a rifle in his stomach and said, "Try to come aboard and I'll blow your guts out." Tiny says, "Go ahead. These guys will take care of you." The guy put the gun down, and the longshoremen went aboard and routed the scabs. Les Clemensen, who was standing right there, told me this story.

So that's the kind of guts and the kind of leadership Tiny offered. He gave me a five-year education before he retired in 1970. I was getting paid my wages, and it probably cost the company money. But they ended up making money because we produced opportunities for that company and for everybody else.

E. L. [Roy] Perry also learned a lot talking with Tiny. Roy Perry was the Tacoma port manager from 1964 to 1978. He got there at the right time, when the waterfront was changing from the pier concept to container terminals. Here we were, a little chickenshit port that didn't have nothing but a lot of land. Perry got federal money to subsidize the building of terminal complexes. He hired the right people, had the right work ethic, modernized the port, and worked closely with us.

Our cooperation with Perry started with a raw rubber project he promoted in the mid-1960s. We never had rubber before. It's a dangerous, difficult commodity to handle. The longshoremen worked their asses off but were only producing eleven to twelve tons of discharged rubber an hour. We weren't going to be able to survive because other ports were producing eighteen to twenty tons an hour with the same amount of men. So we got together with Perry to consider what to do.

As a result, the longshoremen sent three or four people around the United States with two or three people from the port to study the different places handling rubber. They went to the Great Lakes and to Hampton Roads, Virginia. When they came back, the port bought new equipment and improved the system of processing rubber through the warehouse. In eight or nine months we were producing twenty-four tons an hour, four tons better than most ports. Before we were done, Tacoma was the number one importer of rubber in the United States.

Here's another example of how we cooperated with Perry, this time in the late 1960s. Perry was not afraid to come to our union meetings to speak. That's not normally done by a port manager. He got a contract for Panasonic electrical products to come through the Port of Tacoma. Before the first shipment, he came to a Local 23 meeting and said, "If you guys see things you want, steal like hell off the first Panasonic ship, because it'll probably be the last."

When he left the meeting, we hired the best damn police force the waterfront has ever seen—the longshoremen themselves. If you monkeyed with anything on a Panasonic ship, you were told by the guy next to you, "Put it back. Don't open the box. You're screwing with our jobs."

Soon we had one hundred people working on Panasonic stuff. We developed a container freight station just for Panasonic. In eight years we only lost one transistor radio. Panasonic changed their whole distribution system and made Tacoma one of their key places in the entire United States, all because there was no pilferage here. We had all this Panasonic work until the 1990s, when they restructured distribution again.

We got all these jobs, of course, because of a cooperative attitude on the part of Perry and the Port of Tacoma and because the longshoremen wanted to increase their work opportunities. I even started to estimate the amount of man-hours it took to work certain products. Then Ginnis would tell the employers, "We want this kind of cargo." He had 'em going out lookin' for cargo that would produce us more man-hours. I don't know whether anybody else ever done that, but that's what we did.

I retired in 1993, but for three years before that, I chaired a coastwise safety committee made up of port officials and longshoremen. My kid, Ross, was killed in a waterfront accident in 1989, and I wanted to do something about it. I ended up being vehement about trying to protect longshoremen. I did get the Port of Tacoma shook up bad enough so they put a guy on the International Safety Organization, a clearinghouse for safety ideas for big equipment.

When Harry Bridges died in 1990, they had a big memorial in San Francisco. I was no longer Local 23 president, but I held a memorial simultaneously at our hall in Tacoma. I was also the emcee. We had a real large crowd, and the last place in the world you'd think they'd have a large crowd is in Tacoma, because a lot of the old-timers didn't particularly care for Bridges.

Some people were always loyal to Bridges, though. One guy, Ernie Tanner, was prominent for that. He was the only black worker on the Northwest Joint Strike Committee in 1934. He had to be 125 percent, and he thought Bridges was the right guy. During the mid-1990s I lobbied to name the University of Washington, Tacoma, Labor and Ethnic Studies Center after Tanner.

In my case, I realize that without the ILWU I wouldn't have a pension, medical benefits, and stuff like that. There are several ILWU people I credit. Bridges was the top leader, but there were a lot of other people who also pushed the right buttons and did the right things. Once I even told the union here in Tacoma—I said it at an ILWU convention, too—that if I had it to do over again, I would've voted to go into the ILWU, realizing now that the things I feared in 1957 didn't exist.

IKE MORROW: TACOMA'S SOUL TRAIN ENGINEER

The testimony of Isaac (Ike) Morrow, a legendary black longshore worker on the Tacoma waterfront, reflects Local 23's independent, enterprising spirit. Morrow, who started on the waterfront in the early 1960s, later convinced the employers to adopt innovations that made the Port of Tacoma a thriving modern facility.

He also labored to bring his fellow workers of all backgrounds together. In recognition, Tacoma's African American Longshoremen's Association awarded him a plaque naming him "Head Engineer of the Soul Train."

Isaac (Ike) Morrow

I was born in a little place called Frogsville Bottom in Choctaw County, Oklahoma, in 1940. My dad's family was sharecroppers, but by World War II, my dad couldn't survive sharecropping and he couldn't find other work in Okla-

Ike Morrow at the Port of Tacoma, Washington, 2004. Photo by Harvey Schwartz.
ILWU Library.

homa. He came north when he was recruited to work at the Hanford nuclear
project in eastern Washington. His first day there, he worked mixing construction mud. He had no idea what the Hanford project was, but he knew he was
making more money than the nothing he was making in Oklahoma.

The real beginning for our family was eastern Washington. My dad was
special. It took him almost two years to get his whole family up north. He had
five kids, just like I did. I was brought north when I was four or five years old.
My dad would get a little money and drive south, and in those days if you
were black, you didn't stop at a Motel 6 or nothing like that. You'd stop for
gas and keep on going.

It took my dad three trips to bring his whole family north. He taught me
many things, like how to work and all about responsibility. He said, "If you're
man enough to make a baby, you've got to be man enough to take care of a
baby." And that's what he did. He didn't just leave us down south.

My dad taught me how to deal with discrimination, too. He said, "Don't cry
about discrimination. You look at the mirror in the morning. You know you're
black, and therefore you have a problem. Your job is to figure a way to get around

that problem. You got to go over it, around it, or through it, or sometimes you got to put it on its ass." That was my daddy. I've lived my life by that rule. In other words, I didn't turn everything into a black-and-white issue. If you didn't like me, I dealt with it, and I never used anything for an escape.

Dad always had at least two jobs, maybe three. My mom worked until I was thirteen or fourteen. We always had food on the table. One day, to beat the heat and the cold in eastern Washington, dad just packed us up and came over here to Tacoma. He was a natural-born heavy equipment operator and wound up working twenty-five years for McChord Field. I guess I am my father's son, because that's what got me goin' on the waterfront—my ability to handle equipment. In my early days in Local 23, I became a real good crane driver.

I went into the Marine Corps in 1959. That's how I got on the waterfront when I got back to Tacoma. James Cook, a guy in my marine outfit, was a reservist from here who worked as a longshoreman. He asked me what I did for a living. I told him I worked in the bar at the Winthrop Hotel. I'd worked my way up in another place from dishwasher to bar manager. Cook asked me what I made, and I told him. Then he asked me if I ever thought about being a longshoreman. "Come on down," he urged, "and try it some time." And I did. That was forty-two years ago.

I started coming down to the waterfront when I had a chance—a day here, a day there. When I went home from my first day throwing these big flour sacks, there was nothing left in my tank. My fingers were raw, and every joint in my body ached. It was a horrible day, but I refused to quit.

At first I hated the waterfront because it was dirty and the people were so rough in those days. But it was good money, and I got lucky and made the bench, which meant you became a permit man. I got picked, I eventually learned, partly because of my work attitude and partly because they mistakenly thought I was the grandson of a legendary longshoreman named Barney Ruckers.

Actually, the only thing that kept me on the waterfront is that I got pissed off. Once the guys realized I didn't belong to anyone, they kind of ostracized me. Nepotism was strong back then. For six months hardly anybody would talk to me or teach me anything. The black guys ostracized me same as the whites. So I decided I'd show them. And that's why I'm still here today!

I came to love the waterfront. Eventually all four of my sons became long-shoremen. They earned their way in through a high school program. When I started I was just a little shit, a 145–pounder tossin' 150–pound sacks and

450–pound bales of pulp. It was never easy, although it didn't take me long to start to get it. My wife's support helped, too.

Then I ran into a black guy named Willie Lee. One day, he says, "I'm goin' to show you how to be a longshoreman." And he would yell and scream and harass me. I was with that man so much he made me a damn good longshoreman. It seemed like all the black guys then were huge—six feet two inches, six feet three inches, 240, 250. Here I was 150 pounds. I couldn't muscle it like the big guys. So Willie Lee taught me how to use every ounce of my body for leverage.

To use your body, you had to use angles. One time we had this 450–pound bale of pulp wedged in tight on its edge. These big guys were down in the hold sweating with peaveys trying to get it in place. Finally, Harvey Matthews, the hatch tender, came down. He wasn't a big guy. There were two bands holding that pulp that you could get your hands on—one in back, one in front. Matthews reached back with two hands, grabbed the bands, squatted down, humped the bale with his body, picked it up, and shoved it in place, using his legs and everything. That's leverage. I never forgot that lesson.

Back when I was still new, you didn't talk with your mouth because they'd send you down the road. I can recall how this white old-timer, Bud Mostrom, used to show me so much disrespect. One day he asked this other young man to work a pulp ship with him. We were the only two younger guys there. Mostrom looked me right in the eye and said, "I picked a young stud, because some of these kids can't handle it."

I was seething. I told my partner, Willie Lee, "OK, you big mother—Willie weighed 275—today we're goin', and we ain't stoppin'." We humped and hollered all day long. That last hour we took sixty ton of pulp in fifty-five minutes. Then we had to go to chow and come back. I had thrown so hard my arms locked up. I said to Willie, "What am I gonna do? Listen to this SOB talk some more?"

Well, I went back, and Mostrom approached me and said, "Hey, kid, you're all right." After that he always talked to me in a positive way. It wasn't that he couldn't stand me. I guess I just had to prove myself. That's how most of those old-timers were.

Years later, when women began to come on the waterfront, I thought "no" at first. Then, as the work became mechanical and gentrified, I said to myself, "Well, that's what they once thought about you," changed my mind, and decided I'd never hard-time women on the waterfront. In fact, I've come to admire them.

I had my own little civil rights movement on the waterfront in the 1960s, teaching people to respect me. Every time I'd see the pictures of the dogs and the hoses attacking blacks in the South, I'd get mad, and Lord help the first guy who crossed me the next day. The union itself wasn't prejudiced, but we had our individual problems on the waterfront.

For instance, just after Martin Luther King died, we were working rubber when our gear broke down. Back then, you waited for repairs. I heard these white kids down below from where I was. They were talking about shooting black people. Foul names came up. I got madder and madder. Finally I exploded. I grabbed a bear claw, which is like an axe handle with a triangle end with nubs to pull the rubber. I jumped down twelve feet to where these guys were and landed on boards. It sounded like a gunshot. I screamed, "Come on!" I'd tried to hold it all in, but I'd had enough. I got these four guys in one corner, and I was going to kill somebody.

All of a sudden, I heard this soft, caressing voice. "Take it easy, Ike. It's not worth it." It was Dick Tulare. He was six feet four inches, 280 pounds, a gentle giant. After much talking, he finally touched me and massaged my shoulders. I sighed, looked at those guys, looked at Dick, and said, "Thank you, brother." He was a white guy. Tulare kissed me on the side of my head and said, "Let's go." He led me upstairs.

There was no more noise from downstairs the rest of the night though! That'll be in my mind as long as I live, because I was about to commit murder over words. Later on, we all became good friends.

I became a foreman in 1972. Because I'd seen a Chinese seaman killed in a container-lashing accident, I made myself one of the best lashing foremen on the waterfront. Back then, the company that asked you to be a foreman—in my case, Stevedoring Services of America [SSA]—generally was the company you ultimately went steady for.[13] I always thought I'd become an SSA man, but they kept dangling jobs in front of my face and those jobs would disappear. Finally, in 1981, the Port of Tacoma approached me, and I said, "I'm going to take their steady job."

The Port was the first company that had enough courage to look past my color and look at my work ethic. That's why I'm so loyal to them. They're as big jerks as anybody else, but they gave me that first shot, and I've busted hump for them. That's why, around 1983, I worked hard to give the Port its start toward its North Intermodal Yard, which is an accomplishment I'm very proud of.

Isela Linares of longshore Local 13 at work on the southern California waterfront. ILWU Library.

Here's how the intermodal program came about. In the early 1980s our biggest line was Star Shipping. They'd come into town and dump three hundred cans [containers] at Pier 4 where I was foreman. The next day there'd be forty-six Burlington Northern [BN] truck drivers at our gates plus our regular traffic. We'd be overwhelmed, with everybody pissed off and the customers unhappy. One day I'm in my office, and here is this Star agent, Judith Novik, talking about taking her business someplace else. So I told her, "Maybe I can help."

"Where," I asked, "are these guys going?" She said, "Up to Tukwila" where the BN rail yard was. "Well," I says, "why can't we make rail delivery right here instead of putting all those trucks at our gate?" She said, "Why can't we? Let's give it a shot." We talked to management. The Port had a little rail setup with twenty-one cars in the North Yard and ten elsewhere. We had house and dock tracks. I said, "I'll make it work."

I talked to all the longshoremen. The Port gave us the next ship. We had all these railcars waiting when the ship discharged. Fast as the cans got on deck, we loaded the cars using straddle carriers [strads]. Our tallest strads could maneuver right over the cars. It worked beautifully. The pressure was off the doggone gate.

Then, after months of success, the BN said, "That's enough. You're not going to get any more railroad cars. You're cutting into our load center profits." That really ticked Judith Novik off. I don't know where she applied pressure, but six months later they relented, and I got those cars again.

After that, it just kind of blew up as people got interested. Maersk Line came to town because of our intermodal yard. Everybody up and down the coast had little mom-and-pop operations with a few conventional cars, but no intermodal dock. But here the Port started expanding in our North Intermodal Yard because Maersk bought into Tacoma's program.

When Maersk got to town, they initially took the car-loading process out of our hands. This was really insulting. We'd been loading railcars successfully for years. Maersk fumbled around for several months. The last train they loaded was three hundred cans in sixteen hours. That seemed the proper time for me to step in.

"Look," I said, "just give us three sorts of containers—twenty-footers, heavy forty-footers for bottoms, and light forty-footers for tops—and get out of our way." What they were doin' was flooding the yard with different kinds of equipment so nobody could move. Our adjustment cut out all that traffic. The next week or so, we moved 571 cans in one shift. Then we started setting records like crazy.

Of course, every system in the North Intermodal Yard was put together by the ILWU. At first nobody knew anything about loading railcars. But we'd have a meeting, me and my guys. And they just worked their asses off. Now you've got all those lines—Evergreen, Maersk—because we were so productive. It's been a boon to Tacoma and to the men. Once we got up and cranking, it opened doors for the entire coast, too. But we were the grandfather of them all.

I had a terrific crew of drivers, ground men, and clerks in those early days. My six crack pioneer strad drivers were Harry Dixon, Dave Ginnis, Roger Marshall, my son Terry Morrow, Ramo Natalizio, and Tony Tomal. We used to give synchronized shows loading railcars before we attracted customers. Our

Straddle carrier
working at shipside,
North Intermodal Yard,
Port of Tacoma, 2004.
Photo by Harvey
Schwartz. ILWU
Library.

strads were painted orange, so the group got nicknamed the Orange Angels. Early on, we also employed a great top pick driver to complement our strads. His name was Signal White. There should be a statue of those "Magnificent Seven" drivers, as they were called, down at Local 23.

The zenith was 1987. We set a record of 937 lifts in one shift. We've done over 1,200 moves in a shift since then, but that 937 was made with just three tracks and six three-high machines that could go over railcars. Later we had eight tracks and more strads. Some of those 937 runs were over two miles long. When I look back on it now, it still blows my mind.

After a while, most guys called me Pops. They seemed to dub me a kind of

Straddle carrier driver, North Intermodal Yard, Port of Tacoma, 2004.
Photo by Harvey Schwartz. ILWU Library.

a father figure. White guys, too—even more white than black—would ask me
to counsel them. I wanted to help, and I didn't believe in polarization, which
is horrible. I tried to get guys together. We formed the AALA so guys could at
least have somebody to talk to.

Our union back in those days lacked any line of communication, even for
white guys. If you had a problem with a foreman or a guy, who did you talk
to? I tried to get people together so they could talk and solve problems. In the
1980s some black guys got transferred up here from Portland, which was racist.
They had chips on their shoulders. I tried to settle them down and urge them
not to make every situation a black-and-white issue, because every situation is
not that way. Eventually the AALA awarded me a plaque in appreciation of
my work. That really touched me.

One situation I think was racist was when the employers delayed my son
Tim's promotion to foreman. He is smarter and stronger than me, but they kept
passing him by. It's almost like there was a "no more than three" black foreman
rule, unspoken, and there were already three black foremen. The last time they

passed him over, he was high on the list, so the day before the hiring process began, they changed the job criteria so it excluded him. I threatened to test the [legal] waters. Two months later they hired more foremen and took him in.

Looking back, this waterfront has been good to me. It's given all my sons a job. And the waterfront is about the only place I know where a man, especially a black man, can be as much of a man as he wants to be. That's worth its weight in gold. Sure, there are racists on the waterfront, but the union is not racist. If it was, how come I was so successful? And how come my son Terry was elected dispatcher, one of the most powerful jobs on the waterfront? How could Willie Adams get elected International secretary-treasurer? You get those votes because the union people respect you, not because you're white or black.

Today [2004] we have many new people on the waterfront who don't know anything about unions. If you're going to come into this industry, you have to be taught where you have been, where you are now, and where you are going. You have to be taught the longshore way. We can only do this by education. I think the 2002 West Coast longshore lockout was a wake-up call to us. Now everybody knows we're here and what we control. We better be ready for the next contract challenge. Don't sit there thinking you're a fat cat. You'd better be ready for a fight.

DEFEAT AND VICTORY IN CANADA, 1935–1966

In 1935 the Canadian longshore workers in Vancouver, B.C., struck to end the hated shape-up. They lost that battle, as they had a similarly bitter confrontation in 1923, and suffered a decade of company unionism. Then, in 1944, they voted to join the ILWU.

The Canadians developed new power and solidarity by winning a pivotal strike in 1958, becoming autonomous within the ILWU the next year, and taking a principled stand in 1966. Gordon Westrand, Craig H. Pritchett, Roy C. Smith, and Dave Lomas, all former ILWU Canadian Area presidents, tell Canada's story.

Gordon Westrand

I was born in Vancouver, British Columbia, in 1946. I'm president of the ILWU Canadian Area, and I'm the son and the grandson of longshoremen. I grew up a couple or three blocks from the Vancouver waterfront. We lived in the Hastings East area, which was a working-class neighborhood. In those days Vancouver was not as big a port or city as it is now, and you lived close to the port.

I started longshoring in 1965. My family was mostly what my father, who is called Gordie like me, and my relatives would have called "soldiers." They were always the first ones to take part in union activities, but none of them ever aspired to go into the union political system or into union offices. Yet in 1973 I started attending union executive board meetings to see how they worked. I ran for executive board in 1974, barely lost, and won the next year. After that, I held several positions. I became president of the Canadian Area in 1992.

Charles Westrand, my grandfather, started working in Hasting's Mill of Vancouver in 1906 as a longshoreman loading lumber onto ships. His nickname was "Charlie the Fish." Coming from Sweden, he was a very capable fisherman. He fished and went longshoring from 1906 on and went through several waterfront strikes in the early part of the century and in the 1920s. He had several sons by the time the big strike happened in 1935.

My grandfather died in 1938, but my father and many in the family told stories about him. Longshore work in the early part of this century was very hard. It was lumber loading mostly—heavy fletchers [large, long, squared timbers] and heavy timbers worked in very tight, confined areas. It was all hand-stow.

In the late '20s, when many docks started to appear in Vancouver, they had the shape-up way of dispatching. My father tells how his father used to go down to the Canadian Pacific Railway dock and a place called Pier H. The foreman or the straw boss would go out and pick those people who he wanted in particular. Then he had a certain number of tokens, and he'd throw the tokens out in the middle of the crowd. The person who fought the hardest to get a token would end up becoming one of the workers for that day.

If you never got picked, or never got a token, you started running. If you ran hard enough, you could get down to Ballentyne Pier in enough time for their pick and their shape-up system. So you were under total domination by the employer. This continued into the '30s, and a desire for union control over dispatching became a major goal among the longshoremen by 1935.

In the '35 strike my aunt's husband, Jack Kelly, used to do all the shoe repairs for the strikers. My grandfather would go out fishing all night, and then he'd go picketing during the day. He had three sons who were on the picket line with him.

At the time of the strike my uncle Carl was a semiprofessional boxer. He was what they called "a young buck" in those days, and there was what they called "the goon squad." There were many incidents on the picket line where scabs were either beating up or abusing strikers. If the scabs were billeted off of the docks—and many times they were billeted right on the docks—my uncle Carl and sometimes other people would go around and repay those individuals for transgressions against some of the union members.

In 1935 there were a lot of interrelationships with the families. My grandfather would make sure that certain families got fish. Those families in turn would make sure that he got vegetables. But it was still tough times. The strike went on for six months. My father remembers going to bed hungry at night. Maybe fishing was bad, or the fish had to be sold for the rent. My grandmother would give all the younger kids a slice of bread and sprinkle it with sugar. That was supper. But she wouldn't give it to the kids until just before they went to bed, so they went to bed with something in their stomachs.

My family was in the march that ended in the Battle of Ballentyne Pier on June 18, 1935, when the Vancouver police fired tear gas at the strikers and charged them. My grandfather was clubbed down at least once. My uncle Carl was clubbed down and knocked unconscious four times. I got reassurances that each of the four times he left his mark with the police officers in question.

The Battle of Ballentyne Pier was a setup. The strikers had been marching in an orderly way to confront the scabs who were going to work. When the strikers got down there, they were not in a position to see that there were a large number of mounted police officers present. They also didn't see that there were two 50–caliber machine guns placed on a flat deck, which was rolled out to confront the picketers.

When the police charged, they forced the strikers up Powell Street. There were signs in many windows there that said "We support the strikers." The police fired tear gas into these grocery stores and other buildings. The whole battle was uncalled for. It was provoked by the police and the employers.

The strike was lost because of the scabs. In 1935 Canada was in the middle of a depression, as the U.S. was. People were willing to do despicable things to other people by taking their jobs and taking away their security, even though the strike itself had the support of the general public.

The strike was broken by the simple fact that the employer was able to keep his operation going. In the U.S. during the big '34 strike—in San Francisco especially—the longshoremen were able to stop the flow of cargo. In Canada they were not able to do so. After the flow of cargo continued, the strike broke itself.

My grandfather, as many on the blacklist, got a phone call asking him to come back to the waterfront in 1938 when there was a lack of qualified long-shoremen. He refused to return. Nobody in my family returned to the waterfront until after he died of cancer later that same year. My uncle George never returned to the waterfront.

A lot of the things I heard from my family are not necessarily things that history would contain. I heard of the kinds of problems a regular striking family had—things like how do you feed the family? My father tells the story of how he'd go down to the butcher shop in '35. In those days liver was not something the butcher sold; he gave it away. Usually he gave it to a person with a dog for dog food. It seems that that was the time my father and his brothers and sisters acquired a taste for liver.

Those are the kinds of stories I heard. This goes into my philosophy in regards to the ILWU and what the whole movement is about. What is important is the individual, the "soldier" out there who turns around and puts himself and his family in peril and through hell to better not only his conditions on the job but also those of other workers. The thing I'm so proud of with my family is that my grandfather and three of his sons, at a time in history in Canada when it was practically unheard of to have a job, never mind to be striking against that job, made the kind of commitment they made, saying, "This is wrong and we are not going to stand for it." That is something to be proud of.

Craig H. Pritchett

I was born in 1924 in Westminster, just outside of Vancouver. I'm a fourth-generation Canadian. My dad was a shingle weaver, a longtime union member, and a founder and president of the IWA [International Woodworkers of America]. So I knew intimately my dad's connections with the building of the CIO and about his deportation from the U.S. during the organizing days of the IWA. I was familiar with the name Harry Bridges long before I ever became a union activist in the longshoring industry.

In March 1944 the Vancouver longshoremen voted what had long been a company union into the ILWU. I was in the Canadian army then, training to go overseas. They gave me a leave to come home, and I went to the inaugural meeting when they installed the charter of the ILWU in Vancouver,[14] because there was a bunch of longshoremen there and I figured I'd get a drink! After the meeting they got to congregating, and they said when I come home from overseas, there was a job for me if I wanted to come down on the beach. So I took 'em up on it.

While the ILWU charter was installed in '44, there were still a lot of people from '35 there who had gone through picket lines. When I came in, there were lots of young veterans coming in, but the old-timers who had controlled the union through the company union days still held office.

The old-time Vancouver longshoremen were initially anxious to get into the ILWU because the work petered off during the early war years. Most of them felt that by being with the ILWU, you'd be with a whole coastwide operation. They felt that shipping was mostly American shipping anyway. There wasn't too much Canadian shipping then except for the Canadian Pacific Railway ships, which were blown out of the water in wartime.

So the move to join the ILWU basically arose out of a fight for a share of the work on the West Coast. By March 1944 deep-sea work had come damn near to a standstill. The Vancouver workforce had dropped from eight hundred down to two hundred to four hundred men. When the old-timers agreed to join the ILWU, they were desperate and lookin' for anything. Soon the young veterans did move in there, though. So the transition to new officials was an ongoing thing, which in the end wound up with a proper ILWU leadership.

Roy C. Smith

I went to work on the waterfront in 1948, but I didn't get into the union until 1954. We were casuals, equivalent to longshore B-men [or permit men] in the U.S. We got all the rough work: heavy fletchers, heavy sacks of wheat, 260-pound sacks of sugar you had to handle by hand and on your back, copra, timbers and logs. All cargo down below was stowed by piece. You struggled on every job. In 1956, two years after I got into the union, I was elected to the executive board of Local 501, then the deep-sea longshore local in Vancouver.

I was president of the local during the 1958 British Columbia longshore strike, which was the most serious confrontation since 1935. Our two main issues were the eight-hour day and pensions. I wanted us to hang out for a meaningful pension, a trusteed pension where there was joint control. The

Canadian longshore workers lining up to take a strike vote, Vancouver, B.C., 1958. *Left to right:* C. Vanvolkingburgh, C. Latourneau, J. Olsen, Bill Korp, Jim Henderson, Geoge Hazelwood, Louie Charboneau, Bob Hansen, Fred Hamm, Bruce Walker, Fred Somolenko, and poll clerks R. Cope and Bob Blemme. Photo by Basil King. ILWU Library.

eight-hour day was just as important, but we had a flimsy pension that was completely controlled by the employers. We never knew how much money was in the fund.

The 1958 strike was a real landmark in the history of the waterfront in British Columbia. It was the first major strike the longshoremen won. In the big '23 and '35 strikes, the union was broken. Our modern union really started growing out of that '58 strike. Before, we were still basically a company union, which we had been literally until 1944.

In Vancouver we had been in the employers' Shipping Federation hall for many years, and in our discipline procedures, the joint union-owner Labor Relations Committee wasn't operative. The employers had a joker they hired— an ex–army colonel—who did the disciplining! If a man was guilty of a little infraction on the job, he had to go see Colonel Bailey. So we got rid of all that as part of the '58 strike.

We also told the employers they had to get their hands the hell out of our agreement. There was a clause that our membership was restricted to eight hundred members. The employers had to agree to any other members coming into the union. We got rid of that. During the strike there were a lot of nonunion men working steady on the grain ships. We informed the employers that they were coming into the union. The employers flashed the restrictive clause on us, but to no avail.

The consolidation of the scattered Vancouver locals into Local 500 in 1966 sprung from all this. We were having amalgamation meetings for the locals in the Port of Vancouver starting around 1956. It started to gel after the 1958 strike. The first bit of organization was to amalgamate the five deep-sea locals. There were five separate agreements prior to 1958. The '58 strike let us put them together.

During the strike we had a committee working on the structure of the Canadian Area and working on a constitution, so we would be ready later to set up the Canadian Area. This we did in '59, when we had our first convention. This movement to achieve autonomy within the ILWU was aimed at strengthening our union in Canada, because we couldn't always rely on the International. We had to have strength in our own organization. All that we had prior to organizing the Canadian Area structure was a district council with no real authority and an International representative who had no support from the local membership.

Gordon Westrand

The 1958 strike was a significant turning point for Canada because it seemed to bring everybody together. It had a common issue—pensions—that everybody could relate to. As a young kid then, it was my job to carry thermoses of coffee down to the picket lines. There was even a bit of a carnival atmosphere there. One fellow had a quarter horse he would bring in to give all the kids rides back and forth on the picket line. That indicated the longshore family atmosphere then.

The '58 strike was the real birth of the Canadian ILWU. In the '40s and early '50s there was nothing to really bind us, to say this is what we're all about. The pension strike in '58 did that. This was the first strike the union people really felt they won. I think some of the people walked out of there feeling "I'm the toughest son of a bitch in the valley because I'm ILWU."

Dave Lomas

People figure we always had Canadian autonomy within the ILWU structure, but it's not the case. We never had a problem getting autonomy with Harry Bridges around. He used to tell us, "When you're ready to put on your long pants, let us know." Getting complete autonomy wasn't done in one jump. It took a long time. We didn't start to transfer the jurisdictional and financial aspects of the union up here until the early 1970s.

Craig H. Pritchett

I was the founding president of the new Canadian Area in 1959. We took the old District Council and gave it some meat and a constitution with the blessing of Harry Bridges, Bob Robertson, and Lou Goldblatt, the ILWU International officers then. We put together an organization the employers had to meet head-on.

The push for autonomy in the '50s was part of a national struggle in Canadian unions for disaffiliation from the U.S. We raised the question of autonomy within the ILWU because we didn't want to break our International ties and tradition, but we still wanted to stay in the mainstream bid for Canadian sovereignty.

There was the whole question of Canada having its own national policy based on its own constitution, not on the American constitution, including our own court system, injunction acts, and labor laws. We never moved for disaffiliation, because we had an International that recognized that Canadian autonomy was something the union should be fighting for. That really consolidated the union here, and then you couldn't kick the ILWU out of Canada with a ten-foot pole.

The other thing we did at the same time to unify the union was that the leadership of the Canadian Area took the position in the 1959 negotiations and through into 1963: Pensions for all. Now that meant pensions for ex-scabs, too.

We got pensions for all the guys who went into the service, who went to work in the shipyards because there was no work on the waterfront early in World War II, who lost their jobs because of the '35 strike but had come back into the industry, and who had scabbed in '35. We never differentiated, and we were able to hold the union together by saying, "The past is gone. Close the book; move ahead." All the slogans we had at those early Area conventions led to that direction.

In 1966, when I was the Canadian regional director, I promoted the amalgamation of several locals in Vancouver into one longshore unit, Local 500. The advantage was the consolidation into one agreement. I didn't consider warehouse as something out in the barnyard, or grainliners as something different from longshore. It was a changing industry with new methods of shipping; I thought we should bring 'em all together. If we hadn't of gone that road, we'd have been crafted out of business.

I spoke industrial unionism to them rank and filers. The old-timers wanted to hang on to their slings and winches. I told them, "You're crazy—you won't be around." The young guys overwhelmed 'em; they made the decisions at the meetings. The warehouse guys were all twenty-two to thirty-five years old. They could see the changes. They all wanted to get on forklifts, they all wanted to drive machines. She was a comin' for you, and I'll tell ya, she'd a been all contracted out if we hadn't pulled the union together.

Roy C. Smith

In 1965–66 there was another crisis when the employers withheld the proper pay for statutory holiday work that our members had been collecting for years. So on Victoria Day in May 1966, we refused to work the waterfront. The employers had achieved injunctions against me—I was then president of the Canadian Area—and nine local presidents. We were told to order the men to work on statutory holidays. We refused, saying we would not do so until the employers paid the proper amount.

We accepted jail in lieu of fines that June. We were put in the paddy wagon and taken to the Vancouver City Police Jail. We spent a night there in the big drunk tank. The following day we were taken out to Okalla, a provincial jail, with mounted police escort. One young Mountie had his hand on his gun all the time. I suppose he figured we were a slew of Al Capones. We were there for five days. In that jail, we managed to have an Area executive board meeting!

We decided we were going to stick together. We had the deputy warden promise us this. When we were sent to the minimum security camps on the Chilliwack River, they split us up. We protested and kept reminding them of the promise, and after three days they got us all back together again. We were in three weeks when the federal minister of labor promised to bring the dispute

ILWU Canadian Area President Roy C. Smith and nine local presidents upon leaving minimum security confinement, 1966. They were jailed for defying an anti-union injunction. *Back row, left to right*: Les Copan, Laing Mackie, Smith, Bill Foster, and Vince Shannon. *Front row, left to right*: Ed Pilford, Bill Laurillard, Don Garcia, G. W. (Stan) Ball, and Dave Mason. Photo by Don Leblanc. ILWU Library.

before parliament, the B.C. Federation of Labour paid the fines, and we were released. The following fall, parliament amended the Statutory Holiday Act to cover all longshoremen.

I'm damn proud of myself and the others involved in these things, and of our membership, because at that time, when we took something back to the membership that was a worthwhile program or position, and something had to be done about it, the membership was always there. If you haven't got the membership behind you and involved, the employers know that, and they just laugh at you, whether you are in negotiations or whatever in hell you are doing.

Dave Lomas

We went through all those tumultuous periods and came out with a united organization here in Canada. But we can't forget the past, because we still have struggles ahead of us. We've got new people in the union who may not know this history, and we have to educate them to understand that those kinds of problems can come up again, and we have to be able to defeat them. We have to know the history so we know where we're going.

THE INLANDBOATMEN'S UNION JOINS THE ILWU, 1978–1987

In 1980 the 3,700 members of the independent IBU voted to affiliate with the ILWU.[15] This made strategic sense for the IBU, especially given the ILWU's commitment to union democracy, a concept IBU members had long fought for.

A year later, a tragedy occurred in the Northwest when agents of Philippine dictator Ferdinand Marcos murdered Gene Viernes and Silme Domingo, the democratic reform leaders of Seattle's predominantly Filipino ILWU seafood processing Local 37. In 1987 the IBU absorbed Local 37 as IBU Region 37. Six years afterward, Terri Mast, Domingo's widow and a Region 37 stalwart, became the first woman national officer of an ILWU affiliate when she was elected IBU secretary-treasurer. The cause of union democracy seemed vindicated.

Our story here begins with the IBU's 1980 Washington State Ferries strike, for that struggle was key to the original IBU-ILWU merger. After 1980 much attention remains on Washington, although the IBU also had a presence in Alaska, California, Hawaii, and Oregon. Don Liddle recalls the Washington ferries dispute and its results. He and Burrill Hatch then describe an important IBU shipboard strike over health and safety seven years later that severely tested the union. Liddle and Hatch were both important IBU officers.

Don Liddle

I was born in Davenport, Washington, in 1938. My stepdad was a staunch union guy. In any household he was in, you was going to know about unions, because that was what he talked about. He got me a job in a feed mill in Tacoma, Washington. The Butcher Workmen's Union was there. Everything my stepdad told me over the years about the union suddenly made a lot more sense now that I was on that job.

After two years, I got laid off from the mill and come to Portland. I worked in a rubber mill for ten years as a member of Local 504, United Rubber Workers. I held all the local offices—president, secretary-treasurer, shop steward. I was fired for union activity and got my job back through arbitration, but my days were numbered. So I started lookin' around and found out they were hiring at Western Transportation. That was an IBU bargaining unit. I applied and was hired there in 1969.

At Western I did dock warehouse work, loading and unloading barges of paper products. Over the years a number of people who went to work at Western had also worked at that rubber mill. They started askin' me if I'd be interested in runnin' for union office. I was elected vice president for the Columbia River Region in 1975.

In the late 1970s the IBU was affiliated with the Seafarers International Union [SIU]. The IBU national president, Merle Adlum, wanted the IBU to give up its autonomy and become part of the SIU's Atlantic and Gulf [AG] District.

In my opinion, it was not in the best interest of the IBU members to merge with the AG District and lose control over our local affairs. We wanted to continue to have a democratic union, where we elected our people. The AG District did not have union democracy like we had. They didn't elect their business agents and patrolmen like we did. Those people were all appointed.

There were also conspiracies between Merle Adlum and some of the officers of the IBU to give our jurisdiction to the AG District. In 1978 they allowed the SIU and Crowley Maritime Corporation to throw two hundred southern California IBU guys out of their jobs and then replace them with SIU–AG District people.

So we had an enormous philosophical difference between factions over where this union was goin' and what it was going to be. Because of all that, in 1978 I decided to run against Merle Adlum for IBU president. I was elected and took office in early 1979.

After I became president, we continued to meet and negotiate with the SIU International and the officers from the AG District about gettin' those southern California jobs back. The SIU held out carrots: "Maybe something could be worked out." But there were always conditions, and eventually the SIU said,

"We can do this and this, but you're gonna have to merge with the AG District within a year."

While this was goin' on, they again took some IBU jobs away, this time in Santa Barbara, and assigned them, through backdoor deals, to the AG District. Well, in our affiliation agreement with the SIU, our rights were spelled out just like in our later agreement with the ILWU: If the SIU took work from IBU members and assigned it to other parts of the International, or to people outside the International, that would be grounds for us to disaffiliate. So I held an IBU executive council meeting in October 1979, and we voted to disaffiliate from the SIU. Our IBU convention unanimously ratified the decision that December.

The SIU tried to raid us in a number of areas after we went independent. They attempted to take over our members in Alaska and Hawaii. We took it on with state-supervised elections. Their argument was, "Don Liddle and his Executive Council took you out of the AFL-CIO, out of the house of labor." Our argument was, "Yeah, but we're free to continue to have the kind of union we want." And we won overwhelmingly.

In April 1980 we had a serious confrontation with the Washington State Ferries system that indirectly led to our affiliation with the ILWU. The ferry system was determined to have part-time people who would only work during peak hours. We were very opposed to an open-ended part-time employee situation. Of course, there was money. Our membership had not been keeping pace with the cost of living. The other big issue was hiring practices. We wanted the hiring hall for people to gain access to Washington State Ferries employment. The ferry system wanted no part of that.

During bargaining, when it was apparent there might be a strike, Fred Peil, the state negotiator, told me, "If you strike, I'll have you in jail." I said, "I don't think you can do that, but have at 'er." That broke the meeting up. So that threat was out there the last couple weeks of bargaining. When the strike deadline arrived, our seven hundred ferry system members voted to reject what the employer had on the table, and we went on strike.

The next thing I knew, I was up before King County Superior Court judge T. Patrick Corbett in Seattle. He told me to order the membership back to work. Well, I had no authority as IBU president to force anybody to go to work. I said, "I can't do that." He said, "You'll do that or you'll stay in jail 'til you do." Myself and Larry Miner, our secretary-treasurer, then went to jail.

Corbett said jail was not going to be much fun, and he was right. Here you are in there, just being confined, knowing all those members are out there being very supportive, but their livelihoods are on the line. They need your help, and there's no way to get to 'em. There's nothing to do, and if you've got something to worry about, which I had, and Larry Miner had, you just sit there and worry.

When we went to jail, we had some of the things resolved. We got hiring through the union. We had the part-time issue resolved. We agreed to a formula where they could have a few part-time people. I know wages weren't resolved because after John Burns, our attorney in Seattle, got me out of jail in a day and a half, I remember going back to bargaining over wages.

This is about when Jimmy Herman got involved. He was the ILWU president then. He wanted me to contact him. I did, we met, and things happened.

I told Jimmy what the issues were, where our membership was, and why we were doin' what we were doin'. He said the longshoremen had just had a meeting and wanted to help. One thing led to another, and the longshoremen shut down the waterfront in Puget Sound. That got the talks going and got the settlement done.

There's a great appreciation from myself and the IBU membership for Jimmy Herman's help. Beyond that, what Herman and the ILWU did was what you were supposed to do in those days. That's the way union people thought: "If we can do something to help shove this thing off dead center and help these workers, we should do it."

There was never any talk about or hint at any condition attached to that help. Herman made that real clear from the first moment because there were a number of unions wanting us to affiliate with them. He said, "There's no strings attached."

The strike came out very good. We got some raises with cost-of-living factors hooked on 'em: "Not less than 9 percent," which amounted to over a dollar an hour back in those days. We're talking about some really good raises over a three-year contract. Hey, we were only on strike for twelve days. I was really proud of that outcome.

After the strike the state legislature instituted civil service. It was to be implemented at the end of the contract.[16] I told Jimmy, "What if I talk to the governor and tell him that you, Jimmy Herman, are suggesting that they create a blue-ribbon panel of labor, politicians, and ferry system people to study the

ILWU International President Jimmy Herman (*left*) and Martin Jugum of Seattle longshore Local 19 picketing in support of striking IBU Washington State Ferries workers, 1980. Photo by Vic Condiotty/*Seattle Times*. ILWU Library.

possibility of not implementing that law and replacing it with a process where we still have collective bargaining, but with binding arbitration instead of the right to strike?" He said, "Anything is better than that nonsense."

I talked to the governor, and that blue-ribbon commission became a reality. Out of that commission we were able to adopt some legislation to replace that civil service stuff and preserve the essence of collective bargaining.[17]

While we were an independent organization, we developed some great relationships with the unions that offered us affiliation. But I always had a great deal of respect for the ILWU, Harry Bridges, and that whole tradition. The ILWU was my first pick for affiliation, although I never professed that until mid-1980 when we got to the point where we really needed to do something to put some foundation under our union.

I started raising the issue of affiliation at membership meetings up and down the coast. We had two special meetings in every region, and I attended every one. At the second meeting we would vote on which organization the members would prefer. The ILWU was the uncontested favorite. I was having talks with Jimmy Herman, obviously, about this. I talked to some of those other unions, too.

Then we had a mail ballot vote of every member asking whether we should affiliate with the ILWU, the number one choice in those meetings. It passed with 82 percent in October 1980. The ILWU International executive board officially approved the affiliation the next month, and we became the IBU, Marine Division, of the ILWU.

We never were concerned that "We've gotta affiliate with the ILWU because if we get in a beef, they can really impact for us 'cause we're right on the water with them." We believed that would be there whether we were affiliated with them or not. But we believed therefore that we should belong to that organization! "Hey," we felt, "they can help us. We ought to be in the family with them. We ought to be there for them."

Things went along okay until February 1987, when the IBU got involved in a long strike against Crowley Maritime Corporation. Eight hundred people went out in a beef focused mostly on Puget Sound and San Francisco Bay. The issues were manning, pay, health and welfare, you name it.

The employer wanted to go from five IBU members aboard oceangoing vessels to three, and from three MMP members to two. Then Crowley wanted to merge classifications. For example, they wanted a classification such as able-bodied cook, who would sail as an able-bodied seaman but would also cook. So manning was by far the biggest issue, although they also wanted to cut wages.

Manning is a safety issue because you have fewer people aboard the vessel to make up tows. The links in the anchor chains they're makin' up tows with are ninety pounds each. That's each link. It's heavy, dangerous work because you have all that weight and you have equipment to work that weight. And that equipment can tear you apart.

So it was a huge safety issue. Where the people had been workin' four hours on and then eight hours off, they would now be working six hours on and six off. So you could be at sea for up to ninety days by the contract—in reality it was usually thirty to sixty days—and in that whole period of time you would never be able to get eight hours of continuous sleep.

Although we got great help from the ILWU longshore division, 1987 was a hard and expensive strike for the IBU. We had to fly people around to picket different situations, then fly them home. As the strike dragged on, it got bitter. It lasted nine months. You wondered if it would ever get over.

By the end of March, the MEBA [Marine Engineers Beneficial Association] in San Francisco told us they were no longer going to honor our picket lines.[18] This was a big setback. Still, our members were strong and tough for months. It was an honor to be around them. They lasted until the bitter end. Then we did what we could to get ourselves well and fight again some other day. Now [1996], we're nine years down the road, and the IBU is still here and as strong as ever.

Burrill Hatch

My earliest job was workin' for Foss Maritime in 1949, when I was seventeen. We were running up to Alaska to bring down gold ore from a mine in Canada. We barged it down to Tacoma Smelter. I was an oiler on a tug with a fourteen-man crew, which is extinct now. That included officers, unlicensed personnel, and a cook and messman.

In the '50s I worked for Chicago Milwaukee Railroad. They used to have the last steam tug in Puget Sound. It towed railcar barges from Seattle to Port Townsend. I was an able-bodied seaman on that tug—I did maintenance and stood wheel watch—until it was taken out of service about 1955. Then I went to work with Foss Maritime and soon ended up on Chicago Milwaukee–owned railcar barges being operated by Foss. I worked there probably fifteen years. I was always IBU. I only belonged to one union my whole life.

About 1971 I became national secretary-treasurer of the IBU and held that job for seven and a half years. Then I was out of office for eighteen months and worked as a tankerman. In 1980 I came back into office as Puget Sound regional director. That was my job at the start of the Crowley strike of February 1987. As required by my position, I was a key figure on our negotiating committee and did a lot of the negotiating.

In 1987 the IBU officers went on the same strike pay that the members were getting. After two months we went on the same kind of austerity program as the men did. That was a good solid way to be, because the strike lasted for nine months.

Don Liddle left the IBU presidency before the strike was over. I'd been speaking for the union and ended up having to conclude the strike myself. Crowley Maritime told me, "Either you send those people back to work or they're all fired." In addition, about forty of our people went back to work for Crowley by themselves, crossing the picket line. So I capitulated. I put it before the membership, and they voted to go back to work.

After the strike, under the ocean and coastwise agreements, many of our vessels were reduced from eight to six men. On the inside boats that stay in the harbor, they were reduced from six to five. Under the new system, the engineer would have to come out on deck during the captain's watch and handle lines. This is not what engineers think they should do, and I agree. Employers call that economy and meeting the competition. I call that by a different name.

Still, in 1987, I was not going to lose a whole company, nor was I going to just sit there and watch all our Crowley people get replaced. It was just one of the difficult situations you find yourself in by being a union officer. You have to make those decisions sometimes.

I became president of the IBU at the strike's end and retired from that post in 1993. I've seen a lot, some of it good. For example, about the time of the '87 strike, some of our San Francisco Region people did great pioneering work in toxic fume control around our vessels. Their idea was to stop deadly fumes from venting all over the place. Jeff Quam-Wickham was a tankerman who was one of the people who worked on this. He pointed out that this problem existed on Crowley's barges and really everywhere.[19]

Now, of course, we're going through a period where the unions are relatively weak compared to what they were thirty years ago. But people at some point are going to wake up and recognize that the employer is taking advantage of them and their families.

The Dispatcher or any union newspaper should have a program where they teach our young people what has come before them. All the information they get about the 1934 strike, and how bloody that was, is through word of mouth or by some newspaper. They're probably not gonna believe the newspaper, but the facts are there.

I can remember a company I worked for. To get seniority, you had to work continuous months. They would fire you every five months so you never got seniority. That rule has been changed dramatically. It became something like you gotta work 120 days in twelve months, any twelve months, not a calendar year. Your seniority goes back to the first day you went to work.

The reason this was changed was because the companies were sinful back in those days. And they always like to return to that form. As long as we keep them on the right road, and we keep our young people educated as to where they have to be, then I don't think we're gonna have any problems.

MARY WINZIG: THE POWELL'S BOOKS ORGANIZING DRIVE, 1998–2000

Powell's Books of Portland, Oregon, is the largest independent book company in the United States. Mary Winzig was a key figure in the 1998–2000 organizing drive that brought Powell's into the ILWU. She also served as the founding president of the newly chartered warehouse, retail, and allied workers Local 5 that represents Powell's four hundred booksellers.

The ILWU Powell's drive into the U.S. service economy is somewhat reminiscent of the California warehouse "march inland" organizing campaign covered in chapter 4. But Powell's is also a distinctly Pacific Northwest story.

Mary Winzig

I was born in Houston, Texas, in 1964. My parents were Republicans, but odd Republicans. They told me never to cross a picket line. When President Reagan fired the air traffic controllers in 1981 for going on strike, my parents said, "That's not a good thing." So I learned something about labor from an early age.

I got interested in politics as a student at the University of Texas. There was an anti-apartheid drive because UT had money invested in South Africa. There was a free speech movement because they were arresting people for speaking on campus during non-designated hours. I met folks from Central America, and I joined the UT Committee in Solidarity with the People of El Salvador.

In 1987 I went to Washington, D.C., for a big protest march against Reagan. Going to school during the 1980s, when Reagan was president, opened your eyes if you were not blinded by business school. After college I worked for Pueblo to People, a Houston group that helped cooperatives in Central and South America sell their goods for a living wage.

When I was twenty-eight, I came to the Northwest, partly for the cool climate. I hate hot weather. If you want to know about global warming, go to Houston. Besides, I was really tired of Texas. The state was getting so conservative! I worked at 23 Avenue Books in Portland for two years. Then, in 1995, I got a job at the Burnside Street store of Powell's Books.

During orientation at Powell's, the human resources guy, who was the owner's cousin, said, "I just want you to know that there was a union drive a couple of years ago, but we don't need a union here." Immediately I thought, "Oh, if you're willing to say this right off the bat, you must really need a union."

What I heard about that union drive was that they tried to organize just the big Burnside store, which is just one of several Powell's shops. They realized too late that they needed to organize the rest of the company. They never did get enough pledge cards signed to get a union certification vote with the National Labor Relations Board [NLRB].

What happened to us was that we felt desperate. Management pulled so many things all at once that we had the momentum and the anger to sustain us.

I started working at Powell's right after they computerized. Powell's went from a fairly small family business to a multimillion-dollar corporation. There began to be a split between management and the workers. Management began thinking more about the bottom line, more about themselves than about what the workers needed. When I started at Powell's, upper management would say hello, talk to me, and even help me shelve. But as time went on, management pulled away.

By the time we unionized, management didn't have personal relationships with us anymore. I think this worked to our advantage, because they were so out of touch. It also helped that we liked each other. We got stronger as we went along. We became family. I don't think management had that.

Michael Powell, who owns the company, is a liberal. To his credit, he opposes discrimination and censorship. But people need a living wage. After I'd been working at Powell's for five years, despite stunning performance reviews, I was making eight-something an hour. People who had been there longer were making only fifty cents, seventy-five cents more.

It's great to be against censorship, but when people are having a hard time making rent, an employer has to come to grips and do right by his workers. If you are going to be the planet's bookstore, get online, and be a multimillionaire, you need to give people their fair worth. Michael Powell wasn't doing that.

We felt degraded, too, when the company restructured our jobs. Before, we were working in areas we understood and enjoyed. But suddenly I would be shelving in railroads or automotive that I didn't know jack about. I couldn't help customers anymore. This sort of thing happened across several departments at the Burnside store, which had the most Powell's employees. Many of us saw what we'd liked about working at Powell's disappearing.

What affected every employee, though, is that they eliminated the compensation group made up of workers and managers that had set up a plan to get people equal compensation. They decided instead to give us small raises based on merit, which in many cases meant raises based on favoritism.

Friends of mine and I talked about how we needed a union. Other people in the Burnside store were having similar conversations. Many of us felt we had nothing to lose. We were making crap wages, and even if we got fired, we felt we could always make crap wages somewhere else.

When they eliminated the compensation group, Marty Kruse said, "Let's meet at Ringler's Annex, the bar down the street, and discuss what we're going to do." I wasn't at that initial meeting, but some of the people I had talked to were. Those who attended decided, "Let's start a union."

I was at the next meeting, which was in September 1998. We invited the United Food and Commercial Workers [UFCW], the IWW, and the Teamsters to meet with us at the same time. This was a little naive. It put the union people on the spot. We met at a private house late at night after Powell's closed. Weirdly, the cops showed up. I thought, "We're getting watched already!"

There were thirty of us at the meeting. These people ultimately became the organizing committee, but at this point, we didn't know what we were doing. People were all talking at once. Finally one guy took charge and had us introduce ourselves. The UFCW and the Wobbly organizers answered some questions, but things didn't seem quite right yet.

Then Jobs with Justice suggested we try the ILWU, which was democratic and represented a bookstore in San Francisco.[20] In October we met with Michael Cannarella, the ILWU Columbia River organizer, at the longshore Local 8 hall. Some of our group had looked into the history of the ILWU and learned about its militancy and support for different causes. When we met at Local 8, Michael gave a good spiel, and those of us who were there decided to sign cards that night.

Once the main organizing drive started, the company held a series of meetings with the workers. These were commonly at the Powell's corporate office. Michael Powell would sit there with his top managers and ask how come we didn't take our concerns to him, his door was always open. But he'd been a very private person until the union drive began. Then he was like, "Hi, how are you?" We thought, "Where are you coming from? Where were you?"

Peter Olney, the ILWU organizing director, Cannarella, and Paul Bigman, the Puget Sound organizer, predicted that the managers would have these meetings. They said management would tell us they were sorry and if we just didn't unionize things would get better. We told the workers who were skeptical of us that this would happen. When it did, those workers felt, "Wow, they know what's going on." It made us look smart. That helped us in many ways.

One way it helped was in overcoming this class thing that existed. Many people working at Powell's had college backgrounds. Some said, "Longshore? I've been to college. Why do I need a dockworker to represent me?" This was even though some longshore workers made five or six times as much money as Powell's employees. It also helped that Bigman had gone to Reed College, because a lot of people from Powell's had gone to Reed.

It was hard talking to some people, especially in other stores away from Burnside, where we had no contact at first. Some folks at the technical books store complained, "Here's this union being thrust upon us." Finally, at one of the management meetings, I stood up and said to those people, "You're mad, but don't blame the union, blame me. I was one of the first to bring in the union." That felt kind of like outing yourself. I thought, "Can't go back now!"

Michael Powell shook his head and looked over at me like he was thinking, "Oh no, a voice of reason." I was taking responsibility. It was not what he wanted to hear. Others of us went to management meetings held at various stores. They said, "If Michael Powell's going to give his spiel, well, here's our spiel." This was quite brave and wonderful.

The company also sent letters to our homes. We never got letters before, but now managers sent letters signed with their first names. One letter identified us as the wrong union. Our members said, "You're telling us the union is bad, and you can't even do the right research?"

When we were organizing, we had people we called "communication stewards." We had stickers I labeled "Peter Olney papers," because Peter loves those stickies. There were charts with people's names and locations, and we would pick workers to talk to. I had a group of ten or twelve. When we were making decisions or having a meeting, we would contact those people to let them know what was going on.

We got help from the outside from progressive community groups like Jobs with Justice and Art and Revolution. ILWU longshore Local 8 and marine clerks Local 40 from Portland and longshore Local 4 from nearby Vancouver, Washington, were always at our picket lines and rallies. Some of us wore punk clothes, and we looked different from waterfront workers, but they would be there with their banners. Their nickname for us—which they didn't tell me about until 2000—was "the Bisexual Vegan Union." This was all in fun. They were really supportive.

In December 1998 we started wearing union buttons. I gave one to Billy Bragg, the singer, when he came into the Burnside store. He said, "Mary, you're doing Woody Guthrie's work." That was inspiring. At a concert that night he dedicated his song "There's Power in a Union" to the Powell's workers. This led to our first mention in *The Oregonian*, the Portland paper, which is usually no friend of unions. That felt like, "Okay, you've gone another step. You just got to keep going."

In early 1999, when the NLRB election for union certification got closer, the company sent out more letters. They said how costly dues would be, so we kept announcing that the workers voted on the dues. We had to do a lot of education to counter their misinformation. In April we won the election, 161 to 155. I think it was so close because people are afraid of the unknown, even though there might a better future with a union.

But as soon as we won and reality set in, people came forth to help us. Some who had voted "no" and had refused to wear a button or a sticker were willing to serve on our bargaining committee. It came down to "Who do you trust more, management or us?" People could see that we had their best interest at heart. It helped, too, that when we put together a bargaining team, we made sure there was equal representation throughout all the stores and locations. We elected one person each from Beaverton, Hawthorne, tech, travel, and Hoyt the warehouse, and I think two from Burnside. We didn't want it to be Burnside-centric.

The company employed Larry Amburgey, a union-busting lawyer, to bargain with us. He sat across the table and insulted our team. Amburgey was there to take the heat off Michael Powell and to stall the process. One of the best things we did is have open negotiations where any Powell's employee could watch. I think that idea, which was brilliant, came from Peter Olney. People could see how their coworkers were being treated. It also put pressure on management because they could see thirty or forty workers trooping in.

We asked for better wages, reinstatement of the compensation group, the same health care, the union shop, and a successor clause. Michael Powell fought long and hard to try to have an open shop. We tried to tell him he was putting himself in the same company as George W. Bush, who supposedly he didn't like. Ultimately we were able to come to a compromise, so a limited number of people who didn't want to join the union could stay out. Fewer than twenty signed up for that, and later some of those joined the union anyway.

We had to have a series of demonstrations and short strikes before we finally got a contract. Once Art and Revolution, which does visual street theater, made these huge puppets for us. We staged the marriage of the puppet Larry Longshore to the puppet Michael Powell. Larry Longshore was holding a union contract. At the same time there was a carpenters' union conference in town, and three hundred of their people joined our rally.

The Teamsters helped us, too, by sending their truck around the block at the Burnside store blaring really bad '80s music. Some of the more friendly middle managers, who actually did the work on the floor, said, "If that truck goes by one more time, you'll get that contract!" We also used a lot of written material that Marcy Rein, *The Dispatcher* reporter, prepared for us.

In April 2000 management was still stalling. The ILWU International convention was coming to Portland during May 1–5, and somebody on the union side said to Larry Amburgey, "You should sign an agreement before May. You don't want the convention protesting you." Larry said, "Take it to the streets." So we did.

Management underestimated us again. A lot of amazing things happened convention week that turned the campaign around. On May Day there was a parade headed for the Burnside store. The cops yanked the permit and started beating people and trying to run them down with their horses, motorcycles, and four-wheelers. All the Powell's stores were on strike over an unfair labor practice issue, and a lot of us were there. The Burnside store was still open though.

Later that day, at four o'clock, all the ILWU convention people marched from their hotel headquarters toward Powell's. I went with them. Powell's was surrounded by cops in riot gear. I could see my coworkers being pushed up against the wall by cops with bully clubs and shields. Helicopters were overhead. It was horrible and scary. It looked like a war zone.

As we marched up, Brian McWilliams, the president of the ILWU, approached the head of the police. The cop said, "There's just a bunch of anarchists across the street." Brian looked at him and said, "Those are our people. We're going across." We started to march. Some cops took a few swings, but there were more than four hundred ILWU people with us, so the cops moved away. When

Mary Winzig, in cowboy hat, and Local 5 pickets during the Powell's Books strike, Portland, 2000. *Left to right:* Winzig, Jenny McKenzie, Gin Enguehard, Dee Dee Hall, Kristi Lovato, and Mira Brockelman. Photo by Bette Lee. ILWU Library.

we joined our people across the street, everybody was clapping and cheering like liberation was at hand. Powell's shut down early. That made people believe what a union can do.

The opening ceremonies of the convention were the next morning. About fifty of us from Powell's walked in, and everybody was chanting, "ILWU." I'll remember that for the rest of my life. I gave a speech about the people I was working with and the union we were joining. The convention passed around ILWU tote bags, and the delegates filled them with money for strike relief. On May 4 the convention marched to the Burnside store again, and we held a hands-around Powell's rally with the ILWU delegates. We shut the store down once more, too.

We went on strike again on Memorial Day, and people who had never worn a button or even signed a petition were walking the picket line. I knew then we were going to win. We went into federal mediation, and now negotiations were totally different. The workers couldn't watch this time, and the mediator negotiated between the two bargaining teams that were in different rooms.

The contract proposal agreed upon called for an 18 percent raise over three years. We retained our health care. Now there was a grievance procedure, so we couldn't be fired at will. The compensation group was put back in place. We didn't get the successor clause we wanted, but I don't think Powell's is going anywhere. We got a profit-sharing program, so if a customer goes through our Web site, we get a percentage of the sale price. The vote in favor of the contract that August was 293 to 37.

After we won our contract, we were on the cover of *The Oregonian*. Of course, that contract symbolizes much more than its various clauses. We have a sense of community at Powell's now that we never had before.

When I visited the International library in San Francisco, there was this glass table with all these medallions that looked like they came from when Harry Bridges was around. Beside them was a Local 5 button. I thought this represented such a blending of past and future, longshore workers and booksellers. Today, unions have to expand their jurisdiction to survive. It clicked for me then that what we had done together was pretty cool.

4

WAREHOUSE AND COTTON COMPRESS

CALIFORNIA

THE ORIGINS OF THE ILWU'S WAREHOUSE DIVISION GO BACK TO THE UNION'S early days. To protect its flanks during the 1934 strike, the ILA began organizing marine terminals in Alameda, Berkeley, and Oakland and waterfront warehouses in San Francisco. Work performed in these facilities was often close to longshoring. If these workers unionized, the shipowners would not be able to use these places to recruit scabs or move scab cargo during future disputes.

Soon after the 1934 strike, Local 38-44, the ILA's new warehouse unit, got contracts with many Bay Area waterfront storage companies. But when the local asked to renew its contracts in late 1935 and early 1936, the employers refused. They said they could not afford union wages and conditions while dozens of uptown warehouses remained nonunion.

ILA 38-44's response was to unionize the uptown facilities. The organizers called this the "march inland." By 1938 what had become warehouse Local 6, ILWU, in northern California was 8,500 members strong.

Partly because of Teamster competition, the ILWU did not match its northern California inland gains elsewhere on the Pacific Coast. It did establish a viable warehouse local in southern California and a cotton compress beachhead on the Los Angeles waterfront. The latter provided a platform for the union's eventual extension into compressing in California's Central Valley.[1]

THE "MARCH INLAND" IN THE SAN FRANCISCO BAY AREA, 1934–1938

Our story begins with the union's early organizing on the Alameda, Berkeley, and Oakland side of San Francisco Bay. Howard Shirley, Joe Chambers, Paul Heide, and Ray Duarte review the warehouse local's origins there. Joe Lynch, who, like Paul Heide, later served as a Local 6 officer, recalls the march inland in San Francisco.

Howard Shirley

In 1932 I started to work at Encinal Terminals, a combined dock-warehouse in Alameda. They told me to come down and wait out front. When they could use me, they'd let me know. They called that the shape-up system. Sometimes there'd be one hundred men. Sometimes there'd be twenty or thirty.

When there was work along the terminals, they'd come out and make up a gang at the front of the dock. If trucks came in that needed unloading, they'd get you for that. As railcars showed up, they'd build gangs to unload the cars. When they needed longshore gangs, they'd pick gangs for that.

I weighed 145 pounds, but I was physically fit. You had to be. We used hand trucks with so-called monkey boards. That's a V-shaped board that went under the blade of the hand truck. When you loaded up your truck with canned goods, you could extend the load on it. You'd put one case on the bottom and crisscross eight more on top for a total of nine cases.

Then you'd pull the truck over and wheel it. You had from 500 to 650 pounds on a monkey board. There was a high pace of work. When you got through at the end of the day, you knew it. You had to get the work out. If you didn't, particularly in the days of the shape-up, you didn't last. There were too many men out there that wanted a job.

When the '34 strike took place, I used to go down and visit with the long-shoremen and sometimes get them some coffee or doughnuts. They knew I'd worked at Encinal. I wanted them to be sure I was out there because some of the fellows stayed in during the strike. So I wanted to be sure they saw me, and that's why they gave me a '34 strike clearance card.[2]

When we started, the wages were fifty cents an hour around the clock. After the '34 strike, they were one dollar an hour and a dollar fifty overtime.

Joe Chambers

In 1930 I did standby work at Encinal. You'd stand out in front of the joint; it's the old shape-up crap. The work essentially was loading and unloading railcars, to and from the docks. Car to ship was stevedoring. Sometimes you'd work from nine o'clock until ten or eleven, and he says, "Well, that's all, come back tomorrow and see what's doin'." You're neither here nor there. You work and you starve anyhow. It paid fifty cents an hour in 1930.

They were signing them up ILA in '33. Most of them at Encinal signed in the longshoremen's local. When the terminals were first organized, there was a tremendous bone of contention. Harry—the longshoremen—dropped contention for the terminals of the East Bay and left them to the warehouse local.[3]

The terminals had a definite waterfront flavor though. Very early on, there was even a little friction against anybody who wasn't from there. I'm talking about the other places, like Haslett warehouse. Ray Heide and his brother Paul—they were early organizers—come from Haslett's.

In 1933 I went to the University of San Francisco and played football, but I quit on May 9, 1934, the day the strike started. I went to the beach to hang out with the guys. They could tell who was missing—the son of a bitch might be scabbing. Alameda wasn't that big of a community. They had brought in scabs. They used an old sailing vessel, *The Star of Finland*, as sleeping quarters.

After the strike I went to work at Plant 48 of California Packing Corporation near Encinal Terminals. The organizers were coming over to follow up on Encinal. Jack O'Conner, an organizer, come walking by. I was working in a car. He said, "When the hell are you guys going to join the union?" I said, "When the hell are you coming in here? When are you gonna sign us up?" So O'Conner come in and says, "How many of you guys want to sign up?" We didn't do it in the open, but we signed them up.

There had been very little growth from the '34 to the '36–'37 strike.[4] Mostly it was near the waterfront or tied to it. Crockett, California, where the big waterside C & H sugar plant was organized in 1935, was the same as us. In '36 organizing took off as an inland march. We were picking up people in the '36 strike. I think we went in a few hundred people. We come out of there, well, hell, you couldn't count 'em. We had grocery warehouses and this big paraffin plant—they had three hundred or four hundred warehousemen alone out there.

Paul Heide

I went to sea a little over six years. During the last trip I was on, I shipped out a month before the longshoremen went on strike in 1934, and then it became a maritime strike. The shipowners cut off the news because they didn't want to agitate us. They kept us on the East Coast on a familiar easy run. They wouldn't send that ship back to the West Coast for fear it would be tied up. I was the ship's delegate for the Marine Workers Industrial Union.[5] I guess I became the ship's delegate because I was the most vocal of the bunch.

I finally got to Oakland in August 1934. My brother, Ray, was working for Haslett Warehouse Company part-time. I just shaped up along with the other men, and I would be picked now and then. I was making an average of ten dollars a week. Soon my brother and I were sent to Standard Warehouse, a place Haslett had leased.

The first day I was at Standard, the gang boss kept coming into the railcar where I was working. We were unloading big sacks of sugar. He would say, "You're five minutes behind." I finally said to the warehouseman I was working with, "What the hell is he talking about? We're five minutes behind what?" There were a number of ways of speeding up the work.

At Standard my brother and I worked as high-pilers. We'd pile heavy sacks up ten high for storage. The wages for an eight-hour day were $3.50. That figured about forty-three cents an hour. They would generally give people who showed up some work so they could keep a large group of men hanging around. That's how they would maintain the shape-up—by giving everybody a little bit.

I got active helping the union organize and was hired to organize on commission in January of '36.[6] In the middle of '36, I became a combination organizer and business agent, which I had been anyway. I had already typed contracts; we didn't have any office workers then.

To organize, we'd simply contact the people on the jobs at their lunchtime or whenever they were free, or put out a leaflet and have a meeting at a nearby location. We never had any difficulty in those days. It was still the aftermath of the maritime and general strikes of '34. The employers were not anxious to get into trouble.

One of the first places we organized was El Dorado Oil because we already had the El Dorado Terminal in the union. So it was logical that the El Dorado plant in Berkeley should be organized. There was this older man, a big, tall white

Warehousemen high-piling heavy sacks by hand, 1937. Bags like these often weighed one hundred pounds or more. Photo by Otto Hagel. Copyright 1998 Center for Creative Photography, University of Arizona Foundation.

guy in his late fifties or sixties. He had just one question when we had the organizing meeting in an old vacant store by the plant—that was if we took in everybody without discrimination. When we said, "Yes," he said, "Okay, folks."

When we were organizing, if there were black people working, they came into the union just like anybody else. At the Colgate plant in Berkeley, it was a little different because all the black members worked on the cleanup crew.[7] There were several black workers on the East Bay marine terminals in the mid-1930s, so we always had black members in the local, since the terminals were the first to be organized.

At Albers Milling in Oakland there were women working filling lines and men doing warehouse and operator's jobs. We just signed up the men at first. Then it became crazy that we would have a place organized but a number of the workers—just because they were women—would not be organized. So we signed up the women. At first we had separate meetings for men and women, just for a short time. Then we had meetings all together.

Ray Heide (*right*) and, to his right, Paul Heide, California State CIO convention, San Francisco, 1945. ILWU International Vice President J. R. (Bob) Robertson is fourth in from the left, and to his left is ILWU International Secretary-Treasurer Louis Goldblatt. ILWU Library.

During the '36–'37 strike we did a lot of organizing. There was a volunteer organizing committee, and we signed up all kinds of people all over the place. The warehouse union grew from eight hundred to over three thousand when the strike ended in early 1937. When the '36–'37 strike started, we had $10,000 in the treasury. After it ended, we had $30,000, although we had given $10,000 to the longshoremen. We gave to any labor group that was fighting to get organized or to win a strike. We helped them all out.

When the L.A. Spring and Wire strike of 1936 was on in Oakland, we organized the warehousemen, and they served as a way for the United Auto Workers to organize the production people, because we shut off the loading and unloading. There were times when other unions would be organizing and they would have trouble with the employer—he'd fire somebody and they would put up a picket line. A lot of times we'd just clear our hiring hall—everybody would go out on their picket line. They could always call on us.

The first time I was charged by the cops with anything serious was during the 1935 lockout at Santa Cruz Packing Company in Oakland. We'd just organized the place. Bob Moore, another organizer, and I were arrested and charged with throwing a switch with intent to derail a train. We were acquitted by a jury in superior court. The women's auxiliary was organized during that period—at least a small part of it in the East Bay—and they put out leaflets to get people to attend the trial.

During the 1936 L.A. Spring Company strike, I got a telephone call to come out right away. I drove out and parked directly across the street from the Oakland plant. It had to be a frame-up. The police wanted me out there so they could work me over. Those were the days when they had an anti-picketing ordinance. They did away with it later. Captain Brown was in charge of the Oakland Police Department's Eastern Office Division. He hated labor organizers.

Anyway, there were two cops in front of the L.A. Spring plant. One of them walked over when I parked. He said, "You can't park here." I said, "Why not?" He said, "Because Captain Brown says so." I said, "Well, screw Captain Brown!" He took out his club and almost broke my arm, he hit it so hard.

"Get out of the car," he said. I stepped out and he hit me in the back. I knew he was trying to get me to do something so I could be charged. He said, "What are you coming out here, starting trouble for?" He took his club and punched me in the rib cage. I'd trained as a boxer, and I hit him by automatic reflex before I realized it. I punched his teeth and cut a hole right through his lower lip. Then the other cop stepped behind me and hit me over the head and split my scalp open. I was bleeding all over.

They took me to Highland Hospital and put me in one of those barred rooms. They charged me with resisting arrest and battery. I had a trial in municipal court, and the jury found me guilty of battery but not guilty of resisting arrest. If you can make those two things fit together—I've never been able to understand how they figured that out. I don't think the judge believed this cop. He sentenced me to ninety days, suspended. So, it really didn't amount to anything, and we won the beef, got the contract, and were satisfied.

Ray Duarte

When longshore work started after the '34 strike, they started the terminal group up in Oakland. The first group of warehouses they organized after were the grocery houses. In the first part of 1935 my brother Chili [Charles] got me a job at Haas Brothers, a grocery wholesale house where he worked. In the latter part of '35, the union started organizing. We signed applications in '35 and got initiated in '36.

When we organized, all these grocery warehouses were in the same area. Maybe that was one of the reasons they figured they could organize them the fastest. The company found out about that. Naturally, they're going to try to keep organization out. They immediately raised everybody.

I had already got one salary increase from fifty-five dollars to seventy-five dollars a month. And, man, they raised it to one hundred dollars a month. But it didn't work because we knew the other benefits that we were asking for. We had no overtime. If we had to take inventory on a Saturday or Sunday, you'd come in, but you didn't get paid for it. You were just under their thumb. If you made the wrong move, if they didn't like the way you looked. . . .

There must have been some discussion that the ILA was interested in getting these inland grocery houses organized. That's where the first little light started showing that somebody was interested in organizing, although we had been talking about it in very hushed tones since the '34 strike was on. We were labor-minded to begin with, and we figured somewhere along the line we're going to get involved.

We used to go next door to Western States Grocery to use the trash incinerator. One day I was there with Ray Fisher. We knocked on the door, and the guy opened it up. He says, "Hey, when are you guys going to get organized? There was some guy out in front here this morning, and quite a few of the guys signed up over here in Western States."

Ray Fisher says, "Yeah, I saw that guy out there. He talked to me, too. He said he was going to come over and see us later on." So I asked, "What do you mean, later on today? During the morning or at night?" Ray says, "He said he'd come over and see us." So we waited around, and that afternoon we all went out and sat in the car, and nobody came by!

The next morning we came to work and Ray Fisher comes in. He whispers, "Come here, I wanna show you guys something. That guy was out there, that business agent, Ray Heide, and he gave me these applications. You guys gonna sign?" We says, "Well, what the hell, Western States is gonna sign. We might as well all sign together. If they get 'em all together, they'll present it all at one time and we ain't got nothing to worry about. Let's sign the damn thing!"

After we got organized, Chili and I were quite active. The various parts of the local were coming together. The East Bay setup was Bob Moore, the Heide brothers, and Vincent Sharkey. They were mostly the organizers.

Chili and I were real interested in everything that was going on. We went to every kind of meeting they called. If it was just a little get-together meeting, we went. If it was a meeting of the whole group, we went—to learn. We never participated because we hadn't been initiated yet. But after we got initiated, we found out, "Hey, now we can participate." We ran for offices. Chili made the executive board, and I made the investigating and grievance committees the first year we were in.[8]

Joe Lynch

During the 1934 strike I was very sympathetic. See, I knew all these San Francisco longshoremen. They were Irish and Swedes. They were my buddies. I was playing soccer for the Vikings then, and we had five longshoremen on strike. My dad and I talked about the strike; he was a trade unionist. And the longshoremen in our Mission District neighborhood swore by Harry. They were church-going Catholics, but they didn't buy this red-baiting shit.

Ralph Dawson came up to our joint, Lipton's Tea Company, and organized us. It was Christmas week, 1936. We signed up right after New Year's, 1937. We said, "Jesus Christ, what took you so long?" We hadn't the faintest idea what the union was doing, but we knew organization was just a matter of time after the '34 strike was over and they started moving uptown.

See, the organization took part on a very planned, systematic approach. You had commercial warehouses strung along the waterfront from the Hyde Street pier over to Islais Creek. Then you had cold storage warehouses. Behind those you had mills, feed, flour, and grain. Behind those you had grocery—big grocery, with fifteen hundred people—and that's the way they organized. Gee, it was terrific.

Then came hardware, paper, and the patent drug industry, and then coffee, tea, and spice in '37. Liquor and wine came in '38. Then it was a mopping-up operation after that. By World War II the union had under contract, either wholly or partially organized, forty-six different industries in warehouse, distribution, production, and processing.

Management was very nervous after the '34 longshore strike. Before the organizers came—before Dawson—our Western Division manager called a meeting. He said it looked like there were going to be union organizers around. "If you guys decide to join a union, it's all right with us," he said, "but we'd like an opportunity to pick a union for you." Well, I says, "We want that one on the waterfront!"

Then seven other guys spoke up and said, "We want that one." The manager asked, "You all go along with what Joe says?" They said, "Yes." He said, "All right, boys, if that's the way you want it, that's fine with us. When the organizers come up, send them to me." I was on the negotiating committee. We signed an agreement in April 1937. Soon I was elected steward for ILA Local 38–44.

At Lipton's, fifteen men had joined the union in January 1937. There were also twenty women who were not organized until August or September. After we signed our April agreement, they came to me and said they were anxious to get into a union, too, so I organized them. These were some of the first women to come into our union.

SAM KAGEL: REPRESENTING THE UNION, 1934–1939

As an advocate for the warehouse local in San Francisco during the latter 1930s, Sam Kagel participated in the march inland on a daily basis. He describes that experience here.

Sam Kagel

In the 1930s there were lots of warehouses in San Francisco. The city was a big distributing center. You had public warehouses and warehouses in grocery, drug, hardware, and coffee. All of them were part of the waterfront, really. Right after the 1934 strike, most were still unorganized. But soon there was a conscious decision to move off the 'front and on to the warehouses. And for good strategic reason. They were easy pickings, too, because they were paying forty-five, fifty-five, sixty-five cents an hour with hardly any other conditions. Those wages were low even for the Great Depression.

Eugene Paton was one of the San Francisco warehouse organizers. He was an extraordinary guy. I remember how Pat got recognition at this one warehouse that specialized in packing fancy Italian olives and stuff like that. Pat had the workers organized, but the employer wanted to go to the NLRB for an election. Congress had recently passed the National Labor Relations Act [NLRA], or Wagner Act, of 1935 that set up the board. Well, Pat said to me, "This guy wants a vote. Okay, we'll give him a vote."

I went to the plant with Pat. He asks the guy, "You want a vote?" The guy answers, "Yes." Pat says, "Well, come on out to the gate." Off we go. Pat has the steward with him. He turns to the steward and says, "Tell the guys to come out." They start coming out, and Pat tells the employer, "Count 'em." That was the vote—the whole company! There must have been a hundred persons working there. They didn't stop work. They just walked out and walked right back in. The employer had his "vote." He recognized the warehouse union immediately.

At most other places where the people were organized shortly after the 1934 strike, the employer either knew it and accepted it or, once in a while, asked for a card count. There was an atmosphere for union organizing in those days. People were eager to sign up, and many employers got it. But this guy was so adamant that it had to be a formal vote under the Wagner Act that Pat got a little pissed.

The public warehouse was the first employer group that we sat down to negotiate with. Wes Howell headed a key company in that group, and he represented the employers. It had taken us a long time to get an agreement to meet. It was a real touchy deal. I can still see Wes Howell sitting on one side of the room across from Pat, myself, and the people from the union. Well, there had been a movement within the warehouse local at the time that there should be an audience of workers. So we had an audience about two or three rows back.

I was the economics guy with the proposals. Therefore I started the meeting. All of a sudden one guy in the audience stands up. He says he wants to say something. Everything stops. He starts, "My wife passes the Roos Brothers clothing store on her way to work. She sees all the wonderful clothes in the window and she believes we should have enough money to buy them." The place was stunned, 'cause this guy was not part of the negotiating committee and he was not an officer.

Finally the guy sat down. With that, Wes Howell said, "I don't think we should continue with this meeting." It took another four or five weeks to get back into negotiations. After that, we didn't have an audience. We just had a negotiating committee that represented the warehouse persons in a particular plant and any officers of the union who wanted to be present.[9]

Once a place was organized, the employer would sit down and negotiate seriously or we'd have a strike. In those days we had a lot of strikes going all the time, and not only in the warehouse industry. There were strikes on at Safeway, department stores, hotels. During the whole period between '34 and 1937–38, there was hardly a time when there weren't four, five, or six strikes going on. All of this union activity, of course, was inspired by the longshoremen winning the 1934 strike. That victory gave backbone to a lot of people to organize.

For example, how come the department store clerks got organized? Well, around 1937, the longshore union's new warehouse local went on strike at Woolworth's dime store in San Francisco. One of the clerks working there was a young woman named Marion Brown, later known by her married name as Marion Sills, labor leader. She was talking to the warehousemen on strike. From that, she got an idea of what the hell a union was all about. Ultimately that led her to call a lot of people working in the big Emporium department store, and they arranged to have meetings at night. Bingo! You've got an organization going.

In the early organizing years, 1935, '36, '37, there were two basic issues that always came up. This was all part of the march inland, when everybody was organizing—hotel workers, grocery clerks—not just our warehousemen. One issue was that the unions wanted to have the right to arbitrate discharge cases. The employers wouldn't agree to that. The other issue was the unions wanting to have the shop closed, which was legal in those years. A closed shop meant that only union members could be employed in a plant.

One day while there was a grocery strike going on, "Navy" Bill Ingram called me up. Ingram was the football coach at UC Berkeley who had his players scab on the longshoremen during the 1934 strike. He'd been dumped as coach and had been appointed head of labor relations for Safeway. He wanted to know what this closed shop thing was all about. Obviously, his background was not in labor relations!

I knew Ingram didn't care about the union's point of view. You think he'd be happy with the idea that the union wanted to be secure so it could beat the ass off the employers every year? Of course not. So I told him a union was like his business. You had to have a certain amount of money to survive. You've

Harry Bridges (*foreground*) leading ILWU contingent up Market Street, San Francisco
Labor Day parade, 1939. ILWU Library.

got rent, secretaries, and so forth. He listens. Then he says, "I can understand
that." Well, that grocery strike finally ended, and we got the closed shop.

During a lot of other strikes, including warehouse ones, I would talk until
I was blue in the negotiations. There would be no progress. Eventually I would
say, "Listen, why don't you call up Bill Ingram and discuss it with him?" I can
tell you now that Bill Ingram settled more closed shop provisions for the unions
than we ever got by economic strength.

About the discharge deal, well, we finally got it through the employers' heads
that if you don't have some kind of internal machinery to settle these beefs, the
unions would have to strike every time there was a discharge or a suspension.
Many of the employers could ultimately see that, 'cause it made sense. That's
how we got arbitration clauses written into so many of the early contracts.

As is generally known, the shipowners tried unsuccessfully to bribe Harry
during the 1934 strike. I even cited a Matson Navigation Company source on

this in a memoir I wrote. Still, in my experience, there were actually very few underhanded efforts to end labor disputes in those early days, or even after. Our area of the country was always pretty clean.

One time, though, I was in a San Francisco saloon called The Streets of Paris. This was 1937, '38. I was waiting to meet with a guy who was coming from a union meeting. It was after ten o'clock at night, and there was hardly anybody in the place. I was sitting there reading the newspaper when three guys came in. One was a little short stubby guy. The other two were great big monsters. They walked straight up to me.

I looked at these two big guys, who were what we called "goons" in those years. They were dressed in long black overcoats called "bennies." I said, "What can I do for you?" The short guy answered, "I'm here to settle the strike with Owens Illinois Glass." At the time I was representing the warehouse union in negotiations with that firm. I came back, "I have no authority to settle that strike. What is your interest in it?"

He said, "They used to supply me with bottles during Prohibition." I asked, "What's your name?" He said, "Waxie Gordon." So I'm looking at this guy who I now realize is a notorious gangster from back east. I didn't know what the hell was going to happen. I offered, "Do you want me to arrange a meeting with the union?" No, he didn't. "Well," I said, "I'll be in my office tomorrow if there's anything you want." And they left.

I immediately telephoned Jack Shelly, the secretary of the San Francisco Labor Council. He said, "I'll take care of it." He called the chief of police, whose men visited Gordon at the St. Francis Hotel, where he was staying. They asked him what he was doing in town. He said he was there to introduce a new cleaning process.

The police then saw that he went out to the airport. They put him on a plane headed east. He indicated he was going to stop off at Reno, so they alerted the Reno cops, who wouldn't permit him to get off the plane. So off he went. That was the end of my experience with the gangster Waxie Gordon.

A little later, in August 1938, there was a big industry-wide lockout of all the Local 6, ILWU, warehouse employees in San Francisco. By then, the West Coast longshore and warehouse workers had left the ILA, which they were affiliated with from 1934 to 1937, and formed their own new union, the ILWU. Most of the city's six thousand warehouse people were now covered by Local 6 contracts.

The contracts in different groups in the industry—the grocery houses, coffee houses, and so forth—had different termination dates. We used to go from one group of employers to the next, trying to get a better deal in each set of negotiations. This was called "whipsawing." The employers finally decided they wanted one master contract in the whole industry to stop the whipsaw.

So the employers as a whole locked out all the Local 6 workers in the city by moving a boxcar containing nonunion products from warehouse to warehouse. That car became famous around town as the "hot boxcar." Local 6's members wouldn't work its contents. The whole industry remained down for two months, with the local insisting it would not give up the whipsaw or accept a master contract. That lockout was front-page news for weeks in San Francisco.

I used to discuss the situation daily with Pat, who was now president of Local 6. We always got the early editions of the *San Francisco Chronicle* to read Paul C. Smith's blasts at us. Smith was the editor of the newspaper. He had not been an unreasonable, anti-union guy before. Finally we decided we would write him a letter asking him to be mediator. He accepted.

Paton and I knew that when we got into mediation, we would end up with a master contract. There was no way we were going to get the employers to agree to permit us to whipsaw. But we didn't sit around and say, "Hey, they won." You don't do that. You suddenly come to the realization that, "Are we going to stay out another sixty days with nothing happening and we've got our people not working?"

Interestingly, Harry thought we should take the master contract all along. He sided with, for Christ's sake, Adrien Falk, one of the main employers. We had a public meeting with the world there, and both of them were arguing for the master contract. We used to call them, in fun, "the Bridges/Falk Axis" after the Hitler/Mussolini Axis. Anyway, from the beginning, Harry said, "You guys are going to have to agree to a master contract." And so we did. We also got some decent concessions in the arbitration proceedings that settled the details of the master contract in 1939.

Around this time the ILWU boycotted the export of scrap iron to fascist Japan to protest that country's invasion of China. I participated in the picket lines down on the waterfront. My point here is that this boycott was not related to negotiations or contracts. The ILWU was always socially minded, and not just the ILWU.

The union movement never said, "All we're interested in is how much money we're getting today," because labor by its very history was part of a social movement. It always asked, "Who the hell got schools? The eight-hour day? The five-day week? Who was concerned about children working?" Despite all the contracts, that's what it was all about. It was about concern for all people. That's why the ILWU boycotted the scrap iron and I was on the picket lines, protesting what the Japanese were doing to the Chinese.

BROTHER HACKETT: RANK-AND-FILE ACTIVIST, 1936–1939

Local 6 veteran Brother Hackett describes work at McKesson-Robbins Drug Company in San Francisco during the 1930s. Hackett served on the local's grievance committee for decades. After he retired, he volunteered countless hours in the 1980s to care for the Local 6 archives.[10]

Brother Hackett

I was born in San Francisco on September 5, 1914, two days ahead of Labor Day. So you can figure I was born to be a labor man. My father worked in the shipyards and was in the boilermakers union from 1910 to 1925. Later he worked for the city and paid dues into the Laborers Union for forty years. Even after he retired, he still kept up his membership.

I got out of high school in 1931, during the Depression. There was no work to be had. To make money, I gambled: blackjack, poker, dice. I used to make fifteen dollars to twenty dollars a week. When I went to work at McKesson's in September 1932, I made less! The job was as an errand boy. I made eight dollars a week, about thirty dollars a month. The warehousemen weren't gettin' much better. Four years later, in '36, just before the union came, I was only making thirty-eight dollars a month as a checker.

They had started cutting wages about 1930, taking 10 percent here and 10 percent there. After the third or fourth cut, your three dollars a day was down to two dollars a day. But before the union, people took the wage cuts. Better 10 percent cuts than no job at all. You were in a position where you couldn't bargain. The boss was in the driver's seat, and you had no choice.

When I was a checker in early 1936, there was no hourly rate. They gave you that thirty-eight dollars a month, and that meant all the work they could get out of you for that. You'd work your regular eight hours, then they'd come up to you at four thirty, a quarter to five, and say, "We're working tonight. Here's half a buck. Go get dinner and get back here at six. We're working 'til ten." They'd do this two, sometimes three times a week. And you had to be at work at eight o'clock the next day. Then they'd bring you in on Saturday 'til two. We were putting in a hell of a lot of time, and we were getting practically nothing.

I first bumped into the warehouse union in March or April 1936. I had a feeling there was something going on with a few whispers here, a little group there. I finally approached somebody and got 'em to confess: There was a union in the offing. You think I wasn't going to jump for it? I said, "Sign me up!"

The early organization was sub rosa. Then we were told by the union, "Tomorrow, everybody wears a union button." The people who started the union and the people who joined it were very discreet, so the company was caught completely by surprise. Once we hit 'em with the buttons, then the union said, "We represent your people."

If the union had sent a letter saying, "We represent your people," the company would have laughed, "That's a farce." But when you looked out at the warehouse and you found better than half your warehousemen wearing buttons, *and* you got a letter, then you said, "Hey, these guys aren't kidding."

The company tried to stem the tide of unionism. They said, "We'll take care of you. Times are getting better, we'll give you a few more dollars." They gave us a raise, but it wasn't that great. Our pay went from forty dollars to forty-five dollars a month, still ridiculously low wages. It was all a facade. They were just trying to con us.

McKesson's also fired two guys. They figured, "Fire a couple, put the pressure on the rest of 'em, and they'll fold." This was July, August, or September 1936, when the last of us were initiated into the union. Word spread through the warehouse, "They fired so-and-so. What the hell we gonna do about it?" People said, "Let's not work until they bring 'em back." It was a spontaneous thing. Next thing you knew, everybody just sat down.

At this point the company either brought those guys back or we lost our strength in the house. If we gave in, those guys would have been gone, and somebody else would have gone the next day. But we were all committed. We figured, "They're going to pick us off two at a time. Let 'em pick us all off at once, and if they do that, they're dead." After two or three hours the word came around, "They're bringing 'em back." That gave us a hell of a lift. First taste of unionism, our first act, and damn it, we beat the company! Boy, that made us feel twenty feet tall.

We went into negotiations in September or October 1936. We created a rank-and-file committee to formulate demands. I was part of the group. Our idea was, let's get recognition, which the union office will get, and then go for wages. We put in for seventy-five cents an hour. We took this figure back to the house. We didn't have a formal meeting to accept the demands of the committee. We just came back and said, "We're gonna ask for six bits an hour. Is that all right?" The guys said, "Sure, that's fine." It was rather sloppily done, but it was rank-and-file unionism.

The company stalled us in negotiations. We pulled the pin, and out we went. We carried the rest of the drug houses out, too, and finally most of the city's warehouse industry was out between the end of October 1936 and January 1937. The brass at the hall did the negotiating for us. We were concerned primarily with keeping the place closed and doing our picket duty.

We came out on the streets, got some wooden boxes together, and sat on 'em. There weren't any specified shifts. You stayed on the picket line until you got tired and went home. Sometimes it was two or three days. Nobody wanted to go home because what was the point of going home? The action was down here. I was down there for a week. I only went home to bathe and come back.

We had some boxes that were good-sized crates. We'd set 'em up on end for a windbreak, get a fifty-gallon drum, scrounge some wood, and make a fire. It was cold—this was November and December. At this same time, the Maritime Federation of the Pacific was on strike, too, including the longshoremen. They had a soup kitchen down on the Embarcadero, four blocks from us. We'd go down there and eat dinner—beans, hot dogs, and salad. We'd go in shifts, three guys at a time.

When the strike was settled, we'd nearly doubled our wages. Now you had a feeling of dignity. Before, you were just a machine, a nonentity. "Now," you could say, "you can treat me as a man, not as a damn dog." Now they *asked* you to work overtime, they didn't *tell* you to work overtime. And we got a seniority list, which meant you couldn't fire someone indiscriminately.

The steward system was set up now, too, so you had somebody to go to bat for you. A union steward could go to the superintendent and say, "This guy's working as a checker and he's only getting order filler's wages. Get him checker's wages." Or "That work is too heavy for one man. Put two or three men on the job."

After the 1936–37 strike everybody organized. You went around the neighborhood on your lunch hour, found somebody havin' lunch, and started talkin' to 'em. If they didn't belong to a union, you asked 'em what wages they were getting. When you found out how little they were being paid, you'd say, "We just joined the warehouse union, went out on strike for a lousy couple of months, and doubled our salary." The guy'd say, "Just lead me to it."

See, there was a tremendous surge then. We had a meeting every week. There was always fifteen, fifty, or a hundred to two hundred people being sworn in. The people were just waiting in the weeds for somebody to hit them with a stick. It was just like a great awakening or a crusade.

In 1938 McKesson locked us out with the rest of the warehouse industry. When the lockout was over, the warehouse union got the master contract they still have. In 1938 we didn't have twenty-four-hour picket duty. It was just day shifts. They had too many men at McKesson, so they picked five or six of us and threw us down the street to Mutual Drug. There was some scrap wood around, and we built ourselves a little shack. We built it so we could take it apart because the cops would come around and say, "Get that thing down." We fixed it so we could break it down and put it back again right after the cops left.

About 1938 to 1939 there was another incident that showed our new militancy. The company said it was absolutely necessary that we work Saturday. Nobody wanted to work Saturday, but fine, we work Saturday. I took Monday off. The next time they said everybody work Saturday, I took Tuesday off. I did this with a couple of other guys. The idea was, everybody who worked Saturday, take Monday or Tuesday off. Soon everybody was doing it, always working Saturday, but only working four days during the week.

Finally the superintendent says to me, "I see that every week you take a day off." I said, "As long as you insist on making us work on Saturday, I'll work Saturday, but it doesn't cost me anything, it costs you. You're paying me time and a half for Saturday, and I'm only losing a straight day." Did something hit the fan? The minute he took that to the other managers, the order came out, "No more Saturday work." And everybody was happy.

By the end of the 1930s our stewards ran the place. They were more important than the foremen. If you had a beef, you went to the steward, not the foreman. If you had to say, "This guy is making me work twice as hard because he isn't doing his part," the steward would walk over and say, "Look, brother, you're making it tough on the other guys. Straighten up or we'll cite you before the grievance committee."

On the other hand, the foremen didn't dare push, because they were union people under our jurisdiction! We set it up so the foremen were not supervisors but working foremen. If you were a foreman, you *asked* your union men to do things. You didn't stand behind them with a whip, or the steward would say, "Treat your men properly, or they'll have you down to the union hall."

BILLIE ROBERTS HENDRICKS: UNION PIONEER, 1936–1951

In the 1930s–40s, Billie Roberts Hendricks was widely known to Bay Area warehouse union members.[11] She joined the warehouse local during the march inland in San Francisco and persevered as a staunch ILWU advocate for the next fifteen years.

Billie Roberts Hendricks

I grew up on an Iowa farm. I'm seventy-six now [1982]. My mother was the only one of eight children not born in a log cabin near Prairie View. My grandmother rode to Iowa in a covered wagon, and my grandfather went through the Civil War as a Yank with the Eighth Iowa Cavalry. We've got family trees until it comes out of your ears. Some of my relatives wanted to join the Daughters of the American Revolution, but I never joined. It's so stuffy!

My parents were married in 1904. They weren't rich, but they owned their farm, eighty acres of corn, oats, and livestock in Van Buren County, Iowa. My folks raised me to be a little lady and marry a "professional man." Well, by age seventeen, the farm was choking me. I would wake up and see the sun come in over the cornfield and settle over the cornfield. The world was my oyster, but there was nothing to do, just grow up and pick flowers in the summer. We were five miles out of any little town.

I'd read books where you get out and see the world. I wanted to leave the farm, be on my own and go to school. My father wanted me to stay home and raise chickens, but that didn't appeal to me at all. So I went to Lawrence, Kansas, where my Aunt Lucy took me in, and I went to college. I wanted to be a schoolteacher. You didn't have to have a college certificate to do that in those days. So I took a teaching job when I was nineteen or twenty.

For two years I taught grade school in the small Kansas towns of Bayshore and Heifer. I had to sign a paper that I'd go to church at least twice a month.

Billie Roberts Hendricks and daughter Sallie, San Francisco, 1945. ILWU Library.

Remember, this was rural America in the 1920s. I was supposed to stay in the village of Bayshore, and I couldn't smoke, get married, or go out with high school boys. After I won a five-dollar box of candy in a local lottery, the school board charged me with gambling. So when I was invited to my uncle's in Chicago, I went. I took a job there and stayed for eighteen months.

In Chicago I met a man who was twenty years my senior. He'd been married several times, once to a silent-movie star in Hollywood. He was selling and traveling from coast to coast when he wasn't drinking. He said, "If you want to go to Los Angeles, I'll get you a little house with red roses around it and you can pick oranges off the trees." I quit my job in the middle of the day, got married, and came to California!

That's when the big 1929 crash came. The Great Depression shot my husband's sales business. At first I couldn't get a job. I'd go to those big all-night markets they had in Los Angeles, where vegetables were a penny a bunch, if you had the penny. I would go to Elysian Park and look under the trees where the lovers were, and pick around and maybe find a dime.

I finally got a job in a little scab restaurant. Everything in Los Angeles was scab then. Each time I called the order in, the short-order cook would give me a punch on the backside. That incensed me to death. Now, I'd curse him back, after all my years in the ILWU. Then, I just went home and told my stuck-up college husband. He said, "You must have encouraged him." Imagine!

We came up to San Francisco in 1932. A lady I knew said, "There's jobs opening in this whiskey place." That was around 1933. The first job I got, and it was before we were organized into the union, was at South End Warehouse. After Prohibition was repealed in late '33, the foreman opened his own place, Distillers Distributing. He asked several of us to go with him, including me, and I went. These were small businesses. It was before the big companies started, like Schenley's and Hiram Walker's.

At South End Warehouse, I got thirty-two cents an hour for eight hours' work, if I was lucky. If you were wanted for a second shift, it was eight hours more at thirty-two cents an hour. All we got between shifts was coffee, no meals. There was no such thing as hours-a-week or overtime. But mostly, we'd go in and work a few hours, and then they'd say, "There are no more orders. Go home." We'd work two hours, sit there and wait two more hours until the mail came, and then go home.

I worked on a line with a big machine, and it would drive you crazy. We pasted labels on whiskey flasks and put the bottles in cases, twenty-four to a case. If you wasn't careful, if the boys didn't get it right, the glass would fly. The floors were wet. You had to wear certain shoes. You wore your own gloves. These were old warehouses. Sometimes they weren't even heated. After they were union, you had clean uniforms supplied and you bought your own shoes. They supplied gloves.

Before the union, the women that worked the fastest got to stay the longest. Then the boss would come along and say, "Fire all the old bags, and keep all the pretty ones with pretty legs." Here the poor old gals were working their tails off and needed the money and was better workers. You never knew when you were going to be let out and when you weren't.

When the three-day San Francisco general strike came along in July 1934, everybody was out. The town was ours. We were just on top of the world. Nobody dared tell us we were poor. We knew we were going to win. There was nobody quitting and saying, "We can't make a living, we'll go someplace else." During the long maritime strike, before and after the general strike, I was working at South End Warehouse. When the National Guard patrolled the waterfront following the police killings on Bloody Thursday, the longshoremen gave me a pass to go through. The women weren't organized yet, but they weren't anti.

Actually, it was our dream to be unionized. Imagine belonging to a group like the longshoremen that stuck up for your rights, saw that you had seniority, and saw that the boss couldn't harass you or sleep with you. Harry Ludden, the foreman at South End Warehouse, used to say, "Come out to my house tonight." We didn't dare say "no." We were tired, but when we were invited to the boss's party, we went. Once he made us all get down on our hands and knees and bark like a dog for our plate of supper!

The first group of organized warehouses we heard about was the coffee houses. We went down to the hall to get in the union. But the work wasn't too steady. We would go to the hall and be dispatched out to work.

During the years right after the 1934 strike, people flocked to the warehouse local. All the Italian women from North Beach rushed down to join the union. Those were the years the longshoremen worked to start other unions going. They inspired everyone. The garment workers and the flour workers were organizing. Everybody wanted to get their home base, just like the longshoremen.

My first union meeting must have been about 1936. The women would just listen back then. We did think our organizers—Gene Paton, who became a wonderful Local 6 president in 1937, Lou Goldblatt, the Heide brothers, Bob Robertson—were "it." And Lou knew how to get things rolling. He started our steward system. But we didn't have much of a voice. The men would make all the rules. There was nothing we could do but be a rubber stamp for them.

Between 1937 and 1942 the women had their own separate meetings. Our male Local 6 leaders weren't much interested in women's problems in those early days. Neither was Harry, although we were thrilled when he came to meetings. The men thought "the girls" were only going to work until they got married or made some extra money. I was on the Women's Division executive board, but we didn't have much real power. We didn't meet with the men until we bellowed. Then we got amalgamated with them. We wanted to be known as workers. I never knew about this equal rights amendment business. I always thought I was a worker.[12]

Sometimes when we were dispatched out of the union hall for jobs, we were sent to a place that wasn't organized. We would talk union to the workers. Then we would vote to get the union in. We were called Red Hots because we organized. The bosses hated us. We had some pretty rough times. Whenever anybody struck, we were on that picket line. This little Judy Anderson always had a long sock with a Sweetheart Soap bar in it. If she was bothered by scabs, they'd get hit with a "sweetheart."

My husband and I divorced before very long. Then I married a man named Roberts. While I was working at Distillers Distributors, I became pregnant. When my daughter Sallie was eighteen months old, Roberts left me to marry someone else. But by then, I had a good Local 6 job and was determined to keep care of my little girl.

I became interested in a group called Working Mothers with Children. As my daughter grew up, for the next seven or eight years, I went to every meeting they had. There were several Local 6 people who were interested in child care, including Tillie Olsen and Hazel Drummond.[13] Hazel wrote a column for *The Dispatcher* in the mid-1940s. We'd meet with the board of education and rant and rave about getting a center for working mothers' kids. All the unions sent delegates, including the longshoremen.

Right at the end of 1939 or in 1940 I went over to Schenley's Liquors. It was just starting up. The union wanted volunteers to go in and help organize the place. One of the officers asked me to go. The company was avid to get workers. We just went down and asked for a job. We succeeded in organizing Schenley's into Local 6, too. I'd been working at the MJB Coffee warehouse packing tea bags on a belt line. It was a wrench to give up your seniority in a house, but I did.

When the bosses figured out I was organizing, they called me "that red button girl" and gave me the dirtiest job there was. I was stuck off in this washroom, standing up all the time washing bales and bales of dirty rags with glue on them and then passing them along. When the other workers put the labels on the bottles, they had nice clean cloths to wipe the extra glue off. In this job, though, I sometimes got to walk up and down the line and, when I wasn't caught, talk union.

I also got on every Local 6 committee I could. We had a publicity committee that put out a little magazine on yellow sheets. We would send these yellow sheets around to everybody so they'd know what the other shops were doing.

I was on our uniform committee, too. Each of us got a cap and a white, starched uniform for parades. On Labor Day, we were out in force on Market Street. We'd pass the reviewing stand and then get a walk-away shrimp cocktail down at the beach. We were the proudest things you ever did see!

Usually when there was a committee meeting, I'd take my daughter with me. The Local 6 hall was our second home. Everybody knew Sallie at the union. From nine to four, while I was working at Schenley's, I could leave her at the St. Francis Day Home, which was close to where I lived. It only cost me thirty-five cents a day. Otherwise Sallie went everywhere with me. Of course, if there was a night meeting or a potentially dangerous situation, someone else would take care of her.

About 1940 there was a particularly rough strike at Euclid Candy Company. We had joined the picket line and were walking back and forth across the company's door when the cops dove in. They weren't nice cops and they were on horseback. We tried to put our arms together and keep walking. They kept pushing with their horses. A horse's hoof almost stepped on my foot. One of our boys had a pocket knife, and he gave the horse a jab to make it move away.

The Local 10 longshoremen showed up to reinforce the Euclid picket line. They were all in their white hats, work shirts, and black jeans. That was kind of an ILWU uniform. The cops saw this one longshoreman I recognized who was always an organizer. They said, "All right, Hendricks, step back." That was the first time I ever heard the name of Hendricks. I thought, "That guy's for me." He wasn't afraid of the devil. At Easter, anybody else would bring his sweetheart an Easter lily. Not Frank Hendricks! He brought an Easter basket with a bunny in it for my baby. We were married in 1943.

When the United States got into World War II in the early 1940s and most of the men went into the service, I took what had been considered a man's job. I got a marvelous wage and I was now called a "receiving clerk." This was at Schenley's. The boss said, "Are you afraid to go downstairs to shipping and receiving, you and Alice Moore?" We weren't. Alice became a shipping clerk. We each got our own little office.

I used to get this solution that came in five-gallon cans. It went over the top of the liquor to keep the government stamps intact. I took in supplies for the machine shop, too. All the boys were helpful, although there was one old man who used to say, "Why don't you girls go home and raise your family? Why

Labor Day, Stockton, 1947. ILWU Library.

do you want to do men's work?" What an old son of a gun he was. We had to live, you know?

I was also quite into the blood donor scene during World War II. This was around 1944 to 1945. They needed blood for the wounded. I represented Schenley's, Local 6, and the San Francisco Industrial Union Council, CIO, in this big contest to elect Queens of the Purple Hearts. When you gave a pint of blood, you cast a vote for queen. I got four hundred votes for four hundred pints donated. We had it so well organized in warehouse. There were big signs that said, "Vote for Billie Roberts." I gave a lot of blood myself, too. You'd think I was a mainliner. But I had lots of blood. I was a strong person.

When Schenley's and all the other liquor houses closed down in 1951, I went to work in a top-grade restaurant at the Clift Hotel and became a member of the AFL waitresses union. They were a very so-so outfit. You didn't have to go to union meetings. In early Local 6 days, we couldn't wait for our two meetings a month. But in the waitresses union, if you didn't want to go, you just had to pay your month's dues. They thought I was the craziest thing they ever saw because instead of paying for someone to picket one of the restaurants, I went and picketed after my job. They never heard of anyone getting out and walking again after she'd walked all day.

Of course, I was always in political action as a good Democrat. When Franklin Delano Roosevelt was running for president, Sylvia Maker from Local 6 and I took pamphlets around. We walked for blocks to put flyers in front windows. It didn't occur to us to charge. The waitresses union didn't care who was running. They didn't care if you voted or not. It was very different.

The waitresses, too, always worked for tips and were jealous of each other. There wasn't that comradeship like we had in the ILWU, where you knew that you belonged. You weren't fighting alone. All of my life, for the last thirty or forty years, I've remembered those Local 6 kids. They were like the buddies, I guess, in a war. We were together against the enemy every day.

I love the ILWU. I'm so proud of it. I don't know what life would have been for me without the union. It was certainly a wonderful way of life. When you were a schoolteacher, you had to get out and wrestle your own job, or go in all dressed up to see the boss, with him looking you up and down wondering what kind of a lay you were. But it was nothing seeing the boss after there was a union and we got our dispatch hall.

I never got into anything before where I thought the workers would get their just desserts. When I was in college, they used to say, "What good are unions? They're only for stupid people. Anybody with any ingenuity can get their own job." You know, stuff like that. But when I found out these workers were organizing, I thought it was beautiful.

MAKING IT WORK IN SOUTHERN CALIFORNIA, 1936–1950

In Los Angeles activists founded an ILA warehouse local in 1936. The next year it became Local 26, ILWU. Three pioneer ILWU organizers recall those early days. Northern California's Paul Heide worked in Los Angeles for several months in 1937. Lou Sherman and Loyd Seeliger served as Local 26 officers well into the post–World War II years.

Local 26 made significant headway despite tension with the Teamsters over turf and politics that lasted until the ILWU and the Teamsters reached an accommodation around 1960. Due partly to its skirmishes with the Teamsters, the L.A. warehouse local never attained the numbers that warehouse Local 6 boasted in northern California during 1945–46, when the Bay Area union temporarily reached nineteen thousand members and had associated units in a number of regional towns. Still, by 1941, Local 26 had a membership of six thousand.

During the latter decades of the twentieth century, Locals 6 and 26 had great difficulty maintaining their numbers. Plant closures or relocations and internal difficulties were largely to blame.

Paul Heide

In May 1937 the ILA sent Bob Robertson, Ralph Dawson, and me to L.A. as Pacific Coast District warehouse organizers. We had helped unionize all the inland houses in the San Francisco Bay area. The L.A. warehouse local, ILA 38–134—it became Local 26, ILWU, in September '37—had organized most of L.A.'s drug warehouses since its chartering in October 1936, but there was still a lot more to be done.

We went down there with a kitty of twenty thousand dollars. See, ten thousand dollars had been put up by the Bay Area warehousemen, and ten thousand dollars was matched by the district to hire additional organizers. We had some volunteer organizers, and we hired a number from the L.A. port's longshore local, including L. B. Thomas, Elmer Mevert, and Don Cox.

We had organizing meetings almost every night of the week. Anybody could come from any of the houses. We'd be at the office about eight o'clock in the morning. The workday would last until we were through with the organizational meetings at ten or eleven o'clock at night. We had four thousand workers signed up before the Teamsters started raiding us. Then we lost several places.

We had cards made for different industries we had organized in the Bay Area. We'd put down the conditions we had there. Then we'd drive down the street in the L.A. industrial area. There would be three on a crew. One organizer would drive, and the other two would hop off the car and go right through a plant before the managers had a chance to stop us. In the plant we'd pass out our cards. Sometimes we were right ahead of the superintendent or some stooge who'd be chasing us out.

Lou Sherman

In the mid-1930s, when I was in the Teamsters, a guy named Loyd Seeliger and I organized a dissident movement in Local 208, the general truck drivers' local in L.A. The Teamster International moved in and took away our autonomy. They threw out the officers and appointed International representatives. Loyd and I were on the Teamster shit list then. We were charged with being subversives, reds.

In 1937 the warehouse organizing committee—Robertson, Heide, and some other guys—hired Loyd and myself to try to develop the Teamster rank-and-file movement to counter the Teamster raids. It didn't last. The Teamsters clamped down.

At this point the committee decided to keep us on as organizers. After about three weeks they decided to cut back. I went to work for Brunswig Drug, a place our L.A. warehouse local had already organized, and stayed there for two and a half years. But they decided to keep Loyd as an organizer. He was one of the best.

When I was working at Brunswig Drug, a couple of years went by with relative peace there until 1940. Then the drug industry went on strike for ten weeks. I was personally involved. My job was to raise money, buy food, and package it for distribution to strikers. When the strike was over, Brunswig fired me.

The local went to bat for me, there was an unfair labor practice charge, and finally the company was willing to throw in the towel and settle. They didn't want me back, but they were willing to pay several weeks of back pay to get rid of me. As soon as my beef with Brunswig was over, I was hired to work for the union again organizing. I organized anything I could put my hands on until the war came and I went into the army in 1943.

After the war I was elected secretary-treasurer of the local. I held that job for a long time. Around 1950 there were hard times for four or five years. There were new confrontations with the Teamsters, who raided us in L.A. and seized any opportunity to prevent us from expanding. There was adverse publicity given to the ILWU as a result of the constant red scare then.

Labor Day, Los Angeles, about 1946. ILWU Library.

We survived, and through it all we were in accord on one thing—we were part of the ILWU with a fine tradition and we were going to make it work in southern California even though we weren't longshoremen. We always regarded ourselves as independent and equal to the longshoremen—we admired and respected them, and we loved them because they were great trade unionists—but we had an identity of our own that we were very proud of.

Loyd Seeliger

I left home when I was thirteen. This was around 1919. I went to work for a contractor out of Riggins, Idaho. The IWW was strong then. They was in all the construction work and logging camps. I learned from the old Wobblies about job action. That meant a surprise attack—a quickie strike—on the employer.

Later I worked on the waterfront at San Pedro, not very long. I come into L.A. because it was the Depression and you couldn't get a job. Maybe you got one day off the waterfront. L.A. was nearly an unorganized town when I come here. You talked about a union, and you was a real rebel.

In 1937 the warehouse organizing committee hired Lou Sherman and me to organize in L.A. We'd been thrown out of the Teamsters, and they'd heard about it. The warehouse union organized the drugs and the mills first, and a big hardware house.[14]

All this time we were fighting the Teamsters. They'd come in and try to take over through the boss, who'd say to the workers, "You're supposed to be organized. Join this union, don't join that red organization." They said we was Communists.

Organizing at California Mill, I'd wait outside and let the workers come out. Then I'd collar one or two of 'em. I'd ask them why they didn't join the warehouse union. They'd say, "We'd organize, but they'll fire us." I'd say, "We'll keep it a secret."

I'd take a guy, go home with him, talk to him and his wife, maybe for two hours. I'd convince them that the union movement was the only thing—but they had to be quiet until we got enough people organized so they wouldn't get discharged. So we organized the wives right along with the employees.

At California Mill we got more than half of 'em organized. We went to the labor board for certification. The employer fired 'em all. So we set up a picket line. We also planned on breaking L.A.'s anti-picketing ordinance. The L.A. Police Department's "Red Hynes Squad"—named for its anti-labor captain, William F. Hynes—would come down to the picket line and take me to jail. Our lawyer, Leo Gallagher, would put a bond up and I'd be released. I think they took me to the police department to book me eleven times in one day.

Finally my case went to the state supreme court and broke the anti-picketing ordinance. At California Mill we won the strike and got a contract. The employer called me. "Come down here," he said, "I want to talk with you, you SOB."

I went to his office, and he said, "You've cost me half a million dollars." I said, "I haven't cost you nothing. You've cost yourself something. Your men need good working conditions and a contract. They haven't got nothing, no holidays, no vacations of any kind." Of course, that was before health and welfare come on. So he said, "Okay, we'll sit down."

I said, "Here's the contract." We had it already written out. It had one week's vacation. If we got a week's vacation in those days, we was doin' damn good. It had five days of sick leave. It had time and a half for over eight hours and for Saturdays and Sundays. They never had time and a half before.[15] It had a good grievance procedure to be taken up with the stewards.

A little while after the drugs and the mills was organized, we went after the L.A. scrap workers. This was in 1940 and 1941. The Teamsters didn't want the scrap industry then. There were blacks, Mexicans, and Jewish people working in those places. The Teamsters didn't care about them. The scrap workers were getting twenty-five cents an hour, no overtime, no conditions at all. The employers took so much advantage. If they had a lot of work, they'd keep their employees until nine o'clock at night, straight time. We felt these workers were ripe for organization.

We organized M. F. Berg's scrap rag place first. There were six guys in there that was very militant. They was so mad at Berg. They wanted to get organized, and they wanted to shut this damn place down if they didn't get some money. But M. F. Berg knew he'd been gettin' away with murder. He doubled their wages, put 'em on an eight-hour day, and gave 'em time and a half after that. We got a good contract with him.

We took these six guys, made an organizing committee out of their whole house, and organized all the rest of the scrap industry. If those six guys would call all the other M. F. Berg workers, they all went. They'd surround a plant. We wouldn't let the workers come out until they all signed applications. We'd go from plant to plant. And we doubled their wages. The M. F. Berg workers were mostly Mexicans and blacks. I think the six guys was all Mexicans. They were wonderful. We had a ball with these guys.

During World War II [1942–45], when I was in the army longshore battalion, the drug workers and Berg and our other scrap yards stayed in Local 26. We lost the mills. But after the war, the local did a pretty good organizing job.

I came home from overseas in 1946, got elected business agent for the port, and organized National Metals there the next year. It had two hundred to three hundred people at one time. And the local had a hell of a good guy in L.A. by the name of Chet Meske. He went out and organized a lot of different kinds of houses in different industries.

UNIONISTS FIGHT FOR RACIAL JUSTICE, 1942–1960

Local 6 has long been known for its diversity and its lack of discrimination, but these things did not come easily. Fannie Walker, Virginia Wysinger, and

Lillian Prince, three African American women who began work at the Colgate manufacturing plant in Berkeley during World War II, describe their early experiences.[16]

Then Ole Fagerhaugh, a white worker who became an International representative, and Curtis McClain, the local's first African American business agent (1960) and president (1969) and the ILWU's first African American International secretary-treasurer (1977), recall their battles against discrimination during the post–World War II period.

Fannie Walker

I was born in Louisiana in 1904. My grandmother raised me. My grandfather was a sharecropper. I come up pretty hard. You worked in the fields in early morning and evening, when it was cool. I was twelve when I started. Growing up, I did housework. You didn't make but a dollar and a half a week. The first job I had was twenty-five cents a week washing dishes for two old maids.

I came to California in 1940, got a job at Colgate in 1942, and retired there after twenty-eight years. At first I worked on a conveyor machine, packing washing powder and soap. You'd case so many hours and make boxes so many hours.

We had really nice foremen. They had to be nice to you because you were in the ILWU! When foremen would be nasty in different departments, the union steward went to bat for you. When different foremen would be sort of high style because they wanted to make a name, they just couldn't, because the ILWU cut 'em down pretty close.

I was the first black woman at Colgate. Early on, the white women had little mean things they would do. You'd put your lunch on the table. They'd take your lunch off the table. They would put your food on the floor. So I just went and put mine on the table. I said, "Now, the first one put my lunch on the floor, I'm gonna fight." So then they let me alone. I told them, "I'm going to stay here. You're not going to make me quit." The next day this girl brought me a sweater. We were friends from then on.

The treatment of black people by the whites changed a lot. It changed a lot on account of the union, because they had stewards in different departments. If anything went wrong, you'd report it to your steward.

Virginia Wysinger

I was born in New Orleans in 1905. I came to California in 1930 and worked in homes until 1942, when I heard about the union and got hired at Colgate. I got into reconditioning soap products, cutting the bad boxes that come off the line, putting the soap powder into another box, and putting it back on the line. I was the first black woman to work in the wash powder department. Fannie Walker had been there for about a month in another department.

Early on, sometimes the white girls would push the soap down so you had to stop the machine. The soap was coming out of the machine, and they'd stand there and push the soap so you didn't get it in the box. Of course, the girl running the machine wanted to know why! But that was about all of it. Soon, the whites got used to us because quite a few of us began coming in.

In the beginning there was a difference between men's and women's work and wages. Then I didn't have any feelings about this, I was so glad to get the work. It was better than doin' housework.

Lillian Prince

In 1944, when I was twenty-one, I came to California from Oklahoma. I got work through Local 6 in twenty days, went to Colgate in 1946, and stayed for thirty-five years.

I was the first woman that ever done cans on Colgate's Ajax line.[17] It was supposed to be heavy, men's work. The men didn't think I could make it, but I made it like a champ. I done cans for four years. They thought a women couldn't bring those loads, but I was bringing loads on a dolly, pulling them myself. They'd be up over my head. We had a thing you stuck underneath there, and you could pull this load down and roll it on your dolly and bring it into the line.

I was on the house committee. We fought for better working conditions. We'd go to committee meetings and sit down with the company and talk with them. We got a lot more things this way that we didn't get in the contract. These were what you call "added on to."

When I went to work it was more black than it was white. I'm going to say it like this, and you know I was at Colgate all these years: Local 6 made it possible for blacks to get where we got. If it hadn't been for the union, we wouldn't have made it. I've been a union member since I've been in California, and I'll still fight for unions.

Ole Fagerhaugh

I made my seniority in 1949 at Owens-Illinois Glass of Oakland. I was elected steward about a year later. We were 150 warehousemen in a plant that had 1,400 workers. Amongst our 150 members there were three blacks. In the rest of the plant there was one black—in Oakland, a city with a large black population. To explain this, I'll give you an example.

I was around the dispatch hall on my day off. This was about 1950. I heard a conversation between our dispatcher and Charlie Kinsey, the personnel manager at Owens. "I need seven men for Monday," Charlie said, "but don't send me any n——ers."

The dispatcher laughed, "Ha, Charlie, I gotta take 'em off the board, but you know you don't have to keep 'em." That explained everything to me as far as the warehouse went. And, of course, if they could do that with the warehouse union, what could they do with the company-oriented glassblowers' union that had much of the rest of the plant?

I got our committee together. There were five of us, including two Hispanics. I said, "There is something disgraceful going on that's a danger to us all." I got agreement on a program. I said, "I want you to send me every dispatch that comes out here. I will tell them, 'Look, if you get laid off, ask the foreman why. Then come and tell me.'" We kept a record of it for nine months. The picture was not pretty. No black made seniority although 50 percent of those dispatched were black. They'd keep them a couple of months, just short of making seniority, and lay them off.

One Monday morning here comes seven new people. There were three blacks and two Hispanics. Later they laid off the blacks and the Hispanics and kept the two others. I said, "Now is when we move." I called the dispatcher and asked him if there were any calls for new people. He said, "Yeah." Then I got the committee together and marched over to the personnel office and said, "We want a meeting."

Bud Owens was the president. He and the personnel manager said, "We better get the warehouse foreman." We said, "We are charging a violation of the contract." I pulled out the records I'd kept for nine months. I said, "The most recent thing is you hired X number and you sent them all back except two Caucasians, and you've got a call in." They said, "We have a right to do that under the contact. We can lay anybody off before ninety days." I said, "Wait a minute. The contract says the company may for any reason lay off anybody prior to seniority. What we want to know is the reason."

So they asked the foreman, George Gower, "Why did you lay this one off?" Gower, who was from Georgia, said, "I just didn't like the man's attitude." My committee was riled. Al Martinez said, "What do you mean, George, you don't like his attitude? He didn't take off his hat and say, 'Yeah, boss'?" Owens's face got brilliant red. He looked over at Gower! Come to the next guy—I'd started on the three black guys. Gower stuttered, "Damn, he's too short." Then I asked, "How tall is Johnny, Al?" He was a little Portuguese guy who stood about five feet and had worked there for fifteen years. "Well," Gower said, "we can't have them all short."

We got to the third one, and Bud Owens interrupted, "Wait a minute, that's enough. We'll take these men." I got on the horn, called the union dispatcher, and said, "Wherever these guys are, pull them off the job and send them out to Owens." They came out the next morning.

We broke their f—in' back. They never tried it again. And we didn't just break their back in the warehouse. I was in contact with this guy in the packing room, and he started getting busy. Well, it happened so fast after that—they realized the game was up. I put the NAACP on their tail, too, and they started a pressure campaign. In one year you wouldn't recognize the place.

Curtis McClain

In 1946, shortly after I left the military, I was hired on a temporary basis by Schmidt Lithograph, a multiunion house in San Francisco. They had a crew of sixteen or seventeen warehousemen, but they had a total work force of six hundred. I was the only black there.

When the person who was to return from vacation had an accident, John Munson, the company supervisor, asked me to work steady. He also kind of pissed me off by implying that I would either come late or wouldn't show up. "Don't forget," he said, "we always start at the regular time." I went into the paper seasoning department where work was heavy, hot, and dusty. Although it was the last place I wanted to work, I needed the job, so I stayed for fourteen years.

I liked working out of doors in the bull gang, which handled freight cars and trucks. This job paid more money on a straight-time basis, you had an opportunity to work overtime, and you could operate a lift or a jitney. But when I asked to be sent to the bull gang, I'd be told I was too important to be moved from the paper seasoning department. Someone else would then come in from the hall, would just happen to be white, and would work the bull gang and get the overtime pay.

As I acquired seniority in the plant, I tried to get into the trades as an apprentice, but that's where you really encountered the old runaround. You didn't get into the lithographers' or the printers' union. You didn't get into the electrical department. I saw many people come in, begin an apprenticeship, and become journeymen. I had electrical training, but I was never allowed into the trades.

So I was interested when a black caucus developed in Local 6 in 1947. We decided to meet on an informal basis to discuss problems that affected blacks and other minorities in the local. We discussed grievances we thought were not being handled properly. We often heard of people being bypassed for jobs. At that time you did not find blacks in the vast majority of the good classified categories.

There were also certain discharges we felt warranted greater attention from the officers. At least we felt this grievance was not being aired quickly enough. I'm not saying the union did not pursue discharges as such. But not all officers pursued them as they should have. So we wanted to band together, so it was not just one person approaching the officers or going to a meeting to deal with a problem.

When I say "we," I am referring to other black rank-and-file members of the union. There were no outsiders. All the people who attended these meetings were dues-paying members of Local 6. We started very small. There were five or six of us who met first and exchanged ideas. We expanded to twenty-five or thirty on the San Francisco side of the Bay. We had a close working relationship with white rank-and-file members in the local, but there were no white brothers in the caucus.

We reached twenty-five rapidly. I think we could have expanded to a much larger number if we had chosen to. The union was changing. There was a large influx of black people coming into the union. World War II was over. The shipyards were closing down. The warehouse industry offered a means of people obtaining employment.

Some of the new people had been stewards or had held leadership positions in other unions and were not satisfied just coming to membership meetings and playing the role of voting rank and filers without giving input into policies and programs. So we could have expanded the caucus to almost any number, but it remained small because we chose to keep it small. It was a group we thought we could work with.

When we formed, we had in mind to get organized for political purposes within the union. The term "black caucus" was really a name white trade unionists called us. We were not too upset because they called us a black caucus—after all, it was a group of black people coming together to discuss problems. But we constantly called ourselves the Frontiersmen. This was a club we set up so if we were questioned, there would never be any problem, because we sponsored dances and parties. We tied ourselves in with social activities within the community.

Clearly, though, the purpose of the Frontiersmen was to organize so we could elect an Afro-American to a full-time position and address the grievances taking place. I was the person elected as business agent in 1960. But there were appointments—field representatives, organizers—made prior to my being elected when some of the longshoremen joined with us to approach the International.

The first Afro-American organizer appointed was Roland Corley in the Redwood City division of Local 6. Also, the union began to have shop committees push more for promotions by seniority. This had been union policy all along, but in reality it had not necessarily worked out in the past.

At the time we formed the Frontiersmen Club, it was sorely needed within the local. We did a great deal of good, not only for the black union members, but for the union as a whole. We learned some of the fears and concerns of the union people, both black and white. After serving its purpose, there was no need to continue with the organization. It dissolved after fourteen years. Things had worked out as they should have been, in a more democratic fashion. We were now working together on the job, forming good house committees and a strong steward system, and electing people who were going to work for the whole union.

LEROY KING: THE EQUAL RIGHTS STRUGGLE AND LABOR POLITICS

After experiencing racism in his youth, former ILWU Local 6 secretary-treasurer, northern California regional director, and International representative

LeRoy King fought discrimination for six decades. He also specialized in expanding the ILWU's influence in the wider community and in the political arena beyond the union.

Leroy King

I was born in Fresno, California, in 1923. My background is African American, Cherokee, and Irish. My father worked for the Southern Pacific Railroad for forty-five years. He laid bricks in them steam engine boilers.

Fresno was a racist town when I was growing up. We lived on the other side of the tracks, the west side. We went to school with mostly Mexicans and blacks. You couldn't go across the tracks until later years when they broke segregation down. The police was very rough back then. At the theaters in town, we had to sit upstairs. The whites sat downstairs.

In 1941 I moved to San Francisco. We had our own segregated thing in the city's Fillmore District then. A bowling alley and a theater were nearby. That section was for whites only. They talk about the South, but you had the South right here in San Francisco. The struggle for breaking this down came after World War II.

In the early 1940s I learned how to weld and be a boilermaker at Kaiser Shipyard in Richmond. The boilermakers had a segregated union then. I was at Kaiser for a little bit, then left there and worked at Marin Shipyard in Marin City until I was drafted into the army.

Basic training was at Fort Sill, Oklahoma. I'd never been south. When we got to Brownwood, Texas, they said we could no longer all eat together and that the blacks had to get in the back of the train. That was the first time I felt Southern segregation.

At Fort Sill I was put into an ammunition supply unit. It was segregated, too. We couldn't have a gun, we couldn't have nothing. All we could do is handle ammunition. In 1944 we went overseas and moved up near the front lines. We were loading trucks and supplying ammunition like the devil. German planes flew over regularly to drop bombs on us. Through all this, our unit remained segregated.

After the war we sailed home to a camp in New Jersey. People were friendly on the ships going overseas and returning, but the racism came back at that New Jersey camp. Any time a couple of blacks would go by some of these white

Three warehouse Local 6 stalwarts picketing in San Francisco, 1971. *Left to right:* Curtis McClain, Keith Eickman, and LeRoy King. Photo by Sid Roger. ILWU Library.

guys' barracks, those whites would come out and taunt them. One Saturday we had so many fights—we had to fight every day.

When the young blacks left the army, they challenged segregation and changed San Francisco from being a racist town. We had demonstrations on Fillmore Street and along Auto Row. All that was led by these young black soldiers who came back. They felt like me—I served my country; I did everything I could to try to make this a decent place and make sure we got rid of fascism. So when we came back home, we figured there'd be some change.

I got discharged, came back to San Francisco, and went down to the department of employment. There I met Julius Stern, who was recruiting for the ILWU. He sent me to warehouse Local 6. I went out to Edward's Coffee and worked in the warehouse unloading one-hundred-pound green coffee sacks. I'd stack them up for the roasters. There was various other work—roasting, blending coffee, loading boxcars. But my first job was unloading that green coffee. I was at Edward's for four years.

Two progressive Local 6 white guys, Henry Glickman and Clarence Paton, used to hold meetings every noontime near Edward's. This was before the warehouse strike we had in 1949. They'd organize demonstrations, have people stop work, all that stuff. Not many blacks were active in Local 6 then. Those two guys were trying to get the young blacks involved.

Glickman used to say, "You gotta go to union meetings, you gotta do this, you gotta do that." This got me interested in the union. My interest peaked when four hundred of us got fired after a stop-work protest over grievances the coffee house refused to settle.

In 1951 I married Clarence Paton's daughter Judy. I met her at the California Labor School that closed in the mid-1950s.[18] Clarence's brother, Eugene Paton, was the president of Local 6. He'd been one of the union's key leaders before the war. So that's how I got really involved.

I began to get into politics, something I'd always been interested in. My folks were very religious, and their church was active in politics as a way to get certain things done. I got mostly into San Francisco politics, like the mayors' and supervisors' races.

Around the same time, the union started a systematic church-labor movement where we worked with the black churches getting politicians elected. Bill Chester, a black leader out of Local 10, became ILWU northern California regional director in 1951. He led the church-labor effort, and I was part of it. So were Ed Becks, Revels Cayton, Roland Corley, Curtis McClain, and Richard Moore.

The right wing tried to attack our church-labor program with red-baiting in the McCarthy era. The Right didn't like Harry Bridges or our union. They didn't like it when we got Paul Robeson concerts in black churches after he was denied at the San Francisco opera house. This was about 1947. Paul was a great black singer who was associated with the Left. We took up his cause. I remember how my wife and all the women stood guard around Paul at the Booker T. Washington Hotel.

Dave Beck, the Teamsters International president, used McCarthyism, too, when he raided Local 6 in San Francisco around 1950. I was put on as an International organizer to help stop the raid. That job lasted about a year and a half. I went around making sure our warehouses were organized, and I got the churches and the community to support the ILWU.

The Teamsters kept picketing us, so we mobilized our membership. Finally there was a big battle at United Grocers. Paul Heide led us. He was a great Local 6 organizer and leader from the 1930s. Paul hit this Teamster, George

Pedrin, over the head. Blood spurted everywhere. Pedrin and a few others had left Local 6 to join the Teamsters and raid us. That battle broke the Teamsters from picketing any more of our warehouses.

When my wife and I first got married, we tried to get housing in San Francisco. But as soon as the landlord found out we were an interracial marriage, we'd get kicked out. Luckily, Vince Hallinan owned some apartments. He was one of our attorneys in the early 1950s during the trial of Harry Bridges and two other ILWU men, Bob Robertson and Henry Schmidt. I was northern California chair for the Bridges-Robertson-Schmidt defense committee. One day I mentioned my problem to Vince, and he gave us housing. We had moved nine times the year before that.

My major early thing in Local 6 was serving on the board of trustees. I did that for about fifteen years in the 1950s and 1960s. Betty DeLosada and I led an effort that brought the local's finances under more rank-and-file control.

The black guys also organized a group to get more of us involved in the union. It was about ten or twelve. This was around 1950. Basic guys was Roland Corley, Curtis McClain, Revels Cayton, Leon Cooper—mostly young blacks. Bill Chester helped us from his post as regional director. We were called the Frontiersmen. We took on some issues to make sure we'd get some black leadership in the local.

The first big struggle was over running for office. To get elected business agent, you had to run for an individual slot. Eliminating these A, B, C, and D business agent slots meant everybody would have to run at large. The way it was before, guys who had not had opposition for years just campaigned for that one guy we ran someone against. That blocked out the black candidate.

Keith Eickman supported our position. He was a young white guy coming up then. Keith became a business agent with our backing before we could get a black elected. Then, at this big membership meeting, Keith spoke out from the officers' platform saying to eliminate A, B, C, and D. He was one of a mixed, progressive group we had in the local.

It was a big fight, but we broke up the A, B, C, and D system. Candidates now had to run at large, so everybody had to run on his own. We got newer people in and gave 'em an opportunity. In 1960 Curtis McClain became the first Local 6 black to get elected business agent. The next year I was appointed International representative.

During the 1960s civil rights movement, we had a big demonstration when these four young ladies were killed by a bomb in a black church in the South.

We had about sixty thousand people march in San Francisco. This was part of our church-labor movement.

When Martin Luther King, Jr., came to San Francisco in 1967, we had a big thing around him. Local 10 gave him an honorary membership, and we had a big rally in Oakland at Sweet's Ballroom. Harry Belafonte sang. Bill Chester planned a lot of this, and I was involved. Bill and I were very close. Everything he did, I was right there with him.

I also helped Louis Goldblatt, our International secretary-treasurer, when we set up St. Francis Square, the integrated San Francisco housing cooperative I've lived in myself since 1963. We worked on it for years until it finally opened.

In the late 1960s Revels Cayton, Bill Chester, Dave Jenkins from our union and I met with Joseph Alioto, who was a candidate for mayor of San Francisco. He was a lawyer who had represented the rice growers in the Central Valley. [The ILWU had contracts with rice processors near Sacramento.] He'd been pretty fair, and we knew him. Alioto said, "If you guys go with me, I'll be loyal to the ILWU. I'll appoint blacks to commissions and I'll have somebody black in my administration. When appointments are needed, black and white, I'll run 'em by the union."

So we decided we'd support Alioto, who won and kept his word. He appointed Revels Cayton deputy mayor. Several appointments of ILWU guys to San Francisco commissions followed—Joe Johnson was named deputy mayor after Revels—and we got real influence in city politics.

We've supported and worked with San Francisco's current [2002] mayor, Willie Brown, too, ever since he first ran for assemblyman way back. We wanted some black representation, and he qualified. He was a friend of labor for years in the state assembly.[19]

I didn't want any part of those city commission appointments myself because I liked working out in the community and in the union. But I did get appointed to San Francisco's Economic Development Advisory Council in 1978. I finally agreed to be on the Redevelopment Agency Commission in 1980 after Mayor Dianne Feinstein beat me up about it. I've been on there twenty-two years now.

Feinstein wanted me to help Wilbur Hamilton, a member of ILWU ship clerks Local 34, who became the director of the Redevelopment Agency in the late 1970s. A lot of minority residents of the city's Western Addition got moved out during redevelopment. Wilbur did a good job trying to make sure they got back and into affordable housing. Some of them did, but not all of them.

They'd already been moving people out of another area south of Market Street when I came onto the Redevelopment Commission. This was to make room for a new development called Yerba Buena Center. When I joined the commission, I criticized the use of eminent domain to tell people they had to move.

An ILWU veteran named George Woolf led a group of retired longshoremen and other south-of-Market residents in a movement called Tenants and Owners in Opposition to Redevelopment [TOOR]. They demanded affordable housing. One result was the building of Woolf House, named after the TOOR leader, that provided some beautiful places right across from the Yerba Buena Center.

When I went on the Redevelopment Commission, I was secretary-treasurer of Local 6. I'd followed Bill Chester as northern California regional director in 1969 when he became an International vice president. I was regional director from 1969 until I retired in January 1992, except for 1977 to 1981, when I served as Local 6 secretary-treasurer.

As regional director, I used to travel from Bakersfield to the Oregon border. In the 1970s we took some people into the ILWU from plants around Fresno and Delano. These were mostly white workers at cotton-processing mills.

We also had a big organizing push in Salinas in those days. I worked on that one for seven years. We reorganized Shillings, a company that had moved to Salinas from San Francisco, where they'd been a Local 6 house. We went after a new Nestle Chocolate plant, too. Ole Fagerhaugh and Felix Rivera, two of our organizers, and I stayed in Salinas a lot. There were five hundred workers involved. They were all in Local 6 at one time.

I've also been active for years in the union's regional political action arm, the Northern California District Council [NCDC]. NCDC has often been influential in the state legislature. Once, we got Assemblyman Willie Brown to rewrite a whole bill so it provided better funding and protection for the ferry workers in the IBU. That was in the 1980s, when the IBU had only recently affiliated with the ILWU.[20]

Through NCDC we've also fought for legislation to improve worker safety, workman's compensation, disability insurance, and many other things. We didn't fight just for economics and pork chops for our union. Instead, we used our legislative committee and NCDC to benefit the whole community and to protect things like civil liberties and civil rights.

We relied on NCDC for wider unity with the rest of the labor movement, too. Before 1988, when we were not in the AFL-CIO,[21] Don Watson, another longtime NCDC activist, and I always used to attend the legislative conferences of the California State Federation of Labor. Even back when the other unions disagreed with some of our programs, like our opposition to the Vietnam War, we were there with our recommendations.

COTTON COMPRESS IN THE CENTRAL VALLEY, 1937–1938

The ILWU's cotton compress jurisdiction in California's interior can be viewed as an extension of the march inland. Two years after the '34 strike, workers established an ILA cotton compress local at San Pedro. To protect that local, which became part of the new ILWU-CIO, during 1937–38 the CIO United Cannery, Agricultural, Packing and Allied Workers of America (UCAPAWA) organized compress workers inland from the Port of Los Angeles with ILWU backing. This was a case of left-of-center CIO unions helping each other.

In the 1920s most skilled compress workers in California were African Americans from the South and Southwest. Soon Mexican Americans also became California compress men. For decades, these two groups made up the majority of the Central Valley's compress workers. Most were hired seasonally.

Cotton compressing, which involved reducing the size of five-hundred-pound cotton bales for shipment and storage, was hard, dangerous work in the 1930s. Bales were hand-trucked to the block, which held a huge compressor. Specialized workers—cottons cutters (or samplers); lever pullers, who activated the press; band shovers, who handled sturdy bale holders; and cotton tiers and sewers—worked quickly and skillfully.

George Lee, who was in San Pedro in 1936, Ernest Clark of Fresno, and Tommy Burse of Bakersfield remember nonunion conditions. Elijah Fifer, Burse, and Ollie Lewis recall an early walkout in 1937 and unionization the next year at the San Joaquin Compress Company of Bakersfield. These men were all black workers.

George Lee

Organizing cotton compress workers in the Valley was a little like it must have been to organize in Mississippi. Cotton was a southern industry. The supervisors and foremen were mainly from the South, the whole company leadership

ILWU members working a cotton compress, Central Valley, 1947. ILWU Library.

was southern. Many of the workers had worked in the compresses back in Texas, Oklahoma, and Arkansas. When they followed the industry out here in the 1920s and 1930s, they brought that whole southern thing with them.[22]

Ernest Clark

I was at Anderson-Clayton's new Fresno compress in 1937. They were slave drivers. You would walk through a plant and see a foreman just standing right over atop of a man; he just working for his life, just driving for life. The foreman just be standing right over him, saying, "Do it, do it, do it, do it!" If the man frown, don't say nothing, the foreman'd say, "Go off and get your check!"

You were working for nothing, thirty to thirty-five cents an hour. There was no machinery. Them people was picking up five-hundred-pound bales of cotton, stacked 'em on top of one another, trucking cotton with hand trucks, running all day. You checked in at eight o'clock and you run 'til noon, pushin' that bale of cotton on a truck with iron wheels.

When they first built this Anderson-Clayton plant, some of the sheds didn't have paved floors, just dirt, dust and dirt. And you imagine a hand truck with a five-hundred-pound bale of cotton on it, and you're pushin' and pullin' it through that dirt. Or they'd be loading railcars with bales of cotton off the press—they'd have them piled three high in there, with guys up there on their knees, with three-foot clearance, rolling that cotton around for hours and hours without a break.

Man, with this weather up above one hundred degrees, and the press runnin' maybe 150 bales an hour, they'd have four, five guys up there pushing that cotton around. It was absolute slavery. It killed many a man. I mean, not actually took his life, but just broke down in his back, in the legs, just wrecked men.

Tommy Burse

When I first started at San Joaquin Compress of Bakersfield in 1933, they didn't have no union. If you was a cotton cutter, band shover, tier, head sewer, lever puller, any of those crafts, it didn't make no difference. The superintendent over there, name of Carl West, if he found someone better than you was, he could say, "Don't come back tomorrow. I got a man to take your place." Only after we got the union, we got to the place where we had some seniority.

We had a block foreman out there one year, name of Rip something-or-other. This Rip was a driver; he was a hard man. He wanted everyone to run with them hand trucks. He had this record player by the press, and he would put this whole stack of records on it, mostly what we called colored records, jazz.

Rip would have us runnin' ourselves to death, tripping all over one another to get back to that music. Until they caught on, which was pretty soon, and they made away with that music. That was around the time the union came in. Guys said, "We got a union in here now, we don't have to do all that rippin' and runnin'."

Elijah Fifer

I came to Bakersfield in September 1935 and went to work out at San Joaquin Compress that October. I was from Texas and had worked in compresses a little. That's what got me on pretty quick—I already understood it.

If you did something they didn't like, they'd push you out. The superintendent wasn't as bad as the foreman he brought in, a white man named Tex. He was one rough bugger. I'm glad he came in here because he was so nasty, he made us organize faster.

Tex got off a freight train, just the same as me. He got off there sometime in 1935 and come over here and wanted a job. He didn't know nothing about no press. He was really nice, you know, getting in here. Guys learned him everything, so he got to be block foreman. And then he got tough. If he didn't like a guy, he'd lay him off. He and I could never get along. I don't know why, since I've always been pretty easy with people. He would just keep aggravating. He'd move you around and get you in trouble with some other foreman. He just kept the pressure on all the time.

The speed-up was the worst thing. Tex'd get in and tie cotton like the devil for a few minutes, get the machine flying, and walk away. It was really on account of Tex we walked out. We wasn't asking nothing, and he was just making it so hard on us. We was working ten hours a day, straight time, and if you didn't come in one day, they'd be likely to lay you off for a week.

So in 1937 we got to talking about a walkout—me, Walter Foster, Kenneth Gatewood, a man named Walker, and some Mexican guys. You know, the bunch I was with were in sympathy with all those early '30s strikes. In 1935 we used to go out to support the cotton strike at Shafter, close to Delano. So we knew a little when we started to talk walkout.

We knew we had to be pretty secretive. We had a signal all worked out, which was when the leverman blew the whistle, we just stopped the press. He blew the whistle twice—it was during the night shift, around 10 P.M., and everyone quit. It was pretty surprising. Even I was surprised, because, you know, we were a pretty mixed-up bunch, Mexicans and blacks, and nobody thought we could get this together. Nobody expected S. G. Emby, the lever puller, to walk out with us either, but I knew he would because I had talked to him beforehand.

Tommy Burse

The walkout was at a time of year when they had a lot of work, and for us to stop pressing fouled things up way down the line. So when the superintendent, Carl West, found out that we had quit, he came down out of his office. He cussed at us. He swore all the time. "Goddamn it," he said, "what you want?"

Somebody called out, "Mr. West, we want a nickel more an hour." "God*damn*," he says, "you don't want nothing. I thought you was striking for something. Y'all get back to work."

See, that was before we got the union. We was just getting into it, not knowing how things was going to be. We could have got ten to fifteen cents if we had asked for it, but we were afraid to lose the whole thing. Besides, we thought five cents was pretty big money.

Elijah Fifer

People were afraid that when we walked out, West would fire us all. But there was only a few compresses in the state and help wasn't plentiful like it was in the South with people who understood the compress. We got them in the middle of the season. Head sewers, lever pullers, cotton tiers, they was hard to get. We knew that. We knew all the skilled people had jobs. We did our homework. We didn't go into it just blind.

We didn't have no union yet, so Walter Foster called a guy who worked at the laborers' union. They sent an old black guy out of the waiters' union up from Los Angeles to talk to us. He come up two or three times to tell us to organize and about the advantages we'd get. I heard afterwards that the longshoremen were helping him.

Pretty soon after that, Hursel Alexander, a black CIO organizer from Los Angeles, came up to organize us into UCAPAWA [United Cannery, Agricultural, Packing and Allied Workers of America] Local 272. He was one of the best talkers you ever seen. Everybody liked him. He meant business, too. He'd really fight for the men.

Ollie Lewis

I was working at San Joaquin in 1938 when Alexander came to organize. We were really green, so I tried to learn as much as I could. Hursel was a labor man—he knew all the laws, all the ins and outs. At the time there was John L. Lewis of CIO and other guys like that, and they were trying to school us about the power that labor had. They was mostly drillin' us to be good labor people. And, of course, Hursel told us how they was payin' more in other places.

We voted in the union, struck for three days, and won a contract with better wages, overtime, holiday pay, seniority, and a grievance system. After that, we began to get very particular about the hours, gettin' time and a half and so on. And 100 bales an hour became the production standard—the boss might get 103 or 105, or 97, but he wouldn't be gettin' no 125 bales like he used to. He would get a fair day's work, that's all.

THE ILWU ENTERS THE VALLEY, 1951–1952

The ILWU expanded into Central Valley cotton compressing in the 1950s, initially in Bakersfield and later in Fresno. During 1949–50, the national CIO, stampeded by McCarthyism, purged its most progressive unions for alleged Communism. Those ousted included the ILWU and the Food, Tobacco, Agricultural and Allied Workers (FTA), formerly the UCAPAWA-CIO of the 1930s, which represented Bakersfield's San Joaquin Compress employees. The purge devastated the FTA, but the ILWU stayed strong and aided the isolated Bakersfield unionists in San Joaquin. During 1951 George Lee and Chet Meske, who was white, organized the formerly FTA San Joaquin group into ILWU warehouse Local 26.

Lee and Meske then unionized the nearby Calcot Plant. In 1957 the ILWU used its Bakersfield base to organize Fresno-area compresses as well. Here Lee and Meske describe organizing in 1951. Dave Burciaga, who was Hispanic, remembers that one reason for the ILWU's appeal at San Joaquin was its policy of nondiscrimination. Meske, Sterling Green, who was black, and Lee reflect on a 1952 strike at Calcot.

George Lee

When Chet Meske and I were organizing in the Valley in 1951, we'd go to the plant at noon, find the key skilled people who had influence, and talk to them at night to get their point of view. We'd put out a leaflet and go back and ask 'em how the leaflet was received among the workers. If something was wrong, we'd correct it in the next leaflet.

We met at Kenneth Gatewood's house in Bakersfield. He was a key person at Bakersfield's San Joaquin Compress, and he was the strongest guy in the Valley. San Joaquin was the first place organized into ILWU Local 26 because of Gatewood and his friend Elijah Fifer.

At these meetings we'd tell the workers, "These people are robbing you, stealing your labor. They gettin' rich, and the only protection you have is to act in unity. You can't stand alone—you have to have a union to support you."

The workers trusted me. I'd worked in the industry and was considered one of their own. They were black and Mexican, and Chet was white, but he did all right because he spoke the workers' language. He knew what it meant to suffer and be punished.

Chet had spent a lot of time in New Orleans. He was able to relate to how unjust it was there. And he had a unique way of organizing. Chet went to people's houses. He'd sit down at their table, eat their food, and make himself part of them. Most organizers want to talk to a guy in a restaurant or on the picket line. Chet would visit a guy at his house and stay for hours. Most people don't find the time.

Chet Meske

Many organizers would call a meeting in the hall right away and push cards under people's noses. I'd get one or two names, and I didn't want more than one or two on the first initial meeting. Then I'd get another two, and I'd get additional information. So when I'd call a big meeting, I'd know the ins and outs within that plant. I'd know the grievances, what the workers were getting, and what I could offer.

Another thing in my favor was that we had a cotton compress organized in Local 26 on the L.A. waterfront. The Valley compress workers knew about the conditions we had in the harbor. Some of them originally came from that area. So it got around. That helped. And I had strong guys on my side like Gatewood and Fifer.

Dave Burciaga

I was working at San Joaquin Compress in Bakersfield in 1951 when the AFL butchers' union and ILWU Local 26 were on the NLRB [National Labor Relations Board] ballot to decide representation. The butcher guy, Hudson, came over once. I asked him, "How many Mexican and black butchers do you have in your union working at the stores?" He tried to bullshit me. I said, "No, answer me." He walked away and never came back to San Joaquin. The butchers got on the ballot, but they didn't get any votes.

Chet Meske

At Calcot Compress in Bakersfield we got a contract, but when we tried to renew it in 1952, we had trouble. We had a negotiating committee of five, and we walked into the office. F. W. Frick, the president of Calcot, said, "We're not going to negotiate with you. Who the hell are you?" He opened the desk drawer, took out a gun, and asked, "Why don't you get out of here before I use this?" I'd keyed the guys in ahead of time that if we don't get anywhere, we're gonna walk out.

So we walked out of the office with our hands up. The workers saw that, and right away the steam was cut off. About two hundred men followed us out the gate. We set up a picket line. Then they started importing white scabs from the South.

I tried to persuade the scabs not to go into the plant. When they were in front of Calcot in cars, I opened one car's door and started talking. The driver began to move ahead slowly. The sheriff was waving them in.

I twisted this guy by the ears, then reached for a guy in the back seat. The cop pulled me out, and the scabs drove in. I didn't know it, but the owners were prepared. There were photographers on the roof snapping pictures right and left. All the newspapers were there. So I was hauled away and had to go to court and pay a fine.

Sterling Green

When the '52 strike came, I was the chief steward at Calcot. They brought them scabs in here in boxcars. They fixed the place out at the plant for 'em to sleep and eat. The scabs were some of everything—white guys, Mexicans, a few blacks. Maybe twenty-five or thirty scabs came. Some left. They said they didn't know they was comin' into something like that.

I was the picket captain during the strike. Our guys was very good, although we had one man, "Papa" Hayes, a lever puller, who slipped in to work. He tried to get me to take a gang into the cotton yard and sample and tag cotton. Then trucks would bring it in. I said, "I ain't gonna do nothin' like that. I'm with the men."

George Lee

For a while after the '52 strike Calcot still didn't want to recognize Local 26, and they wouldn't give us a decent contract. They fired a lot of people who the

NLRB ordered reinstated with back pay because the company had violated the law against discriminating against people involved in union activity. The company was also ordered to recognize Local 26 and bargain in good faith.

Eventually we got the union shop at Calcot. G. H. Mullins, the superintendent, said, "George, I'm tired of fighting you and Chet. I got a car, I got a plane, but goddamn it, I can't keep them if I keep fighting you and Chet, 'cause I can't prove I'm doin' my job! So I won't put it in the contract, but every card you show me, I'll deduct the dues." So we went for that for a long time.

Sterling Green

After the '52 strike Calcot tried to cheat us out of the back pay the NLRB told them to give our members. The boss offered to pay me mine but said, "Don't say nothin' to the rest of 'em." I said, "No, you're goin' to pay all of us." So he paid.

Then he tried to fire me. "Don't be for you," he said, "I wouldn't have to pay all these men their back pay. You're fired." And he just walked away. But I knew he couldn't fire me, 'cause if he did, the whole union would have got in behind him. So I kept workin'. He didn't come back, never did bring it up again.

The union was still strong after the strike. Anything come up, all I had to do was tell the company I'm gonna stop the works. And the men were willing to stop. They always told me, "Green, whatever you say, we're with you." I know from that they was strong.[23]

5

AGRICULTURE

HAWAII

LATE IN WORLD WAR II, THE ILWU BEGAN ORGANIZING HAWAII'S SUGAR AND pineapple plantations. The union wanted to strengthen its waterfront position in the Islands by unionizing agriculture, Hawaii's economic center at the time. Beyond this strategic concern, ILWU leaders knew that the Islands' agricultural workers had been exploited for decades, deserved better, and might respond positively to unionization.

Still, organizing Hawaii promised to be a tall order. The union's foothold on the waterfront, never very strong in the 1930s, had become more tenuous during the early war years when the Territory of Hawaii came under military rule and labor rights were pushed aside. (Hawaii did not become a state until 1959.)

The division of Hawaii's agricultural workforce into segregated ethnic camps also challenged efforts to organize. Perhaps most important, the union would be up against Hawaii's Big Five, a tightly knit group of holding companies with great economic and political power that had controlled the Islands' plantations and run them like medieval fiefdoms since the end of the nineteenth century.[1]

Yet, during 1944–46, the organizing drive succeeded overwhelmingly. It also brought a complete social, economic, and political transformation to Hawaii that dramatically improved life for thousands of workers and their families.

CARL DAMASO: UNION HERALD, 1930–1940

Carl Damaso was a Filipino immigrant sugar worker and contract laborer who tried to help bring unionism to Hawaii's agricultural fields a decade before the ILWU's late wartime and postwar triumph. His years of struggle culminated with his becoming president of the Islands-wide ILWU Local 142 between 1964 and 1981.

Damaso suspected that the multiethnic unionism the ILWU eventually brought to the Islands was the only kind that could survive. Still, he supported attempts at single-nationality organization as they came along during the mid-1930s. The planters responded by firing Damaso and blacklisting him, or labeling him "do not hire." He finally found work on the Honolulu waterfront, where he became an ILWU longshoreman in 1946 and served as an Oahu ILWU official from 1950 to 1963.

Here Damaso focuses on pre-ILWU working conditions and the organizing efforts he backed in the mid-1930s. His story reveals the difficulty and heartbreak of trying to bring union representation to the Islands in those years.

Carl Damaso

I came to Hawaii when I was fourteen years old, in 1930. My first destination was as a plantation worker at Olaa Sugar Company on the Big Island of Hawaii. There was no union there. It was really hard for the workers.

Most of the Filipinos in Hawaii then were concentrated in field work. They were sugarcane cutters or cane railcar loaders. The plantation management just set the price. You could say nothing. If you raised a question about wages or any sort of grievance, the managers would throw you out.

I had all kinds of objections to how things were. There was this big segregation. The Filipinos were concentrated in one camp, the Japanese in another camp. The Portuguese were the first-class citizens. They got the better jobs. Despite this segregation and other bad conditions, you couldn't fight back much. People were scared. You had to obey what the company said or be out of a job.

My first dream was to be organized under one strong union, but there was no unified labor organization for plantation workers in 1930. By 1932 Pablo Manlapit was trying to organize the Filipino sugar workers, but his organization

Cutting sugarcane, Hawaii, 1953. ILWU Library.

wasn't too liberal. I felt that if we were just organizing Filipino workers, it didn't make sense, because the Filipino group alone could not succeed in a strike in the sugar industry.

Manlapit did not have too much success organizing just Filipinos. Most important, though, the workers were beginning to realize that labor organization would be all right, but not strictly on the basis of one race, as had been the case in Hawaii before.[2]

In 1934 the managers began asking me what I did after my days of work, and especially on Sundays, our one day a week off. After working hours and on Sundays, I'd devoted time to Manlapit. The managers wanted to know if I was interested in becoming a "liberator." I told them, "That's not my plan."

By 1934 I was one of the fastest cane cutters in Olaa. The field boss said if you were fast, you deserved an incentive. I figured I was supposed to get a bonus. But on payday it didn't come to me. That went on and on. So I worked faster. Then one day I felt rotten, so I just worked at the pace of the old guys.

The field boss said, "What are you doing? That's not the way you work every day." I told him, "I can't work fast 'cause I'm not feeling good. On top of that, I've been cheated many times. You didn't live up to your promise." He started swearing. I asked him, "What do you want me to do, kill myself?"

I had no choice but to argue with him. He was calling me a bastard and every damn thing. Finally I hit him with a sugarcane. I tried to explain about the situation to the plantation managers, but they didn't want to listen. They said, "Pack your clothes and go. We don't need you anymore."

That afternoon and night I met with workers from all the various Olaa Sugar Company camps for miles around. The next day half the people didn't show up to work.

The managers called the police. The cops said I had to leave the camp or go to jail. So I told 'em, "I got no money, I don't have a place to go. Give me time to call the Philippine government to find out what they can do. I have to try to settle this as a labor dispute or else go back to the Philippines." They gave me until the following day.

The Philippine government sent over one of their resident commissioners. We had a meeting with the Olaa managers. They agreed to reinstate the strikers without any charges, except for me. I was fired.

I stayed in a secluded place, but one afternoon I had to go to the camp where I had belonged because I had my parents there. I had to sneak in to eat with them. Somebody knocked at the door. My brother opened it up. It was the head of the plantation camp police plus two government cops. I couldn't even finish my meal. They just said, "You need permission to come in here." They grabbed me and locked me in jail for forty-eight hours.

Now I had to leave the Big Island. I had no money, but my friends and my brother raised forty bucks for the twenty-two-dollar boat fare to Maui plus eighteen dollars extra for me and my wife. We'd just been married. At Maui I didn't get a job for five months.

In early 1935 I got a job at Wailuku Sugar Company. I worked there as a cane cutter. It was the same old story, hard work for a dollar a day. You'd start work at six in the morning and go to six in the evening. They pushed the incentive idea again: "Cut a little bit faster, you'll get an incentive." But I knew it was the same old story.

Then the workers began to realize that this was too much. There were meetings in the clubhouse of two hundred to four hundred people to discuss what we could do. I sat down at one meeting like an innocent guy and didn't say a word. But one guy found out I was from Olaa. He started addressing me. I told him, "The only way we can improve our working conditions is to stay together and appoint someone to bring grievances to management."

I never knew that during the meeting, the Filipino camp police was sneaking in the back of the clubhouse. The next day, at five thirty in the morning, the camp police came knocking at my door. They said, "Pack your clothes and go to the manager's office."

When the manager said I'd have to leave the camp, I asked him, "What about my wife and kid? Can they stay here this month?" My wife had given birth to my son in late 1935. The manager said, "No, everybody must go, kid and all." We didn't even have a chance to pack. My wife was crying, but they just put a lock on the door and said, "Get out."

I went over to the local plantation office. The man there said, "I wish I'd known before I hired you that you were the instigator of the strike at Olaa." I was let go and was blacklisted. After that, my wife left me and took my kid with her. I had no chance to try to bring him up. That was the hardest thing.

I applied for jobs, but they wouldn't hire me. I tried to make a living shooting pool. Finally, in late 1936, I got hired at Hawaiian Commercial and Sugar Company. The man there said, "We'll put you to work, but any false move you make, that's it."

Then Antonio Fagel came along. He led another nationalistic Filipino organization, the Vibora Luviminda. That label came from a Filipino patriot's nickname plus the letters for key areas in the Philippines. One Sunday, Fagel's organization held a meeting that I attended. I asked, "Why organize only a Filipino group? We should involve all the other groups."

One morning in April 1937 all the cane cutters lined up and nobody moved. The workers had been cheated on wages. Twelve hundred of them engaged in a spontaneous sit-down strike. They were just sharpening their cane knives and wouldn't move. Nobody said a word. The assistant manager arrived in his Cadillac. He said, "Work, or you guys are all fired."

I didn't want to be seen by the assistant manager. But my mind and heart were pleading to fight for the common cause. So I negotiated for the guys. But the assistant manager said, "You guys should get a wage cut. You cut yourself. If you don't want to work, we'll make a cow pasture out of the sugarcane field, and you guys can go."

Then everybody went home. The strike was on. In the morning the camp police and the managers came to my house. They said, "We know the workers believe you. We'll give you a good job and a new car to drive. You'll join the camp police. Just convince all these guys to go back to work." I thought, "I'm not going to be a pig for you people." I said, "Give us our demands. That's all I'm asking for."

The third day of the strike they drove me from the camp. The camp police came, and I was strong-armed out. Soon all my leaders were evicted from camp, too. Finally they forced many strikers away. We were thrown onto Kahului Beach at the Maui Dry Goods Store.

The strike became a major confrontation that lasted three months. [Fagel assumed leadership as the strike progressed.] We tried to mobilize all the surrounding plantation guys to back us. We said, "Our struggle is yours. Whatever we come out with, you guys will benefit also."

We did sign a contract, but after the strike some in our leadership betrayed us. The agreement we'd reached went to the dogs. One guy entered Maui management. He got a gold car and joined the camp police. I was the only guy of my group who was unable to go back to work. Again I was blacklisted.

I took a ship to Molokai to look for a job there. I went to the pineapple camp at Hoolehua where I had friends. At two thirty in the morning, a camp manager knocked on the door. He asked, "Is Calixto Damaso here?" That was my name before I became a naturalized citizen. I answered, "I am, sir." He said, "Everyone pack your clothes, get out. This plantation is not a hotel. Move or I'm going to call the government police to lock you guys up."

We went to Kaunakakai. I labored there fishing for three months during late 1937. But I had no clothing, no food, no nothing. In 1938 I went to Honolulu. I told my friends, "As soon as I leave, try to find jobs. Don't say I was with you." They got jobs then. I think the managers decided, "As long as Damaso is not with you, we'll give you guys jobs."

I applied for a job at Waimanalo Sugar Company. The manager opened a drawer. There was my picture taken during the '37 strike. He said, "We're not hiring." When I heard they hired thirty-eight people the following day, I went back to see the manager again. He said, "You were the ringleader in '37. You think I'm going to hire you?"

I couldn't find a job, basically, in late '37, '38, and '39. This went on until 1940, when I got employed as a truck helper at the Ready Mix Concrete Company. Then I got a job for a year with American Stevedoring. During the war, 1942 to 1945, I worked for the Honolulu navy supply depot.

In 1946 I applied to Castle and Cooke Terminal as a stevedore and got hired. I was now an ILWU longshoreman. At Castle and Cooke I attended ILWU meetings, but because of my past record, I just sat and listened until we took a strike vote in 1949. Then I got active again. In 1950 I got elected Oahu longshore business agent.

When I was in the ILWU, I began to realize that my dream had come true. I started from the hard nuts of the laboring group, but now the workers were respected. And they realized that the only way for them to do better was through unity and understanding more about everyone.

JACK HALL: ISLANDS ORGANIZER, 1934–1951

Jack Hall was a major figure in ILWU history. He played a crucial role in bringing union power to the Islands and was Hawaii's ILWU leader from 1944 to 1969, when he was elected International vice president. Hall died in office at San Francisco in 1971.

Hall was a young Sailors' Union of the Pacific activist when he made Honolulu his home port in 1935. In 1937 he began organizing plantation workers into the CIO with ILWU backing. The following year, with the ILWU-CIO and the SUP-AFL feuding, he was expelled from the SUP, beaten by a Honolulu detective, and told of the Hilo Massacre on the island of Hawaii, where police shot and wounded fifty-one unarmed IBU and ILWU strike supporters.[3]

Undaunted, Hall kept organizing until World War II, when the declaration of martial law in December 1941 led to the suppression of union activity in the Territory of Hawaii. Strict general orders froze wages and suspended the NLRA and employer-employee contracts. Union membership plummeted. But in spring 1944, with military rule being relaxed, Hall became Hawaii ILWU regional director. Under his leadership the ILWU unionized nearly twenty-five thousand sugar plantation workers during 1944–46.

The ILWU quickly united Hawaii's diverse work force—Filipinos, Japanese, Portuguese, Chinese, Native Hawaiians, Puerto Ricans—into a multiethnic movement. The planters had imported various national groups over time as agricultural laborers.

In part to solidify the union's successful new multicultural approach, in

1947 Hall pushed toward the consolidation of scattered ILWU units into what became the powerful Islands-wide, multiethnic Local 142 four years later. Here Hall covers his early days in Hawaii.

Jack Hall

Many Hawaiian seamen were involved in the 1934 strike, which I happened to get into starting around Bloody Thursday, July 5. That was the day I hit San Francisco, coming up from Los Angeles. My ship tied up in L.A. and did not go on to San Francisco, so I went up by bus. I got there in time for all the excitement. The strike continued after July 5, and the Hawaiians were involved in large numbers. They ran almost as a group in San Francisco and were considered the toughest gang of guys on the waterfront when it came to going after scabs—"strikebreakers" as they call them politely.

Matson Navigation Company's schedules in the 1930s were such that a ship coming to Hawaii from the West Coast would hit Honolulu, then make every outport and come back to Honolulu, generally before going back to the coast. So it was quite common for people to get off in Honolulu and be replaced by others who had just continued to work around the islands. Of course, these people had local contacts, and the story of the 1934 strike was being spread.

In some Hawaiian ports, wages for longshoremen were as low as twenty-eight cents an hour before the waterfront in the Islands was organized after the strike. The Hilo, Big Island, longshore group included in those early days many Hawaiians and others who had gone to sea on Matson ships and were quite militant. They began the first efforts toward organization and were successful in 1935—after a series of job action strikes—in getting recognition from the company at Hilo and in getting some form of a contract.

It was not a very good contract, but at least it established some load limits that were comparable to West Coast load limits. These remained unchanged in Hilo until the 1960s. So Hilo, as a group of longshoremen, were always the most militant. I've always considered them the guys that really got started in the modern-day labor movement in Hawaii.

In most other areas people were frightened. This was particularly true in the ports on Kauai, which were run at Nawiliwili, Ahukini, and Port Allen and over at Kahului on Maui. There were no real efforts at organization in Kahului

Jack Hall speaking to sugar workers, Hawaii, about 1963. ILWU Library.

until after or toward the end of World War II, when military controls on labor went off and all the other ports were organized.

There were many outstanding leaders, but many of the rank and file were taken in by company paternalism. For example, even in the days at McCabe, Hamilton and Renny Stevedoring Company in Honolulu, when the guys were only making five and ten dollars a week, I remember Jack Guard, the manager, making sure that when anybody was broke they could come up and get five or ten dollars to feed the family.

Of course, those men were all indebted to McCabe. It took three elections to get representation rights there. But the Hilo group, on the contrary, I think primarily because of a close affinity to the seamen and so many of them being ex-seamen, had a militancy that was uncharacteristic of the rest of the Hawaiians.

Organizers came from Hilo to Honolulu in 1935 to assist the people in Honolulu that were trying to unionize. Guys like Harry Kamoku, Pat Ikeda, and a couple of others came up at the expense of the Hilo longshoremen. It was five dollars in steerage on Inter-Island steamer then.

I first came to Honolulu to stay in 1935. It's been my home base ever since I returned there from a trip to Port Allen after the 1936–37 maritime strike. When we had that strike, the SUP leaders on the mainland wanted us to bring the ships back, but I held up the *Lurline* in Honolulu. I was SUP sailors' delegate aboard. I said, "Who wants to be in San Francisco in November and December?" So we ended up with twelve ships tied up, including the *Lurline*, and about eleven hundred seamen on the beach.

This had a tremendous impact on the community in Honolulu. Strike headquarters was at the old St. Louis College down on College Walk that Bishop Alencastre had made available. So we had all the facilities there, and people were able to get by. We had a lot of quiet support from the community.

One of the best ways to get a few bucks for beer money, I soon found out, was to get a bundle of *Voice of Labor* newspapers and go around selling them on Hotel Street and in all the bars. The newspaper was five cents. I could always get a quarter or a dime or a half dollar. Eating was tough, but we made out a lot better, I'm sure, than they made out in some of the ports where they were fighting the rain and the cold.

After the '36–'37 strike, I made one round-trip to the coast on the old *Maui*, came into Honolulu, and found out that Port Allen had walked out. The whole port was shut down. The longshoremen called the SUP hall to see if they could get some help in setting up a union now that they were all on strike.

I was available, and Maxie Weisbarth, the SUP agent, asked me if I'd go to Port Allen. So I went over, and in a few days we were able to get the thing resolved with recognition and an initial contract. That contract wasn't much by today's [1966] standards, but it did recognize the Port Allen Waterfront Workers' Association.

Fortunately, somebody had had a little trade union experience—not an awful lot, I had only been a ship's delegate. Of course, I had put out the *Voice of Labor*, or helped put it out. I took it over shortly after that. Ed Berman was the guy that did most of the work on the *Voice of Labor* when it started.

The modern-day effort to unionize Hawaii's plantation workers began in March and April 1937 when Filipino labor leader Antonio Fagel, together with a number of close associates, one of whom was Carl Damaso, made efforts to organize the people on the island of Maui on a nationalist basis.

They came to the SUP and asked for help, so a couple of us went over and joined them in street rallies. There were some tremendous crowds with tremendous enthusiasm. We were, of course, trying to get them to move toward a multiracial union.

There were a number of people, particularly among the older Japanese, that were supporting the Filipino unionists, giving money through people they could trust. That organizing effort ultimately ended up in a strike. Lots of criminal charges were brought up. Although the strike was settled with a temporary victory in terms of wages, they didn't have the organizational structure to continue, and a lot of people were blacklisted and arrested. Some of the strike leaders sold out. But there was such a demand for organization among these people that word got out throughout the Islands.

The first real success in plantation organization came on Kauai later in 1937. It was an outgrowth of the organization of the longshoremen there, who had a close association particularly with workers at McBryde Sugar Company. They all had the same employer. This time the Japanese took control of the organizational efforts, although one of the very active Filipinos, Mauro Andaya, was the president over there.

We set this up as a CIO organization, Local 76 of UCAPAWA-CIO. We organized everybody, mill workers and all. At one point, McBryde had almost two thousand employees, and we had most of them signed up. Workers at the adjoining Kauai Pineapple Company were brought in soon. There Dick Bell, who was the manager, recognized the union.

At McBryde we had to go to the NLRB [National Labor Relations Board] to get recognition. Old John Waterhouse at McBryde wasn't about to recognize any union if he could get away with it. Len Wills, who was head of the NLRB in Hawaii, suggested we file just for those people that were clearly covered by the NLRA [National Labor Relations Act]. So we did file for a very narrow unit and a unit much narrower than the board finally handed down in the elections held at the tail end of World War II.

We won that McBryde election in 1940 and eventually got a contract at least recognizing the union and its right to handle grievances, have some protection against discrimination, and get some measure of job security. Not much more.

That was the beginning, and from McBryde we branched off into the adjoining plantations, Olokele and Kekaha to the west and Koloa and Lihue toward the east. The movement spread out primarily because the union was well established in the McBryde and Kauai Pine and Port Allen areas and had already become a political force. So we were riding high by 1940.

People with time on their hands and not much else to do really worked hard to organize. We used to go right into the camps, even though they had trespass laws, and defy them to throw us out. Sometimes they would take you out, but we went back in. Actually, I haven't been subjected to any violence since before the war, but there was a hell of a lot of it then. There were two occasions when they were out to knock me off on Kauai that have been confirmed by informed sources.

By 1941 we thought we were strong enough to win an election at Kekaha and lost it by a handful of votes. We had considerable organization developing at Koloa, and by developing, I don't mean just signing people up. We used to have lots of meetings and lots of interest. Meetings used to go on for five and six hours. In those days they had to be conducted in three and sometimes four languages, including two Filipino ones. You had to have discussion in Japanese and Ilocano, in English for the younger workers, and sometimes in Visayan.

On the Big Island we didn't do anything until we started this big drive at the tail end of '43. I was working for the Territorial Department of Labor then. But we consulted, and the longshoremen in Honolulu donated five thousand bucks out of their treasury and put on a task force to go to work down there, because you could feel it coming. People wanted to organize. They were very resentful of the wartime labor controls.

So this group of longshoremen went down there and started flying all over the island, barging into mills and shops, looking for contacts. There was some damage, because they were saying all you had to do is join the ILWU and you get longshore wages. We corrected that later on.

Finally the ILWU International sent Matt Meehan to Hawaii. Matt had been secretary-treasurer of the union in the '30s. He had known of me, and we spent some time together. When he left, he appointed me the regional director for the Islands. I started work in 1944. They also sent down Frank Thompson, who had been with Lou Goldblatt in many organizational campaigns in the West in timber and mining when Lou was secretary-treasurer of the California CIO [1937–43]. When Frank and I were given adequate funds, we just went step-by-step methodically. Didn't take long before we signed them all.

I think Olaa plantation on the Big Island was the first place to get complete organization. But we weren't concentrating on any one plantation. Initially the concentration was on the Big Island, although there'd been movement toward organization on Maui and Kauai, where our prewar beginnings had been eroded by military rule. Olaa went very fast. They had a cohesive group of young people, what they called the Surfriders. These young guys, like Saburo Fujisaki, put that one into shape first.

By the time the NLRB got into the picture to hold hearings, we had every plantation on the Big Island except Waiakea Sugar, where the company had signed a backdoor deal with the AFL covering the mill workers. Of course, we went ahead and organized the field workers.

In the big 1946 Hawaii-wide sugar strike we had meager resources, but the people had meager resources when they were working, too. In fact, in the '46 strike, many people were doing better than they lived normally. Many had had a very low diet in an attempt to save a little money. During the strike, there was a communal type of living. The first plantation communities here were ideally constructed for that. So when everybody was eating the same, some of their living standards slightly improved.

We, of course, enforced multiracial leadership, irrespective of abilities, which bothered some people, but you can't survive without multiracial leadership. We had everybody in the leadership in one fashion or another, and everybody felt a part of it. The employers didn't think we would survive, but I don't think they knew their own people.

When the employers saw they couldn't break the '46 strike, some of them wanted to fold. C. Brewer and Company, one of Hawaii's Big Five corporations, was hurting so bad they forced a settlement. It went far beyond the original demands in economic gains. After that, the employers figured, "Let's see, change the complexion of Congress, develop the Cold War, and McCarthyism." Perhaps they could break the union on a red-baiting campaign.

They began to hammer away and find every renegade they could. The 1947 so-called Ignacio Revolt on the Big Island—a red-baiting attempt to split the union—was directly financed by the employers. We know that from people that were on the inside and later broke from them, like Jacinto Conol, who gave us information about what was going on. We made out a program with Hilo that everybody was going to vote on to see if we would all stay ILWU. We threw all our forces into getting down to the rank and file. When the vote was over, we were still in business.

In 1951 I was indicted under the Smith Act.[4] The charge was advocating subversion. I think all these attacks just strengthened the union. Now [1966], there's a tremendous loyalty in the union for the leadership. I don't think they like everything, but they know what's happened. Nobody's going to get taken in by that sort of thing in this union in Hawaii anymore. It's historical fact made clear to every new member through the education program for leadership and union participation. So we have a tremendous ability when we go into negotiations. We don't have to look behind our shoulders to make sure the troops are there. We know they are.

LOUIS GOLDBLATT: THE ILWU TAKES ROOT, 1943–1946

Another major ILWU figure, Louis Goldblatt, served as the union's International secretary-treasurer from 1943 to 1977. He was known throughout his long career as a brilliant strategist and master negotiator. One of his most notable achievements came in the late 1950s when, following twenty years of ILWU tension with the Teamsters, he engineered a joint ILWU-Teamster warehouse bargaining council in northern California.

A former University of California graduate student, Goldblatt became a San Francisco warehouse worker shortly after the 1934 strike. He was elected vice president of ILWU warehouse Local 6 in 1937. During the next six years he served as secretary-treasurer of the California state CIO. In February 1942, two months after Japan's attack on Pearl Harbor, he told a congressional committee that the federal plan to intern U.S. mainland Japanese Americans was "hysteria and mob chant."

Upon taking office as ILWU International secretary-treasurer in 1943, Goldblatt evaluated the union's position in Hawaii. His analysis led to the big organizing drive and to his own subsequent role as a key figure in the Islands. Here he focuses on his early thinking about Hawaii and the union's initial success.

Louis Goldblatt

In 1943 I began to consider organizing in Hawaii beyond the waterfront jurisdiction we had in Hilo and Honolulu. I took office then as International secretary-treasurer and started going through material on the background of various locals.

We had gotten started in Hawaii in the organizing of longshoremen, first in Hilo around 1935 and then in Honolulu. In 1938 they took a bad setback in Hilo in the IBU Inter-Island Steam Navigation strike, with a number of people shot up and hurt. I read about the ILWU's long waterfront strike at Port Allen in 1940 that lasted damn near ten months. It got to the point where all the workers were living under a huge tent. The union salvaged recognition and little else. The thing that struck me was that in no case had we really made it over the hump.

In the case of Honolulu, they signed some sort of a makeshift agreement, which never became truly effective because in 1941 World War II came along, and that brought military rule to Hawaii. As far as the military was concerned, unions might be around, but you don't pay any attention to them. There had been some initial organization of plantations, mostly under Jack Hall's leadership. Still and all, we had never been able to get an effective base.

I recall doing a lot of reading on Hawaii and its closed structure. Not just longshoring, but everything from land, to banking, to insurance, to factories, to supplies, to shipping was dominated by the Big Five corporations. One of the conclusions I reached was that longshoring played a different role in Hawaii than it did on the mainland. Instead of being a general industry of longshoring, in Hawaii longshoring was just a branch of the Big Five.

Jack Hall and I later had lengthy discussions. We had both reached the same conclusion, namely, that by tackling longshore first in an effort to strengthen and widen organization in Hawaii, we would not succeed, even though longshore had the very direct appeal of being tied in with the same industry on the West Coast and had been organized and gotten ILWU charters in the 1930s.

Anyway, I was thoroughly convinced that Hawaii ought to be given a whirl. Initially we sent down Bill Craft, a longshoreman from Seattle, who reported that the workers wanted a union, and not just for the waterfront alone. We sent another old-timer, Matt Meehan, who had a distinguished record in Portland. He came back with a more detailed report and a positive recommendation that the individual who knew the greatest amount about the economy of Hawaii and about trade unionism and had already done a great deal of work was Jack Hall.

We hired Jack as regional director in 1944, and that's when organization really began. For a while we were sending all of our supplies by ships through seamen we knew. We didn't trust the mail. We opened a small storefront down off the waterfront in Honolulu. I think it was the street just before Maunakea, where the flower vendors are. That was the headquarters until we got going.

My first trip to Hawaii was in 1944. I remember going down there in the *Maunakai*, a big tub that carried fourteen thousand tons of cargo. It was awfully slow. When it did ten knots, that was good. It broke down during the trip, so an extra day was lost. They had put doghouses, sort of, on the afterdeck and carried a few passengers. Getting plane transportation was out of the question at the time with the war still on.

That's when I first met Jack. We hit it off well. There had been a lot of correspondence before then, back and forth, stressing the importance of trying to tackle the Big Five at its roots—that would be the land, agriculture. We agreed that the basic source of their power was sugar and pineapple. It was towards the tail end of the war, and the atmosphere of military rule by then was not that tight. So we began not only the rebuilding of the longshore union but mainly going after the plantations.

Resentment had piled up around the plantations and all through the society on the manner in which manpower had been handled during the war. A number of people wanted to get out of the jobs they were doing, like laundry jobs, and go to work in Pearl Harbor where better jobs were opening up. The military had frozen people on these laundry jobs so the colonel could have his shirt washed.

That was the situation when we got going on the organizational push. We began putting some money in. We decided we needed a guy in the field like Frank Thompson, who was as good an organizer as this country has ever seen. He was quite a character, an old-time Wobbly, a hardy, efficient guy with an endless amount of energy.

Frank worked well with Jack, although they didn't see too much of each other because Frank spent so much time in the field. As soon as the initial breakthroughs began and the word went out that the union was signing up people, everybody got into the act. There was a real wave of organization.

The waterfront fell into place very quickly. There wasn't too much of a problem there. At that point we had to do some heavy-duty thinking. Do you sign up everybody? What is the purpose if you can't follow through? The signing up itself is a very preliminary step toward genuine organization.

The big decision we had to make was, how wide could we scatter our forces? We only had so much money and manpower. Ultimately, the conclusion we had reached did not change—namely, we wanted to make the break primarily in sugar and secondly in pineapple.

We decided that we could not repeat the mistakes made in the past. Jack and

I knew a great deal about the whole background of lost racial strikes, if you want to call them that. So under no circumstances would we have a racial strike, no matter what the rate of speed in organizing one group as against another.

The Japanese were an active group and organized very quickly. The Filipinos were not too far behind. They would move with a lot of strength once they felt they were getting a straight and honest shake and that the union was going to do exactly what it promised, or try to.

We were spending a fair amount of money organizing, but it wasn't a lot, even for the time. I think we paid Frank seventy-five dollars a week. I don't know that Jack got much more. The whole thing was a very low-paid operation. With a few organizers, supplies we sent from the mainland, plus the volunteers who pitched in, I'd say that if you had to compare it to any organizing push in the history of the country, the cost of organizing one worker must have been one of the lowest ever.

I remember that in 1944 Frank did something very novel. Before NLRB elections for union certification took place, he would go to these plantations one by one and conduct a rehearsal election. He would put out a sample ballot, call a meeting, and say, "We are going to vote. Everyone gets a secret ballot." If the vote came out, say, 695 to 4, he'd say, "Okay, there are four people we've got to find. They somehow got screwed up." Well, the NLRB election results speak for themselves. We had entire plantations that voted unanimously.

In the fall of 1944 they had elections for the Territorial legislature. Jack had always been interested in the political offshoots of the whole economic situation in Hawaii, and particularly the domination of the legislature by the big employers. The legislative representatives were practically just stooges of the Big Five. Legislative sessions sounded more like a Gilbert and Sullivan show than a genuine legislature.

Well, in the '44 elections, under Jack's lead, we endorsed a great many candidates, and the results were highly favorable. One of the commitments we had where we made endorsements was that we would get a Little Wagner Act for Hawaii. We did get a Little Wagner Act in 1945 out of that legislature. It provided for collective bargaining elections for all agricultural workers. This included a lot of people not covered under the Wagner Act that Congress had passed ten years earlier to set up the NLRB.

Voting for candidates recommended by the union in '44 was a direct offshoot of the whole organizing campaign. It was also one of the beginnings of the sociological breakthroughs in Hawaii. It took a while before you even had the sociological breakthrough of some of our workers going into Waikiki just to have a drink. In those days that was a rare thing.

Waikiki was the tourist section. That was for *haoles* [whites]. Our guys felt they belonged down in the Kalihi district, River Street, a different section of town. I had to persuade guys to join me for dinner at the Tropics, which was then across from the Royal Hawaiian [Hotel]. So this was also the beginning of the sociological breakthroughs.

A lot of the plantations toppled into place, but the one outfit that did present a bit of a problem was Waialua Sugar Company on Oahu. Waialua had always been a very prosperous plantation with a good piece of land and plenty of water. It paid more than the other plantations. I recall getting a telephone call from the manager, John Midkiff, asking whether I would be interested in coming out for dinner. I said sure.

I think Jack Kawano of the Honolulu longshore local was with me that night. Midkiff was very pleasant. When we got through dinner, he got down to business. He said, "Look, I know what you fellows are after, you want the dues. I'll make arrangements where I'll send you the dues each month." I said, "We are not interested in the dues." He said, "Of course you are, that is what unions are all about."

I said, "No, we are interested in getting everybody organized. An organization means something else than collecting dues." He said, "Well, I don't think my people really want to belong." I said, "We know the general atmosphere around here and that you pay a bit more, and a lot of people feel pretty loyal on that score, but we're still convinced they want the union, and given a proper chance they'll join." He wasn't convinced. Plus he had this thing in his head we couldn't budge—the union wanted the dues, and if the union got the dues, what do we want to kick about?

When we got back, we sat around and talked about the conversation. We decided the only thing to do was bell the cat. The following Sunday we sent a group of organizers out there with cards. We said, "Start going house to house. If company cops or anybody else tries to stop you, call at once and we will have the lawyers run out there." There was no interference of any kind, and I'd say within a week or ten days we had Waialua organized. That was the only place I can recall running into real difficulty.

The workers lived in company camps on isolated plantations. These camps were divided in most cases by racial groups. That is the way the people themselves would talk about it: "Oh, that's the Filipino Camp, that's the Portuguese Camp, that's the China Camp," and so forth. As I said, though, we had made the decision that certain past mistakes would not be repeated. One would be no racial strikes. That meant there had to be a new interpretation of unit leadership, because if you are not going to have a racial union or racial strikes, you had to, if necessary, force integration of the leadership from the beginning.

Now I know better than to figure that issuing a union ruling on integration brings about integration. It's a much more deep-going thing. But you have to start someplace, and that's where we started. The instruction given to Frank when he set up the units was to get as many groups as possible represented.

A Japanese was almost always elected chairman, partly because the Japanese had a better command of English and partly because they had been extremely active in organizing. Frank would have the election for chair, and a Japanese would be elected. Right, nominations are open for vice-chair. Somebody would nominate another Japanese. Frank would say, "Nope, you've got a Japanese already. Now you've got to get somebody else. Nominate a Filipino, a Portuguese, a Chinese, or anyone from the other groups on the plantation." Not all of these situations were completely happy, let me put it that way.

But whatever doubts or reservations any groups might have had about the program of integration disappeared entirely with the 1946 sugar strike. The '46 strike brought all the groups together as a fighting force, where they won a major struggle for their life—we'd either get over the hump or that was it.

During the strike, when it came to discipline, doing picket duty, eating in the general soup kitchen, and the families all mixing, a great change took place. I'm not saying racial division disappeared entirely from the social scene in Hawaii, but I am saying that whatever there remained in the way of racial feelings in the union really went out the window with the '46 strike.

Another major problem, but more of a tactical one, was that we were determined that we would not have plantation-by-plantation strikes or island-by-island strikes. If we had to fight, it would be all the plantations down at one time.

The theory had developed during the earlier Japanese and Filipino attempts to organize that the workers on one plantation would strike and all the others would pitch in and help them. That's like trying to match dollars with the

ILWU workers demonstrating in Hilo, 1946 sugar strike. ILWU Library.

employers. There is a certain point at which you are going to go broke—you don't have the reserves. So we decided that that was a fundamental mistake that had been made. The key to the thing would be industry-wide bargaining.

Our first sugar contract in 1945 was just a sort of holding action, a recognition thing with maintenance of membership. It was just to get a contract under our belt. This had nothing to do with the major decision we had made that if it ever came to a beef, we would take it on as an industry. That decision finally was implemented when we deadlocked with the employers in 1946.

By that time we figured we had to put on a major push for enormous change and get rid of the prerequisite system, where the workers got poor company housing and rudimentary supplies and medical services instead of cash. We wanted to move toward a genuine kind of unionism where we'd build up the grievance machinery and get contract provisions such as no discrimination because of race, creed, or color. In other words, we had decided we wanted the framework of a genuine labor agreement. And in '46, of course, the policy was, when we struck, we shut it all down.

You could do something when you had the whole industry down that you couldn't do before when there had been piecemeal strikes. We knew how, in the past, the employers had evicted people from the company camps. When the '46 strike took place, we notified the employers that if they evicted one family, everyone was going to empty out and go to the county, city hall, or state building and camp out and tell them, "Okay, you feed us." I think the vision of the twenty-four thousand to twenty-five thousand workers we had pulling that off at one time must have given those employers the horrors. We could have done it, too. We had the discipline and the steam. There were no evictions.

In the '46 strike guys set themselves up fishing, hunting, and growing small gardens. The employers got over this business of ever evicting anybody, and the men all knew that if you couldn't pay the rent, you didn't pay the rent, and you simply owed it, that's all. One thing winning the seventy-nine-day '46 strike taught the sugar workers was that they could be damn self-sufficient and they could take a long beef if they had to. They could survive.

FRANK THOMPSON: FIELD ORGANIZER, 1944–1946

Californian Frank Thompson was the union's chief field organizer in Hawaii during the great 1944–46 unionization drive. Profiting from earlier union experience in the Sacramento Valley, he personally organized thousands of the Islands' Filipino, Japanese, Chinese, Native Hawaiian, Portuguese, and Puerto Rican workers at numerous sugar and pineapple plantation camps.

Frank Thompson

In 1934 I started putting together what later became ILWU warehouse Local 17 here in Sacramento. Going back into the '20s, I organized for the IWW in the logging camps. I worked in them camps a good many years. After 1929, during the Depression, I supported the unemployed councils and the Cannery and Agricultural Workers Industrial Union [CAWIU]. We'd go see Lincoln Steffens, the famous muckraker, when he was still alive in the early 1930s. He was living down at Carmel with his wife, Ella Winters, who was a progressive writer herself. We'd put the bum on them for money when we wanted to put out a leaflet or feed somebody.

Around the beginning of 1935 I was approached by the guys in the Pacific Coast District of the ILA. The ILA had a bargemen's local on the waterfront in Sacramento. They were out on strike and needed help from somebody who'd had a little experience. I stayed with them until the strike was won.

After the bargemen's strike we put on a big drive to finish up organizing warehouses here [Sacramento]. We'd started in '34, stalled in the early spring of '35, but got going again by midyear. In November of '35 we got our first contract. We've been in business ever since. I stayed with Local 17 until '44, when the ILWU International asked me to go to Hawaii.

They had sent Mat Meehan down there, the longshoreman out of Portland. He was there a couple or three months and indicated he had no desire to stay. Lou Goldblatt, the ILWU International secretary-treasurer, was looking for somebody else that could go down there and do 'em a job. He asked me if I'd go. I told him, "Things are in pretty good shape in this local. I'll go on down and take a whack at it." That's how I went to Hawaii.

I went down there as regional director, but after looking the thing over a week or two, I decided they didn't need no regional director. That is, they didn't need me, anyway. I decided I'd rather go out to organize the outside islands and let Jack Hall stay in Honolulu and take care of being regional director.

The first island I went to was Hawaii. I went down there on a ship under blackout conditions because World War II was still on. It took all night to get to Hilo from Honolulu. I made a visit up Hamakua Coast and over to Olaa. Then I went back to Honolulu. The next visit I made was over to Kauai. All our organization there had been smashed since Pearl Harbor was bombed and military rule came in. We had to pick up the pieces from there.

We started the drive in Lihue, Kauai, particularly the big plantations. The rest of 'em fell into line as we went along. One time the manager of the Lihue Plantation invited me to take a trip. He had a dandy yacht, and he went fishing way out for swordfish. I refused to go. You get on the guy's boat, maybe he dumps you overboard. That'd be one good way to get rid of Thompson.

The union was definitely attractive to the workers. In many cases, from the time a guy was born until he died, his whole life was run by the plantations. In other words, life was a form of serfdom, a peonage. On the Big Island, at a lot of places, if some worker had a friend in another plantation and he wanted the guy to come see him, he had to get permission from his manager. And the other guy had to get permission from his manager to go over to see the first guy. The workers were used to this, but a lot of 'em resented it. So anything they could do to improve their wages and things of that kind, why, they were for it.

One thing that helped us organize is that during the war the workers were frozen to their jobs in all the outside islands. They couldn't go to Honolulu even to work in defense unless they got a permit, and they couldn't get a permit because the manpower committees wouldn't allow 'em to. The authorities had to keep men on the islands to run that sugar 'cause sugar was considered war essential. So we weren't organizing people one day and then having to reorganize a place over again the next day. The workers were all stuck there.

Another element that helped was the background of the union sailors coming ashore in Hawaii at the various ports and talking to the sugar workers and other people about the '34 strike. The maritime workers were probably among the world's best organizers back then because of the nature of their travels and the people they came in contact with. They could carry a message quicker than a newspaper.

Beyond this, the missionaries and planters had given the Hawaiian workers a pretty good primary school education. Consequently the people weren't illiterate. They could read what was going on. So they finally got the idea that going ILWU was one way to solve some of their problems. I knew this whole psychological background was there, too. I could feel it all the time. Coupled with the fact that when you organized a plantation, the people stayed there, why, very few of 'em got away from us.

Of course, the conditions on some of the plantations were pretty rough, too. At Ewa on Oahu, they had a good facade. Any visitor would be shown the front part. But in the back, they had open sewers. The toilets were in the house, but the offal would run down this wooden tube right through the camp. This was right alongside where people were walking. It's a wonder they didn't have typhoid or something. We raised hell about that and about housing, but during the war the plantations didn't do a hell of a lot about it. They couldn't get the materials even if they wanted to. But when the war was over, we put the heat on and the plantations began to clean up some of these backward places.

In Hawaii you had to deal with these different racial camps the planters had set up, but I'd had a lot of experience with racial groups in California before I went to the Islands. In the Sacramento Valley you had Filipino and Mexican agricultural field workers. You had people who in many respects were similar to what you got in Hawaii. I'd helped these different groups in the CAWIU all the way from 1929 on.

I spent hours up in the mountains in Hawaii, particularly around Hilo. All along the Hamakua Coast, you'd go in there around quitting time in the afternoon. The Filipino workers didn't want to be bothered right away. The first thing a guy did was get that fighting cock. Pretty soon another Filipino would come along. A chunk of dough would go down, the roosters would hit the ground, and zing-zing, it's over. Then you could sign 'em up. You learned that pretty early.

The Filipino workers spoke either Ilocano or Viscayan, but we really didn't have any trouble with language. Most of the guys understood what was going on. You'd use pidgin English, and those that didn't understand, why, one of the other guys with you would translate pretty easily.

After we organized several Big Island plantations, there was a NLRB hearing. The employers screamed that the workers were agricultural and were legally excluded from the NLRB, which could only certify nonagricultural bargaining units. The hearing was in Hilo in October 1944. In January 1945 a decision came from the NLRB in Washington, D.C., directing NLRB elections in about a dozen plantations and ordering two units giving us everything out to the end of the railroad tracks, or out to the flumes. They even gave us the bargaining rights on the guys that worked a horse pulling a stone boat loaded with sugar-cane. The NLRB called them "transportation workers."

Basically we got anything that was transported from the field. One bargaining unit went right into the mill. The second one covered the bull cooks, the storekeep-ers, the janitors—all the basic camp personnel. I think we held our first election in February 1945 at Olaa. Then we had other elections right on up to Hamakua Coast. I think we ended up down around Naalehu, or Pahala, south of Hilo.

The next election we held was over in Maui. Then we moved down to Oahu. They were still holding elections on Kauai about the time I left Hawaii for the first time. This was in 1945. Of course, we won almost all of the elections quite handily. After that, and after the passage that same year of the Hawaii Employee Relations Act, nicknamed the Little Wagner Act, that covered agricultural workers, the plantation owners said, "Look, there's no use having elections. If you sign up the people in the agricultural fields and think you've got a majority, see the plantations manager. If you can show applications signed by 51 percent, we will recognize you." That's how we got the agricultural units in.

Workers voting in an ILWU election, Hawaii, about 1947. Their diversity and enthusiasm for union democracy shine through. Photo by Toshi. ILWU Library.

Like I said, I left the Islands for a while, but I came back on V-J Day, August 15, 1945. I wasn't gonna go back, but things got rough, so I hustled back and stayed until the end of August 1946. The problem was that the workers were having a little dispute among themselves, a little disunity you might say.

Some of the guys on the Big Island and the Jack Kawano faction in Honolulu was whipping up a little storm. Jack Hall was having to keep the peace. I figured out a scheme whereby we'd send a lot of these people out of the Islands so they couldn't engage in divisiveness. I called Harry Bridges and said, "I wish you'd blow a little smoke and tell these guys how good they are. Tell 'em you'd like to give 'em schooling and you're inviting them to the mainland as students." This is what he did.[5] When they came back from the mainland, they were different people.

The guys had been green, and they had figured things should gel a lot faster than they did. But things just gel so fast and no faster. The first contract they had in sugar wasn't much to speak about, and they were pretty dissatisfied about that. But it was a start. Some of the red hots expected more in the way of benefits than what they originally got.

Going into the 1946 sugar negotiations, we pretty well figured there'd be a strike. During the war the sugar planters tolerated us to keep the war going, and 'course we got quite a boost when we got that NLRB decision. But what we got in that first contract in 1945 was goddamn little, and the sugar planters had no desire to do real collective bargaining. So with the war over, we knew what we were faced with. We either moved with the whole bunch and did a job on those planters or they'd run us out of business.

To prepare, we had a lot of educational meetings. We knew one of the questions in the workers' minds was, "How do you feed this bunch of people?" So Bob Robertson, the ILWU International vice president, and I exhorted the workers that we're gonna have to set up kitchens, send some of our people out to sea to catch fish, and send others into the hills to do some hunting if there was anything running around loose up there to shoot at. In the meantime we'd organize to ship rice to the Islands from the outside. We prepared for a long siege. When the strike came, it lasted for three months, and all the planning paid off.

A bit before the strike, the Hawaiian Sugar Planters' Association recruited six thousand workers from the Philippines as potential strikebreakers. I was there the day the first group came ashore in Hilo. We'd sent John Elias and another Filipino guy, Joe Dionas, down to the Philippines on a freighter. They could speak the language and tell the guys about the union. Between the both of 'em, when the Filipino workers come down that gangplank, they had these big blue ILWU buttons on.

The Filipino guys had all been organized into the union on the way over. [The CIO Marine Cooks and Stewards Union provided memberships for several ILWU advocates so that they could complete the organizing at sea.] Those goddamn planters were around there looking at all these guys, figuring what they were gonna do to our union. When those employers saw those ILWU buttons, man, their faces dropped a foot and a half. So then we raised a lot of hell because the accommodations the planters had for these people were the same as you'd do for cattle, only worse. We had a hell of a demonstration over that one.

When I left Hawaii that second time at the end of August 1946, it was the eve of the sugar strike. Back on the mainland I spent a good deal of time with

Virginia Woods, one of the research workers in the ILWU. We were the ones who got the rice for the sugar strikers. First we got a commitment on rice from the rice mills over here. You had to go through the maritime commission to get a ship, and the guy sitting on that commission was an ex-shipowner. No surprise, we couldn't get our own ship, but we got enough space on this one vessel to get the rice to Hawaii.

The psychological idea of the rice was to show that the union could not only organize the people, but it could also deliver, because the Hawaiian workers were always fearful that the employers would starve 'em to death. Going back fifty years, the employers had starved many people to death in those islands during strikes before. So when our rice came through, it had a hell of a psychological effect. And, of course, the union won the strike, got some important concessions, and survived in the Islands.

A powerful red-baiting campaign against the union got going the year after the '46 sugar strike. A lot of the workers didn't pay any attention to it. It didn't have the effect that was expected. The workers in Hawaii remained pretty true to the people who had organized them.

With the drive for union organization, I think the moment had arrived in Hawaii when things that had been brewing over time came to a head. The workers were tired of living in a sort of island reform school. That's what I would call living on a Hawaiian plantation before the union, where people were treated like kids who can't leave or go over the wall. Since the ILWU broke that, most of the workers remained loyal to it despite the red-baiting.

LOUIS GOLDBLATT: COLD WAR BATTLES, 1947–1960

Here Goldblatt comments on developments in Hawaii after the landmark 1946 sugar strike. He reviews early Cold War challenges, two important strikes in the pineapple industry that revealed the union's initial vulnerability and the ultimate resiliency of its multiethnic constituency, and the coming of mechanization to Hawaii's agricultural fields.

Louis Goldblatt

In 1947 red-baiting was going on and was picking up steam. Amos Ignacio, then ILWU Big Island Division vice president, charged that the union was dominated by Communists. He tried to lead people out of the ILWU and to build a separate union of Hawaiian workers. I think Harry Bridges might have been down during one of the sessions when we were kicking the thing around. We said, "Look, there is no reason why we shouldn't bring this thing to a head in a hurry." Remember, we had won the '46 sugar strike. We felt we had the strength.

The idea occurred to us—Why not have a special convention, and why not have it right where the so-called Ignacio Revolt was supposed to be taking place, in Hilo? We took over the armory. Jack Hall and I were at that convention, which was held in early 1948. It was called the Hilo Unity Conference. We decided we wanted Ignacio at the convention so he could present all of his arguments in favor of breaking away from the ILWU. We tried to get in touch with Ignacio. All of a sudden, he disappeared.

So why let go of a good thing? We sent out hunting parties—different groups of guys—to look for Ignacio to convey the message that he had nothing to be concerned about. He would be politely treated. He would be given a full audience to come down to the convention and say his piece. But nobody could find Ignacio. He never did come to the convention.

We took the red-baiting discussion head-on in Hilo. I said, "Look, we're not Communists, we're unionists. We are also the kind of union where people can believe as they please. They can be Democrats, they can be Republicans, they can be Communists, they can be Catholics, as long as they are good union people."

This was the only time I ever used a letter I had gotten from Dillon Meyer. Meyer became the head of the War Relocation Authority after the Japanese Americans had been evacuated from the West Coast and set up in camps early in World War II. He was determined to try to empty out those camps and get people back living a normal life. So he was quite a hero to Japanese Americans on the West Coast. After the war I got a letter from him.

Meyer said he was reviewing the records of Representative John H. Tolan's congressional committee hearing held in San Francisco around March 1942 to consider if the Japanese should be evacuated. I had decided I would testify against the evacuation. I was the only trade unionist who did. Well, Dillon Meyer sent me this letter that my testimony had stood like a beacon light in the whole hearing.

I read the letter at the '48 convention. Then I said, "I want you to think for a minute as to who your great friends were in Hawaii who said a word of protest about the Japanese American evacuation on the West Coast. Here you've got the *Advertiser* newspaper supporting the revolt against the ILWU. Where were

The ILWU's key leaders meeting in Hawaii, about 1955. *Left to right*: Jack Hall, Harry Bridges, and Louis Goldblatt. ILWU Local 142 Archives, Honolulu.

they in 1942? What were they saying? How about all these company agencies, how about all your politicians?"

By that time, as far as the Japanese at the convention were concerned, they were solid as rocks. The Filipinos were good, too. It went to a referendum, and the vote was overwhelming to stay in the ILWU. That ended Ignacio for good. We came out of that stronger than when we went in. This held us in good stead when other red-baiting attacks came along, like in 1949, during the big Hawaiian longshore strike for wage parity with the West Coast, where red-baiting was practically the sole instrument of the employers.

One of the outstanding features of the '49 strike was the rather minimal effect that the red-baiting had on our members compared to the degree of the onslaught, with its "Dear Joe" [Stalin] editorials and one headline after another. The fact

Strikers and their families, 1949 longshore strike, Ahukini Pier, Kauai, Hawaii. Photo by Senda Studio, Lihue, Kauai. ILWU Local 142 Archives, Honolulu.

that we had gone through some struggles, including the '48 convention, meant that the guys were pretty well inured to this stuff. In retrospect, I'd say that the '48 convention was a good thing and the referendum vote even better.

In '47, though, we did take a kick in the pants on pineapple. We lost a big strike that year. Several factors were involved. There were a lot of seasonal workers with whom the union had no contact. The industry would bring in about ten thousand seasonals to work in the pineapple canneries in the summer. A lot of them were college and high school students who depended on the season for that extra couple of bucks to go to school. They went through the picket lines.

The field workers stayed absolutely solid, like out in Waipio. In places like Lanai, nothing budged. Yet the seasonal workers were so much of a larger group, that in terms of proportion of numbers, the support did not appear to be there. The preliminary work of trying to get to them had not been done.

There was also an unfortunate fascination with striking at the peak of the season. But if, at the peak of the season, there are a lot of seasonal workers coming in over whom you have no control or no contact, then the peak of the season doesn't mean a thing. There has also always been a question in my mind as to whether the harvesting is more important than the cultivation. In some ways, striking in agriculture during the cultivation period might be more effective because you have a stable workforce that, if you organize effectively, should be very tight.

We decided we had to settle and back up—patch up the mistakes we had made, strengthen the organization, do a little bit of getting to the seasonal workers. After '47 the pineapple employers enforced plant-by-plant contracts. We recouped, but it took a while, until the Lanai pineapple strike in 1951. I happened to be down there when that strike began. We had just finished up some small negotiations in pineapple, but we really didn't negotiate. The guys were pretty well forced to the wall and had to take what the employers offered.

I recall a meeting with the Lanai guys. They said, "Do we have the right to strike?" I said, "Sure." They said, "We don't want to take the contract. We are not going to." I said, "The employers want to go plantation by plantation, and there is no question—they are able to make it stick. It will take a while before we are strong enough to handle it."

They said, "Well, that's not the question we asked. Do we have the right to strike?" I said, "Yes, but you're not going to be able to spread the strike. If you shut down Lanai, you can't picket the canneries in Honolulu. We don't have the power to shut them down effectively. We'll help you as best we can, with money, with bumming [food and solicitation] committees, and so forth. But if you strike Lanai by itself, if you think you can get by in less than four or five months, maybe six, forget it. It'll be a long beef."

They went right back to the same question, "Do we have the right to strike?" I said, "Yes, I've told you that." That's all they wanted to know. The next thing I knew, the strike was on, and sure enough that strike lasted a long time—about six or seven months. I found out more and more about the real issues as the strike went on. Partly it was a business of having something rammed down their neck which they didn't want. They were independent thinking.

There were also all kinds of peripheral issues I knew nothing about. For example, some of the Filipinos brought over in 1946 had been assigned for Lanai. After they had been at Lanai for a couple of years, and made some friends, they all stuck very close together. Then the Hawaiian Pineapple Company, which owned the whole island, decided they had brought over an unnecessary number.

The company notified these people one morning that they were being laid off and put them on a plane out that afternoon. Offhand that doesn't seem very big, but this rankled the other Filipinos. The company wouldn't even allow these guys time enough to have a party with their friends, a going-away deal. They didn't allow anything—pack up, get out.

The Lanai workers had a couple of other grievances, little tiny grievances, not big grievances. The company had decided, between '47 and '51, that they had the upper hand and they were going to use it. So the grievance committee meetings were hopeless, and the guys said, "To hell with arbitration. We are going to wait until we can get even."

Well, the strike went on a long time. I had the feeling that with these guys, if you offered to sink the island, they'd say, "Fine, you got a deal." One day we got a call from Jim Blaisdell, the employers' representative. Jack Hall and I joined him at the Tropics in Honolulu. He said, "What will settle it?"

"There is only one way," I said, "that I know of settling this strike, and that is to get together a settlement that goes beyond Lanai. You open up all the pineapple contracts. Instead of the guys on Lanai getting twelve cents as they'd demanded—the other guys had settled for eight—they will get fifteen cents. All the other pineapple outfits will get the fifteen, or an extra seven cents. There are a whole string of grievances here that will go to an immediate grievance machinery. They will be settled in grievance and will not go to arbitration. The industry goes back into collective bargaining as a group and stays there."

The next day there was a call from Blaisdell. The agreement was put together. I went over to Lanai and asked Pedro de la Cruz, the Lanai leader, to have his committee come around so we could meet with them. I said, "This is our recommendation." The only important question that came from them was, "There is nothing wrong with what you agreed to—it's fine—but are you telling us that all the workers who didn't strike are going to get the extra seven cents?" I said, "Yep." They said, "That's no good—they didn't fight. They're not entitled to anything."

"The key issue here," I said, "is that these employers have been able to ride roughshod and run broken field through the pineapple industry since 1947. Finally you turned it around. You showed them—okay, you wanted to run broken field, you can also get a single-island strike. They've lost over 25 million bucks from their Lanai crop. It's gone. They'll be lucky to salvage the second crop. So what you've done is force them back into industry bargaining."

I concluded, "You've won something for yourself and for everybody else in the industry. But more important is the unity." They huddled among themselves. Finally they said, "We'll recommend." Sure enough, the Lanai members ratified the agreement. The pineapple industry went back into industry-wide bargaining.

Another major issue we faced in the early 1950s was mechanization in agriculture. I had conversations with Jack Hall about this even before mechanization had much of an impact, probably in 1946. As far as we were concerned, mechanization would not only be inevitable, we saw nothing wrong with it, providing the workers were taken care of. As far as I am concerned, there is nothing socially uplifting in hand-cutting sugar cane—you're just fighting dirt, dust, and bugs. It is some of the most difficult work in the world.

So we knew mechanization was coming along. How to take care of the people, that was the key. Here I think the union did some real pioneering. The idea was to shrink the workforce from the top. We had all kinds of single guys, particularly Filipino workers, who had been in Hawaii for twenty or twenty-five years. Originally they had come down there for three years, and twenty-five years later, they were still looking for that ticket home. There was no question as to how they felt. But at the same time, they were often also broke.

The big things that were written into the sugar contract in the 1950s were very substantial severance pay and a reparations allowance, which included transportation home, and a complete cash-out provision on all pension rights. A man was able to leave Hawaii for the Philippines with anywhere from ten thousand dollars, fourteen thousand dollars, to sixteen thousand dollars. Now that doesn't look like a lot of money, but in 1950, '51, '52, it was. To many a worker, this was more than enough not only to make the trip back but also perhaps to open up a little store or just lead an easy life in the town where he came from.

If there was any one industry where a shrinking of the workforce took place with a minimum of hardships, it was sugar.[6] That's where our contract was novel. I don't know of anyplace else where the contract was written out in these details. And I would say that if any person was responsible for doing a lot of work on this thing—including a lot of the heavy-duty mathematical work—it was Jack Hall. He was awfully good with a pencil.

We took up some of the slack in employment by organizing in the growing postwar tourism industry on the Outer Islands, those outside of Oahu. In the late 1950s we explained our thinking to Art Rutledge, the Teamster leader in Honolulu who often obstructed our efforts. Hotels in Honolulu were Art's. But we told him, "Look, so far as the Outer Islands are concerned, the hotels are something we have pioneered in the organization of those outside islands. There was nothing organized there, not a thing. We're the ones who knocked over the sugar and pineapple plantations. They're shrinking. Our people are looking for jobs in other areas. When these hotels open up, that is where they're going to have to go to work. That is our *kuleana*, our area."

THE NEW UNION AND THE ISLAND OF LANAI, 1946–1947

The ILWU organized the pineapple island of Lanai in 1946. As Goldblatt attested, Lanai's workers held fast during the Hawaii pineapple strike the next year, although the ILWU lost overall. On Lanai the workers rebuilt the union to prepare for future battles.

George Martin, a former Big Island ILWU divisional director and International vice president, recalls Hawaii in the 1940s, including a summer job he had on Lanai in pre-ILWU days. Secinando Bueno, a picket captain during the 1951 strike, and Pedro Castillo, later a Lanai ILWU officer, describe working conditions at Lanai in 1946–47 and the union's beginning on the island.

Some positive developments did come out of the 1947 strike loss, and these are recalled here by Kenji "Sleepy" Omuro, a 1946 sugar strike activist and in 1947 president of ILWU Local 148 on the Big Island; Hiroshi "Molokai" Oshiro, Lanai strike soup-kitchen manager in 1951; Shiro Hokama, an early Lanai organizer and 1951 Lanai finance chair; and Joaquina Ohashi, who helped the union regroup after 1947.

George Martin

I was born in 1924 on the Big Island of Hawaii. My parents came from the Portuguese-held island of Madeira. My dad worked for one of the sugar companies, got in a battle with a boss, quit, and went to work for Hawaii Consolidated Railway, where he stayed from the 1920s until 1946.

When I was growing up in the Big Island, they had segregated ethnic camps where there was sugar plantation housing. The camps had public baths; it wasn't pretty, with whitewashed lumber, cracks in the walls, and leaky roofs.

The intent of the companies was to keep people divided. The Portuguese were paid a little bit better. They became supervisors or got jobs like mule wagon operator. The others were given a little lower jobs on the totem pole and less wages. The best jobs were for the so-called *haole*, the Anglo-Saxon, western European, Scotchman, Englishman. He'd be the superintendent, the machinist, the engineer, the office personnel man.

I was in high school when World War II began, and I went to work for Automated Sugar Company as a mechanic helper. Once you went to work for the sugar companies, they wouldn't release you. They controlled the political scene and the legislature. They were in command of the banks, transportation, the utilities companies, and the draft boards.

When I was nineteen, during the war, I volunteered for the merchant marine. I told them who I worked for, and that was it. They never took me. The only guys who got out were ones who were active in the union. They got drafted.[7]

In 1944 I joined the union when a couple of the longshoremen approached us. I asked my parents, "What do you think I should do?" because if you mentioned the word "union" in front of the employers, it was like mentioning the plague. My dad said, "Join! We've had enough trouble with these goddamn plantations." So I did.

Almost immediately I became active and helped to organize even before we had a contract. I'd go out late at night, in some cases way up in the camps. You had to be very secretive, because as soon as the employer finds out, you'd get fired. They wouldn't care what the law said.

I was a heavy-equipment mechanic and a steward at the sugar company when this new migration came in 1946. The Big Five sugar companies recruited six thousand Filipinos that year. The first sugar contract we had territorial wide was in 1945. It wasn't a very good one, but it was there.

The following year we'd be negotiating a new contract. We appealed to the employers not to recruit six thousand Filipinos, because the war was over and they'd be hiring back the returning veterans. The war labor shortage would disappear. The employers said, "No." In anticipation of a strike, they thought they'd hire six thousand Filipinos as strikebreakers.

So we had our own Filipino guys go on the ships that were going to bring these people in. We did this through cooperation of the CIO Marine Cooks and Stewards. We sent our guys on the ships as crewmen. We signed up all the Filipinos as ILWU members before they got to Hawaii.

They got there a couple of weeks before the strike. We opened up soup kitchens and fed them. Not one of them scabbed on us, and we won that first statewide sugar strike. Strikes before that in Hawaii were not successful because they were racial strikes. The Filipinos would strike, the Japanese and Portuguese would work. The Japanese would strike, the Filipinos and Portuguese would work. We did things differently.

Lanai got organized about 1946. It was a pineapple plantation private island. Anyone coming in and out of the island was screened. There was fear even though we were organized. It was a real plantation town.

I worked in Lanai for one summer after my first year in high school, in 1940. We stayed in what they called "the single man's quarters." It was like a barracks. We had a dormitory with open baths. You got up early in the morning—lunch was already made for you. They used to serve us sardines, and during the day it got so awfully hot that you'd eat the sardines and you'd get sick. So we had the runs. I never ate sardines again, I swear to God, until I was about forty-five.

I brought home $114 for those three months. We were working overtime, too. We'd start at seven in the morning, and we'd get through at five o'clock in the afternoon. We'd pick pine for eight hours, and then we'd load trucks for a couple of hours. It was all hand-picking. There was no machinery in those days.

You'd pick the pineapple up, put it in this canvas bag, and take it to the end of the row. You'd dump it there. When you finished that row, you'd chop the ends off. Then you'd put it in boxes. The supervisors were pretty tough. They'd say, "Keep moving." They were on your back. It hardened me up, I'll tell you that. Several kids got fired because they'd talk back.

When one of those pineapple leaves pricks you, it's inevitable, you're gonna get an infection. It got swollen, and boils would come. You'd go into the company clinic, and the doctor would just tell you, "Bend over," and they'd squeeze it out, and that was it. They'd put a patch on and say, "Go home." In the front you had canvas pants over your trousers, but in the back there was nothing to protect you.

Secinando Bueno

At the end of 1945 I was working as a checker in a military depot in the Philippines. This job might end anytime, and in the Philippines it was hard to land a job. Also, in the Philippines Hawaii was noted as "the money bag of God."

My uncles came to Hawaii, and they had better living conditions. Young boys of my age talked about maybe becoming workers in Hawaii. Finally that was true, because the Hawaiian Sugar Planters' Association opened an office to recruit workers to come to Hawaii and work in sugar and pineapple. I decided to go.

I was used to riding boats, but many others were seasick. One man died. They just threw him in the ocean. We sailed from the Philippines in January 1946. It took sixteen days before we landed in Hilo. From there we were transferred to Lanai, and we started work on February 2, 1946.

But prior to our landing in Hawaii, some of the crew—Portuguese and *haoles*—explained what a labor union is. They told us what a union can do for working people. To me, it's amazing that I was one of those guys who already signed for ILWU membership when we reached Hawaii.

Later some men from longshore came to Lanai and organized the ILWU there. I attended every meeting as soon as the union was organized. When I first got to Lanai, I did picking, weeding, manual jobs. In that first year we got forty cents an hour.

They gave us a house with four bedrooms and a kitchen. The company wanted us to move out of the house and into the "citizens' quarter." We never moved, and they were not able to force us. The citizens' quarter was an area surrounded by two-bedroom houses with a communal restroom and shower.

Even in my house, at midnight I had to go use the restroom in the citizens' quarter because all those houses never got complete toilets. The company owned the houses and the citizens' quarter. Housing was free at the beginning, but as the union demanded more, they took that away.

Pedro Castillo

I came to Lanai from the Philippines in 1946. My first job was picking pineapple. When we were new here, the bosses tried to push us to work as hard as they like. They'd tell you to pick faster or cut the top faster. If you were not able to go beyond their standard, they'd tell you, "Go, go a little bit more."

In 1946–47, there were only a couple of work breaks. There were no portable toilets—you just went all over the place.

There was no picking machine in early 1946. The picking machine came in late 1947. When the machinery came, we felt lighter than carrying the pineapple, and we produced more. In the early part we worked six or seven days a week.

When the machine came, they reduced the working days to five. We made smaller money at first, but because of wage increases under the ILWU we earned more money later.

I joined the ILWU six months after arriving in Lanai. The union organizers went house to house. I was happy to receive them. I understood the program to have better wages and working conditions.

I asked the organizers: "Can what you are telling me be done?" They said, "To unite everybody, that is your power. If the workers want to achieve benefits, you have to stick together and strike the company." We had different opinions among different nationalities, but when we joined the union, and the platform of the union covered the differences of the national groups, we united the people.

Kenji "Sleepy" Omuro

I had experience building the strike machinery for the 1946 sugar strike on the Big Island, so I was sent to Lanai to help coordinate the pineapple strike in 1947. Lanai became a special deal because it was like a company "owning" that community, and we had to lick the problem and make sure democracy came to the island.

I think these guys became so militant because of the closeness of the community on Lanai. They lived socially as one close-knit group, not only at work, but in every way else. Other plantations were close, but not like that. Maybe this was because other plantations were more scattered into different camps.

At first Lanai's secondary leaders could not accept that the industry-wide '47 strike was lost. They said, "Lanai, we're gonna stay out, we're gonna beat those punks." We explained that it was nothing to be ashamed about that a strike is lost. "We lost," I argued, "not because of you guys on Lanai, but because certain parts of our pineapple union were weak." We said it was better to consolidate and fight another day.

Hiroshi "Molokai" Oshiro

Guys like Hashimoto and Shiro Hokama started organizing Lanai from the very beginning, just after the war. They went house to house and signed up people. Hashimoto had a lot of guts. You didn't just go out and try to organize a union on these islands, where everything was controlled by the company.

Pedro de la Cruz was in charge of a section of field. For a Filipino, being a field boss was all right. But he started working with the guys on the union and became the leader.[8] There was another guy, an organizer from outside named Kealoha. He was the one who talked to me.

The first strike—1947—we lost. But we won something, if not in wages, then in getting the guys together and making the union much stronger. There was one big incident that made us feel unified. We heard a barge was coming in to pick up the pineapple stored at the harbor in Lanai. We set up a picket line.

The harbor foreman, who'd been a crane operator before, was on the crane. There were two *haole* boys, young supervisors, hooking up the pineapples. The whole union gang ran there and started throwing punches. The company men all jumped into the water and swam out to the boat. The pineapple didn't get moved.

There was an anti-union guy there taking pictures with a movie camera. I was in the film. They charged the guys who were in action. I got charged. They just took our names and released us because the union guys were there to get us out.

Shiro Hokama

The beautiful thing I'll always remember about the '47 strike is this: We had some guys involved in beating up two scab truck drivers. If we weren't able to raise seven thousand dollars bail money, these guys would be shipped to Maui for the courts. We got the local to send us a check for seven thousand dollars. The bank was closed. They wouldn't open to cash the check.

The cops wouldn't accept checks unless it's cashier checks. So Pete de la Cruz had to call a session, pass the hat to try to raise the money, but he couldn't raise enough. There was one Japanese old man—he never believed in banks! He had four thousand dollars cash in his house. He came up with the four grand we needed.

Pete de la Cruz made the membership know that this old Japanese man brought up this money. That did a lot to make the Filipinos realize that this union is all of us. This started getting a closer working relationship between the Filipinos and the Japanese. "We" were part of "them" now.[9]

In 1947 we knew we got smashed. Still, okay, the union is our only means. And the management knew we were willing to take them on if we had to.

Joaquina Ohashi

I got my last name when I married George Ohashi, an ILWU unionist who was Japanese-Portuguese. But my people were from the Philippines. I came to Lanai from Maui in 1941, when my mother left my father. I was eleven years old. My stepfather came to Lanai in 1945. He was a pineapple field laborer. After he got paralyzed by a stroke in 1951, my mother started to work in the pineapple fields herself.

I was twelve when I started to work in the fields. You belong to a gang. The gang is under a foreman. You joke, you rib each other. You're yelling at each other, you're laughing. You're not by your own self.

I liked high school in Lanai. It was small. We only had forty-one in the class. The big shots—field bosses—sent their kids out to school. They had money. And some of the managers and other people who lived on Snob Hill sent their kids out, too. We had separate crowds. We didn't mingle with the kids from Snob Hill. The supervisors' kids went around by themselves.

When I was sixteen, I helped the union reorganize after they lost the 1947 strike. I was a contest queen—I was popular. I was with this Filipino group. They said, "Hey, Joaquina, come on, help us. Get some folks to join the union."

Every girl the union recruited represented a nationality. I represented Filipinos, and there was a girl who represented the Japanese. We went house to house and asked people if they wanted to sign up to become union members. I didn't know anything about unions. I just did it because I wanted to help. And my mother told me, "You gotta go!"

VICTORY AT LANAI IN 1951

When the Lanai workers struck independently of the other islands in 1951, they won a victory for the whole union. Shiro Hokama, George Martin, Bill Alboro, who was 1951 ILWU leaflet and mail circulation manager, Hiroshi "Molokai" Oshiro, Pedro Castillo, Leonora Agliam, and Elizabeth Pokipula recall the strike and its legacy. Agliam and Pokipula also testify about pre-union conditions and the situation of women on Hawaii's plantations.

Shiro Hokama

In '51 there was company-by-company negotiations. That is one of the reasons Lanai struck. I was the finance chairman. Before the strike, International officers Lou Goldblatt and Bob Robertson and Hawaii leader Jack Hall talked to me. They said, "You guys can't take them on. If you strike, you are going to need over twenty thousand dollars a month. You guys can't afford that."

So at the membership meeting I'm the only one telling the guys, "Hey, we're in no position to go on strike." I'm defending the International and the local. When the vote came up, a bare majority decided to strike.

Pete de la Cruz was for the '51 strike. He had a better understanding of what his people wanted, or what he thought was needed for this island. When the vote was taken, I'd lost. So, okay, we go on strike. I said, "Goddamn it, we gotta win this strike now." Before the decision is made, you say your piece. But once a decision is made, you do whatever you can to make it work. Otherwise we'd all end up dead.

George Martin

In 1951, when Lanai struck Dole for seven months, the other islands contributed food and money to the Lanai strikers. We felt the employers were out to break the union on Lanai.

We thought we had to win to put the employers in their place because we'd have future battles with them, with the Big Five, Hawaii's dominant companies—the employers were all interrelated in pineapple and sugar. It was a crossroads of where this union was going to go.

Bill Alboro

When the '51 strike came, I was working in the fields, picking. I was a steward. After one month I was made circulation manager, putting out leaflets and mailing cards asking for help. I had guys writing, typing, stenciling, and mimeographing—I was just the manager.

There were committees for hunting, fishing, and bumming. Everybody had something to do. De la Cruz organized all this. Everybody had his share of jobs. If people didn't do a job, they lost their food allowance for the weekend.

Pedro de la Cruz
addressing pineapple
workers, 1951 Lanai
strike. ILWU Library.

In 1951 we felt we were going to gain or going to lose everything. People said, "Go for broke." It was also only us on strike, while all the rest of Hawaii's pineapple employees were working. I felt kind of bad about that, but I figured if we could gain something out of this, it would be better for everybody.

Hiroshi "Molokai" Oshiro

During the 1951 strike I was in charge of the soup kitchen. There were a lot of families on the borderline. They wanted the union, but they were scared. That kind of family we'd try to convince by giving them a little more food. The strike went on for half a year, so we felt that if we help them now, when we go back to work these guys are going to be strong union guys. I was right, because when we came back, they became good union members.

During the '51 strike my wife was a nurse. She had a continuous job at the hospital. She contributed half her pay to the union. I was lucky. She understood what I was doing.

Pedro Castillo

After the 1947 strike we stopped calling the field boss "sir" or "mister," but the relations between the company and the working people were still bad. You'd tell the bosses something, they didn't respect you. If you had a problem, they didn't listen.

Before the '51 strike I was driving a tractor and breathing all this dust. They gave us a respirator that was worse than without one, because it was not tight. But if you complained, they didn't listen. If you told them a better way to work, they wouldn't recognize what you were telling them. They didn't recognize you as a human being. This was a main issue for the 1951 strike.

During the '51 strike we set up a bumming committee to go to the different islands, to the different units of the union, to ask for food and money. We had no strike fund in 1951, but we never starved, because the other units gave us support.

After the 1951 strike, because we got what we wanted, we were happy. The bosses treated us better. They started to mingle with us at social affairs. They settled some grievances. They began to treat us more as equals. They saw that doing things their way didn't work. They learned that they had to listen to us.

The Lanai '51 strike is really the history of the state of Hawaii because the other pineapple companies were working and only Lanai was on strike. When we got the Lanai settlement, the other islands benefited. Whatever we negotiated, they also got.

Leonora Agliam

I was born in Lahaina, Maui, in 1926. My father picked pineapples. He and my mother were from the Philippines. When I came to Lanai, I had just started school, so I grew up here.

When I was going to school, we did seasonal work. They'd send us home at two o'clock. We'd put on our work clothes, go to the labor yard, and go out to the fields and pick. We used to trim the top of the plant. It was so cheap. They paid fifty cents a day. But it was the only way we could get some extra money. This was about 1938. I was twelve.[10]

After the eleventh grade I quit school because my father and mother were separated. I was the oldest still at home. My father was the only one working.

He told me to quit school. I did not want to. I only had one more year to go. But I had to go to work out in the fields.

I got married in 1943 and stayed home. I couldn't go to work because I was having my children. But I began to work in the fields in 1950. Then came the 1951 strike, and I still couldn't work.

The '51 strike was hard at the beginning. Then we got used to it. We couldn't buy anything we liked. I explained to my children that we just had to eat what we got.

During the strike we had meetings night and day. You got to listen to what people had to say. To me, it was good. I enjoyed it. The women helped with whatever needed help. We stayed the whole day. We took turns on phone calls, and we had some ladies in the strikers' kitchen helping cook breakfast, lunch, and dinner. While waiting for mealtime, they had volleyball. My children thought it was a party.

After the 1951 strike I began to work in the fields regularly. The union needed a steward. I didn't want to become one, but because my husband, Catalino "Pete" Agliam, was a good friend of Pedro de la Cruz, our '51 strike leader, he pushed me into it.

As stewards, we'd go to leadership meetings. They always stressed safety. We'd go back to the gang and tell them they were supposed to keep covered, especially with goggles. And as a steward, I asked all the members of my gang to come to union meetings. A lot of them talked dialect, but I told them to come anyway to understand better instead of just hearing about things from other people.

Picking, there's a lot of bending. If you're not used to it, your back hurts. When the pineapple plant is low, your back is sore. There is a right way to bend, and every so often you'd stand and stretch. You have to get used to doing it like us. We had no time for exercises to help our backs. When you're working out in the fields, that's your exercise.

For years I stuck to picking. Our gang was all women. We were mostly Filipino—we had a few Japanese and Hawaiians. The ladies would talk and laugh and joke. We'd laugh the whole day so we don't get too tired. Sometimes we'd talk about our husbands, our children, and about what goes on around Lanai.

I changed jobs in 1981. I got this better job as an irrigation worker from my seniority. They posted it, I signed up, and I got picked. I didn't miss being on a gang. I think I had enough of picking pineapples all my years.

I still remember when the union got organized. We felt good because we got somebody to back us up. When we got problems out in the fields, we cannot trust the bosses, we just gotta do what they say. So when the union was organized, everybody felt better.

Elizabeth Pokipula

I was born in 1922. My father was Hawaiian. He worked as a mule man in the fields, cultivating with a mule. After they no longer used mules, he picked in the fields. My husband was also Hawaiian. He was a stevedore, and then he operated a high lift.

When we went to school, kids worked pineapple during vacation. When I was twelve, I went out there to work. The men took off the crowns. We'd count and stack it up. They used that for planting. They had slips. We'd stack up the slips. By the time I got through with my pile, the others were all gone, they were so used to the work. I was too slow. So I only did it for two days. I never worked in the fields again as a child.

I never liked the work out in the fields. But then times come when you get too many children and you need money, so you have to go out there and work. I had five children. I started working after the 1951 strike because of the kids.

In 1951 they needed more workers, because for seven months no one had worked, so grass was covering the pineapple. I laid all the grass down, "hoeing it" they called it, but there was too much grass to hoe. Sometimes we made only two lines a day. We crawled on our knees and laid the plants down. After we cleaned up, the fruits started coming up. Then we started picking. Eventually I became the steward for the harvesting department.

My gang was all women in the early 1950s. Later they mixed it up, men and women. In our gang, everyone would get together. It was just like one big happy family. In those days we used to push the old ladies—we worked and we helped each other. We'd pick theirs if we were stronger than them. She'd pick hers, but we'd help her pick.

AH QUON McELRATH: UNION SOCIAL WORKER

Ah Quon McElrath was a highly respected Hawaii union pioneer who served for years as Local 142's social worker. In the 1990s McElrath became a member

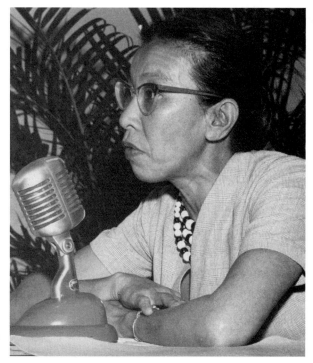

Ah Quon McElrath testifying before the U.S. Senate Subcommittee on the Medical Care of the Aged, Honolulu, 1961. Photo by Robert Choy. ILWU Library.

of the board of regents of the University of Hawaii. During the early twenty-first century, she remained a frequent and forceful speaker at key ILWU conferences and conventions until she passed away in 2008. Here she recalls her role in the union's early days and assesses the ILWU's social impact in Hawaii.

Ah Quon McElrath

I was born in 1915 at Iwilei on Hawaii's capital island, Oahu. My mom and dad came from China. Dad came as a contract laborer. My parents had seven children. My father died when I was five. We did everything we could to survive.

We lived near the beach where we picked *kiawe* beans and dried bones to sell to the fertilizer company. My brothers shined shoes and sold newspapers. There was no gas stove, so we would find firewood to get our outside stove going. We lived by kerosene lamps. We didn't have electricity.

All of us started working in the pineapple canneries when we were twelve or thirteen years old. There were no child labor laws then. I packed and trimmed pineapple and picked eyes out of the so-called jam. I worked in the cafeteria, which was supposedly the gem of jobs, because you made twenty-seven and a half cents an hour as against eighteen cents an hour packing pineapple. In season, we worked twelve hours a day. That was how we supported the family and got back to school during the fall.

Education was extremely important to me. I felt it was a window to the world, and that being able to read, write, and speak English—my first language was Chinese—offered special opportunities. I became the editor of the school paper in intermediate school and decided to concentrate my efforts on learning the English language well.

I went to the University of Hawaii during the period of the Spanish Civil War in the late 1930s. The cause of the anti-fascist side affected many of us. We felt we had a part because we boycotted Nazi Germany and fascist Italy. I also joined an activist group called the Inter-Professional Association in those pre–World War II years before the ILWU came to Hawaii in strength.

In 1938 Jack Hall was arrested during the Inter-Island Steam Navigation Company strike. I remember when somebody came to our Inter-Professional Association meeting and announced, "Jack Hall has been beaten!" That strike culminated in the August 1, 1938, Hilo Massacre.

Early in the game I met Bob McElrath, who I married in August 1941. He later became the ILWU information director for Hawaii.[11] I met him through Jack Hall in the latter 1930s when I was helping Jack with his organizing newspaper, Voice of Labor. I would put labels on and, since I'd worked on newspapers through intermediate and high school and the university, do some corrections of stories.

Sometimes those guys didn't have any money. I'd go out and buy them stew and rice. Although I was volunteering, I'd had five jobs when I was a senior in college, and I'd put away a few dollars. So when those guys needed a meal, I always had a little money with me.

During World War II union organizing stalled in Hawaii when the military declared martial law. But in early 1943 Bob, who had been working on the waterfront repairing ships, set up the independent Marine Engineering and Dry Dock Workers Union. I helped him organize the tuna packers. Because Bob's was the only union setup going at the time—Jack Hall was then working for the Hawaii Labor Department—Bob was on the front lines.

Those early cases of organizing, which I went through with Bob, to me were definitive of a lot of things that followed with the organizing of the ILWU in

Hawaii at the end of the war on as broad a basis as occurred. People saw what Bob had done and began to ask, "Why can't we get the same things?"

The ILWU's success in organizing thousands in 1944 came about because exploitation was perceived by the two major ethnic groups, Filipinos and Japanese, and because the ILWU was able to use the leaders in the ethnic work camps to sign up people without the bosses knowing about it. We knew the ILWU was a union that was devoted to nondiscrimination, and that there was no need for us to repeat the mistakes of earlier organizers, who in past decades created associations of only Japanese, Filipinos, or whatever group it might be. So we set up one union made up of all ethnic groups under the ILWU.

A good deal of what I did early on was as a volunteer. I'd had experience as a social worker with the Department of Social Security even before the attack on Pearl Harbor, but during Hawaii's April 1946 tidal wave crisis [Hawaii was hit by a devastating tsunami that April] I was not employed. I volunteered my services to the union to do the investigations of need, because the entire union was collecting money to give to families that suffered a death or the loss of a home or personal belongings. I also worked with families to get them to understand what it meant to help each other in times of disaster.

This was the prelude to what needed to be done during the long '46 sugar strike, which was a major test for the ILWU in Hawaii. I did a lot more work then by getting recipes from the Department of Health for the soup kitchens, visiting the kitchens, and talking to the families about how important it was for the kids to continue school and about what arrangements we could make with creditors and the parochial schools.

Another crisis started in 1947 when Ichiro Izuka published a red-baiting pamphlet that was inherently a move to separate out various ILWU groupings so they would become independent unions.[12] This move failed, but we felt a great need to close ranks. When the Izuka pamphlet came out, we still had a number of locals devoted to sugar and to industrial groupings such as pineapple and miscellaneous trades.

We decided that, for the strength of the union and its members, it was better to have one consolidated local. Then we could send out the same message to all units. We would have solidarity in political action. People would have an opportunity to come together and discuss what it was that concerned them in their various industrial groupings. That's how we eventually became Local 142 in a consolidation process that began in 1947 and concluded in 1951. We ended up with one big local of longshore, sugar, and pineapple, plus, later, the super-markets, hospitals, and hotels.

In 1954 I was hired as ILWU Local 142 social worker. The union had moved into the area of negotiated medical plans, pension plans, later on dental plans, and a whole slew of social legislation that required the interpretative work of a social worker. Because I had done volunteer work during the 1946 tidal wave and the '46 sugar and '49 longshore strikes, the local's leaders realized that a social worker could perform valuable services, including things elected officials could not do.

As social worker, I ran an educational program. I talked to members about things they needed to know beyond collective bargaining, like how to access services available from private and public agencies. During the 1960s and 1970s there was much educational work to equip our members to get help.

Lobbying the state legislature was also part of my social work for the union. I worked for increases in public assistance, and I used to testify for the ILWU about human services issues. Of course, some of the things we did at the legis-lature were more forward in terms of social legislation than any union could usually hope for. We helped push through a Little Wagner Act for Hawaii's agricultural workers in 1945 and, later on, improvements in workers compensa-tion and unemployment insurance as well as a temporary disability insurance act.[13] These were exciting things that went to the nub of the existence of work-ing people and their families.

The ILWU was also successful in providing inexpensive housing for our members. For just one example, at Waipahu, on the island of Oahu, we were able, by forming into a private nonprofit housing organization, to get federal funds to build a cluster of homes for individuals of low income as well as seniors, so they could rent homes in public housing.

Looking back, it is clear that what the ILWU accomplished in Hawaii was truly remarkable. In a short time we raised wages two and three times what the workers had received before, and we gave them a measure of control over their working lives. The Republicans and the sugar and pineapple growers had held unchecked power for decades. Then along came this little union, and it was able to upset them and disperse that economic and political power. Never before had this happened in Hawaii.[14]

Despite recent problems, our union remains determined. One of the good things to come out of the recent attempt by some of our hotel employers to freeze our wages and take away a lot of our benefits has been a renewed consolidation of our solidarity. The union has picketed these organizations, and our members have said, "We will not give back. We will not go for our taking a bigger bite of the health care premiums, nor will we go for a cutting of benefits in our plan."

We should teach our younger members the history of the ILWU to reinforce and enhance the contributions their forebears made to building a stable economy in Hawaii. This would also give to young people a way to get rid of the stereotype of the so-called Asian mentality, which is an inability to get together to fight concentrated power. The other reason why it is important to learn history is the old thing about not repeating the mistakes of the past. By learning our history, we can develop new ways in which to enhance our personal lives as well as the collective lives of working people.

ABBA RAMOS: FILIPINO ACTIVIST, 1946–1959

Avelino (Abba) Ramos was a warehouse Local 6 business agent and an ILWU International representative who served the union in California for years. He came to the mainland from Hawaii, where he grew up on a Big Island plantation. Ramos was a product of the efforts of ILWU planners like Hall, Goldblatt, Ah Quon McElrath, and others to encourage and train local leaders in the Islands from the mid-1940s on. His testimony here illustrates the success of this policy.

Abba Ramos

I was born on the Big Island of Hawaii in 1934, the year of the San Francisco general strike. My dad was a sugar worker. My parents came from the Philippines in the 1920s as contract laborers. We were a family of ten. While growing up, the kids knew we were on a plantation.

Plantation life was paternalistic, yet very exploitative. We were money poor. Hunger was not the problem. Hawaii grows an abundance of food, and the growing season is all year around. So the plantation owners utilized that. They made the workers feed themselves and gave them very little remuneration for their labor in the planting and harvesting of the sugar crop.

The sugar companies owned the plantation store, too. They would carry over the bill the following month, plantation-system style. You couldn't buy outside the plantation store. There was no other choice. Since they were related to the Big Five companies of Hawaii that had total control of the islands' economic structure, the sugar companies brought in all outside supplies themselves from the mainland.

There were camps on the various plantations. The camps were separated by ethnic groups because of language barriers. But like Jack Hall used to say, the one mistake the missionaries made was that although they kept people segregated, they sent their children to the same school, and we all came out speaking pidgin English. Now we could communicate with one another. That brought the ingredient of eventual unity.

My dad, Marcelino Ramos, was an activist. He was involved with the strike of Pablo Manlapit's Filipino labor union in the 1920s. Manlapit was framed and deported, and the strike failed. My dad was exiled for a couple of years. He worked under another name on the island of Kauai. He finally got back to the Big Island. He was not given formal amnesty, but he did get back to work.

The workers organized on ethnic lines in the 1920s. So the employers would use one group against another. They'd give one group a little more money, give them a raise to come to work during a strike. If the Japanese went on strike, then they would use the Filipinos.

There were efforts to organize Hawaii in the 1930s, after the 1934 maritime strike on the mainland. Then during World War II everything was put on hold. Hawaii was under martial law. But at the war's end it didn't take long for the ILWU to organize—the workers were just waiting for the opportunity. The big strike in sugar came a year or so later.

On the verge of the 1946 strike we were living at the camp at Hilo Sugar. I was the kid who used to wait for the ILWU organizers. They held secret meetings underneath the Japanese church. They would wait until it was dark so the camp boss couldn't see who was coming. The union steward would say to me, "Abba, you wait down at the road. When you see this little car come up, you gonna see two *haole* guys coming out of there. You escort them up here. Go the back way."

I'd take 'em around where you wouldn't be seen, and take 'em underneath the Japanese church. The *haole* guys were Henry Schmidt and Frank Thompson, the organizers. Even Jack Hall and Lou Goldblatt used to come up into the camps. As a kid, I never quite understood things fully, but I got twenty-five cents to stay up on the porch at the church. There was a bell, and if I saw any of the camp bosses, I was supposed to ring it and put the union guys on notice. Then they would make like they were just having a poker game.

When my dad would get together with his friends in those days, they would talk about the oppressiveness of the employer—about some of the *lunas*, who were the straw bosses, and about the superintendents. And sugar work then was hard, backbreaking labor, with no mechanization. It was all done by hand-cut. The men would say, "What are you going to do? You can't swim back. You're in the middle of the Pacific Ocean!" These guys in fact were really held hostage.

During the '46 strike we ate better than when my parents were working. We had a soup kitchen, all the ethnic groups would get together, there were reports from the various picket captains, there were hunting, fishing, and gardening committees, and it was a luau—for us kids, anyway.

When I was growing up, the struggle became more intense. There'd been a long, bitter strike in 1946—which we won—but the employers still didn't give up trying to bust the ILWU in the Islands. This was when the McCarthy period was developing. The employers got to some people. The struggle for unity was still there. The employers tried to divide and destroy the leadership of the union and discredit the union movement by using Communism and the red scare.

The schoolteachers then were mostly pro-employer. They'd say, "These guys are trying to teach the overthrow of the government." I'd say, "That's not the way I see it. All they're trying to do is help the sugar workers, help us. They haven't said anything bad." They'd answer, "You don't know." They'd just put you down.

An FBI guy came to the house. He was trying to discourage the Filipinos away from Harry Bridges. He said, "This guy Bridges is a big Communist." My father's response was classic. He said, "I don't know what you talk about this Communist. Me no go school, me no understand that. But now I got better pay, I have insurance. Is this Communist? Then give me some more."

By 1948 I ventured out from the Big Island. I went to Oahu to live with my uncle, who was a longshoreman. In Honolulu I was influenced by the ILWU education department under Dave Thompson and Ah Quon McElrath. Ah Quon encouraged me to read. I spent hours at the ILWU library with the transcripts of the Harry Bridges hearings. I met Anne Rand—the International's archivist, not the conservative writer—who set up the library in Hawaii. These people answered my questions and opened my view politically. I got most of my education from them.

Serving line, ILWU soup kitchen, 1958 sugar strike. ILWU Library.

I went back home to the Big Island after high school and worked on a sugar plantation during 1952–54. I started in the weed sprayers' gang, what we called the "poison gang," and became a steward. I ended up becoming the herbicide mixer in the plant. The previous person died, and no one bid on the job. But I didn't want to stay in the fields—they was too rough! I bid on the job and got it.

They used 24–D, a Dow Chemical defoliant. We had a lot of the old standard, arsenic, too. It came in wooden drums with no labels. No employer was telling you anything about this stuff then. But I knew it would be bad to breathe the poison, so I always used fans to blow the poison away from me, and I mixed outside. George Martin was then ILWU division director. I called him and said, "I want masks and all that." He said, "You're right," so we got masks and a couple of fans.

Then I went back to Oahu, and Ah Quon encouraged me to take the test for college. She gave me a study plan, and I'd spend time at the ILWU library. I took the test, was accepted, and graduated from the University of Hawaii at Manoa in 1958.

I always said that when I finished college, I wanted to work with the union. So Dave Thompson sent me to see Henry Epstein, the territorial director for the

United Public Workers [UPW]. UPW was organizing in Hawaii with the aid of the ILWU. I was hired and became the first "local, born-in-Hawaii" organizer for UPW. We started with eight hundred members. By the time I left in 1962, we had over five thousand.

There was a major ILWU sugar strike in 1958. I think this was the last effort by the sugar companies to see if they could weaken the union substantially. They finally realized they couldn't do it. Then began the process of merging the sugar mills because of more technology and new methods of processing.

Although the employers were resigned to us in 1958, they did make one last-ditch effort—they did not want statehood for what was then the Territory of Hawaii. They would have preferred a commonwealth, like Puerto Rico. Under a commonwealth, the employers would still have tremendous impact because of their economic power. Jack Hall and Lou Goldblatt explained at several meetings that this was an important issue. "We're going for full-blown statehood," Jack said, "and all the rights that go with it."

The most important thing was political empowerment and democracy. Under Hawaii's territorial regime, you could elect your territorial senators and house of representatives members, but the governor was appointed by the president. With statehood came direct election of the governor. We wanted to have direct representation in Congress, too. We got statehood in 1959. I still don't think the union is given its proper recognition in the striving to turn the old feudalistic Hawaii into a modern-day state.[15]

In 1962 I transferred to warehouse Local 6 in San Francisco. The challenge, for me, was now out there on the mainland. I'd always wanted to venture out, to try to swim in that water. I made seniority at the old San Francisco Grocery warehouse and got elected steward.

I'd been trained in Hawaii by some of the best teachers that any trade unionist could find. So I got active in Local 6—I attended all the meetings, raised issues, joined committees, got elected to the local executive board, and won election as a business agent in 1974. In the mid-1980s I was appointed International representative. But I still consider Hawaii home. I say that I've been in exile in California these last thirty-some years. But it's been a good exile, thanks to the union.

6

POLITICS
THE OLD LEFT

MUCH HAS BEEN SAID AND WRITTEN ABOUT THE MANY TRIALS OF HARRY
Bridges, who was repeatedly accused by government officials of being a Communist Party member. These Cold War–era charges stemmed from Bridges's
outspoken, militant style, his success as a labor leader, his open admiration of
the Soviet experiment in Russia, and his legal vulnerability as an Australian
immigrant. Nothing was ever proved, and in 1955, after twenty years, the government ceased its near-constant hounding of Bridges.

On the other hand, little has been published about those ILWU veterans of
the Old Left who were once active in the American CP, their Party-sponsored
activities in the union, or their sincere dedication to the union's cause. This
chapter addresses these oversights and chronicles the role of CP-ILWU members
in shaping the union's inclusive, progressive agenda.

KEITH EICKMAN: IDEALISM AND DISAPPOINTMENT

*Keith Eickman retired as warehouse Local 6 president at the end of 1982 after
twenty-five years as a union official. Eickman shared the youthful idealism as
well as the eventual disappointment of many people who belonged to the CP
from the 1930s to the mid-1950s. His testimony, laced with self-reflection and
humor, reveals his lifelong dedication to social justice and to the ILWU.*

*Eickman entered Local 6 in 1941 and served as a steward, a business agent,
secretary-treasurer, and president. He was still active as president of the West*

Bay (San Francisco) Local 6 Pensioners' Club when he passed away in 2006 at the age of ninety-three.

Keith Eickman

I was born in Edmonton, Alberta, Canada, in October 1913. My mother was from Scotland, and my father was of German parentage. They got divorced, and I usually lived with my mother, but in 1930 I came to San Francisco to live with my father. I've been in the city most of my life since then. I went to Mission High School here my last two years and graduated in 1932, right in the middle of the Great Depression.

Millions of people were unemployed. My father worked for the Pacific Gas and Electric Company. He never lost his job, but his pay was reduced. It took me two years to get work myself. I finally got a job in 1934 running a Burroughs bookkeeping machine at the Rosenberg Dried Fruit Company in Santa Clara, California.

With so many people out of work, I was convinced there was something wrong with the system. I was looking for something that would give me answers to the problems of society and life. Then I met these young people at a night school in San Jose. They were members of the Young Communist League [YCL] in Santa Clara County. The YCL was the junior section of the American CP. I recall being impressed with the YCL slogan, "Life with a purpose."

I joined the YCL in January 1936 and became quite active. There were some romantic tendencies about the YCL. I was joining an organization that was against the capitalist system. The Communists wanted to replace capitalism with socialism, which promised to divide the wealth of society more fairly.

We were really the most sectarian group in the world. We sang revolutionary songs, like [singing] "Fly higher and higher and higher, our symbol is the Soviet Star." This, I thought, was marvelous. I liked the songs, I liked to sing, and I liked the people. Our attitude toward the U.S. was contemptuous, even toward the good things about it. We were sectarian in that sense.

Through YCL, I got involved with the organization of Santa Clara County's cannery workers. Then a drive started to organize the dried-fruit workers in the Rosenberg plant into the militant new UCAPAWA-CIO. UCAPAWA was set up by the CIO in 1937. This was when the AFL and the CIO were bitter rivals.

As an office clerk at Rosenberg, I was not a member of the plant bargaining unit. Still, armed with the virtue of my beliefs, I announced to everyone in the plant that the production workers should join the CIO rather than stay in the conservative AFL affiliate that then represented them. This was not received by the employer with great enthusiasm.

The workers in the plant weren't in a position to support me. But I was young and brash and thought I possessed the wisdom of the world. I was going to pass on all of my information to these lucky people. Well, they did not join the CIO but remained in the AFL. Subsequently, they did become part of the ILWU-CIO in Santa Clara County, but that was a few years later.

Eventually, Rosenberg laid me off. They said it was for lack of work. Unemployment insurance had just come in, so I ran out my unemployment.[1] There were no jobs, but I wasn't looking for a job very strenuously because of the excitement of being active in the YCL. We did all kinds of things that seemed very important, like going to meetings every night.

Then I got hired under the New Deal's WPA. I was given various WPA jobs around San Jose. Some were pretty stupid, but they did give you enough to live on, and you could survive. Once I worked in the Stanford University labs counting fish scales. Apparently this determined some factors about the fish, but I can't remember what.

I quit one WPA job to attend the 1939 American Youth Congress [AYC] in New York. The YCL in Santa Clara had formed a local Youth Council, and I became the secretary and a delegate to the AYC. The AYC was not a revolutionary organization. It was just trying to improve conditions for young people so they could go to school and get jobs. It had a certain amount of influence in the United States until World War II. Attending the AYC meeting, I think, shows how I always did work of a broader nature than just being a member of the YCL.

That is, I always tried to work with other people. I wanted social betterment for its own sake, but also I had the idea that by doing this, we really were developing some concept of the revolution. I thought the revolution was just around the corner. I remember a friend who said, "You know what? The revolution is going to be within two weeks." We were very young at the time. But I was always very cautious in my analysis. I said, "I don't think so. I think it will take five years." So I gave what you'd consider the very conservative estimate! He was the real radical. Well, the revolution didn't happen in two weeks, and it didn't happen in five years either.

Although I was rather naive in my mid-twenties, I did have certain questions.

In 1939 the Nazi-Soviet Pact caused me some anguish. That was when the Russian Communists signed a nonaggression treaty with Germany that allowed Hitler to start World War II without fear of Soviet interference. But I was able to overcome my anguish because I believed that the Soviet Union knew best. That is what I was told by the CP. I'd gone to confession and received the answer I wanted to hear.

In 1940 I went to work for Westinghouse in San Francisco as a Burroughs operator.[2] But I really didn't like office work. In August 1941 I decided to get into the warehouse industry, where they were hiring. The U.S. wasn't in World War II yet, but the work situation was improving because of increased defense spending. In the building where I was employed, there were some Local 6 members. They were making more money than I was as a Burroughs operator. I thought, "This is ridiculous." I quit my job, went down to the hiring hall on Clay Street, and got on at Zellerbach Paper company.

In those days the warehouse industry was not mechanized at all. Zellerbach had enormous cartons of paper, thirty-six by forty-two inches, and they weighed an awful lot. Everything had to be stacked on the floor, but there were no mechanical contrivances to lift those cartons up. So you'd build a pyramid. You'd start at the bottom and lay it over until you got to the top. The only way you had of moving anything around was to use a little four-wheeler. There were no forklifts or electrical devices of any kind.

When I went to work at Zellerbach, they put me with one of these old Italians who was built like a moose. Local 6 had a lot of Italian workers then. This man was very strong, and I wasn't. I got on one end of this cart, and he got on the other. The next thing I knew, I was flying with the carton. So they put me on something I could do. It was all heavy stuff, but it wasn't this 150 to 200 pounds.

I became active in Local 6 immediately. Joe Orlando was the steward, but the job didn't mean that much to him. Of course, I was just panting to be steward. Joe could see it. It wasn't any big political or personal issue with him. In 1942 he just said, "Why don't you be steward?" Everyone else agreed. So I became the steward, and I practically reached glory. I was elected secretary of the Local 6 stewards' council in 1943, but the war cut that career short. One month later I was drafted. I served in England, France, Belgium, and Germany in an army railway battalion. In June 1946 I got discharged.

Shortly after the war I became a member of the regular CP. When I got out of the army, the union sent me to the CLS [California Labor School]. The CLS was an institution in San Francisco which was close to the Party. It had a trade union program. I got something out of the classes and then went back to work at Zellerbach as the steward.

A number of the leaders of Local 6 were also members of the CP. Normally there wasn't any basic disagreement over what the Party and the union members wanted, but the Wallace presidential campaign of 1948 was different. Henry Wallace had been vice president under Franklin Roosevelt. Now he was running as a third-party candidate on the Progressive Party ticket with Communist support. This was the election where Harry Truman, the Democratic president, beat Thomas Dewey, the heavily favored Republican. Wallace called for peace with the Soviet Union instead of a cold war.

In Local 6 we passed a resolution in support of Wallace. It was not accepted wholeheartedly, but it was done. I was gung ho for supporting Wallace myself because I thought the American people wanted a third party. Only afterwards did I realize that although there were lots of people at Wallace rallies in northern California, in respect to the whole population there weren't that many. When the actual vote came and Wallace did poorly, I was enormously surprised.

As the steward at Zellerbach I used to bug people an awful lot about Wallace. The day before the election I went around to everyone in the plant and said, "Tomorrow you're all going to go out and vote for Wallace." A bunch of workers were sitting there. I guess by then they were fed up with my enthusiasm and my insistence that I knew what they were going to do. One of the old Italian men said, "You're going to vote for Wallace. We're going to vote for Truman." I said, "But Local 6 has endorsed Wallace, and you're obligated to support the position of the local." He said, "Fuck the local and fuck Wallace. We're going to vote for Truman. Don't bother us anymore."

I've had a lot of lessons in my life, but that was one of the most devastating things that ever happened to me. I really thought all the people in that plant were going to vote for Wallace because I wanted to believe it. After that, I began to examine everything I was doing in regard to political issues and my relationship with people. I think I really began to grow up from that time onward.

In 1949 we had our famous warehouse strike in San Francisco that lasted over one hundred days. By then I had been elected chairman of the steward's council. During the strike I was secretary of the strike committee. Those of us who were in the CP made some mistakes in that strike. One of them is that we made the *People's World* [PW], the CP newspaper, the official organ of the union.

This was a mistake because the majority of the members of the union didn't read the *PW* and didn't want to read the *PW*. I know because I used to sell the *PW*, and the number of papers you could sell at meetings was very, very small. We brought the *PW* around on the picket lines, too. The members would throw them in the garbage can. They didn't want the strike to have some political aspect to it.

There was a certain amount of antagonism among some of the members of the union over the *PW*. That, plus the endorsement of Wallace, laid the basis for a group that was organizing for the Teamsters Union to try to take over Local 6. Three or four Local 6 business agents in the West Bay [San Francisco] went over to the Teamsters and set up this rival Teamsters Local 12. This was close to when the CIO purged the ILWU, too, and another little group emerged in Local 6 that wanted a CIO takeover.[3]

We did lose some members to the Teamsters, but the primary problem was that there was constant fighting within the local. It was like a civil war. After the Korean War started in 1950, some people would whip up hysteria and anti-Communist sentiment at meetings. When anyone who was considered a Communist got up to speak, they would chant, "Communist! Communist! Communist!" The local was being torn apart. It survived, but after this, the role of the CP within the union disintegrated, or at least diminished. The CP just didn't have the same influence within the local anymore.

I stayed in the CP until I was expelled in 1955 on the grounds of "white chauvinism." At the very time that Joe McCarthy was carrying on outside the Party, there was a tremendous purge within the CP. They purged anyone who said anything that could possibly be considered the slightest bit questionable. It became a hysteria within the CP. I had an argument on the floor of the stewards' council with a black Local 6 leader who is still one of my friends. The motion we were considering was not that important, but the Party leaders felt this was an example of white chauvinism, and they expelled me.

They probably did me a favor. I am extraordinarily devoted to concepts and organizations. It would have been difficult for me to voluntarily separate myself from the CP because of my history within it, my background, and the people I knew, even after Nikita Khrushchev's revelations of "the crimes of the Stalin era" in 1956.[4] But they took the decision out of my hands.

Local 6's opposition to the Teamsters continued into the mid-1950s. This was not doing us any good. We were spending too much blasting the Teamsters, and they were blasting us. You don't really build an organization on negative action like that. Then Louis Goldblatt, the ILWU International secretary-treasurer, started the concept of the Teamsters and the ILWU working together in northern California warehouse negotiations. This was a wise and sensible decision that helped both of us from the latter 1950s onward.

In the mid-1950s I remained very active in the stewards' council and on negotiating committees. I ran for business agent in late 1957, won a close race, and ended up serving from 1958 to 1970. Those years included a lot of the Vietnam War, which the union opposed. At the same time, we supported the battle for integration. I was never the big hero, but I played my part in those activities.

I became Local 6 secretary-treasurer in 1970 and was unopposed for reelection three times. But when I ran for president in 1977, the CP put every effort they possibly could into backing their own candidate against me. Evidently, it was important to the Party to have enough influence to gain the presidency of Local 6. Yet I got 51 percent of the vote and won against three other candidates.

Understand that I don't want to indicate in any way that I regret my period in the CP. It had an important impact on my life. The Party gave me an understanding of the class relationship of society. It gave me a political attitude that made me different from any of the officers in the union who didn't have that background. I don't think they understood politics to the same degree. I would not want to belong to the CP now because I don't want to belong to an organization in which the decisions are all made from above. Still, my life in the Party laid the basis for whatever role I played in Local 6.

JACK OLSEN: ACTIVIST AND EDUCATOR

Jack Olsen was a CP activist in the union's early days. During the 1940s he served as a Local 6 business agent and education director. He argues that the CP's presence and militancy had much to do with the union's consistent backing of progressive causes. The ILWU's commitment to political nondiscrimination and union democracy clearly allowed for this.[5]

In the early 1950s the employers excluded Olsen from warehouse jobs because of his politics. Local 6, then under severe duress, was unable to help, despite the ILWU's tradition of sheltering victims of discrimination.

Olsen survived as a typographical union Local 21 printer. He had once taught classes in the CLS, though, and in 1974 he became the first director of Labor Studies at the City College of San Francisco. Olsen, who passed away in 1989, was married to the celebrated author Tillie Olsen.

Jack Olsen

When I was one year old, I was brought to the U.S. from Russia, where I was born in 1911. Like most Russian Jewish immigrants of that time, my parents came here to escape the increase of anti-Semitism and oppression in czarist Russia flowing out of the 1905 Revolution. When that first Russian uprising was defeated, the czar's government made the Jews the scapegoat for its problems.

My parents settled in New Jersey but soon moved to Philadelphia, where my father became the recording secretary of the local broom and brush makers' union. Like many people of his generation, my father was excited by the Russian Revolution of 1917. He was not a revolutionary, but he was pleased that the czar had been overthrown. He used to say the Russian Revolution showed that working people could become the heads of governments.

Around 1920 we moved to Alden, New York. My father got involved in the famous Sacco and Vanzetti case. That was my first introduction to radical politics. Sacco and Vanzetti were Italian-born anarchists who were accused of murder in Massachusetts in 1920. They were executed seven years later.

The evidence against Sacco and Vanzetti was so weak that they appeared to be the victims of political persecution. As a high school student in Alden, I attended Sacco and Vanzetti meetings through my father's contacts with radical Jewish workers' clubs. I used to circulate petitions to free the two men.

During 1928 we came out to Los Angeles. In '29, of course, the stock market crash hit, and the Great Depression started. That killed whatever personal dreams I had. I'd planned to go to college, but my father was out of work. That's when I got active in the Communist movement.

I got swept up in the tremendous CP-led demonstrations by the unemployed that occurred in big cities across the country on March 6, 1930. Those were the first mass demonstrations of the Depression. Through my father I met a number of L.A. radicals, joined the YCL, and set out to make a revolution in the United States.

For years I've been called Olsen, but my real name is Olshansky. That's

Jack Olsen (*back row, left*) and warehouse Local 6 publicity committee, C & H Sugar Company strike, Crockett, California, 1949. ILWU Library.

because the L.A. Police Department's Red Squad changed my name on March 6. Another YCL kid and I were walking to the unemployed demonstration in L.A. We had cardboard banners underneath our shirts. The police spotted the bulges and arrested us.

Captain William F. ["Red"] Hynes, who headed the Red Squad and became infamous in history, said to me, "What's a nice kid like you doing associating with these reds?" I stammered, "I got a right to be here." He asked, "What's your name?" I mumbled, "Olshansky." He said, "Did you say Olsen?" I answered, "Yeah." Then the kid with me poked me in the ribs. So that's how I got the name Olsen.

The only job I got in L.A. was shipping clerk at a Woolworth's store. I made fifteen dollars for a six-day week, ten hours a day, and the job only lasted through Christmas. I decided I couldn't help my parents in L.A. I figured I might as well see if I could do better someplace else. So in 1930 I took off and came up to San Francisco.

I liked the kind of people I met in the Communist movement up north. The L.A. movement I knew was concentrated in the Jewish enclave at Boyle Heights. The people there had come from big cities like New York and Chicago, and I was a country boy from Alden. I felt more at home with the seamen and the unemployed kids I met in San Francisco.

Since I was fairly well dressed, which counted then, I managed to pick up odd jobs. I worked a little as a dishwasher and truck driver. Sometimes I got a few days on the waterfront. None of this was enough to make a living, but I did better than most.

In 1932 I was elected state secretary of the YCL by the CP state committee. I'd like to say this was because I was a brilliant guy, but actually the movement, which was growing, grabbed anybody who was energetic and willing. I'm denigrating it a little. I was a bit more vocal than some and had done a little more reading.

State secretary was supposed to be a full-time job. The YCL made a distinction between full-timers and everybody else by saying, "You're a paid functionary." I was entitled to five dollars a week, but I had to raise the five dollars myself! Sometimes I got it, sometimes I didn't.

My primary concern as state secretary was building the organization— putting out handbills, holding street meetings, conducting campaigns. There were nine or ten places around San Francisco where all kinds of radicals and even the Salvation Army held regular street meetings. Depending on how loud a voice you had, how good you were, and what the issue was, you'd get five hundred, six hundred, seven hundred unemployed people standing around to hear you. We'd always pass the hat. If there was anything left after you paid for leaflets, you had some money to work with.

The whole thrust of the Communist movement, of course, was in its claim to be the party of the working class. The idea was to provide leadership. Because there was a long history of militancy among longshoremen and seamen, the CP focused on the waterfront. You were ashamed of yourself if you didn't hold at least one street meeting on the waterfront every month, if not every week.

When the 1934 strike came along, it was the big thing in every radical's life. My role was outside support. Whatever we could do as an organization, we did. We went out on the picket lines and helped around the soup kitchen. After the strike the CP encouraged people like me to get more active in the unions.

Lots of young radicals—many of them Communists, not all of them—got swept up in the feeling that there was a need for union organization. Quite a few helped carry through the longshore union's march inland in warehousing. Some became ILWU leaders. These people came out of a sense of idealism. The new unions systematized hiring, too, and that made it easier for young radicals to get in.

In 1936, when I was twenty-five, I felt I was getting too old for YCL youth activities. I joined the regular CP and decided to see what full-time work I could get. I'd already done quite a bit of casual waterfront work. I recall pushing a hand truck loaded with five or six sacks of coffee that weighed 110 to 120 pounds each. The docks were not well maintained, and you were always hitting ruts and bumps. You'd tear your guts up trying to keep the load from getting dumped.

By this time I knew my way around the warehouse local hiring hall. I got dispatched to a job at U.S. Steel, stayed a year, and got my book as a full union member. In late 1937 or '38 U.S. Steel moved off the waterfront. I decided to switch jobs and got on at Merchants Ice and Cold Storage. Merchants was hard physical work, but I was young and didn't mind. What I also didn't mind was working in the freezers, which used to bother a lot of guys so much they wouldn't take jobs in the ice houses.

In those days the CP set up Party clubs on an industry-by-industry basis. There were warehousemen's, seamen's, and longshoremen's clubs. Each club had its own officers and its own delegates to the CP county committee, a literature agent, and an education director. In warehouse we had clubs on both sides of San Francisco Bay. They used to meet and first take up political issues like the anti-fascist cause in the Spanish Civil War, the current election campaign, or an ongoing legal defense case.

Second, there was always discussion of functioning in the union. Did we have the strength to introduce a resolution? What should our demands be when our union contracts expired? The Communist groups always considered the question of union leadership. Should any of our people run for a particular spot, like negotiating committee or executive board member? Who should we support for office, whether a Communist or not? These preliminary discussions were a tremendous help to us when we went to our union meetings. In effect, each club functioned as a Communist caucus.

To get things done, we tried to get official backing. In the ILWU, which preached democratic unionism, the officers were relatively easy to get access to. Generally there were three or four CP members who were liaisons. We'd go see the president of Local 6, the business agent, and the stewards to try to line up support.

There was always strategy to consider. Could we get a resolution that would ultimately go before a general union meeting introduced through the executive board? Could we get one of the officers to sign it so it didn't come just from the Communists? We might draft the resolution so it suited the officials. When it came time for the union meeting, our guys lined up on the floor behind the microphones to speak for the resolution. Or somebody on the officers' platform would speak for it. There were varying approaches.

The ILWU consistently took positions that were left of where other unions stood. I think the Communist clubs made a difference here. The presence of Communists helped put Local 6 miles ahead of the rest of the labor movement in things like opening up to black members even before World War II. But we also had to think about our limits. For example, had a Communist club come to a meeting and said, "We want an endorsement of the Soviet Union," we would have had our ass ripped off.

I joined the Local 6 publicity committee, helped with a big organizing drive at the Lathrop army depot near Stockton in the late 1930s, spoke out at union meetings, and got the reputation of being a red hot. During the major 1938 warehouse lockout in San Francisco, I was down at the union hall and out on the picket lines every chance I got. Several CP people felt I ought to bid for leadership. The guys in the ice houses were pressuring me to run for business agent, too. So in 1939 I ran and got elected. I took office in 1940.

The first arbitration I had was against the Paris Beauty Supply Company of San Francisco. We'd dispatched a young black woman and a young black guy to the place. The employer was a Southerner. He didn't want to keep them. His excuse was, "I've got nothing against black folks. Why, if I could afford to build them separate toilets, I'd be glad to have them working here."

The local put on a lot of pressure against that sort of thing in 1939–40, and the Communists made an extra-effort issue of it. You can point to many things about the Communist movement that aren't so honorable, but its early insistence on racial equality and its idea that blacks and whites should unite was one of the most honorable things it did.

I went into the army in 1944, during World War II, and got discharged in late 1945. The next year the union asked me to become the full-time director of the Local 6 education and publicity department. In 1946 the local had the money for such a program. It had more than fifteen thousand members. I'd helped develop the Local 6 publications and done other publicity work before I went into the army. This was right up my alley.

As director, I was in charge of our monthly bulletin, got out press releases and strike publicity, had each division put out its own mimeographed publication, and set up classes, theater groups, sports teams, and social activities. This was a job that could have taken two or three more people, but I got a lot of rank-and-file help. By 1948 we had eighteen thousand members. We were a thriving, jumping local. I worked my ass off, but it was an exciting, fun time.

I was still active in the CP. I don't think I would have gotten the publicity and education job without Party support. The CP was then a pretty powerful influence in Local 6. People used to come to it for election campaign support who were not even members, knowing full well that the 150 or so Communists in San Francisco played a real role in who got elected. CP support was something everybody went after, including people who were in opposition to the Party.

There was an awful lot of support for the Left in the union up through the Henry Wallace Progressive Party campaign for the American presidency in 1948. The Communists supported Wallace, who ran on a platform that opposed the coming of the Cold War. The Wallace campaign generated a lot of broad enthusiasm in Local 6. We had a committee of two hundred, and they weren't all Communists. Unfortunately, the support for Wallace disappeared when election day came.

On the heels of the election came the long and costly 1949 Local 6 warehouse strike that had mixed results. The next year Dave Beck, the Teamsters Union president, poured a million dollars into a raid on the local. He was able to lure away some of our business agents and dispatchers. They went on his payroll and led the attack against us, saying we were unpatriotic. Basically the attack was straight red-baiting.

At the beginning of the Teamster raid the guys who went to work for Beck were still not out in the open. They would come to our meetings, which became very stormy, and say that the local should get rid of the Commies. Ironically, some of those guys had supported Wallace earlier on. Of course, because I was a Communist and made no bones about it, and because I was handling publicity and education, I was one of their main targets.

To defend against this, the local leadership suggested that I resign, and I did. The local was beginning to have financial problems anyway. But that was only the beginning. Shortly thereafter, these guys, who were still an internal Local 6 group, put out an election handbill. I took it to a typewriter expert who proved that it was typed in the Teamsters Local 860 office. That brought the whole thing out into the open. These guys also put out a leaflet that said "Who is Olshansky?" It implied that I was a Russian agent of Stalin.

When the crisis came, the black membership of the local was solidly at our side. They knew the job the ILWU had done in opening up to them. Young people like LeRoy King and Curtis McClain came to the forefront. We put LeRoy on as an organizer to try to beat the attack back. When the actual raid started, the internal Local 6 group took a hike and established Teamsters Local 12. Then came the campaign to save our houses from being taken over by them.

Immediately after the raid started, the Local 6 officers told me, "Get your ass back on the job. We need publicity." We conducted an intensive campaign against the raid with posters and weekly bulletins. The Teamsters were only able to take away 250 San Francisco members. But it was a very turbulent period, and when the whole thing was finished, the local was broke. We had to do away with the publicity and education department.

I went back to work after that, but I had a hell of a time getting jobs. I'd walk into a shop and they'd say, "Olsen, we're glad to have you." But there was a rule that an employer could lay you off anytime in your first ninety days. So twenty-four hours later I'd get laid off. This was also the beginning of the closing of various shops. I couldn't make a living. I had to find work outside of Local 6.

About 1951, '52, I left the CP. I felt the Party had lost its viability as an American working-class force. There was an exodus from the ILWU Party clubs, too. This was the period of the start of the disintegration of the entire American Communist movement. It was unable to react properly to events or to provide leadership.

But in the beginning the Communists in the ILWU had been a part of the building of the union, and they had been accepted. They influenced people on the leadership and union-meeting level. Down through the years, too, the ILWU has been a refuge for radicals who were run out of everyplace else. As a result of the policy of the ILWU to protect everybody regardless of political affiliation, many were able to get work, to stay, and to influence the membership.

Thus, the Communists had enough of a presence and enough personal contact to talk to the other workers and bring up issues in the warehouses and shops. They set a tone, and they got a lot of support from the workers on the job. To me, that's the key to why the ILWU was always a radical organization.

DON WATSON: UNION STALWART

Don Watson belonged to the CP between 1948 and 1956 and was an ILWU ship clerks Local 34 member for thirty-eight years. He retired in 1993 after decades of volunteer work for the ILWU and other progressive unions. He consistently campaigned against McCarthyism and racism early on while championing universal social and economic justice. The trajectory of his long career suggests the level of commitment that frequently characterized members of the Old Left. In retirement, he assists the ILWU's lobbying program and plays a leading role in the Southwest Labor Studies Association (SWLSA), the Copra Crane Labor Landmark Association, and other worker education groups.

Don Watson

My father, Morris Watson, was a newspaperman. I was born in 1929 in Evanston, Illinois. My father had a newspaper job there with the Associated Press [AP]. Soon after I was born, the AP sent my father to New York, where I grew up. In New York my father covered major stories and was considered one of the AP's best reporters.

In 1933 my father read an article by the famous columnist Heywood Broun, who said he wanted to organize a newspaper reporters union. My father heeded Broun's call and became one of the American Newspaper Guild [ANG] founders. He was also an ANG International vice president.

During 1933 my father became the lead ANG organizer at the AP's New York office. In retaliation, the AP put him on the "lobster shift" in the middle of the night. They fired him in 1935. So the ANG filed an unfair labor practice charge under the new NLRA. This became one of a group of cases that went to the Supreme Court and resulted in the NLRA being declared constitutional in 1937.

Late in the 1930s my father became active in New York's left-wing American Labor Party. Consequently, I got interested in politics, and it became part of my development.

In 1942 Harry Bridges visited New York. He persuaded my father to move out to San Francisco that fall to become the founding editor of the new ILWU newspaper, *The Dispatcher.* I was thirteen years old, and Bridges was fascinating. He had this supercharged, forceful personality, was very political, and liked to talk about going to sea.

I went to sea myself in the summer of 1946, the year before I graduated from high school in San Francisco. World War II had just ended, and the whole world was moving on ships. The first trip I made was on a troop transport, the *Marine Jumper*. I was a utility man—a pot washer and potato peeler. That first trip I sailed as a permit man. I joined the MCS-CIO in 1948.

I really got involved in political activity around '48. I met people in the MCS who were Communists. I'd read the famous Communist William Z. Foster's big book on labor, including the 1919 steel strike he'd been in. I thought Communists were good trade unionists and felt that I'd like to work along with them.

In 1948 Henry Wallace ran for president on the Progressive Party ticket. Wallace campaigned for peace with Russia and got enthusiastic support from the Left. I handed out Progressive Party leaflets, went to meetings, signed people up on petitions, and did anything needed to help Wallace.

The MCS officially endorsed Wallace, but late in the campaign I noticed all these MCS members wearing Truman buttons. That didn't seem good. On election day Harry Truman, the Democratic president, upset Thomas Dewey, the favored Republican. Unfortunately for the Left, Wallace did poorly.

I was also involved with the MCS pre-strike committee in 1948. The MCS was allied with the ILWU and struck along with the longshoremen that year. President Truman slapped on an eighty-day injunction to stop the strike under the new Taft-Hartley Act. I went to sea on the *General Gordon* during the injunction. When I got back, the strike was on. I sold the CP newspaper, *The People's World*, at all the picket lines that dotted the San Francisco waterfront.

In 1950 I was at sea on the *President Cleveland* when the Korean War broke out. This right-wing guy called a special stewards meeting. He attacked the MCS leaders because they questioned the war, as did Bridges. I got up at the meeting and defended the MCS officers by saying they had done a lot for the people and we should listen to them.

I made two trips to the Pacific on the *President Cleveland*. The second time I was screened off the ship when the *Cleveland* returned to San Francisco. Screening was part of the government's McCarthy-era program of denying employment to leftist seamen and even politically moderate maritime union activists. The program was administered by the U.S. Coast Guard.

While I was disappointed, I knew that the Coast Guard had extended its screening to the Far East, but not to the area between San Francisco and Hawaii. So I got a job on the *Lurline* run to the Islands. After the third trip about fifteen of us were screened at once. We came down the gangplank and had our pictures taken.

The Coast Guard held hearings on Sansome Street in San Francisco to review screenings. I gathered six to eight stewards to come to my hearing. Some of them vouched for me. But the Coast Guard hearing officer just went through the motions.

I got involved with the Committee against Waterfront Screening. Even though I was young, about twenty-one, I was elected secretary. The committee chair was Albert James, a black longshore leader from ILWU Local 10. We held our meetings at the MCS hall in San Francisco. People from the ILWU and other maritime unions came.

I did the day-to-day work for the committee. I've found through the years that whenever I got on a committee, I usually became chair or secretary very rapidly. Generally this happened because nobody else wanted to do the work with as much devotion as me.

The big activity we had was a daily picket line at the Coast Guard head-quarters. Every day I supplied the leaflet. One I wrote in early 1951 says "Screening since July 1950 has denied thousands of maritime workers on both coasts the right to work." Sometimes I'd have a whole leaflet on some individual case. I also wrote about various ships cracking in two to show that the Coast Guard was spending more time screening seamen than working for safety.

We kept up our daily picketing for months. Some of the screened seamen got longshore work. The dispatchers at ILWU Local 10 would call the MCS hall when they had extra jobs. For a while we even got dispatched out of the ILWU Local 2 ship scalers hall.

In 1951 I was drafted into the army. I was sent to Fort Ord, California, for basic training. They had these "information and education" sessions, really political talks. This one guy described what he called the Communist conspiracy. He had a chart of this Communist octopus that was going after our country, and Harry Bridges was a major portion of his talk. And I'm just sitting there.

I didn't discuss politics, and I did all the marches and all the basic training. But that October I got a letter from the Department of Defense that contained what they called "derogatory information" about me and my parents. One charge said "Your father is a Communist who has been active in Communist affairs since 1935." They gave me thirty days to make a rebuttal in writing.

I went with my father to the attorneys for the ILWU, and we did make a response. Part of it said "If it is the policy of the U.S. Army to set sons against their parents, I do not intend to follow that policy." Finally I was given a questionable General Discharge under Honorable Conditions, although I had done every assignment the army gave me. Some years later, after a class-action suit, they sent me a revised Honorable Discharge and told me to destroy the other form.

After the army, I came back to the Bay Area and started doing the same things I was doing before I went in. Over the next two years I worked for the Independent Ironworks in Oakland, but as soon as the day was over, I'd go down to the MCS hall to see what was happening. I still went to meetings and volunteered to help the seamen.

In 1950 the MCS had been expelled from the CIO for its left politics. The NLRB called a bargaining election in 1954 but removed the MCS from the ballot because the top MCS officers didn't comply with the non-Communist affidavits then called for under the Taft-Hartley Act.[6] To support their officers, the members voted "no union."

A new NLRB election was called the next year, and this time the ILWU stepped in to appear on the ballot. The stewards voted ILWU. However, the NLRB allowed other West Coast unlicensed seamen to vote in the same election, burying the ILWU vote. During the campaign Bob Robertson, the ILWU vice president, asked me to help with a stewards' edition of *The Dispatcher*. I put a lot of effort into it, but all was lost due to the politics of the time.

In 1955 I decided I would like to be an ILWU ship clerk. I didn't have a strong upper body, so clerking seemed better than longshoring for me. Emmett Gilmartin, the clerks' assistant dispatcher, gave me a permit card. This saved me, because the dispatcher, Jim Roche, did not like screened seamen. But Roche was on vacation. When he returned, Roche dispatched me anyway, although I was not his favorite.

There were many types of clerk jobs in the mid-1950s. Every ship had a different amount and kind of cargo. Today most of the work involves containers. But the time I'm talking about was even before the extensive use of palletized loads and lift trucks, which became the dominant features on the waterfront in the 1960s.

In unloading 1955–style, the clerk told the longshoremen where to put the cargo. A ship's crane would unload sling loads of cargo from the hatch to the dock, where they would be placed on a series of four-wheel trucks. These four-wheelers were attached to a vehicle called a "bull." The bull driver would haul the four-wheelers inside the dock, where longshoremen would grab cases and put them where the clerk instructed.

At times there would be a cornucopia of goods for us to sort. We used to have piles of boxes all over Pier 29 of various sizes and types. The dock would end up looking like a Woolworth store. We had to build aisles or put small lots of cargo back-to-back or put large lots in piles. You had to figure out how much space was needed and where to put things. If you did it wrong, everybody would come down on you.

A major part of the job was receiving and delivery of cargo on and off trucks and railcars. A clerk supervisor at the front of the dock would assign an arriving Teamster to drive to a section where he loaded or unloaded. When a clerk received cargo, he counted it carefully. Then he would chalk mark the pile, including his count and the name of the loading ship.

In 1955 Jim Roche was the power in Local 34. He was the clerks' dispatcher who did not like screened seamen. Roche didn't like black people either and wouldn't dispatch them. He was a baseball fan. He was known for bringing in white ex-ballplayers and dispatching them to jobs.

An opposition faction arose around Jim Herman when Roche got sick about 1960. This was when Herman emerged into leadership. He was very articulate, lined up a following, and got elected local vice president and then president. He made some dramatic changes, like seeing that a good amount of blacks came into the local. I was in a lunch group that supported Herman in the early 1960s.[7]

About this time I got active politically in the California Democratic Council [CDC]. I'd left the CP in 1956 after Khrushchev's famous speech criticizing Stalin was followed by the Russian invasion of Hungary. That told me the Party was not going to change. I felt relieved by my decision, which actually came when the CP wanted to advance me toward leadership. Instead I joined the Young Democrats and then the CDC. In both organizations we backed the election to public office of up-and-coming candidates like Phil and John Burton and Willie Brown.[8]

Around '62 the ILWU set up its own political group, the West Bay Legislative Committee. Bill Chester was the chair. I was elected vice-chair because they wanted a clerk in the post. In the late 1960s I ran for election to the Local 34 executive board. I made it on the second try and served for twenty-four years, including nineteen as chair.

Jim Herman and I were both from the MCS and had fought the screening program. We also both actively supported the farmworker union movement in the 1960s, and that became the basis of our relationship. In the mid-1960s Whitey Kelm and Herb Mills of Local 10 started a five-dollar-a-month club in support of the farmworkers' organizing drive.[9]

I'd met Dolores Huerta, the vice president of the United Farm Workers [UFW], and had been impressed. I joined the club. It lapsed, and I started it up again. Herman was very helpful, and the local gave me sort of an official status.

Starting in 1967 or '68, Local 34 had yearly Christmas collections for the UFW. As the head of this effort I'd go around to every pier on the waterfront and collect money from the clerks and longshoremen. The overwhelming majority gave. This continued into the mid-1970s. We also had a monthly labor caravan that brought food and money to the UFW headquarters in Delano, California.

I was so involved with the UFW that I became kind of an honorary farmworker. During the 1970 lettuce strike in Salinas, I walked the UFW picket lines. In the early 1970s I started putting in only eight hundred hours a year on the waterfront. I spent most of my time helping the farmworkers. I was very close to the UFW's San Francisco boycott house and volunteered many hours there. Often I would care for Dolores Huerta's children while she led UFW demonstrations or spoke publicly.

During the 1971 coast longshore strike Herman called for a Local 10/Local 34 Joint Longshore Strike Assistance Committee [JLSAC]. He said, "I want Watson to be the secretary." That was it. Everybody agreed, and I became the secretary. While the strike was on, I went to a UFW rally in Sacramento. I asked Marshall Ganz and Jim Drake, two farmworker leaders, if there was a little something they could do for our strikers. They said, "I think so."

The next thing I knew, they put together this huge food caravan for us. This long grape truck came to the San Francisco waterfront from the Central Valley. There were several trucks from Salinas. They had all this produce. Maybe 150 farmworkers arrived, too. They visited the Local 34 hall and then went down to Local 10. It became a giant event.

This, more than anything else, made my waterfront reputation. I was the secretary of the JLSAC, and all of a sudden this help came, and it was on such a vast scale. It took hours just to unload those trucks. While I got the credit within the ILWU, the farmworkers really outdid themselves. I was amazed.

Around 1975 I started doing a lot of volunteer research for the UFW legal office in Salinas. This returned me to an interest in labor history. I did research

Don Watson and United Farm Workers supporters picketing Safeway, San Francisco, 1969. Identifiable ILWU people (*from left*): Bert Donlin, holding UFW flag; Elaine Black Yoneda, petition in hand; Watson (*center*), with petition; Joe Figueiredo, holding "Huelga" sign; and Allen Ohta (*far right*), leaning in. ILWU Library.

papers on fruit tramp shed workers from the 1930s to 1970 and on lettuce mechanization. I interviewed farmworkers, union activists, and growers and made presentations to meetings of the SWLSA.

My interest in farmworker history led me to cofound the Bay Area Labor History Workshop [BALHW] in 1980 with a scholar and UFW volunteer named Margo McBane. I had little academic training and was working in isolation without much feedback. If you don't have that, you need some kind of a forum for discussion. If you want something and there's no organization, you go ahead and organize it yourself. That's what I did, and the BALHW is still going strong today.

In 1978 I became the Local 34 delegate to the ILWU's regional political arm, the NCDC. Four years later NCDC president LeRoy King asked me to take on the job of NCDC secretary-treasurer, and this broadened to include legislative lobbying at the state capital in Sacramento. I remained with these duties until I retired in 1993.

Although I'm thankful that ILWU longshore members, including clerks and retirees, have good medical and pension plans, others are not so lucky. We are all facing ongoing privatization, deregulation, and huge tax cuts for the wealthy, along with growing state and national deficits, all of which hurt working people. That's why I've decided to continue to offer my lobbying skills to help the ILWU program in Sacramento.

Detail of "Solidaridad Sindical," fresco mural by Pablo O'Higgins, 1952, ILWU
Memorial Association Building, Honolulu. Photo by Robert Wenkam. ILWU Local
142 Archives, Honolulu.

EPILOGUE:

"AN INJURY TO ONE IS AN INJURY TO ALL"

IN 1974 THE LIBERAL TV JOURNALIST BILL MOYERS INTERVIEWED HARRY BRIDGES. An excerpt from that interview is reproduced here, courtesy of Thirteen/WNET New York, as a final testimony to the ILWU and to the universal message of unionism.

HARRY BRIDGES AND BILL MOYERS: AN OLD SLOGAN

Mr. Moyers: *What got you indignant, Mr. Bridges, as you were a young man, traveling from port to port, looking at the working conditions in this country? Where did you get your sense of outrage?*

Mr. Bridges: *I wouldn't say it was a matter of being indignant or outraged. It was—I was taking care of myself. To take care of myself, I had to line up with other people and help take care of them. It was one of those things. You know, well, you had a slogan: "Workers of the World, Unite!" It's still a good slogan. It's an old Marxist slogan. Still use it. That's how simple it was: "Workers of the World, Unite! You got nothing to lose but your chains." It's still as good as the day it was said. We still operate that. At least, I tried it.*

Mr. Moyers: *What was the old "Wobbly" quote?*

Mr. Bridges: *Same thing.*

Harry Bridges addressing a longshore Local 10 meeting, San Francisco, about 1960. Photo by Otto Hagel. Courtesy ILWU Library. Copyright 1998 Center for Creative Photography, University of Arizona Foundation.

Mr. Moyers: *"An injury to one . . ."*

Mr. Bridges: *"An injury to one is an injury to all." That's still good today. That's still one of our slogans that we use.*

NOTES

INTRODUCTION

1 The IWW anticipated a time when "one big industrial union" of all workers would lead to the end of discrimination and capitalism. See Melvyn Dubofsky, *A History of the IWW* (New York: Quadrangle, 1969). In *Workers on the Waterfront: Seamen, Longshoremen, and Unionism in the 1930s* (Urbana: University of Illinois Press, 1988), Bruce Nelson demonstrates how Depression-era maritime laborers inherited the rebellious spirit that had animated the IWW. The IWW and ILWU slogan goes back to the Knights of Labor, which used the phrase "An injury to one is the concern of all." See Kim Voss, *American Exceptionalism: The Knights of Labor and Class Formation in the Nineteenth Century* (Ithaca, N.Y.: Cornell University Press, 1993), 81.

2 Nelson Lichtenstein, *State of the Union: A Century of American Labor* (Princeton, N.J.: Princeton University Press, 2002), 149, 154.

3 Ibid., 274.

4 Several writers beyond Lichtenstein have analyzed labor's recent decline and have offered suggestions for recovery. Examples include David Brody, *Workers in Industrial America: Essays on the 20th Century Struggle*, 2nd ed. (New York: Oxford University Press, 1993), 229–66, and *Labor Embattled: History, Power, Rights* (Urbana: University of Illinois Press, 2005); Bill Fletcher, Jr., and Fernando Gapasin, *Solidarity Divided: The Crisis in Organized Labor and a New Path toward Social Justice* (Berkeley: University of California Press, 2008).

1 LONGSHORE: THE SAN FRANCISCO BAY AREA

1 For an informative overview of longshoring in San Francisco before contain-erization, including work culture and union history, see Robert W. Cherny, "Longshoremen of San Francisco Bay, 1849–1960," in Sam Davies et al., eds., *Dock Workers: International Explorations in Comparative Labour History, 1790–1970* (Burlington, Vt.: Ashgate, 2000), 1:102–40. Cherny is currently completing a biography of the ILWU leader. For a brief overview of Bridges's career, see Harvey Schwartz, "Harry Bridges and the Scholars: Looking at History's Verdict," *California History*, 59 (1980): 66–79. On the frequency of general strikes in U.S. history, see Victoria Johnson, *How Many Machine Guns Does It Take to Cook One Meal? The Seattle and San Francisco General Strikes* (Seattle: University of Washington Press, 2008), 5.

2 San Francisco longshore workers belonged to the International Longshoremen's Association until 1916, when they left during a strike to form an independent union. The Blue Book replaced that union after a disastrous strike in 1919. This company-dominated group, officially the Longshoremen's Association of San Francisco and the Bay District, was called the Blue Book because of the color of its membership booklet.

3 For a thought-provoking assessment of Bridges's reminiscences of his youth as a sailor, see Robert W. Cherny, "Constructing a Radical Identity: History, Memory, and the Seafaring Stories of Harry Bridges," *Pacific Historical Review*, 70 (2001): 571–99.

4 The shape-up was part of a degrading longshore hiring system, which was generally characterized by favoritism, extortion, and kickbacks. "We were hired off the streets like a bunch of sheep," Bridges said elsewhere of the shape-up, "standing there from six o'clock in the morning, in all kinds of weather." Bridges quoted in Charles P. Larrowe, *Harry Bridges: The Rise and Fall of Radical Labor in the U.S.* (New York: Lawrence Hill, 1972), 8.

5 In the nonunion years, stevedore companies cashed brass checks on vary-ing days and at different hours. Longshoremen might be working for new companies when their old ones were paying off. Or, since so many men worked intermittently, often they were too broke to wait for these staggered check-cashing opportunities. Consequently, loan and extortion rackets like the brass check system Bridges describes flourished on the waterfront during the Blue Book era. See David F. Selvin, *A Terrible Anger: The 1934 Waterfront and General Strikes in San Francisco* (Detroit: Wayne State University Press, 1996), 36.

6 The MWIU was a Communist Party–led, ultra-left organization founded in 1930. It was disbanded in 1935.

7 Two classic studies contrast the ILA and the ILWU: Charles P. Larrowe,

Shape-Up and Hiring Hall: A Comparison of Hiring Methods and Labor Relations on the New York and Seattle Waterfronts (Berkeley: University of California Press, 1955), and Howard Kimeldorf, *Reds or Rackets? The Making of Radical and Conservative Unions on the Waterfront* (Berkeley: University of California Press, 1988).

8 The National Recovery Administration was created by the National Industrial Recovery Act (NIRA) of 1933 as part of President Franklin D. Roosevelt's early New Deal. The NRA industry codes, aimed at revitalizing the depressed economy, invoked NIRA section 7a, which promised workers the right to organize into unions of their own choosing. However, enforcement was weak. The NIRA was declared unconstitutional in 1935, but the section 7a concept was reintroduced that year in the National Labor Relations Act, or Wagner Act, which offered better enforcement.

9 Technically, this was the Twenty-seventh Annual Convention of the Pacific Coast District, ILA.

10 The six-hour day was a share-the-work plan, since jobs were scarce during the Depression.

11 At this meeting, Bridges's proposal of a secret ballot was shouted down. The San Francisco longshoremen then immediately and overwhelmingly rejected the June 16 agreement in an open vote.

12 Bridges's point was that now Matson and the other shippers could no longer sustain the Blue Book's closed shop system. Matson had fired four men for wearing ILA buttons to work. Once they were reinstated, the way was open for the ILA to replace the Blue Book.

13 Other workers, like Henry Schmidt, also testified during 1934, but Bridges was the most prominent union speaker.

14 The year of the interview (1969) accounts for Chester's use of the dated term "Negro."

15 The ILWU backed Brown strongly during his early campaigns. He became a powerful Democratic Party leader in state government and later the first black mayor of San Francisco.

16 Bridges and other ILWU officers once suspended the charter of a unit of an important warehouse local for practicing discrimination. See Harvey Schwartz, "A Union Combats Racism: The ILWU's Japanese-American 'Stockton Incident' of 1945," *Southern California Quarterly* 62 (1980): 161–76. On the conservative opposition to Bridges in his own local, see William Issel, "'A Stern Struggle': Catholic Activism and San Francisco Labor, 1934–1958," in Robert W. Cherny, William Issel, and Kieran Walsh Taylor, eds., *American Labor and the Cold War: Grassroots Politics and Postwar Political Culture* (New Brunswick, N.J.: Rutgers University Press, 2004), 166.

17 The CLS offered classes in everything from collective bargaining to labor theater. It was close to the Communist Party and was supported by the labor movement's most progressive unions. The school was red-baited and forced to close down during the McCarthy period. On the CLS, see Jess M. Rigelhaupt, "Education for Action: The California Labor School, Radical Unionism, Civil Rights, and Progressive Coalition Building in the San Francisco Bay Area, 1934–1970" (Ph.D. diss., University of Michigan, 2005).

18 The term "B man" replaced the union's older name for a probationary worker, or permit man. The 1947 Taft-Hartley Act outlawed preference in employment for full union members as well as union-selected permit men. ILWU longshore workers had been categorized as union members, who had the first pick of jobs; permit workers, who picked next; and casuals, who picked last. So in 1959, when the employers and the union opened the job rolls for the first time after Taft-Hartley, they renamed the first two categories. Full members were now A-men and permit workers were B-men. See Larrowe, *Harry Bridges*, 362.

19 Bridges always had an eye to building the widest possible version of maritime union solidarity. The CMU was his second attempt to institutionalize this vision. The first was the Maritime Federation of the Pacific, established in 1935, which foundered after 1937 when the ILWU and the Sailors' Union of the Pacific became estranged.

20 In a controversial departure from the past, as part of the 1966 longshore contract, the ILWU gave employers the right to hire highly skilled workers on a monthly basis instead of relying on employees from the union-controlled hiring hall.

21 Like many ILWU pensioners, Kelm carried his union dedication into retirement. For eighteen years, he consistently contributed handsomely to ILWU-related cultural, political, and educational causes.

22 Kagel already had some experience. While in law school at Boalt Hall, he arbitrated disputes between the International Ladies Garment Workers Union (ILGWU) and San Francisco clothing employers.

23 At 134 days, the 1971 dispute was the longest waterfront strike in ILWU history. Several ILWU veterans hold that Bridges was slow to settle due to his displeasure with his union's most militant young members, who he felt had pushed unreasonably hard for a strike in the first place.

24 Rubio, a future ILWU International vice president, represented his local from southern California in steady-man arbitration hearings before Kagel. Various steady-man cases were ultimately settled on a port-by-port basis.

25 Rigging to help remove an injured or stricken worker from a ship.

2 LONGSHORE: THE LOS ANGELES AND LONG BEACH HARBORS

1   Melvyn Dubofsky, *We Shall Be All: A History of the Industrial Workers of the World* (New York: Quadrangle, 1969), 474–75. For the relationship of IWW ideas to the maritime union upsurge on the Pacific Coast during the Depression, see Bruce Nelson, *Workers on the Waterfront: Seamen, Longshoremen, and Unionism in the 1930s* (Urbana: University of Chicago Press, 1990).

2   Parker and Knudsen were shot during this raid on the scab stockade at Pier 145 in Wilmington's West Basin.

3   An important combined IWW–International Union of Mine, Mill and Smelter Workers (IUMMSW) strike occurred in Arizona's Clifton-Morenci copper district in 1917. Many of the ten thousand strikers were Spanish-speaking. See Dubofksy, *We Shall Be All*, 371–73, 417–18.

4   This might have been the Clifton-Morenci strike, or another strike from the same period.

5   In 1946 Local 13 voted to drop five hundred longshoremen from registration. Most were black workers who had joined the local during the peak cargo years of World War II, 1942–45. The five hundred got their jobs back in 1949 following legal proceedings. For more on the Unemployed 500, see the interview with Walter Williams, below.

6   L. B. Thomas and Bill Lawrence were key Local 13 leaders.

7   In *Divided We Stand: American Workers and the Struggle for Black Equality* (Princeton, N.J.: Princeton University Press, 2001), Bruce Nelson uses the Unemployed 500 case to call this tradition into question. Taking account of people like Local 26's Seeliger and Newton, though, alters the L.A. picture significantly. On the other hand, for years there was an unofficial color line in hiring at longshore Local 8 in Portland, Oregon. But pressure from the ILWU International leadership and other locals helped to overcome this in the 1960s.

8   Copra is dried coconut meat. The association is dedicated to preserving an obsolete copra crane on the San Francisco waterfront as a tribute to the city's workers. See Harvey Schwartz, "Building a Labor-Community Alliance: San Francisco Unionists and the Coalition to Save the Copra Crane," *Labor Studies Journal* 33, no. 2 (June 2008): 203–12.

9   The Taft-Hartley Act was passed by conservative members of Congress in 1947. It had several passages aimed at crippling labor unions. One allowed the president to temporarily suspend a strike through injunction. Although he initially opposed Taft-Hartley, Truman used this power against the ILWU in 1948.

3 LONGBOARD, SHIPBOARD, AND BOOKS: THE PACIFIC NORTHWEST AND CANADA

1   The spelling of the names of the seven workers who died in 1934 varies in both primary and secondary sources. I have tried to reconcile these differences as much as possible.

2   This incident occurred in late August 1934, about three weeks after the strike ended. The October 1934 arbitration award eliminated all vestiges of the longshore company-union scab hall.

3   On Coos Bay history, see Nathan Douthit, *The Coos Bay Region, 1890– 1944: Life on a Coastal Frontier* (Coos Bay, Ore.: West River Books, 1981), and William G. Robbins, *Hard Times in Paradise: Coos Bay, Oregon*, rev. ed. (1998; Seattle: University of Washington Press, 2006). The town of Coos Bay was called Marshfield until 1944. For simplicity, I have used the town's modern name, as did the workers quoted here.

4   In a 1919 incident known as the "Centralia massacre," war veteran and IWW member Wesley Everest was cornered by American Legion members after a gun battle in Centralia, Washington. He surrendered but was castrated and lynched.

5   The Workers Alliance of America was a union of people employed in emergency work-relief programs. It was especially active during the late 1930s.

6   In 1950 Bridges posted bail during one of the legal proceedings against him, but his bail was revoked when he criticized the U.S. entry into the Korean War. Bridges advocated letting the United Nations resolve the conflict through a cease-fire and negotiations. A court of appeals reinstated his right to bail, and he was freed after spending three weeks in the San Francisco county jail.

7   During the McCarthy period, hundreds of activists like Taylor were grilled before U.S. House and Senate subversive activities committees. Many lost their jobs or had their lives disrupted in other ways as a result.

8   This CIO union was close to the ILWU.

9   Lelli spearheaded Local 23 projects that produced Ronald Magden's and A. D. Martinson's books on Tacoma: Ronald E. Magden, *The Working Longshoreman* (Tacoma, Wash.: ILWU Local 23, 1991), and Ronald E. Magden and A. D. Martinson, *The Working Waterfront: The Story of Tacoma's Ships and Men* (Tacoma, Wash.: ILWU Local 23, 1982). He also ardently supported the founding of the Harry Bridges Chair in Labor Studies at the University of Washington.

10   On the IBL, see Magden and Martinson, *The Working Waterfront*, 141–44.

11   William T. (Paddy) Morris, the key Tacoma ILA leader in the 1920s, was an ILA loyalist who fought bitterly with Bridges and the ILWU in the 1930s.

12   Under the 1972 contract, longshore workers were guaranteed a certain number of hours of employment per week. PGP was set up to administer the plan.

13 As noted in chapter 1, in 1966 the employers gained the right to hire highly skilled workers on a steady basis instead of relying solely on the union-controlled hiring hall for employees.

14 In this instance, the Vancouver longshoremen were given a new charter formally acknowledging them as part of the ILWU. The custom of issuing charters to new groups of workers or to restructured groups of already organized workers is common throughout the labor movement.

15 The IBU had a long history of affiliations going back to its founding as the San Francisco Ferryboatmen's Union in 1918. It was called the IBU and was part of the International Seamen's Union (ISU), AFL, in 1937, when its members voted to join the new CIO. In 1948 the IBU switched back to an AFL-affiliated group, the Seafarers International Union (SIU). It left the SIU thirty years later.

16 Making the ferry workers civil servants would have put several employment conditions under state control and out of bounds for collective bargaining. This was anathema to Liddle and the union's membership.

17 The legislation removed the most debilitating limitations of civil service status.

18 The MEBA is a union that represents shipboard engineers.

19 Twenty years later the ILWU was still trying to get shippers to curb cancer-causing toxic fume emissions at major West Coast ports. See Jeff Quam-Wickham with Gene Darling, "Oil Barges, Tankers and Toxic Fumes," *Labor Occupational Health Program Monitor*, University of California, Berkeley (April–June 1988), 5–9; John Showalter, "Pacific Northwest, Canadian Locals Join Discussion on Port Air Pollution," *The Dispatcher* (July–August 2007), 8.

20 By this time warehouse Local 6, ILWU, had represented workers at Stacey's Bookstore in San Francisco for many years.

4 WAREHOUSE AND COTTON COMPRESS: CALIFORNIA

1 On the warehouse drive in northern California, see Harvey Schwartz, *The March Inland: Origins of the ILWU Warehouse Division, 1934–1938* (Los Angeles: Institute of Industrial Relations, University of California, 1978; reprint, San Francisco: ILWU, 2000). As a dramatic but temporary expansion of the march inland, the ILWU organized several warehouse locals in the Midwest and the South during World War II. The union lost them in the late 1940s and early 1950s during the McCarthy era. In the 1960s, though, the ILWU gained a new inland jurisdiction in the borax-mining complex in Boron, California.

2 A person with a union-issued strike clearance card could travel along the waterfront without being suspected by pickets of being a strikebreaker. Most of

the workers who labored on the waterfront of storage/dock marine terminals supported the longshoremen during the 1934 strike. They were actually close to being longshore workers themselves.

3   Bridges actually wanted to make the East Bay terminals part of the ILA's Bay Area longshore local. He was well aware that marine terminal work bore a close resemblance to longshore work. However, the post-1934 strike arbitration decisions by the National Longshoremen's Board, of October 12 and 17, kept the two separate by defining longshore work quite narrowly. The East Bay marine terminals remained in the ILA and then the ILWU warehouse local for years. Finally, in the early 1960s, they were switched into ILWU longshore Local 10.

4   There were big simultaneous walkouts in both longshore and warehouse during 1936–37.

5   This is the Communist Party union mentioned by Bridges in chapter 1.

6   Initially Heide was paid a commission for each worker he brought into the warehouse local, but he was so successful that he found his profits embarrassing. After a month he asked the local's executive board to put him on a salary basis. The board was happy to oblige. See Schwartz, *The March Inland*, 80–82.

7   Colgate initially had a gentlemen's agreement that barred its black janitors from promotions, but Colgate's union members followed Ray Heide's lead and voted to confront this. In 1939 Eugene Lasartemay became Colgate's first black worker promoted from janitor to a better job. In the 1930s the warehouse local also used its hiring hall to break the color line. If a company ordered a crew dispatched to a job but refused a black worker, that crew and every successive one would return to the hall until the employer relented.

8   Chili Duarte later became a prominent president of the warehouse local.

9   The ending of Local 6's early experiment with fishbowl, or open, negotiations was not particularly controversial. There was also not much of a clamor nationwide for this sort of negotiations.

10 Hackett's first name was Charles, but he always preferred to be called Brother Hackett.

11 Hendricks was known as Billie Roberts during the early part of her warehouse union years. She became Billie Roberts Hendricks when she married Fred Hendricks in 1943.

12 During the 1920s and 1970s–80s feminists tried unsuccessfully to add an equal rights amendment to the constitution. Some working-class women felt indifferent to what they saw as a middle-class cause.

13 The celebrated writer Tillie Olsen was a strong ILWU supporter. Her husband, Jack, was a Local 6 officer. His oral history testimony is in chapter 6.

14 For a profile of Seeliger and the expansion of Local 26 in the 1930s, see

Mario T. Garcia, *Memories of Chicano History: The Life and Narrative of Bert Corona* (Berkeley: University of California Press, 1994), 88–103.

15 The Fair Labor Standards Act (FLSA) mandating time and a half after the forty-hour workweek was not passed by Congress until 1938.

16 Colgate's Berkeley plant closed in the early 1980s.

17 Moved loads of canned products.

18 For more on the left-progressive California Labor School, see "Cleophas Williams: African American President" in chapter 1.

19 For occasional references to the ILWU's progressive social and political role in Oakland and environs as viewed by a scholar of the new suburban history, see Robert O. Self, *American Babylon: Race and the Struggle for Postwar Oakland* (Princeton, N.J.: Princeton University Press, 2003).

20 For more on the IBU, see "The Inlandboatmen's Union Joins the ILWU, 1978–1987," in chapter 3.

21 After the ILWU was expelled from the CIO in 1950, it functioned as an independent union for thirty-eight years. The AFL and the CIO merged in 1955 as the AFL-CIO. In 1988 the ILWU joined that national body.

22 For in-depth discussion of organizing in the South, see Michael K. Honey, *Southern Labor and Black Civil Rights: Organizing Memphis Workers* (Urbana: University of Illinois Press, 1993), *Black Workers Remember: An Oral History of Segregation, Unionism, and the Freedom Struggle* (Berkeley: University of California Press, 1999), and *Going Down Jericho Road: The Memphis Strike, Martin Luther King's Last Campaign* (New York: W.W. Norton, 2007).

23 The ILWU remains committed in the Central Valley. Since the 1990s, it has been organizing warehouse and distribution workers in the California interior, from Sacramento in the north to the inland environs of Los Angeles in the south.

5 AGRICULTURE: HAWAII

1 Edward D. Beechert, *Working in Hawaii: A Labor History* (Honolulu: University of Hawaii Press, 1985), 80, 134; Sanford Zalburg, *A Spark Is Struck! Jack Hall and the ILWU in Hawaii* (Honolulu: University of Hawaii Press, 1979), 16. The Big Five were Castle and Cooke, American Factors (Amfac), Alexander and Baldwin, C. Brewer, and Theo H. Davies.

2 For in-depth discussion of the trials of single-race unions and their ill-fated strikes between 1900 and the 1930s, including information on Pablo Manlapit's initial organizing forays and his surprising but constricted efforts to close ranks with the Japanese as early as 1919, see Beechert, *Working in Hawaii*, 161–232.

3 This incident, among the most notorious in Hawaiian labor history, occurred during an Inter-Island Steam Navigation Company strike by the ILWU and the IBU, who were seeking the closed shop and wage parity with the West Coast (they won neither in 1938). No one was killed on August 1, when police fired upon a peaceful demonstration against the use of scab labor, but several workers were severely hurt by heavy-duty buckshot. See Beechert, *Working in Hawaii*, 263–68.

4 Hall's 1953 conviction was reversed by the Supreme Court in 1958. See T. Michael Holmes, *The Specter of Communism in Hawaii* (Honolulu: University of Hawaii Press, 1994), 190–211.

5 Some lessons were held at the California Labor School in San Francisco.

6 A decade later the union had similar goals in negotiating its longshore Mechanization and Modernization Agreement.

7 Martin had to stay on his job in Hawaii instead of joining the merchant marine. Most Hawaiian workers were frozen on their jobs during the war. Only known union activists "left" jobs; they were drafted when employers wanted them out of the way. Jack Hall got into Territorial government service in 1942 and was not drafted.

8 Pedro de la Cruz, Lanai's charismatic leader, was known as both Pedro and Pete. He attracted a special following because of his unique kindness as a field boss, his good judgment, and his integrity. De la Cruz gave up his field boss position to back the union. He was Lanai ILWU business agent for twenty-nine years and served in the state legislature from 1958 to 1974.

9 This incident helped overcome national division. Secinando Bueno put it bluntly: "In 1946 the Filipinos didn't like the Japanese because of World War II. I had the same feeling." But, he added, "as I became involved in the union, I believed that there is no discrimination. Our aim is to work together. I found out that past is past."

10 Women in Hawaii generally suffered from poor wages, long hours, and few opportunities in the 1930s. For many, this continued during the war, when people were frozen in low-paying jobs and the military suspended the Fair Labor Standards Act. Training seemed beyond reach for many women, too. A 1937 survey showed that 61 percent of young men applying to employment agencies listed no skill or occupation; the figure for women was 89 percent. Beechert, *Working in Hawaii*, 250–54. Seasonal cannery work and field labor provided the main employment opportunities for numerous women at least into the 1940s. Historically, men of different nationalities arrived first to work in Hawaiian agriculture. But the percentage of women employed in the canneries and fields rose as immigrant families were reunited. In 1946 about 65 percent of cannery workers and 10 percent of field laborers were women. (Women were a larger proportion of field workers before the

1946 importation of six thousand Filipino men.) Beechert, telephone interview, June 27, 2007.

11 Bob McElrath followed Hall as Hawaii regional director in 1969. Earlier he was involved in one of the ILWU's legendary Islands episodes. In 1951 Bob McElrath and Hawaii ILWU educational director Dave Thompson arranged for the former to secretly tape-record an FBI visit to Thompson's house. During the visit two FBI agents asked Thompson to convince Hall to split Hawaii's unionists from the mainland ILWU in exchange for release as a Smith Act defendant. McElrath and Thompson subsequently played the tape on Hawaii radio. (Dave Thompson and Frank Thompson were not related.) See Zalburg, *A Spark Is Struck!* 334–36; *The Dispatcher* (July 1995), 9.

12 Ichiro Izuka was a former Communist Party member and Kauai ILWU leader who issued "The Truth about Communism in Hawaii," a thirty-one-page pamphlet, in 1947. The pamphlet red-baited the ILWU. It was widely circulated, in part due to Big Five funding. While it concerned the union, it was not as much of a challenge as the Ignacio Revolt described by Goldblatt. See Zalburg, *A Spark Is Struck!*, 205–17; Beechert, *Working in Hawaii*, 306–8.

13 See Goldblatt's first testimony for a fuller description of the Little Wagner Act (the Hawaii Employee Relations Act of 1945).

14 As Goldblatt noted, the Territorial government functioned at the direction of the Big Five. But under the leadership of Jack Hall and the ILWU, Hawaii politics underwent a drastic change. In 1962, three years after statehood, Hawaii elected its first liberal Democratic governor, John A. Burns, with strong ILWU backing. Burns remained governor for twelve years with ILWU support. Dave Thompson was the ILWU education director in Hawaii between 1946 and 1979. When interviewed by Edward Beechert in 1966, Thompson testified that Burns "said that the ILWU brought democracy to the Islands. What he meant was that the union, for the first time, made it possible for independent, critical opinions to be expressed. It used to be that there were plantations that a Democratic politician could not go into to hold a political rally. He'd have to hold it on the public road." Dave Thompson emphasized that by the late 1950s "for the first time you had the development of an effective two-party system in the Islands. And, of course, it was the ILWU that had made this possible." See Harvey Schwartz, ed., "Dave Thompson: Islands Activist, 1946–1958," *The Dispatcher* (October 2006), 7.

15 While most of Hawaii's sugar and pineapple plantations closed during the latter decades of the twentieth century, the ILWU still exercised economic and political influence in the Islands fifty years after statehood. This was due in large measure to the union's early organizing of the hotel industry on

the Outer Islands, where the union retained an important presence in 2009. The union also helped to keep Hawaiian politics a two-party system with its ongoing endorsements of political candidates that it felt were union- and worker-friendly. Generally, although not always, this meant that the union backed Democrats, who often achieved electoral success.

6 POLITICS: THE OLD LEFT

1 The Social Security Act of 1935 included unemployment compensation.

2 In the mid-twentieth century, Burroughs business machines were standard devices for office accountants.

3 During 1949–50, the national CIO used predetermined "trials" to purge eleven unions it considered Communist influenced, including the ILWU. Devastating inter-union raiding and intra-union dissention followed.

4 Stalin died in 1953. Many American CP members left the Party in 1956 after Russian leader Nikita Khrushchev delivered a famous speech denouncing Stalin's atrocities.

5 In contrast, many authorities hold that, in purging its eleven member unions accused of Communism in 1949–50, the CIO encouraged timidity and bureaucratization in place of militancy and union democracy and so contributed to the late-twentieth-century decline of the American labor movement. See Ellen Schrecker, "Labor and the Cold War: The Legacy of McCarthyism," in Robert W. Cherny, William Issel, and Kieran Walsh Taylor, eds., *American Labor and the Cold War: Grassroots Politics and Postwar Political Culture* (New Brunswick, N.J.: Rutgers University Press, 2004), 15–19; Steve Rosswurm, ed., *The CIO's Left-Led Unions* (New Brunswick, N.J.: Rutgers University Press, 1992), 12–16.

6 The Taft-Hartley Act requirement that union officers sign non-Communist affidavits before their organizations could have access to NLRB elections was a serious blow to several left-led unions. Political tests like this were eventually declared unconstitutional.

7 Herman followed Bridges as ILWU International president. He held that post from 1977 to 1991.

8 The Burtons became highly influential progressive leaders in California politics. Brown, who was very liberal in his early career, was a long-term power in the California Democratic Party.

9 This was an informal, rank-and-file program created to systematically collect money along the waterfront for Cesar Chavez's fledging United Farm Workers.

GLOSSARY

ARBITRATION the hearing and settlement by a neutral party, or arbitrator, of a case in dispute

BEEF a complaint, disagreement, confrontation, or strike

BLACKLIST a "do not hire" list used to exclude unionists from employment

BRASS CHECKS brass tokens redeemed for cash for longshore work in the pre-1934 era

BREAK BULK CARGO hand-worked freight typical of longshoring before shipborne cargo was transported in huge containers

BUMMING asking for contributions of food or money to help sustain workers during a strike

BUSINESS AGENT a local union representative who, in the ILWU, is elected from the rank and file

CANS waterfront name for containers

CARGO HOOK a hand-held tool for moving break bulk cargo; also refers to the big hook attached to a ship's winch system

CLOSED SHOP a work site at which all employees must be union members; the opposite of an open shop, where employees may be nonunion

COASTWISE a shorthand reference to the whole West Coast longshore industry

COMPANY UNION an employer-controlled union, created to avoid genuine collective bargaining

COPRA dried coconut meat

COTTON COMPRESSING the employment of a giant compressor to reduce huge bales of cotton for storage and shipment

DISPATCHER a person who sends people to work sites

FINK HALL an employer-run hiring hall characterized by favoritism, discrimination, and corruption

FLETCHERS long, heavy, squared timbers

FORKLIFT a motorized conveyance used to move, stack, and unstack cargo

FOUR-WHEELER a trailer used for moving large amounts of freight; often attached to and pulled by a vehicle called a "bull"

GEARMAN a specialized longshore employee who works in a gear locker maintaining and repairing waterfront equipment

GENERAL STRIKE a strike in which all workers in an entire city or region quit their jobs

GRIEVANCES complaints about breaches of a union contract that often end up in arbitration

HAND TRUCK a wheeled conveyance for moving freight

HATCH an opening in the deck of a ship

HATCH TENDER an employee who uses signals to make sure dockworkers, hold workers, and winch drivers are proceeding safely

HAOLE a person who is not descended from the original Polynesians of Hawaii; occasionally used disparagingly toward whites

HIGH-PILER a worker, typically in a warehouse, who piles heavy bags of products to great heights without mechanical aids

HIP POCKET RULE a noncontract waterfront job regulation developed by consensus of the workers

HOLD the cargo deck or compartment of a ship

INDUSTRIAL UNION a union of workers in an industry irrespective of their occupations or crafts, in contrast to a craft union

INTERMODAL transportation by more than one form of carrier, such as combined ship and rail service

INTERNATIONAL UNION an umbrella body that ties together or unites a union's various local units

JITNEY a motorized conveyance used to move cargo from place to place

JOB ACTION a quickie strike, or a spontaneous and usually brief work stoppage

KICKBACK extorted payment for employment

LASHING securing or releasing containers on the deck of a ship using large fasteners that are under heavy tension when tightened

LOCAL UNIONS various geographical units that typically are tied together or united under an international union structure

LOCKOUT an employer strike against his or her employees

LONGSHORE GANG a waterfront work group

LONGSHORE HOOK another term for a hand-held cargo hook

LUNA field boss in Hawaii

MANNING the number of workers required for a particular job under a union contract

MASTER CONTRACT a labor agreement covering an entire industry

MECHANIZATION the replacement of human labor with machine power

MEDIATION intervention between conflicting parties to promote a settlement or compromise

PALLETIZED LOADS cargo on portable platforms that can be lifted, moved, and stored by using forklifts

PERMIT MAN someone with a permit from the union to work who is not yet a full member of the union; since 1959, called a "B-man" as distinguished from a full member, or "A-man"

PICKET a unionist posted at a work site affected by a strike to discourage people from crossing a union picket line

PORK CHOP ISSUES nonpolitical union concerns about basic working conditions

PREREQUISITE SYSTEM the supplying of bad company housing and poor medical services, instead of cash, to workers in Hawaii

RAIDING a union taking over workers who belong to another union

RANK AND FILE the members of a union as distinguished from its leaders

SCAB a pejorative name for a strikebreaker

SCREENING a McCarthy-era government program that denied maritime employment to people suspected of Communist sympathies; even politically moderate union activists were often caught in this dragnet

SHAPE-UP an exploitative hiring system in which workers gather in the hope of finding employment

SLING LOAD break bulk cargo loaded onto a large sling and hoisted aloft by winch to be moved into or out of a ship

SPEED-UP forcing employees to work at an unreasonably rapid and often unsafe pace

STEADY GANG, STEADY MEN employees who work for a single company

STRADS OR STRADDLE CARRIERS tall, mobile conveyances that can straddle railroad cars in transporting containers

STEWARD an on-the-job union representative

TANKERMAN an IBU member who loads and unloads oil tankers or oil barges

TOP PICK a mobile container-handling conveyance with a high reach

TRAMP SHIP a steamship that sailed unscheduled from port to port, trying to move or peddle various sorts of products

UNION HIRING HALL an employment system under the control of workers and their union representatives

UNION SHOP a work site in which employees must join the union after a specified period of time on the job

WALKING BOSS foreman

WINCHES shipboard machine hoists commonly used in the pre-container era to lift and lower loads of cargo

WOBBLY a member of the Industrial Workers of the World

A NOTE ON SOURCES

THE DISPATCHER ARTICLES THAT FORM THE BASIS FOR THIS BOOK ORIGI-
nated with an ambitious oral history project the ILWU undertook during
1981–86 in partnership with the Institute for the Study of Social Change (ISSC)
at the University of California, Berkeley. That project was funded by a major
grant from the National Endowment for the Humanities (NEH).

Awarded under the rubric of "the new labor history," the NEH grant
charged the project's staff with looking at the union's past from the worker's
perspective. Rather than focusing, in the traditional manner, solely on top leaders or the institutional record of the union, the project targeted the recollections
of workers on the docks, in the warehouses, and in the agricultural fields.

Daniel S. Beagle had the original idea to systematically collect oral histories
of ILWU veterans. In the late 1970s and early 1980s, Beagle was the editor of
The Dispatcher. For academic guidance and grant development, he consulted
David T. Wellman, then a University of Oregon sociology professor and a
research associate at the ISSC.

Beagle and Wellman became the NEH project co-directors; I was appointed
coordinator. Ultimately, we interviewed 206 ILWU men and women from a
number of the union's locals and bargaining units in California, Oregon, and
Hawaii. Toward the end of the NEH grant period, the L. J. Skaggs and Mary C.
Skaggs Foundation aided our work with a generous supplemental award.

Many of the 206 people interviewed in the 1980s are quoted in this book. I
have, though, listed everyone recorded under the NEH grant. Quoted or not,

every ILWU veteran who sat for an NEH interview contributed significantly to the making of this book and to the union's valuable oral history collection, which is housed in the archives of the ILWU International library in San Francisco.

The great majority of the NEH tapes are full-life histories covering birth date, ethnicity, youth, education, military service, work experience, union activity, and retirement. I adhered to this approach in conducting interviews subsequent to the NEH project. Several later discussions became the basis for *Dispatcher* articles and sections of this book. Those tapes, which are also in the ILWU library, are listed below, too.

The unreliability of memory is always a concern in oral history. In conducting the NEH interviews, we were aware of the need to validate recollections, and we undertook extensive background research in the union's archives to prepare for recording sessions. Armed with traditional historical information, NEH project interviewers were able not only to ask pertinent questions but also to spot problems of memory. For further validation, we routinely interviewed several workers about the same events. I sought to maintain the same level of quality control in my post-NEH interviewing and in using other people's recordings.

The use of oral history recordings or transcripts as the basis for a print publication raises the additional issue of permissible editorial interventions. While producing the oral history articles that provided the basis for this book, I eliminated the questions to make the workers' experiences direct and forceful. I often moved passages around and edited to clarify, to reduce redundancy, and to delete extraneous material, such as false starts. Occasionally, I added or corrected a name, place, or date or spliced in a small detail to keep the reader oriented.

Throughout, though, I worked diligently to retain every interviewee's meaning and tone, or style of expression, since these elements give an oral account creditability and value. I have tried always to follow the advice the eminent oral historian Donald A. Ritchie offered in *Doing Oral History* (1995): "Editing and rearranging interviews for clarification and cutting away tangential material are appropriate so long as the original meaning is retained."

Most of the NEH interviews were conducted by Beagle, Wellman, and me. In listing these discussions, I have indicated the interviewers by the initials B, W, and S. Additional interviewers are identified separately. When an area involved multiple locals, the number of the interviewee's local follows his or her name.

The 1981–86 NEH tapes were originally grouped into five geographical areas. They remain archived this way in the ILWU International library in San Francisco.

LOS ANGELES AND LONG BEACH HARBORS AREA

The workers here were almost all from longshore Local 13, warehouse Local 26, fishermen's Local 33, marine clerks' Local 63, and longshore foremen's Local 94. Exceptions are noted. Gordon Webb (GW) was a central interviewer in a number of Local 33 discussions.

Frank Albano, Seafarers International Union (GW, S); Frank Barberia, Seafarers International Union (GW); Mathew Batinovich, 33 (GW, S); Chris Braiwick, 13 (S); Clara Braiwick, 13 wife (S); Sam Clark, 13 (S); Jim Cobbs, 13 (S); John Espinoza, 13, 26 (S); Lester Gatlin, 26 (B); Lonnie Gibbs, 26 (B); Cleophas Gordon, 26 (S); Pete Grassi, 13 (B, S); Elmer Gutierrez, 13 (S); Preston Harris, 13 (S); Riley Hatcher, 13, 26 (S); Lester Heston 13, 94 (S); Theresa Hoinsky , SIU (GW, S); James Johnson, 26 (B); Arthur Kaunisto, 13, 94 (S); Pearl Kibre, 33 wife (GW, S); Mel Kolumbic, 33 (GW, S); Joe Kordich, 13, 26 (S); Dave Kreiger, 13, 94 (B,W); Al Langley, 13 (S); A. Lesure, 26 (B); L. L. Loveridge, 13 (S); John Mahone, 13 (S); John Martinez, 13, 94 (S); Elmer Mevert, 13, 63 (S); George Mitchell, 13 (B, W); John Mitchell, 13 (S); Joe Monte, 33 (GW, S); Pete Moore, 13, 94 (S); Ruben Negrete, 13 (B); Jackson Newton, 26 (S); Hyman Orkin, 26 (B, W); Thomas Peaster, 26 (B); Felton Reese, 26 (B, S); John Rodin, 13, 94 (S); Archie Royal, 13 (B, W); John Royal, 33 (BW); Antonio Salcido, 13, 94 (S); Connie Gomez Salcido, 13, 94 wife (S); Frank Salcido, 13, 94 (S); Mike Salcido, 13, 94 (S); Ray Salcido, Sr., 13 (S); Loyd Seeliger, 26 (B, S); Louis Sherman, 26 (B, W); William Spruill, 26 (B); Joe Stahl, 13, 94 (S); Claude Stotts, Sr., 63 (S); Frank Sundstedt, 13 (S); Edward Thayne, 13, 94 (S); Joe Uranga, 13 (B, W); Anthony Vidovich, 33 (GW, S); William T. Ward, 13, 63 (S); Paul Ware, IWW (B); Walter Williams, 13 (S); Corky Wilson, 13, 94 (S); Gilbert Zafran, 33 (GW, S)

SAN FRANCISCO BAY AREA

Unionists in this section were all from warehouse Local 6 or were interviewed about that local's history in San Francisco, Oakland, Berkeley, and Emeryville, California. They were all interviewed by me. I was joined in two interviews by Local 6 members John Bennett (B) and Jan Gilbrecht (G). Because I was involved in every interview in this section, my participation is not noted.

Bill Batchan; Joseph Blasquez; Dick Boyer; Chester Bregy; Bill Burke; David

Burgess; Bill Castagnasso; Ray Casazza; Marcelee Cashmere; Joseph B. Chambers; Albert T. Cummins; Sylvester Daniels; Joe Diamond; Luther Dolin; Edith Dracovich; Manuel Dracovich; Ray Duarte; Mary M. Danahey; Homer Dunlap; Keith Eickman; Frank Estrada; Guthrie Ewing; Ole Fagerhaugh; Daniel V. Flanagan (B); Joe Gomes; Lou Gonick; Dave Gonzales; Pauline Goulart; Lou Granzella; Sam Guereque; Frank Guzman; Charles A. Hackett; Hiram Hanspard; Paul Heide; Wilhelmina Heide; David Hipolito (G); Alicia Juarez; Dave Jenkins; Joe Kabush; Charles Kelly; Mary Lacey; Walt Lacey; Teodoro V. Lira; Raymond Lord; Joe Lynch; George Lucchesi; Albie Marino; Lee Martinez; Manuel Martinez; Tony Mello; Joe Mendonca; Ann Milam; Art Nelson; Jack Olsen; Curtis McClain; Walt Reposa; Sneed Reynolds; Jose Rodriquez; Otto Rupe; Virginia Orosco Salas; Frank Shaub; Howard Shirley; Loren Smith; Carl Spitz; Joe Valin; Mary Valin; Matt Vidmar; Fannie Walker; Barbara Whaley; Eddie Williams; Virginia Wysinger; Kathryn Young.

In addition to these tapes, the ILWU International library holds a collection of forty interviews conducted by the Local 6 Archives Project in the early 1980s. That project was coordinated by John Bennett, Tom Edminster, Jan Gilbrecht, Gayle Pearl, Bob Slattery, and other Local 6 rank-and-file members. In 1981, Gilbrecht and Slattery interviewed Lillian Prince, who is quoted here. ILWU librarian Carol Cuenod conducted the interview with Billie Roberts Hendricks, excerpted extensively in chapter 4, in 1982 as part of the Local 6 project.

THE CENTRAL VALLEY OF CALIFORNIA

Most interviewees listed here were cotton compress workers who belonged to warehouse Local 26 (Los Angeles and Bakersfield) or cotton compress Local 57 (Fresno). The few individuals who were not Local 26 or 57 members but were interviewed about the Central Valley are identified as such.

Ethel Alexander, wife of organizer (B); Willie Ambers, 57 (S); Albert Barrios, 26 (S); David Burciaga, 26 (B, S); Tommy Burse, 26 (S); Bill Chester, International officer (B); Ernest Clark, 57 (B, W); German Clark, 57 (B); Victor Cordova, 26 (S); Nonnie Currie, 57 (S); Ben De La Cruz, 26 (S); Walter Eason, 57 (B, S); Parnell Echols, 57 (S); Elijah Fifer, 26 (B, S); Sterling Green, 26 (S); Peter W. Harris, 26 (S); Reece Herron, 57 (S); Edgar King, 57 (S); LeRoy King, regional director (S); Ruben Lascano, 57 (S); George Lee, 26 (B, S, W); Ollie J. Lewis, 26 (S); John Lindsey, 26 (S); Chet Meske, organizer (B, S); Frank Reyes,

26 (S); John Riggins, 57 (B); Tom Robertson, 26 (S); Lommy Sykes, 57 (B); Floyd Taylor, 57 (B); John Valenzuela, 26 (S); James Walker, 57 (S)

COOS BAY, OREGON

The unionists in this section were almost all longshore Local 12 workers in the small lumber port at Coos Bay. The one exception is Valerie Taylor, the Local 12 wife who led the ILWU women's auxiliary. Joe Canale's participation in several of these interviews is indicated by the letter JC.

Bill Armstrong (B, JC, W); Gene Bailey (JC, W); Lewis Barnekoff (JC, W); John A. Briggs (JC, W); Don Brown (JC, W); Robert C. Christensen (W); Harry F. Coolen (W); Henry Hansen (B, JC, W); Gene Hughes (W); Tim Hughes (JC, W); Carl Jacobsen (JC, W); Pete Kromminga (W); Ted Lopez (JC, W); Everett Richardson (JC, W); Harold Scott (JC, W); Clarence Seamon (W); Clarence Simensen (JC, W); Floyd Smith (JC, W); Forrest Taylor (JC, W); Valerie Taylor, women's auxiliary (JC, W); Glenn Titus (W); C. A. Wilmot (W); Howard Young (JC, W)

LANAI, HAWAII

These workers were all from ILWU Islands-wide Local 142. These discussions emphasized the union's experience on the pineapple island of Lanai. Christopher Conybeare (CC) of the Center for Labor Education and Research at the University of Hawaii participated in several of these interviews.

Catalino Agliam (B, W); Leonora Agliam (B, W); Bill Alboro (B, W); Secinando Bueno (B, W); Pedro Castillo (B, CC, W); Adolph DeShay (B, W); Shiro Hokama (B, W); Domingo Javier (B, W); Sam Kaopuiki (B, W); George Martin (S); Antone Mendes (B, W); Don Nishimura (B, W); George Ohashi (B, CC, W); Joaquina Ohashi (B, CC, W); Kenji Omuro (B); Hiroshi Oshiro (B, W); Manual Pavao (B, W); Elizabeth Pokipula (B, W); Adolfo Sanches (B, CC, W); Caroline Sonido (B, W); Jack Zaan (B, W).

ADDITIONAL INTERVIEWS

After the NEH project, I conducted the following interviews, which are stored in the ILWU International library in San Francisco and became the basis for parts of this book: Burrill Hatch (1996); Sam Kagel (1999); Ted "Whitey" Kelm (2004);

LeRoy King (2002), supplement to NEH interview; Phil Lelli (2002); Don Liddle (1996); Dave Lomis (1995); Ah Quon McElrath (1996); Herb Mills (1998); Ike Morrow (2004); Craig H. Pritchett (1995); Abba Ramos (1996), original recording done for the Labor Archives and Research Center (LARC), San Francisco State University; Marvin Ricks (2001); Roy C. Smith (1995); Jerry Tyler (2002); Bill Ward (1998), supplement to NEH; Don Watson (1994, 2004), done for LARC; Gordon Westrand (1995); Cleophas Williams (1998); Mary Winzig (2001).

Several additional non-NEH discussions that formed the basis for parts of this volume were conducted by interviewers other than me. Noriko ("Nikki") Sawada Bridges recorded her husband, Harry Bridges, in the late 1970s; a copy of these cassettes is at the ILWU International library in San Francisco. Robert Martin taped Bill Chester in 1969; that conversation is now part of the Ralph Bunche Oral History Collection at the Moorland-Spingarm Research Center, Howard University. Professor Emeritus Edward D. Beechert recorded Carl Damaso (1966), Louis Goldblatt (1979), Jack Hall (1966), David E. Thompson (1966), and Frank Thompson (1967) for the Regional Oral History Project, which he founded and directed, at the University of Hawaii. The Bridges epilogue excerpt is from the transcript of the Educational Broadcasting Corporation TV program *Bill Moyers' Journal,* January 29, 1974.

The ILWU library in San Francisco also holds some additional non-NEH interviews conducted by me that are outside the scope of this book. I am listing them here with the dates of their recording so that future scholars and students will be aware of their existence: Local 6, Terry Green (1996), done for LARC, Don Ruth (1996), done for Copra Crane Labor Landmark Association (CCLLA); Local 10, Dave Reed (1995), done for LARC, Michael J. Villeggiante (2008), Ralph Zamacona (1996), done for CCLLA; Locals 10 and 91, Joe Amyes (1996), done for CCLLA, Donald R. Riggs (1996), done for CCLLA, Willard Whitaker (1996), done for CCLLA; Local 17, Dick Boyer (1982), Basil Crutcher (1985), Ben Davis (1985), August Hemenez (1982), Dan Mahoney (1982), Ron Medeiros (1982), Claude Thompson (1985), Frank West (1985); Local 19, Hector Goulet (2002); Local 24, Randy Vekich (2007); Local 30, Ray Panter (2008); Local 34, Ken Fox (1999); Local 37 and Inlandboatmen's Union, Terri Mast (1996).

ACKNOWLEDGMENTS

IN COMPLETING THIS BOOK, I HAVE INCURRED DEBTS TO MANY KNOWLEDGE-able and generous people. First, much thanks to ILWU director of educational services, librarian, and archivist Eugene Dennis Vrana. In 1994, Vrana suggested the series of articles for *The Dispatcher*, the union's newspaper, that ultimately resulted in this volume. Since then, his wise counsel has been invaluable intellectually, strategically, and spiritually.

The ILWU International officers and executive board and Coast Labor Relations Committee (CLRC) members have provided great support through the years. In the early 1980s, when *Dispatcher* editor Daniel S. Beagle and Professor David T. Wellman co-directed the union's original oral history project, ILWU International President James Herman and International Secretary-Treasurer Curtis McClain were exceptionally helpful.

Since the 1980s, much direct aid has come from more ILWU people, including former International Presidents David Arian, Brian McWilliams, and James Spinosa; current International President Robert McEllrath and International Secretary-Treasurer William E. Adams; International office manager and executive secretary Linda Kuhn; the late Hawaii Local 142 social worker Ah Quon McElrath; Local 142 archivist Rae C. Shiraki; and retired Los Angeles longshore Local 13 officer Arthur A. Almeida.

Steve Stallone, former ILWU communications director and editor of *The Dispatcher*, provided valuable assistance that helped strengthen many of the oral history profiles in this book. Thanks for their help as well to *Dispatcher* editor Craig Merrilees, retired *Dispatcher* assistant editor Tom Price, retired ILWU communications specialist Marcy Rein, ILWU clerical assistant Frank Wilder, and Kathy Wilkes, who was editor of *The Dispatcher* in the mid-1990s.

Much gratitude is owed to the National Endowment for the Humanities, which underwrote the ILWU–UC Berkeley oral history project during 1981–86. The subsequent, and deeply appreciated, award from the L. J. Skaggs and Mary C. Skaggs Foundation spanned 1985–86. Since the late 1990s, the CLRC has helped by subsidizing important new interviews.

Recently, too, Karla Lutz has made some extraordinarily generous contributions to the ILWU Legacy Fund that were earmarked to support the union's oral history project. These funds have been of great aid to the project and to the completion of this book.

I also greatly appreciate the efforts of the University of Washington Press's two expert readers, history professor Michael K. Honey and political science professor emeritus David J. Olson. Both are former holders of the Harry Bridges Chair in Labor Studies at the University of Washington, which was endowed by ILWU members and pensioners. Each read my manuscript closely and offered many excellent suggestions, which I have tried diligently to incorporate into my text. Honey worked with the editing of the book through several revisions and helped get it into final form. Oscar Berland, too, gave a draft much thought. I hope I have managed to profit from his wise counsel.

Thanks to Professor Emeritus David Brody, my graduate school dissertation director in the 1970s, for his interest and support over the years. I have returned to his lessons many times in preparing my oral history articles for *The Dispatcher* and in the development of this volume. I also appreciate the sage advice of Professor Emeritus Ronald E. Magden.

Edward D. Beechert, professor emeritus at the University of Hawaii, has been particularly generous in making the superb interviews he recorded about the ILWU in the Islands available to me. Harry Bridges's widow, the late Noriko (Nikki) Sawada Bridges Flynn, and Professor Robert W. Cherny of San Francisco State University graciously provided access to her invaluable 1970s tapes of the ILWU founder.

Carol Cuenod, former ILWU librarian, has helped me in numerous ways since I was a graduate student researching the union in the early 1970s. Recently she generously allowed me to use her outstanding 1982 interview with Billie Roberts Hendricks, which is part of chapter 4 of this book.

Several librarians beyond the ILWU have aided my work. These include Lynn A. Bonfield, founding director of the Labor Archives and Research Center at San Francisco State University, and Susan Sherwood, former acting director of that facility; current Labor Archives director Catherine Powell; Susan Goldstein, city archivist, San Francisco Public Library; Joellen ElBashir, curator at the Moorland-Spingarn Research Center, Howard University; and staff members at the libraries of the University of California, Berkeley, the University of Hawaii, the California and Oregon Historical Societies, and the Los Angeles Public Library. Conor Casey and Jeff Rosen of the Labor Archives and Research Center have also been helpful.

For invitations to speak at their schools on interviewing, publishing, and the ILWU oral history project, special thanks to Professors Dan Jacoby, former Harry Bridges Chair in Labor Studies at the University of Washington; Kathy Nasstrom, University of San Francisco; and Donald Spivey, former director of the distinguished lecturer series, University of Miami. I also appreciate being able to deliver related papers to the Southwest Labor Studies Conference and the Bay Area Labor History Workshop. These occasions allowed me to refine some of my ideas about the craft of oral history.

Thanks to Thirteen/WNET New York for granting me permission to use the excerpt from the January 29, 1974, Bill Moyers interview with Harry Bridges that appears in the epilogue. Lylian Morcos of Thirteen/WNET was particularly accommodating. I also appreciate the efforts of photographer Slobodan Dimitrov, who copied a rare picture of Dick Parker for me at the Los Angeles Public Library, San Pedro Branch.

In the 1980s, a number of my students in the Labor Studies Program at San Francisco State University aided the original ILWU-NEH oral history project by doing useful research and making valuable indexes to taped interviews. One, Nancy-Quam Wickham, went on to become a history professor at California State University, Long Beach, and, using the ILWU-NEH tape collection, the author of an influential scholarly article on longshore Local 13. That essay is part of Steven Rosswurm's *The CIO's Left-Led Unions* (listed here in Further Reading).

The other San Francisco State students were Carolyn Aaron, Marcia Addams, John A. Beal, Michele Bignardi, Marilyn Burnham, Michael Burns, Bill Cannon, Manuel Chaffo, Carolyn Davis, Patricia Dickinson, Paul Dillon, Alison Devenere, Shelton Douthit, Sandra Fitting, Meg Goldberg, Cirilio Gonzales, Ron Greenberg, Mary (Molly) Hassler, Arthur J. Heether, Melanie

Heisler, Sanford Hood, David Kaufman, Bill Keast, Michael Lajoie, Emile Lewis, Miriam MacNair, Theresa McGovern, Lisa McLaughlin, Margie Marks, Daniel H. Martin, Richard T. Mead, Raymond Mosley, Jr., Chris Murray, Clara M. Nealy, Scott Olson, Richard Pak, Kathleen A. Riley, Diane Sandrowski, David Saterlie, Carolyn Secrease, Robert L. Sparks, John P. Spriggs, Jon Sternberg, Janine Storey, Ronald M. Takahashi, Jim Tobin, Mary Tramil, Diana Webb, Gordon Webb, Judith G. Wernick, Thomas E. White, Jean Whitehead, and Dennis K. Wong. UC Berkeley student Linda Facio and Antioch College student Julia O'Halloran also worked on the project.

I have received help and inspiration in various ways from many more friends and colleagues, including ILW pensioners officer Richard Austin, ILWU research director Russ Bargmann, Richard Bermack, Charles Bergquist, Joseph A. Blum, J. A. Bowman, Maria Brooks, Paulette Burnard, Claude Caputi, *Voice of the ILWU* editor Mel Chang, Joy Chong-Stannard, Karen Coffey, Willie Collins, Chris Conybeare, Dan Cornford, Howard A. DeWitt, Nathan Douthit, Troy Duster, Jorge Freiberg, Archie Green, Louis M. Isaacs, Richard Kandel, Howard Kimeldorf, Victoria Kneubuhl, Jennie Kogak, Joan Lando, Nancy Legardy, Vance Lelli, Glenna Matthews, Tom McLaughlin, Michael Munk, T. Nyan, ILWU director of organizing Peter Olney, Susanne O'Neal, G. Johnny Parks, ILWU warehouse Local 6 Secretary-Treasurer Fred Pecker, ILWU pensioners officer Al Perisho, Bill Pieper, Adrian Praetzellis, Jeff Quam-Wickham, John E. Rieber, former ILWU International Vice President Rudy Rubio, Ian Ruskin, former longshore Local 13 officer Tony Salcido, Sheena Schwartz, John Showalter, former ILWU research director Barry Silverman, Victor Silverman, Valerie Smith, James B. Snyder, longshore Local 23 President Conrad Spell, ILWU CLRC member Leal Sundet, An Tran, former ILWU International Vice President Randy Vekich, Robin Walker and former ILWU CLRC members Joe Wenzl and Dick Wise. To those whom I have inadvertently overlooked, I offer my sincere apologies.

Special thanks to Beth Fuget, University of Washington Press acquisitions editor, for her interest, suggestions, and support while this book was undergoing review and production. One could not ask for a better editor. I also greatly appreciate the excellent work of copyeditor Laura Iwasaki and the rest of the University of Washington Press staff.

My greatest debt is owed to Marilyn and Dave Schwartz for their love, patience, and understanding during the many years it took me to finish this history.

FURTHER READING

THOSE WHO WANT TO READ MORE ABOUT THE ILWU MAY BE INTERESTED IN the following titles. This compilation was adapted from the "ILWU Reading List," which Eugene Dennis Vrana, the union's director of educational services, librarian, and archivist, prepared for *The ILWU Story* (1997). I have also added recent works. Many of these books contain institutional history and other information that is beyond the scope of this volume.

Beechert, Edward D. *Working in Hawaii: A Labor History*. Honolulu: University of Hawaii Press, 1985. An invaluable history of Hawaiian labor with lengthy sections on the origins of the ILWU in the Islands.

Bernstein, Irving. *Turbulent Years: A History of the American Worker, 1933–1941*. Boston: Houghton Mifflin, 1970. A classic study of labor in the 1930s with insightful sections on Bridges and the 1934 strike.

Brown, Lee, and Robert Allen. *Strong in the Struggle: My Life as a Black Labor Activist*. Blue Ridge Summit, Pa.: Rowman and Littlefield, 2001. A stirring account of an African American man's commitment to political activism and to the ILWU in New Orleans.

Buchanan, Roger B. *Dock Strike: History of the 1934 Waterfront Strike in Portland, Oregon*. Everett, Wash.: The Working Press, 1975. A description of the 1934 strike in the Columbia River region.

Carson, Robert, ed. *The Waterfront Writers: The Literature of Work*. San Francisco: Harper and Row, 1979. Evocative stories and poetry by ILWU longshore workers inspired by echoes of 1934.

Eliel, Paul. *The Waterfront and General Strikes, San Francisco, 1934: A Brief*

History. San Francisco: Hooper Printing, 1934. A review of the year by an
employer representative shortly after the strike.

Fairley, Lincoln. *Facing Mechanization: The West Coast Longshore Plan.* Los
Angeles: Institute of Industrial Relations, University of California, 1979. An
evaluation by a former ILWU research director of the union's acceptance of
mechanization in the late 1950s and the resultant agreements of 1960–71.

Findlay, William. *Work on the Waterfront: Worker Power and Technological
Change in a West Coast Port.* Philadelphia: Temple University Press, 1988.
An analysis of the impact of mechanization on union morale at the Los Ange-
les and Long Beach Harbors.

Fox, Joan, ed. *A History of Federated Auxiliaries of the ILWU, 1934–1984.*
Seattle: ILWU Federated Auxiliaries, 1993. A compilation of histories of the
ILWU's local women's auxiliaries going back to 1934.

Hinckle, Warren. *The Big Strike: A Pictorial History of the 1934 San Francisco
General Strike.* Virginia City, Nev.: Silver Dollar Books, 1985. A collection
of photos from 1934 supplemented with text by Hinkle and a note on graph-
ics by Lisa Rubens.

Holmes, T. Michael. *The Specter of Communism in Hawaii.* Honolulu: University of Hawaii Press, 1994. An account of the attacks on ILWU leaders and
others in the Islands during the early Cold War years.

ILWU. *The ILWU Story: Six Decades of Militant Unionism.* San Francisco:
ILWU, 1997. A completely revised official overview of the union's history,
with eighty new photos, oral history testimonies, and text by Eugene Vrana.

———. *The ILWU Story: Three Decades of Militant Unionism.* San Francisco:
ILWU, 1963. An official overview of the union's history, with seventy-five
photos.

———. *Men and Machines: A Story about Longshoring on the West Coast
Waterfront.* San Francisco: ILWU, 1963. A pictorial essay showcasing photos
by Otto Hagel taken on the eve of mechanization and featuring text by ILWU
secretary-treasurer Louis Goldblatt.

ILWU Local 500. *Man Along the Shore! The Story of the Vancouver Waterfront.*
Vancouver, B.C.: ILWU Local 500 Pensioners, 1975. A history of the Canadian longshoremen told through interviews.

Johnson, Victoria. *How Many Machine Guns Does It Take to Cook One Meal? The
Seattle and San Francisco General Strikes.* Seattle: University of Washington
Press, 2008. A fresh look at major events in U.S. labor history, emphasizing
the long-term influence of the ideas of Thomas Jefferson and Thomas Paine.

Jung, Moon-Kie. *Reworking Race: The Making of Hawaii's Interracial Labor
Movement.* New York: Columbia University Press, 2006. An exploration of
the complex racial and ethnic issues in play during the struggle for unionization in the Islands.

Kimeldorf, Howard. *Reds or Rackets? The Making of Radical and Conservative Unions on the Waterfront.* Berkeley: University of California Press, 1988. A pioneering work of historical sociology that compares the ILWU and the East Coast's ILA.

Lannon, Albert Vetere. *Fight or Be Slaves: The History of the Oakland–East Bay Labor Movement.* Lanham, Md.: University Press of America, 2000. A general regional history by a former ILWU Warehouse Local 6 officer, with several references to the ILWU.

Larrowe, Charles P. *Harry Bridges: The Rise and Fall of Radical Labor in the United States.* 2nd ed. New York: Lawrence Hill, 1977. The most complete biography of Bridges available pending the appearance of Robert W. Cherny's work in progress.

Magden, Ronald E. *A History of Seattle Waterfront Workers, 1884–1934.* Seattle: ILWU Local 19 and the Washington Commission for the Humanities, 1991. A history of longshore unionization in the Puget Sound region.

———. *The Working Longshoreman.* Tacoma, Wash.: ILWU Local 23, 1991. A history of longshore unionization in Tacoma.

Magden, Ronald E., and A. D. Martinson. *The Working Waterfront: The Story of Tacoma's Ships and Men.* Tacoma, Wash.: ILWU Local 23, 1982. An account of the Port of Tacoma and its unions.

Markholt, Ottilie. *Maritime Solidarity: Pacific Coast Unionism, 1929–1938.* Tacoma, Wash.: Pacific Coast Maritime History Committee, 1998. A useful port-by-port description of developments in the 1930s, rich in detail but lacking in sympathy for Bridges and his supporters.

Munk, Michael. *The Portland Red Guide: Sites and Stories from Our Radical Past.* Portland, Ore.: Ooligan Press, 2007. An unusual local history that includes a section on the 1934 strike in the Columbia River city.

Nelson, Bruce. *Divided We Stand: American Workers and the Struggle for Black Equality.* Princeton, N.J.: Princeton University Press, 2001. A reevaluation of the role of race in labor's past with a chapter that questions the ILWU's record in light of the union's Los Angeles and Long Beach Harbors experience in the 1940s.

———. *Workers on the Waterfront: Seamen, Longshoremen, and Unionism in the 1930s.* Urbana: University of Illinois Press, 1988. A prize-winning history of the resurgence of the Pacific Coast maritime unions during the Great Depression that highlights the crucial role of the movement's ideological origins.

Pilcher, William W. *The Portland Longshoremen: A Dispersed Urban Community.* New York: Holt, Rinehart and Winston, 1972. A sociological study of one local's membership.

Polishuk, Sandy. *Sticking to the Union: An Oral History of the Life and Times of Julia Ruuttila.* New York: Palgrave MacMillan, 2003. A moving account of Ruuttila's life as a union activist and journalist for the ILWU in the Pacific Northwest.

Puette, William J. *The Hilo Massacre: Hawaii's Bloody Monday*. Honolulu: University of Hawaii Press, 1988. An account of an infamous police attack on a peaceful union demonstration at the Hilo waterfront in 1938.

Quin, Mike. *The Big Strike*. Olema, Calif.: Olema Publishing, 1949. Reprint. New York: International Publishers, 1979. A classic left history of the 1934 maritime confrontation and the San Francisco general strike.

Raineri, Vivian McGuckin. *The Red Angel*. New York: International Publishers, 1991. A biography of Elaine Black Yoneda, a maritime union supporter during the 1934 strike and a lifelong ILWU activist.

Robbins, William G. *Hard Times in Paradise: Coos Bay, Oregon*. Rev. ed. Seattle: University of Washington Press, 2006. A history of the lumber industry in Coos Bay with several references to the ILWU.

Rosswurm, Steve, ed. *The CIO's Left-Led Unions*. New Brunswick, N.J.: Rutgers University Press, 1992. A collection on organizing, race, and job control in the ILWU longshore division featuring historical essays by Bruce Nelson and Nancy Quam-Wickham.

Schneider, Betty, and Abraham Siegel. *Industrial Relations in the Pacific Coast Longshore Industry*. Berkeley: Institute of Industrial Relations, University of California, 1956. A dated but still useful traditional overview.

Schwartz, Harvey. *The March Inland: Origins of the ILWU Warehouse Division, 1934–1938*. Los Angeles: Institute of Industrial Relations, University of California, 1978. Reprint. San Francisco: ILWU, 2000. A history of the ILWU's northern California warehouse and distribution organizing campaign.

Selvin, David F. *A Terrible Anger: The 1934 Waterfront and General Strikes in San Francisco*. Detroit, Mich.: Wayne State University Press, 1996. A journalist-historian's careful account of 1934.

Ward, Estolv E. *Harry Bridges on Trial*. New York: Modern Age Books, 1940. A profile of Bridges at a famous deportation hearing held in 1939.

Wellman, David. *The Union Makes Us Strong: Radical Unionism on the San Francisco Waterfront*. Cambridge: Cambridge University Press, 1995. A description of waterfront labor and a detailed sociological appraisal of how the longshore contract works in practice.

Winslow, Calvin, ed. *Waterfront Workers: New Perspectives on Race and Class*. Urbana: University of Illinois Press, 1998. Contains an essay by Bruce Nelson on race relations in the ILWU longshore division.

Zalburg, Sanford. *A Spark Is Struck! Jack Hall and the ILWU in Hawaii*. Honolulu: University of Hawaii Press, 1979. Reprint, Honolulu: Watermark Publishing, 2007. A journalist's description of how the ILWU brought sweeping social, economic, and political change to Hawaii.

INDEX

Page numbers in italic indicate illustrations.

International Safety Organization, 132
International Seamen's Union (ISU),
305n15
International Union of Mine, Mill and
Smelter Workers, CIO (IUMMSW),
82, 303n3
International Woodworkers of America
(IWA), 114, 144
Inter-Professional Association, 266
Iraq war protest march, 52
ISU (International Seamen's Union),
305n15
IUMMSW (International Union of
Mine, Mill and Smelter Workers,
CIO), 82, 303n3
IWA (International Woodworkers
of America), 114, 144
IWW. *See* Industrial Workers of the World
Izuka, Ichiro, 267

James, Albert, 43, 48, 290
Japan scrap iron boycott, 115, *115*,
181–82
Jenkins, Dave, 209
JMSC (Joint Marine Strike Committee),
24, 34–35
Jobs with Justice, 161, 162
Johnson, Clancy, 121
Johnson, Joe, 209
Johnson, Roy, 127
Joint Longshore Strike Assistance Com-
mittee (Local 10/Local 34), 293
Joint Marine Strike Committee
(JMSC), 24, 34–35
Jones, B. B., 15
Jones-Rothschild Stevedore, 130
Jugum, Martin, *155*
June 16 agreement (1934), 22–24

Kagel, Sam, 23, 31–37, *35*, 55–59, *58*,
176–82, 302n22

Kaiser, Edgar, 43
Kaiser Shipyard, 205
Kamoku, Harry, 228–29
Kauai Pineapple Company, 230
Kawano, Jack, 237, 244
Kaye, George, 50
Kearney, James, 50
Kelly, Jack, 142
Kelm, Ted "Whitey," 51–55, 293,
302n21
Khrushchev, Nikita, 279, 292
King, LeRoy, 43, 204–11, *206*, 287,
294–95
King, Martin Luther, Jr., 43, 136, 209
Kinsey, Charlie, 201
Knights of Labor, 299n1
Knudsen, John, 67, 72, 303n2
Korean War, 54, 117, 279
Korp, Bill, *146*
Kruse, Marty, 161
Ku Klux Klan (KKK), 63, 64

L.A. Spring and Wire, 172–73
Labor Day Parade (Los Angeles, ca.
1946), *196*
Labor Day Parade (San Francisco,
1924), 31
Labor Department, U.S., 99–100
Labor Party, 288
Labor Relations Committee (LRC),
Local 13, 97
Lanai pineapple strike (1951), 250–52,
259–64, *261*
Langley, Al, 70–71
Lasartemay, Eugene, 306n7
Latourneau, C., *146*
Laurillard, Bill, *150*
Lawback, Art, 72
Lawrence, Bill, 84, 86
Lee, George, 211–12, 216–17, 218–19
Lee, Willie, 135

NCDC (Northern California District
Council), 210–11, 294–95
Negrete, Ruben, 78–79, 79–80
Nelson, Bruce, 299n1
Nelson, Chester, 58
nepotism, 79, 134
Nestle Chocolate, 210
Newton, Jackson, 87–91
New York City strike rally (1946), 53
NIRA (National Industrial Recovery
Act of 1933), 34, 68, 301n8
nitrate, 66
Nixon, Richard, 57–58
NLRB. *See* National Labor Relations
Board
NMU (National Maritime Union),
53–54
North Bend (OR) auxiliary, 117, 118
Northern California District Council
(NCDC), 210–11, 294–95
North Intermodal Yard, Tacoma,
136–39, 139, 140
Northwest Joint Strike Committee,
132
Novik, Judith, 137–38
NRA (National Recovery Administra-
tion), 17, 18

Oakland, 31, 41. *See also* Local 34,
Oakland; "march inland"
Occupational Safety and Health Ad-
ministration (OSHA), 60–61, 99
O'Conner, Jack, 169
O'Grady, Ed, 36
Ohashi, George, 259
Ohashi, Joaquina, 259
Olaa Sugar Company, 221–23, 231
Olden, George, 124
Olney, Peter, 161–62, 163
Olsen, Charles, 28
Olsen, J., 146

Olsen, Jack, 280–87, 282
Olsen, Tillie, 190
Olson, David J., 8
Omuro, Kenji "Sleepy," 257
oral history project, 6
Orange Angels, 139
Orlando, Joe, 277
OSHA (Occupational Safety and Health
Administration), 60–61, 99
Oshiro, Hiroshi "Molokai," 257–58,
261
O'Toole, Richard, 50
Owens, Bud, 201–2
Owens-Illinois Glass, 180, 201–2

Pacific Coast Labor Bureau (PCLB),
33–35
Pacific Coast Maritime Code, 99
Pacific Coast Maritime Safety Code, 62
Pacific Electric, 93
Panasonic, 131
Paris Beauty Supply Company, 285
Parker, Dick, 67, 72, 76, 303n2
Parker, Eddie, 49–50
Paton, Clarence, 206–7
Paton, Eugene (Pat), 177, 181, 189,
207
Paton, Judy, 207
Pay Guarantee Plan (PGP), 129
payroll, brass checks for, 14
PCLB (Pacific Coast Labor Bureau),
33–35
Pedrin, George, 207–8
Peil, Fred, 153
pensions, 98, 147, 148
Pension Trust and Welfare Fund,
ILWU-PMA, 98
People's World (PW), 278–79, 289
"permit men," 302n18
Perry, E. L. (Roy), 130–31
pesticides, 62

sexual harassment, 189
Shannon, Vince, *150*
shape-ups, 13–14, 65, 300n4
Sharkey, Vincent, 175
Shaw, Frank, 110, 112
Shelly, Jack, 180
Sheraton Palace Hotel, San Francisco, 55
Sherman, Lou, 195–96
Shillings, 210
Shirley, Howard, 168
Shoemaker, Bill, 90
Sills, Marion (aka Marion Brown), 178
Simons, Joe, 68
SIU (Seafarers International Union), 152–53, 305n15
six-hour day, 301n10
Skinner, Jasper, 114
Skinner, Kate, 114
sling loads, *10*, 37, 112
slogan, "An injury to one is an injury to all," 7, 296, 297–98
Sloss, Max C., 37
Smith, Paul C., 181
Smith, Roy C., 145–47, 149–50, *150*
Smith Act, 232, 309n11
Social Security Act (1935), 310n1
social work by McElrath in Hawaii, 267–68
solidarity, 7, 302n19
Somolenko, Fred, *146*
South, warehouse locals in, 305n1
South End Warehouse, 188–89
Soviet Union, 277
speed-ups, 37, 93, 214
Sperry, Howard, 24, *28*
sponsorship, 79
SSA (Stevedoring Services of America), 136
Stacey's Bookstore, San Francisco, 305n20

Stahl, Joe, 71–72
Stalin, Joseph, 279
Standard Warehouse, 170
star gangs, 65
Star Shipping, 137–38
State of the Union (Lichtenstein), 7
Statutory Holiday Act (1966, Canada), 150
steady-man issue (monthly contracts), 55, 58, 68–69
Steffens, Lincoln, 240–41
Stern, Julius, 206
Stevedoring Services of America (SSA), 136
steward system, 184, 199, 277–78
Stovall, Edward, 43
straddle carriers (strads), 138–39, *139*, *140*
strength, 127, 135
strikebreakers: 1916, Tacoma, 128; 1935, Vancouver, 143; in cotton compress, 218; in Hawaii, 245; Stahl on, 72
strikebreakers in 1934 strike: in Coos Bay, 111; at East Bay Terminals, 169; Hawaiians and, 227; in Portland, 105–8; in San Francisco Bay Area, 21, 29–30; in southern California, 67, 70, 71, 76, 93; in Tacoma, 130
strike clearance cards, 168
strikes: 1916 Tacoma, 127–28; 1917 Clifton-Morenci copper strike (Arizona), 303n3; 1919 San Francisco, 16; 1923 longshore, 68; 1933 Matson Navigation Company, 18; 1935 Canada, 101, 141, 142–44, 148; 1935 ILA bargemen, 241; 1936–1937 maritime, 169, 184, 229; 1936 L.A. Spring and Wire, 172–73; 1936 longshore,